Q&A

Routledge•Cavendish Questions & Answers Series

Constitutional & Administrative Law

2007–2008

Routledge-Cavendish Q&A series

Each Routledge-Cavendish Q&A contains 50 questions on topics commonly found on exam papers, with comprehensive suggested answers. The titles are written by lecturers who are also examiners, so the student gains an important insight into exactly what examiners are looking for in an answer. This makes them excellent revision and practice guides. With over 500,000 copies of the Routledge-Cavendish Q&As sold to date, accept no substitute.

New editions publishing in 2007:

CIVIL LIBERTIES & HUMAN RIGHTS 4/E

COMPANY LAW 5/E

COMMERCIAL LAW 4/E

CONTRACT LAW 7/E

CRIMINAL LAW 6/E

EMPLOYMENT LAW 5/E

ENGLISH LEGAL SYSTEM 7/E

EQUITY & TRUSTS 5/E

EUROPEAN UNION LAW 6/E

EVIDENCE 7/E

FAMILY LAW 4/E

INTELLECTUAL PROPERTY LAW

JURISPRUDENCE 4/E

LAND LAW 5/E

TORTS 7/E

For a full listing, visit www.routledgecavendish.com/revisionaids.asp

Q&A

Routledge•Cavendish Questions & Answers Series

Constitutional & Administrative Law

2007–2008

HELEN FENWICK AND GAVIN PHILLIPSON

Routledge·Cavendish
Taylor & Francis Group

Fifth edition first published 2007
by Routledge-Cavendish
2 Park Square, Milton Park, Abingdon, Oxon OX14 4RN

Simultaneously published in the USA and Canada
by Routledge-Cavendish
270 Madison Ave, New York, NY 10016

*Routledge-Cavendish is an imprint of the Taylor & Francis Group,
an informa business*

© 2007 Helen Fenwick and Gavin Phillipson

Previous editions published by Cavendish Publishing Limited
First edition   1993
Second edition   1995
Third edition   1999
Fourth edition   2003

Typeset in Garamond by
Newgen Imaging Systems (P) Ltd, Chennai, India
Printed and bound in Great Britain by
TJ International Ltd, Padstow, Cornwall

British Library Cataloguing in Publication Data
A catalogue record for this book is available
from the British Library

Library of Congress Cataloging in Publication Data
A catalog record for this book has been requested

ISBN10: 1–84568–006–5
ISBN13: 978–1–84568–006–0

Preface

We have often come across students who have a sound grasp of legal principles and have put in quite a lot of work on constitutional law and yet do not feel confident when faced with the end of year examination. This book is written in response to the pleas of such students for more guidance as to the best means of presenting their knowledge in the exam, and it is hoped that it may alleviate at least some of the stress they experience. It is written at a time when the very far-reaching programme of constitutional reform introduced by the Labour government is largely in place; it affords extensive coverage to this programme and its implications for the UK's radically changing constitution.

The law is stated as at 15 November 2006.

Helen Fenwick and Gavin Phillipson
University of Durham, December 2006

CONTENTS

TABLE OF CASES

TABLE OF STATUTES

TABLE OF EUROPEAN LEGISLATION

▌DIRECTIVES

▌TREATIES AND CONVENTIONS

INTRODUCTION

This book is intended to be of help to students studying constitutional and administrative law who feel that they have acquired a body of knowledge but do not feel confident about using it effectively in exams. This book sets out to demonstrate how to apply the knowledge to the question and how to structure the answer. Students, especially first year students, often find the technique of answering problem questions particularly hard to grasp, so this book contains a large number of answers to such questions. This technique is rarely taught in law schools and the student who comes from studying science or maths 'A levels may find it particularly tricky. Equally, a student who has studied English literature may find it difficult to adapt to the impersonal, logical, concise style which problem answers demand. It is hoped that this book will be particularly useful at exam time but may also prove useful throughout the year. The book provides examples of the kind of questions which are usually asked in end of year examinations, along with suggested solutions. Each chapter deals with one of the main topics covered in constitutional and administrative law or public law courses and contains typical questions on that area. The aim is not to include questions covering every aspect of a course, but to pick out the areas which tend to be examined because they are particularly contentious or topical. Many courses contain a certain amount of material which is not examined, although it is important as providing background knowledge.

Problem and essay questions

Some areas tend to be examined only by essays, some mainly although not invariably by problems, and some by either. The questions chosen reflect this mix, and the introductions at the beginning of each chapter discuss the type of question usually asked. It is important not to choose a topic and then assume that it will appear on the exam paper in a particular form unless it is in an area where, for example, a problem question is never set. If it might appear as an essay or a problem, revision should be geared to either possibility: a very thorough knowledge of the area should be acquired but also an awareness of critical opinion in relation to it.

Length of answers

The answers in this book are about the length of an essay that a good student would expect to write in an exam. Some are somewhat longer and these will also provide useful guidance for students writing assessed essays which typically are between 2,000 and 3,000 words. In relation to exam questions, there are a number of reasons for including lengthy answers: some students can write long answers – about 1,800 words – under exam conditions; some students who cannot nevertheless write two very good and lengthy essays and two reasonable but shorter ones. Such students tend to do very well, although it must be emphasised that it is always better to aim to spread the time evenly between all four essays. Therefore, some answers indicate what might be done if very thorough coverage of a topic was undertaken.

The Notes

Most essays also provide Notes exploring some areas of the answer in more depth, which should be of value to the student who wants to do more than cover the main points. Some answers provide a number of Notes; it would not be expected that any one student would be able to make all the points they contain, but they demonstrate that it is possible to choose to explore, say, two interesting areas in more depth in an answer once the main points have been covered. It cannot be emphasised enough that the main points have to be covered before interesting but less obvious issues can be explored.

Expressing a point of view

Students sometimes ask, especially in an area such as constitutional law which can be quite topical and politically controversial, whether they should argue for any particular point of view in an essay. It will be noticed that the essays in this book tend to do this. In general, the good student does argue for one side but he always uses sound arguments to support his view. Further, a good student does not ignore the opposing arguments; they are considered and, if possible, their weaknesses are exposed. Of course, it would not be appropriate to do this in a problem question or in some essay questions but, where an invitation to do so is held out, it is a good idea to accept it rather than sit on the fence.

Exam papers

Constitutional and administrative law exam papers normally include one question on each of the main areas. For example, a typical paper might include problem questions on: public order, police powers, judicial review (probably natural justice) and essay questions on: parliamentary sovereignty, conventions, the parliamentary process, the Executive, freedom of expression, judicial review. Therefore, the questions have to be fairly wide ranging in order to cover a reasonable amount of ground on each topic. Some answers in this book therefore have to cover some of the same material, especially where it is particularly central to the topic in question.

Suggestions for exam technique

Below are some suggestions which might improve exam technique; some failings are pointed out which are very commonly found on exam scripts:

(1) When tackling a problem question, do not write out the facts in the answer. Quite a number of students write out chunks of the facts as they answer the question–perhaps to help themselves to pick out the important issues. It is better to avoid this and merely to refer to the significant facts.

(2) Use an impersonal style in both problem and essay answers. In an essay, you should rarely need to use the word I and, in our view, it should not be used at all in a problem answer. (Of course, examiners may differ in their views on this point.) Instead, you could say: 'it is therefore submitted that' or 'it is arguable that'; avoid saying: 'I believe that' or 'I feel that'.

(3) In answers to problem questions, try to explain at the beginning of each section of your answer what point you are trying to establish. You might say, for example: 'In order to show that liability under s 1 will arise, three tests must be satisfied.' You should then consider all three, come to a conclusion on each, and then come to a final conclusion as to whether or not liability will arise. If you are really unsure whether or not it will arise (which will often be the case – there is not much point in asking a question to which there is one very clear and obvious answer), then consider what you have written in relation to the three tests. Perhaps one of them is clearly satisfied, one is probably satisfied and the other (arising under, for example, s 1(8)) probably is not. You might then say: 'As the facts give little support to an argument that s 1(8) is satisfied, it is concluded that liability is unlikely to be established.'

CHAPTER 1

THE CHARACTERISTICS OF THE BRITISH CONSTITUTION

▌INTRODUCTION

This chapter concentrates on six particular issues which arise from the distinctive characteristics of the British Constitution: the nature of constitutions in general and the sense in which the UK can be said to have/not to have a constitution; the significance of parliamentary sovereignty; the nature of constitutional conventions; the principles of the rule of law and the separation of powers; the significance of the devolution settlement; and the desirability of a new codified constitution. These areas are sometimes treated in textbooks as discrete areas, but they are clearly interlinked and will therefore be considered here together. The significance of the Labour government's reform package, including most recently the Constitutional Reform Act 2005, is considered here in general terms, though the significance of the Human Rights Act 1998 is discussed much more fully in Chapters 2 and 9. The sovereignty of Parliament and the impact of EU law on the UK Constitution are fully considered in Chapter 2.

Checklist

Students should be familiar with the following areas:

- the debate about the nature and functions of a constitution; the argument that the UK does not indeed possess one under certain definitions;

- the nature and role of constitutional conventions;

- certain of the most significant conventions: those relating to the exercise of the royal prerogative, to the working of the Cabinet system, to the relationship between the Lords and the Commons and to those regulating proceedings in Parliament;

- the doctrine of parliamentary sovereignty and the modification to the traditional view represented by the impact of EU law;
- the concept of the rule of law and the impact upon it of the ECHR and the HRA;
- the doctrine of the separation of powers, the effect upon of the ECHR and HRA and of the Constitutional Reform Act 2005;
- the benefits and defects of the un-codified UK Constitution;
- devolution to Scotland, Wales and Northern Ireland;
- the constitutional significance of the Human Rights Act 1998;
- the significance of ongoing reform of the House of Lords and of the Freedom of Information Act 2000 for the overall balance of powers within the constitution.

Question 1

Would you agree that there is no justification for distinguishing between strict law and convention in the UK Constitution and that, therefore, conventions should be codified in legal form?

Answer plan

This question is often asked in one form or another and is reasonably straightforward. It requires the student to consider why features of the constitution which are not strict laws should be maintained. It should not degenerate into a list of the main conventions; rather, conventions should be used as examples. Clearly, it is crucial at the outset to try to distinguish between law and convention.

Essentially, the following matters should be discussed:

- is there a distinction between law and convention? Jennings' view contrasted with Dicey's;
- the relationship between law and conventions;
- the nature of conventions: the difficulty of distinguishing binding usage from non-binding usage;
- what justification is there for maintaining the distinction between law and convention, assuming that it exists?;

- the advantages which might be derived from codifying conventions;
- the detriment which might flow from such codification: loss of flexibility and of discretion in adhering to conventions.

Answer

This question makes the assumption that there is a distinction between strict law and conventions, but the existence of such a distinction has been questioned by commentators such as Jennings. Before considering whether any such distinction should be maintained, it should first be asked whether it does indeed exist.

Dicey wrote that conventions could be clearly distinguished from laws, in the sense that no court would apply a sanction for their breach (*The Law of the Constitution*, 1971). However, this distinction was attacked as artificial by Sir Ivor Jennings in *The Law and the Constitution*, 1959, on the basis that law and conventions both ultimately rest on 'general acquiescence'. The distinction put forward by Dicey, however, finds some support in case law. In *Madzimbamuto v Lardner-Burke (1969)*, the Privy Council held that the convention under which the UK Parliament needed to obtain the consent of the Southern Rhodesia government before legislating for that colony had no effect in limiting the powers of the UK Parliament. Similarly, the Canadian Supreme Court in *Re Amendment to the Constitution of Canada (1982)* held that conventions are not enforced by the courts: the only sanctions for breach of a convention are political ones. Most constitutional writers have accepted this distinction between law and convention and the general view may be summed up by Marshall and Moodie: conventions may be described as 'rules of constitutional behaviour which are considered to be binding by and upon those who operate the Constitution but which are not enforced by the law courts . . . nor by the presiding officers in the Houses of Parliament' (*Some Problems of the Constitution*, 5th edn, 1971, pp 22–23). Most conventions are based on usage which continues because statesmen would find it politically inconvenient to depart from it. It may then be argued that conventions depend on acquiescence for their very existence, whereas laws do not cease to exist because they are widely disobeyed. The road traffic laws are frequently violated, but no one doubts that they remain valid laws.

It follows that if, for example, the government was defeated on a vote of confidence in the House of Commons but refused to obey the convention that it should therefore resign, the courts would not recognise this breach of convention by declaring that government ministers were not legally entitled to exercise the powers of their office.

However, having postulated a distinction between law and convention, it must be accepted that there are exceptions to it. In particular, it would be going too far to say, as Dicey did, that conventions are never recognised by the courts. For example, in *Liversidge v Anderson (1942)* and *Carltona Ltd v Commissioner of Works (1943)*, the courts supported the refusal to review the grounds on which executive discretionary powers had been exercised on the basis that a minister is responsible to Parliament for the exercise of his power. In *Attorney General v Jonathan Cape Ltd (1976)*, Lord Widgery CJ considered the doctrine of collective Cabinet responsibility at some length, coming to the conclusion that the maintenance of the doctrine was in the public interest and, therefore, could justify restraint on the disclosure of Cabinet discussions (although no restraint was granted in the instant case due to the lapse of time since the discussions took place). Equally, it must be remembered that not all legal rules are justiciable.

Assuming that to an extent, the distinction between strict law and convention holds good, why, as De Smith asks (in *Constitutional and Administrative Law*, 8th edn, 1998), maintain a distinction at all? Why not codify conventions of the constitution in legal form – either in a statute or as part of a written constitution? Several Commonwealth constitutions have already undertaken this. Codification would have the advantage of clarifying certain of the most significant constitutional rules. The informality associated with conventions may be disadvantageous in that it may sometimes be very difficult, if not impossible, to ascertain whether a certain usage has crystallised into a conventional rule. Of course, some conventions are formulated in writing, such as the agreement in 1930 that the Governor General of a Dominion should be appointed by the Crown exclusively on the advice of the Dominion government concerned, but those that have gradually evolved will often be uncertain in scope and, unlike laws, their meaning will not be resolved by their interpretation in the courts. For example, the conventional powers of the Queen to require a dissolution of Parliament are uncertain. A refusal or assent by the Queen to a request for the dissolution of Parliament might, in certain circumstances, appear not to have a clear basis, making the task of defending her action against the charge of unconstitutionality difficult. This difficulty could be avoided if the constitutional functions of the monarch, including the circumstances in which he or she could dissolve Parliament, were set out in legal form.

Uncertainty arises not only as to the scope of some conventions, but as to whether or not they have come into being at any particular time, or whether it may be said of a custom that it is merely a non-binding usage. For instance, it is a convention that the Queen must give assent to a Bill, whatever her personal view of it. In 1708, the royal assent was withheld from a Bill which the monarch in question, Queen Anne, disapproved of, whereas in 1829, George IV gave consent to a Bill which he disliked. At some point during those hundred years, the convention in question must have come into being. However, it would be impossible to pinpoint the stage at which this occurred; if, during that time, the question had arisen as to whether withholding the royal consent was unconstitutional, no answer would be available to the monarch in question: in effect, it would not be available until after he or she had acted.

Moreover, it is arguable that conventions should be enshrined in law because otherwise they may be more readily violated. Conventions are binding if those to whom the usage applies consider that they are under an obligation to comply with them. But although in practice, many conventions do seem to be regarded as binding, lack of certainty as to the scope or existence of some, as already considered, may lead to behaviour which would be regarded in some quarters as unconstitutional. The absence of an enacted constitutional code means that 'unconstitutional' has no definition. Such a code would mean that unconstitutional behaviour could be more readily identified and would be clearly illegal. If the resulting code were made non-justiciable, its value would largely lie in its clarification of conventions, thereby precluding some disputes.[1]

However, codification might achieve a desirable clarity in some areas, but at the expense of the present flexibility. The interpretation given to an Act of Parliament may evolve over time, but there is still a rigidity associated with statutes which is avoided by conventions. Conventions allow the constitution to evolve and keep up to date with changing circumstances without the need for formal repeal or amendment of law. Further, conventions may not always be followed and, although this can be seen as a weakness, as argued above, it can also be seen as a strength that in certain circumstances, rigid adherence to conventions is not required as it would be if they were enshrined in a legal code. Conventions have been able to lose their binding force or undergo a change in content without the need for any formal mechanism being followed. They may disappear gradually if they are no longer observed. If a convention has been established by express agreement, it may be superseded or modified by agreement. For example, decisions taken by the Prime Minister or the Cabinet about the way the Cabinet is to operate may be superseded by new decisions. Such flexibility has been politically convenient in the past and will, presumably, continue to be so.

The doctrine of collective Cabinet responsibility provides an example of the advantage to be derived from the indeterminate nature of conventions. Under the doctrine, ministers are collectively responsible to Parliament for their actions in governing the country and, therefore, should be in accord on any major question. A minister should resign if he is in disagreement with the policy of the Cabinet on any such question. Examples of such resignation include Sir Thomas Dugdale's in 1954 due to his disagreement with the government as to the disposal of an area of land known as Crichel Down (this resignation is not always cited as an example of policy disagreement, but such appears to have been its basis) and Sir Anthony Eden's in 1938 over Chamberlain's policy towards Mussolini. However, there appears to have been some blurring and weakening of the doctrine dating from the mid-1970s. In 1975, the Labour Cabinet was divided on the question of whether the UK should remain in the Common Market. It was agreed that in the period before the referendum on the question, Cabinet ministers should be able to express a view at variance with the official view of the government that the UK should remain a member of the Common Market.[2]

If the convention of collective responsibility were enshrined in a statute, departure from it, as in 1975, might be less readily undertaken even if the provisions of the statute were made non-justiciable. In any event, it would be difficult and probably undesirable to define the convention, as discretion in complying with it may be said to be endemic in it. Political inconvenience would clearly arise and it might be argued that the democratic process would be endangered if ministers could not at times express their views on exceptionally important issues with some freedom. Therefore, it may be argued that no advantage would be gained by enacting such a statute: such crystallisation of the convention would clearly reduce its value. The example of the convention of collective Cabinet responsibility illustrates the general principle that codification would in general inhibit the main purpose of many of the conventions – keeping the constitution in touch with contemporary political needs.

Of course, in particular instances, the enactment of conventions has been called for after they have been violated; the need for flexibility has been outweighed by the need for clarification and certainty. For example, in 1909, the House of Lords ignored the convention that it must defer to the will of the House of Commons. This led to the enactment of the **Parliament Act 1911**, which defined the relationship between the two Houses and ensured that the House of Lords would defer to the Commons.

In some instances where a convention seems to embody a clear rule, the need for flexibility is certainly less pressing and the argument for codification more compelling. Arguably, certain constitutional functions of the monarch (such as rules governing assent to the dissolution of Parliament and assent to Bills) should be enacted in order to avoid uncertainty as to when the Queen may be acting unconstitutionally.

Thus, it may be concluded that if codification were undertaken, it should be confined to conventions of a sufficiently definite nature which should be codified in order to reduce the potential for disagreement as to their scope.

▌NOTES

1　The argument as to whether conventions once codified should be made directly justiciable could be developed at this point. De Smith makes the point that the courts would be asked to shoulder a possibly intolerable burden if they had to determine questions of extreme political sensitivity. This argument receives support from the experience of new Commonwealth countries which have codified conventions in the texts of their constitutions.

2　A further example could be given to strengthen this argument. Some weakening of the convention appears from the *Westland* affair which, on the face of it, provides an example of its operation: when Michael Heseltine resigned from the Cabinet in 1986, due to his disagreement with government policy, he specifically stated that he did not do so as a result of his perception of an obligation arising from the convention.

Question 2

A number of commentators have argued that, in the only meaningful sense of the word, the UK has no constitution. Do you agree, and has this remained true following devolution to Scotland and the **Human Rights Act 1998**?

Answer plan

Students must set out clearly the argument as to why the UK has no proper constitution, offer a view on it, and then relate this directly to the new state of affairs following devolution and the Human Rights Act (HRA) 1998.

Essentially, the following matters should be discussed:

- the requirements of constitutionalism: power-allocation and power separated by law: power only to be exercised by law; laws to be made in accordance with specified procedures; limitations on the content of laws; entrenched rights;
- the overriding requirement that the constitution be above the power of government and, therefore, not susceptible to ordinary change;
- the application of the above to the UK Constitution; partial compliance but no form of higher law save sovereignty itself; constitutional statutes under the *Thoburn* doctrine?;
- the basic point that the HRA and the Scotland Act 1998 are both susceptible to normal repeal by Parliament;
- the constitutional limitations placed on Scottish government – the European Convention on Human Rights (ECHR), etc; the prospect of constitutional review of legislation;
- the growth of the convention that Westminster Parliament will not legislate in devolved areas without consent;
- the impact of the HRA at the normative level – the identification and partially protected status of basic rights;
- overall conclusions – a limited step towards constitutionalism.

Answer

The claim that the UK has no constitution was originally put forward by Bryce, but has recently been forcefully expanded and restated by Ridley ((1988) 41 Parlt Aff 340). In essence, it distinguishes a merely descriptive definition of a constitution as that body of rules and arrangements which regulates the government of a country and its relations with its citizens from what is argued to be the more important one; one which Ridley believes has been in use since the American War of Independence and the French Revolution, in which the word has a much more specialised and more normative meaning. Under this approach, he argues, there are four particular characteristics which a constitution must have. This essay will consider these characteristics, but will also discuss some more basic characteristics which, it will be argued, a constitution must possess and which are not expressly mentioned by Ridley. This combined set of characteristics will then be used as a measure against which to judge the existence or non-existence of the UK Constitution. The final part of the essay will examine whether the introduction of devolution and the (at least, partial) incorporation of the ECHR via the HRA changes the conclusions previously reached on the UK Constitution.

It is suggested that there are perhaps two essential characteristics or purposes of constitutions, at least as they are understood within the tradition of liberal democracy to which Ridley refers. The first is that constitutions are necessary in order to control the power of the State; the second is that constitutions ensure that the power of the State derives from a legitimate source. As to the first notion, constitutions may be seen to exercise such control in a number of ways. As Schauer has pointed out (*Playing by the Rules*, 1991, pp 118–120), they are power-allocating: they usually distribute power amongst the different organs of government, according to law. This represents a limitation on State power in two ways: first, and more basically, there is a formal limitation: allocation of power in this way means that power may not be exercised arbitrarily by any part of government which finds it convenient to do so, but only by that organ of government which is authorised, and publicly authorised at that, to do so. This, in the simplest sense, is the idea of limited government, or government under law. Ridley does not expressly identify this as an essential aspect of a constitution, but it is submitted that this notion of power-allocation through law is implicit in his first characteristic of a constitution, that it 'establishes' the system of government.

The second aspect of power-allocation is rather more substantive: allocation should offer a more concrete guarantee against tyranny by separating out different types of powers and assigning them to different and separate organs of government. This is the doctrine of the separation of powers which, broadly speaking, demands, first, that each part of government should be separate and to an extent independent of the others; second, that each organ should be vested with only one main function of government; and, third, that each should be able to check the actions of the others. This characteristic is, to a greater or lesser extent, apparent in every single liberal constitution and must therefore be seen as an essential aspect of such a constitution; again, it is implicit in Ridley's thesis.

A further very simple aspect of a constitution is that power must be exercised only through the making of laws. To appreciate the constraints which this requirement places on the rulers of a State, it must be contrasted with a State in which the ruler has the power simply to imprison, kill or confiscate the property of any citizen at pleasure and without warning. Power exercised through law-making is far more constrained: a law is a rule, of general application, which is reasonably certain in its terms and made known in advance. This represents a basic limitation on government because, since the rules must be announced in advance and made relatively fixed, the government cannot simply act as it pleases; instead, it must be able to point to some law justifying its actions. As a concomitant of this, constitutions must not only provide that power must be exercised through law, they will also state the procedures that must be followed to produce a valid law. This not only helps us identify what the laws are, but also ensures that since certain specified procedures must be followed before a law is deemed valid, the government cannot simply declare the law to be what it wishes.

While the above requirements provide a number of formal restraints upon governments, they are rather empty, formal restrictions, since they merely divide power and provide for formalities in relation to its exercise. They say nothing about *outcomes*, about what laws validly produced can say or do. Therefore, liberal constitutions usually limit the power of government in a more substantive way: that is, governments are limited not only as to the *form* by which it must exercise power, but also as to the *substance* of that power. Thus, under many constitutions, there are some laws which the government *cannot make at all*; broadly, those which would infringe what are seen as fundamental human rights. The First Amendment of the US Constitution states simply (*inter alia*): 'Congress shall make no law abridging the freedom of speech or of the press.' This is the notion of entrenched rights – a ring fence around certain basic liberties which the government is not allowed to cross. Most Western countries have constitutions which declare the existence of such liberties and forbid governmental interference with them, except perhaps in cases of grave national emergency.

Implicit in all the above ideas is the notion that constitutions are in some way superior to and beyond government; they state what form the government shall take and what it may and may not do. They are above government in specifying matters which are prior to the formation or election of any government, and they also bind all governments. From this requirement logically flows another: namely, that the constitution should be *entrenched* so that it is not readily alterable by the government of the day. As well as being logically necessary, this requirement is also practically necessary: if the constitution was not in some way entrenched, then any government could simply remove the limitations on its power which the constitution imposed and the basic idea of controlling the power of government would be lost.

We may now turn to the application of these ideas of constitutionalism to the UK. The British Constitution does allocate power amongst the different organs of government. The doctrine of parliamentary sovereignty states that Parliament, and only Parliament, may make laws. Similarly, the judges must give effect to all valid Acts of Parliament and may not question the desirability of their content. In reality, a government with an overall majority will be able to ensure that the vast majority of its Bills will reach the statute books, often with little modification, and may thus be seen to exercise the power formally belonging to Parliament, but this is a matter of political practice, not constitutional law. However, looking a little closer at the idea of allocation of powers in Britain, another more fundamental problem appears: some of the most important powers in the British State are allocated not by law but only convention, that is, a traditional understanding about how things should be done, which is accepted by everybody but which cannot be enforced legally. Thus, in theory, the Queen holds all the prerogative powers of government – to declare war, to make peace, to dissolve Parliament, etc. In practice, of course, these powers are exercised by ministers, either collectively or individually. However, there is no law of the constitution stating that this is the case. The *law* in fact states that all these powers belong to the Queen. The idea that these powers are exercised by her only in a formal way is a constitutional convention only. Furthermore, some of the most important 'checks and balances' in the constitution, required by the notion of separation of powers, exist only by virtue of convention. For example, it is only a convention that a government, if defeated in the House of Commons on a vote of no confidence, must resign: if a government were to refuse to do so, the courts would not declare the subsequent acts of its ministers to be unlawful.

What about controls on how laws may be made and what they may say? Laws may only be made through Acts of Parliament which comply with all specified formalities: resolutions of the Commons alone, for example, are not laws binding on the courts: *Stockdale v Hansard (1839)*. Furthermore, the courts enforce a basic notion of legality: government action impinging on citizens must be justified by reference to some law which empowers the specific act done, as in *Entick v Carrington (1765)*. However, the ability of Parliament to enact what laws it pleases means that it can pass – and does increasingly pass – laws which give government very wide discretionary powers, so that it will be difficult for the courts to find that any particular actions are not justified in law. As to the notion of more substantive limitations on government rule in the form of entrenched rights, we may note immediately that there is no comprehensive system of entrenched rights, and orthodox constitutional doctrine tells us that Parliament is competent to legislate on any matter whatever. However, it has recently become apparent that the courts will not apply Acts of Parliament which conflict with rights deriving from

European Community law (*Factortame Ltd and Others v Secretary of State for Transport (No 2) (1991)*), so that insofar as rights are protected by EU law, they do have a special status. However, EU law does not at present provide a set of basic civil and political rights. It should be noted that a few judges have recently, and mainly speaking extra-judicially, suggested that there may be basic rights and freedoms embedded in the common law, particularly the ability of the courts to engage in judicial review of executive action – a basic requirement of the rule of law – which the judges would not allow Parliament to remove.[1] The most notable recent example was an obiter comment by Lord Steyn in *A-G v Jackson (2006)*:

> In exceptional circumstances involving an attempt to abolish judicial review or the ordinary role of the courts, the . . . House of Lords or a new Supreme Court may have to consider whether this is a constitutional fundamental which even a sovereign Parliament acting at the behest of a complaisant House of Commons cannot abolish.

Nationality, further evidence for this may be seen in the outcry over the proposed clause in the Asylum and Immigration Bill 2002, which sought to exclude judicial review, on all possible grounds, of the new Asylum and Immigration Tribunal so that even blatant errors of law or procedural unfairness could not be corrected in the courts. The Government was eventually forced to withdraw the clause after a huge rebellion in the House of Lords; there were predictions of judicial resignations in the face of such an unprecedented attack on the rule of law, as well as judicial warnings that the courts might even refuse to give effect to the clause.

Of course, legislation removing basic liberties would be in violation of the UK's obligations under the ECHR but, prior to the passage of the HRA 1998, the illegality here would not have been imposed by the UK Constitution as such, but rather by a particular treaty signed by the UK, which was not then binding in domestic law at all, and from which the UK could in any event resile from in its entirety.

Finally, what of the notion that the constitution must in some way be above or beyond the powers of government? One matter – parliamentary sovereignty itself – appears to be a matter of 'higher law', in that it is generally accepted that Parliament is unable to restrict its continuing sovereignty. This point has been thrown into some doubt as the courts have, in effect, allowed Parliament to restrict its own powers to legislate contrary to EU law. Nevertheless, there is little doubt that this restriction is ultimately one which Parliament could remove through withdrawal from the EU and probably also through the simple expedient of stating an express intention that a given Act should prevail over EU law. But, on the orthodox view, no other rule in the constitution is immune from change by an ordinary Act of Parliament, although, as just seen, there have been judicial hints that there are some fundamentals of the rule of law, in relation to which this may not be so. There is, of course, no authority, in terms of decided cases, for such a proposition. Thus, so called constitutional principles are in theory as readily changeable as rules relating to the licensing of public houses. One caveat should be entered to this: the line of reasoning taken in *Thoburn (2002)* in relation to the refusal by the courts in *Factortame* to allow implied repeal to apply to the 1972 EC Act. In that case, Laws LJ held that, whilst Parliament could not bind itself in any way and had not done so in the 1972 Act, the *courts* could and should recognise certain Acts, including the 1972 Act, as 'constitutional statutes'. Essentially these are those which affect fundamental rights or 'the relationship between citizen and State in some general, overarching manner'. The legal consequence of recognising a statute as 'constitutional' was simple: 'Ordinary statutes may be impliedly repealed. Constitutional statutes may not'. Whilst this view still allows for the unlimited sovereignty of Parliament when expressed through express repeal of a previous statute, however constitutionally significant, it does give a means of giving additional protection to constitutional fundamentals, although it is too early to say whether this revised view of sovereignty has won general acceptance amongst the senior judiciary.

Nevertheless, even under this view, Parliament could, at least theoretically, restrict the franchise, through express repeal of the Representation of the People Act and its replacement with a more restrictive statute, thus undermining even basic democratic principles. Hence, the basic notion, noted above, that the constitution should establish the source of governmental power and, in a democracy, establish that source as the people is only partly fulfilled in the UK. The source of ultimate *legal* power in the UK is Parliament, *not* the people. Of course, Parliament has been a democratically elected body since women were given the vote early in the twentieth century, but this requirement is contained only in an ordinary Act of Parliament – the Representation of the People Act. As such, it is subject to normal repeal by Parliament and, as a matter of law, has no entrenched status, even if it is a 'constitutional statute'. The constitution thus does not even provide for a democratic basis for government, if 'constitution' is taken to mean a form of higher law not subject to the standard process of legislative change.

Thus, the 'no constitution' thesis appears to be fairly readily made out, at least if it is taken to mean that 'the constitution' must consist of a form of 'higher order' law. Alternatively, it has been suggested that the UK has a constitution, but consisting of only one rule: 'What the Queen enacts in Parliament is law.' Ridley, however, arguably goes too far in further claiming that the term 'constitution' does not even have a normative or conventional meaning in the UK. He claims that there are no parts of the system to which any special sanctity attaches, so that no one may confidently claim that a given change to the system of government or to the rights of the citizen is 'unconstitutional'. However, if the government were, for example, to procure the passage of legislation allowing for the dismissal by Prime Ministerial *fiat* of any judge, or if a court refused to enforce a statute on the basis that it was sponsored by a political party to which the judge was opposed, commentators would have no hesitation in using the term 'unconstitutional' to describe such actions, although the first would not contravene domestic law. The real problem is not that such hypothetical, drastic actions could not be labelled 'unconstitutional', at least in this sense, but that such confidence would fade in the more marginal cases such as the curtailment of the right to silence (by virtue of the Criminal Justice and Public Order Act 1994) or the enactment of the Prevention of Terrorism Act 2005, allowing for the imposition of draconian 'control orders' on terrorist suspects by the Home Secretary, albeit subject to judicial review.

How far has any of this changed in the UK following devolution and the advent of the HRA? The first point to make is that neither change has, in terms, created any 'higher' system of law. Both the Scotland Act and the HRA specifically affirm that they do not affect Parliament's continued ability to reverse the changes they make, either wholly or in part. Thus, the HRA makes no attempt to entrench itself, and further provides quite specifically that if the courts find a piece of legislation passed either before or after the HRA to be incompatible with one or more of the Convention rights, this will not affect the validity or continuing effect of that legislation (ss 3(2) and 4(6)). The White Paper on incorporation of the ECHR (Cm 3782) states quite clearly that the HRA is not intended to detract from the sovereignty of Parliament in any way. Similarly, the White Paper on Scottish devolution (Cm 3658) proclaims that 'The United Kingdom is and will remain sovereign in all matters', and this basic statement of principle is clearly enacted in the legislation. Section 28(7) of the Scotland Act states that the grant of legislative powers to the Scottish Parliament 'does not affect the power of the United Kingdom Parliament to make law for Scotland'. Westminster may, therefore, still legislate in the devolved areas and may also repeal or modify the Scotland Act itself by ordinary legislation.

These two pieces of legislation introduce substantive, rights-based limitations on governmental power (the HRA) and devolution of that power to a specified region (the Scotland Act). These are matters which in most countries would be part of 'higher' constitutional law, subject to change only through extraordinary procedures themselves specified in the constitution. Instead, the opposite is provided for: following devolution and since the introduction of the HRA, Parliament is still, as a matter of law, able to invade basic rights or the legislative autonomy of Scotland as easily and readily as it may change the rate of income tax.

Thus, on one level, the 'no constitution' attack retains its basic force. But, on another level, its applicability to the UK has become more problematic. To take Scotland first, its Parliament and thus its government for most matters are now limited by what is in effect a codified constitution, made up of the Scotland Act itself, the ECHR and EU law. This is because the Scotland Act provides that Acts of the Scottish Parliament or Executive which are outside the powers devolved to it by the Act or which infringe Convention rights or EU law will be *ultra vires* (s 29), and further that the courts will have what can only be described as a power of constitutional review, being empowered to strike down legislation of the Scottish Parliament or actions of its Executive on those grounds. Of course, in the areas which are not devolved, the Scots continue to be governed by the unrestrained and unconstitutionalised Westminster government and Parliament. However, the day to day experience of the Scottish people is now to live under a government which, in most areas, is constrained by a written constitution which will protect basic rights, specify the electoral system and set the basic shape of government. Those entrenched matters are above and beyond the reach of the Scottish government and Parliament (since neither may alter the Scotland Act itself). Of course, the Westminster Parliament still has the theoretical right to legislate in the devolved areas against the will of the Scottish Parliament and even to abolish the devolved institutions entirely, but no one seriously expects either to occur: the system would be unworkable if Westminster interfered in the devolved matters in this way, while the outright abolition of devolution has become virtually a political impossibility. The Conservative party, which bitterly opposed the Labour plans for devolution from the run up to the 1992 election onwards, has bowed to reality and promised that it will not attempt to reverse devolution. Thus, the day to day experience of the Scottish people is now to live under a codified constitution for the first time.[2]

Moreover, it is clear that the term 'unconstitutional' has started to have a very clear and definite meaning, certainly in relation to the government of Scotland, but also in relation to Westminster. In relation to the former, it now means 'legislation or administrative decisions which violate the legal constraints on the government of Scotland' – there is no doubt as to that. Legislation on rights-related matters now falls to be discussed, and eventually adjudicated upon, in constitutional terms. As to Westminster, as devolution and the new Scottish government have become firmly entrenched, a convention has become established to the effect that the Westminster Parliament will not legislate in the devolved areas without the consent of the Scottish Parliament, just as such a convention developed during the period of the Stormont government of Northern Ireland between 1920 and 1972. Indeed, in a memorandum of understanding drawn up between the UK government and the devolved administrations, it is stated that 'the UK government will normally proceed in accordance with the convention that the UK Parliament would not normally legislate with regard to devolved matters except with the agreement of the devolved legislature', (the so-called Sewell Convention) implying that a convention to this effect was established with the setting up of the devolved legislatures. So far, Westminster has not in fact legislated in the devolved areas without the consent of the Scottish Executive. Of course, legislation intruding into the areas of Scottish competency could not be *legally* condemned by the constitution, but the *terminology* of constitutionalism has entered into the competency of Westminster. Furthermore, this constitutional convention does not suffer from the indeterminacy of other more vague conventions, such as the principle of individual and collective responsibility of government to Parliament, an indeterminacy that allows such principles to be manipulated by the government of the day and undercuts the confidence of any attempts to label a given act as clearly 'unconstitutional'. This is because the Scotland Act lays down in considerable detail the reserved powers of Westminster and thus the powers devolved. Devolution has thus become constitutionalised: in a very concrete way as far as Scotland and its government are concerned; in a conventional but nevertheless real way for the Westminster Parliament.

Much the same may be said of the HRA. We have noted that it is not in any formal way entrenched; nevertheless, for the first time, the rights of the UK citizenry have been authoritatively identified and stated to be fundamental. Executive actions are unlawful if they infringe such rights, unless primary legislation inescapably mandates or authorises the infringement (s 6). *Daly (2001)* confirms that this requires courts to assess for themselves whether Executive decisions have infringed Convention rights, affording a far higher level of protection for those rights than was available under judicial review, although there has been some vacillation about this point in some of the decided cases (see, for example, I. Leigh [2002] PL 265). For the first time, statutory construction fully and unequivocally recognises the importance of basic rights – courts have to read both past and future legislation into conformity with the Convention rights if possible (s 3(1)). Cases such as *A (2001)* and *Ghaidan v Mendoza (2004)* indicate the radical force of this provision, and how far it subordinates normal canons of statutory interpretation to the overriding imperative to uphold Convention rights if possible, though other cases, such as *Re W and B* indicate a less activist approach. Ministers now have to make a statement when introducing legislation into Parliament that it does not infringe Convention rights, or that they believe it does, but they wish to proceed in any event (s 19). Statements of the latter kind would amount to a declaration that the UK intended quite deliberately to violate its Treaty obligations and breach international law; this requirement will inevitably act as a powerful deterrent against the introduction of such legislation. However, an instance of this has already arisen, albeit in relation to a relatively contentious issue of interpretation of Art 10: the UK refuses to accept the correctness of the Strasbourg court's finding that a complete ban on political advertising in broadcasting is a violation of Art 10 and has maintained such a ban in the Communications Act 2003, making a negative (s 19) statement in relation to it when the Bill was introduced. Nevertheless, clear and serious legislative infringements of the Convention are still extremely unlikely, and inadvertent infringements will be avoided by the need to scrutinise the Bill prior to making the statement to Parliament mentioned above.

Meanwhile, ambiguously worded legislation which may infringe rights can be dealt with via the interpretative obligation of the courts noted above. Together, and depending upon how rigorously the courts enforce the interpretative injunction in s 3(1) of the HRA (as indicated above, the cases to date indicate that it is being taken very seriously, though the outcomes vary), this adds up to quite a strong guarantee that legislation will no longer, in practice, infringe basic rights. All this could of course theoretically be removed, simply by repeal of the HRA. However, as with the Scottish Act, this will be highly unlikely, so that as with devolution of powers, basic rights will become to an extent constitutionalised.

In conclusion, therefore, while no form of higher basic norms has, as a matter of law, been created, the effect of the canvassed reforms may in practice be indistinguishable. The basic ability of Parliament to remove so called constitutional guarantees, perhaps only by express repeal, will still remain, at least as a matter of strict law. However, Ridley's suggestion that the concept of 'constitutionalism' at the normative, conventional level cannot be deployed in the UK will lose much of its force, as certain notions of devolved power and of basic rights attain an authoritatively declared basis and – as is likely – become fenced round by strong inhibitory conventions. In that sense, these reforms will inject a modest dose of normative constitutionalism into the UK government and society while leaving us formally still in search of a constitution.

NOTES

1 Students could expand on this, pointing out that recent articles indicate that members of the judiciary, including a very senior member, no longer accept this viewpoint. Lord Woolf ([1995] PL 57) has opined that the courts would not apply an Act of Parliament which purported to remove the power of judicial review from the courts on the basis that this would represent an intolerable attack upon the rule of law, on which the constitution is based. Similarly, Sir John Laws has argued ([1995] PL 72) that not Parliament but the constitution is supreme, and that the 'higher order law' which the constitution represents would inhibit Parliament from successfully assailing fundamental human rights, democratic institutions and the rule of law. He acknowledges that 'constitutional theory has perhaps occupied too modest a place here in Britain', but urges that 'though our constitution is unwritten, it can and must be articulated'.

2 Students could add here that there is some doubt as to whether Scottish judges would uphold Westminster's claimed legislative omnicompetence. In the case of *MacCormack v Lord Advocate (1953)*, the judge suggested that the notion of parliamentary sovereignty was a 'distinctively English principle, which has no counterpart in Scottish constitutional law'. In *A–G v Jackson (2006)*, Lord Hope, the Scottish Law Lord, left open the question whether there are some provisions in the 1707 Treaty of Union, designed to guarantee fundamental aspects of the Union, such as the separate Scottish Church and education system, that Parliament is not competent to remove. Furthermore, the *Scottish Claim of Right*, the foundation of the Scottish Constitutional Convention which laid the basic principles for devolution, affirmed the 'sovereign right of the Scottish people

to determine [their] form of government' – a clear rejection of the notion that sovereignty over Scotland lies with Westminster. It is possible, therefore, that Scottish judges in the future will make findings at least to the effect that devolution, bolstered as it was with emphatic democratic endorsement by the Referendum of 1997, is an entrenched principle which may not be unilaterally removed or modified by the Westminster Parliament.

Question 3

Would you agree that the notions of the separation of powers and the rule of law are entirely overshadowed in the UK Constitution by the doctrine of parliamentary sovereignty? Take account of the impact of the Human Rights Act 1998 in your answer.

Answer plan

This question is very commonly asked. Clearly, the assumption that parliamentary sovereignty is the dominant feature of the constitution should be tested. The question of how far the doctrine has been affected by the UK's membership of the EU should be touched on, but cannot be considered in detail if the other two main issues are to receive adequate coverage. Obviously, it amounts to a very important issue in itself (which is considered in Chapter 2), but it would not be appropriate to examine it in detail here. In considering the doctrine of the separation of powers, comparisons can usefully be made with other jurisdictions, such as the USA. Mention of specific aspects of the Human Rights Act (HRA) 1998, specific European Convention on Human Rights (ECHR) Articles and relevant case law is essential in dealing with the final part of the question.

Essentially, the following matters should be discussed:

- the concept of the rule of law as put forward by Dicey;
- the extent to which the rule of law finds expression in the constitution;
- the doctrine of the separation of powers as propounded by Montesquieu;
- instances in which the doctrine is breached or observed;
- the impact of the HRA and the Constitutional Reform Act on both of the above;
- the meaning of the doctrine of parliamentary sovereignty;
- the weakening of the doctrine which has taken place due to Britain's membership of the EU.

Answer

The question presupposes that parliamentary sovereignty is the main basis of the UK Constitution and that the two other doctrines mentioned do not represent a constraint on it. It will be argued that both these assumptions are overstated, although it will be accepted that parliamentary sovereignty is the most significant feature of the UK Constitution. It will be argued that while the HRA has strengthened aspects of both the rule of law and the separation of powers, its enactment has not affected the basic subordination of both to parliamentary sovereignty.

Before determining whether the rule of law can be said to be irrelevant in the British Constitution, it must be decided what is meant by the concept because the interpretation adopted will clearly affect the issue of relevance to be addressed. The concept of the rule of law as influenced by Dicey (*The Law of the Constitution*, 1971) appears to encompass the following notions: first, that powers exercised by government must be founded on lawful authority as opposed to being arbitrary; second, that citizens should be equal before the law; and, third, that the law should be clear. Can it be said that these notions find expression in the UK Constitution?

Historically, constitutional lawyers in this country have prided themselves on their adherence to the rule of law, as upheld by judges in a number of famous cases. One of these is *Entick v Carrington (1765)*, in which agents of the King, acting under a warrant issued by the Secretary of State, broke into the house of Entick, alleged to be the author of seditious writings, and removed certain of his papers. It was found that because the action was justified by no specific legal authority, it was a common trespass, for which the Secretary of State was liable in damages. If government is under the law, in the sense that any actions it takes must be authorised by law, then since the courts are empowered to make the authoritative determination of what the law is, this must mean that the government is in a sense under (and therefore obliged to obey) orders of the courts, expressed in the form of injunctions. The normal sanction for failure to obey an order of the court is a finding of contempt of court. Perhaps surprisingly, it was only in the case of *Re M (1993)* that it was settled that ministers of the Crown were obliged to obey court orders and risked a finding of contempt if they did not. The notion, expressed in both the above cases, that exercises of governmental power, particularly those which impact upon the liberty of the citizen, must have a basis in law, has now found a powerful reinforcement through the incorporation of the ECHR into UK law through the HRA 1998. The Convention rights are now binding on all public authorities, including courts, which act unlawfully if they act incompatibly with them (s 6(1)). Under s 3(1) of the HRA, 'So far as it is possible to do so, all legislation must be construed compatibly with the Convention rights', though if any primary legislation cannot be so construed, it remains valid and of full effect – the courts are given no strike down power. Certain Convention rights permit interferences with them in limited circumstances: Art 2 (right to life); Art 5 (personal liberty); Art 8 (privacy); Art 9 (freedom of religion); Art 10 (freedom of expression); and Art 11 (freedom of assembly and association). In order for such interferences to be lawful under the ECHR, the government must first show that the interference was 'prescribed by' or 'in accordance with the law', that is, that it had a basis in existing domestic law. In other words, an identifiable legal basis authorising the interference must be shown: mere Executive discretion cannot suffice. It was on this basis that the UK was held to be in violation of Art 8 of the ECHR in the case of *Malone v UK (1985)*. The Constitutional Reform Act 2005 states in s 1 that 'it does not affect the existing constitutional principle of the rule of law', thus giving statutory recognition of its constitutional importance, for the first time.

It could be said that arbitrary power, although apparently contrary to the rule of law as expounded by Dicey, is exercised by ministers in the sense that legislation is often enacted conferring on them a broad discretion to act as appears appropriate in any particular circumstance. Section 365(5) of the Communications Act 2003 (replacing the similar power unders 10 of the Broadcasting Act 1990) provides an example of a very widely drafted discretion: the Home Secretary can order Ofcom, the independent broadcasting regulator, by notice to direct broadcasters to 'refrain from including in their licensed services any matter or descriptions of matter, specified in the notice'. Once a discretion of this width is granted to a minister, might it be said that he can act in a manner which is unregulated by the law? Clearly, in a narrow sense, the minister is acting within the law because the discretionary power is lawfully granted. However, such an answer begs the question at issue. To some extent, it may be said that the minister is indeed able to exercise arbitrary power in the sense that any specific action has no specific legal authority; the only check on such actions is represented by the availability of judicial review. Where the exercise of the power in question would impact on a right protected by the ECHR, as in the example given above (Art 10) then, under s 3(1) of the HRA, the courts will be obliged to construe the power granted narrowly, so that it no longer authorises interference with Convention rights, if that is possible, and to strike down actions which do infringe Convention rights (s 6(1)) unless the statute in question clearly mandates or authorises such infringement (s 6(2)). This will considerably reduce the broad discretion which is *prima facie* granted by such statutes, and which the House of Lords in **Brind (1991)** refused to read as impliedly restricted by reference to the Convention rights. The HRA therefore overrules *Brind.* But where no Convention right is arguably engaged by the exercise of statutory authority, such powers, however broad, will not be affected by the HRA. However, the courts are prepared to invalidate a minister's actions, according to the House of Lords in *Padfield v Minister of Agriculture (1968)*, where he purports to act within a broadly drafted power, on the ground that the actions do not promote the policy and objects of the statute conferring the power. Although the check thus represented by judicial review on a minister's actions may suggest that the rule of law is recognised by the constitution, it might be equally plausible to suggest that such a check springs from the doctrine of parliamentary sovereignty, in that it is designed to ensure that powers exercised by ministers and other bodies do not rise above those of Parliament itself. Certain constitutional writers, such as Wade, have criticised the notion that such a well settled feature of the constitution as the granting of wide powers to ministers can be said to infringe the rule of law.

What of the notion that the law applies equally to all citizens, which implies that no one is above the law? The notion could be attacked by citing numerous exceptions to it. Members of Parliament enjoy complete civil and criminal immunity in respect of words spoken during 'proceedings in Parliament' by virtue of the Bill of Rights 1688, while judges also enjoy various legal privileges. Diplomatic and consular immunities arise under the Diplomatic Privileges Act 1964 and the Consular Relations Act 1968, and these have been left undisturbed by s 16 of the State Immunity Act 1978. However, it might be suggested that these examples of exemptions granted and recognised by law support the argument that the rule of law exists in the UK Constitution, as they imply that there is a need to create exceptions to a general principle which would otherwise apply to all the groups mentioned. It is notable that in *A v Secretary of State (2004)*, one of the key grounds for finding the legislative scheme allowing for detention without trial in Belmarsh prison of terrorist suspects incompatible with the Convention, was that it unlawfully discriminated between nationals and non-nationals.

Can it equally be said that the doctrine of the separation of powers is of some relevance to the UK Constitution, even though it is possible to find instances where it is clear that the doctrine is not being applied? The doctrine, mainly developed by Montesquieu and his followers, encompasses the notion that the three main organs of government are the legislature, the Executive and the judiciary, and that only one class of function should be in the hands of each body. For example, the judiciary should apply, not create, law. Thus, a system of checks and balances between each branch of government will be provided. It is not hard to find examples of the violation of this doctrine. Judges can create law, in the sense that they can declare and develop the common law. Declaring the common law clearly means creating it, as the common law often has to meet fresh situations which have never previously been addressed. In *Shaw v DPP (1962)*, for example, the House of Lords declared that the common law included a doctrine known as conspiracy to corrupt public morals, although no precedents were cited demonstrating that it had ever existed except as a variant of the power exercised by Star Chamber judges to punish offences against conventional morality.

Ministers, who are members of the Executive, sit as members of the House of Commons which is the legislative body. The Lord Chancellor is a minister as well as head of the judiciary and a Law Lord, and is also a member of the House of Lords in its legislative capacity. However, the case of *McGonnell v UK (2000)*, in which the Bailiff of Guernsey, an officeholder with mixed functions similar to the Lord Chancellor's, was found to have violated Art 6 of the ECHR when he sat in judgment in a case involving legislation in the passage of which he had been involved as Speaker of the legislature, spelled the end of the Lord Chancellor's days as a judge, as confirmed in the Constitutional Reform Act 2005, discussed further below. More importantly, it is well accepted by constitutional observers that the Executive can effectively determine the legislative output of Parliament, theoretically a separate body. As Calvert puts it, with perhaps a little exaggeration, 'before the formally dramatic part of the legislative process even begins, almost all the terms of almost all (government) Bills are settled' (*British Constitutional Law*, 1985).

It seems clear, then, that the separation of powers, if interpreted as connoting a rigid compartmentalisation of the functions of government, hardly exists in the British Constitution, and indeed it appears that government could hardly be carried on if it were. However, if the doctrine is not interpreted literally, it may be argued that some aspects of government do reflect a recognition of its existence. Under the House of Commons Disqualification Act 1975, civil servants must resign their posts if they wish to stand for election to the House of Commons, as must professional full-time judges. Further, the number of government ministers permitted to sit in the House of Commons is limited to 95. Moreover, the growing significance of judicial review does not suggest that the separation of powers is irrelevant. Judicial review is generally recognised as an important and necessary check on the exercise of official power. Here again, the HRA has clearly had an impact: s 6(1), which makes it unlawful for a public authority to act in violation of a Convention right, represents a significant shift in power from the Executive to the judiciary. This is not, as some on the Right have complained, a shift in power from *Parliament* to the judiciary because, under the HRA, there is no power given to judges to strike down primary legislation. However, there is a shift from the *Executive* to the judiciary, because for the first time, the courts will be able to strike down actions not because they are outside the powers used to justify the actions or did not follow a fair procedure, but on the substantive basis that they violated human rights: *ex p Limbuela (2005)* is a striking example. The freedom of action of the Executive – the area of discretion it enjoys – is, as a corollary, substantially curtailed. Again, however, this shift in power will occur only in relation to areas of law which touch on Convention rights.[1]

The HRA has already had a more specific impact in terms of the separation of functions between the Executive and the judiciary. An example of what Stevens refers to as 'the casual British attitude to the separation of powers' ((1999) OJLS

366) was the power of the Home Secretary to set sentences to be served by juvenile killers. Under the Crime (Sentences) Act 1997, the Home Secretary set a 'tariff' – that part of a sentence designed to satisfy the demands of retribution and punishment – and upon its expiry, the prisoner became eligible for release by the Parole Board, and would be released unless it was thought that he still constituted a danger to society. In effect, therefore, a sentencing function was being performed by a party politician and powerful member of the Cabinet. A challenge to the Secretary's power to set such tariffs was launched before the European Court of Human Rights, in reliance upon Art 6(1) of the ECHR, which provides: 'In the determination of his civil rights and obligations, or of any criminal charge against him, everyone is entitled to a fair and public hearing within a reasonable time by an independent and impartial tribunal established by law.' In *T v UK; V v UK (2000)* the Court found that the Secretary, as a party politician, could not be considered an Independent' tribunal. The UK was obliged to implement that judgment as a matter of international law. A very similar decision was made by the House of Lords under the HRA in *Anderson (2003)*, in which the incompatibility with Art 6 lay in the like involvement of the Secretary of State in sentencing adult life prisoners. Indeed, the Scottish decision in *Starrs v Ruxton (2000)*, finding that the scheme for appointing temporary sheriffs was unlawful under Art 6(1) because it failed to guarantee their impartiality and independence from the Executive, indicates the bolstering effect which that Convention right may now have on the independence of the judiciary, a vital aspect of the separation of powers. However, it must be recalled that a statute (say) clearly granting a judicial function to a politician (as with the Home Secretary, above) or setting up a scheme for appointing judges that similarly violated Art 6(1) could not be struck down by the UK courts (ss 3(2) and 4(6) of the HRA).

A more systematic reorganisation of the UK constitution, in line with separation of powers principles, has been brought about by the Constitutional Reform Act 2005 (CRA), when it comes fully into force. The Act brings in a number of reforms designed to rationalise the UK's hitherto rather ad hoc arrangements for its highest court, the position of the head of the judiciary (the Lord Chancellor) and his involvement with other organs of government (discussed above) and judicial appointments. In brief, the CRA provides that the Lord Chancellor will cease to be the head of the judiciary; that function is now held by the most senior judge – the Lord Chief Justice (s 7(1)). It provides for a new Supreme Court, to end the anomaly whereby the UK's highest court – the House of Lords – was merely a committee of its upper legislative chamber (its formal name is the Appellate Committee of the House of Lords); this will end the violation of the separation of powers represented by the presence of the Law Lords in the second chamber of Parliament. The CRA also formally brings about the end of the Lord Chancellor's role in the judicial and legislative arms of government; he is no longer a judge and does not now take the judicial oath (s 17), so he will not sit in the Appellate Committee of the House of

Lords or the new Supreme Court; it also provides that he is no longer the Speaker of the House of Lords (s 18), which now chooses it own Speaker. Perhaps most importantly, the Act puts in place a new system for judicial appointments, designed to bolster judicial independence. Previously, the most senior judiciary (the Law Lords, the Court of Appeal judges, President of the Family Division and Master of the Rolls) were appointed by the Queen on the advice of the Prime Minister. High Court, circuit and district judges were appointed by the Queen on the advice of the Lord Chancellor, as were recorders. In relation to the most senior positions (Law Lords and Court of Appeal judges), there was a system of 'secret soundings', whereby the Lord Chancellor would consult confidentially with existing judges at this level as to the merits of possible candidates for promotion. This system had been subject to widespread criticism for its lack of transparency and for its tendency to limit membership of the senior judiciary to a small elite of senior barristers, overwhelmingly, white, male and upper class (see, for example, K. Malleson, (2004) PL 102). Prior to the CRA, a limited, non-statutory reform was undertaken by way of the creation of a Commission for Judicial Appointments, which, despite its name, did not *make* appointments, but oversaw the process. The CRA is a much more thorough-going piece of reform, by creating a full Appointments Commission, with a carefully balanced membership. Lord Mance, an existing Law Lord, has described its composition as 'more nuanced and subtle than any found in any other European jurisdiction' ((2006) 25 CJQ 155). The Commission does not actually appoint, but makes recommendations to the Lord Chancellor, who, in the case of the most senior appointments, then puts these to the Queen, or to the Prime Minister to put to the Queen (the Law Lords). Thus, formally speaking, senior politicians are still involved in the process; however, the Lord Chancellor's power to reject names put to him is restricted; Lord Mance has commented that:

> the Lord Chancellor's powers to reject or require reconsideration [of names put to him] and his obligation to give reasons are restrictive to the point where it seems in practice to be almost inevitable that he will accept the Judicial Appointments Commission's recommendations (ibid).

The Act therefore considerably strengthens the independence of the judiciary, both symbolically and practically, and, it is to be hoped, may lead to greater diversity in appointments. Moreover the Act specifically provides that the Lord Chancellor and other Ministers have a duty 'to uphold the continued independence of the judiciary' (s 3(1) and, specifically, 'must not seek to influence particular judicial decisions through any access to the judiciary' (s 3(5)). It is valuable to have so important a principle both of the separation of powers and of the rule of law (which is heavily dependent upon the independence of the judiciary) enshrined in statute.

Nevertheless, overall, it must be acknowledged that the separation of powers in Britain is less clearly apparent than under some systems. In America, for example, the President and his Cabinet cannot be members of Congress, and the President may veto legislation but may not dissolve Congress. The courts can declare legislation enacted by Congress invalid on the ground that it is unconstitutional. In contrast, it is clear that the UK judiciary will refuse to hold legislation enacted by Parliament to be invalid (as a matter of the UK as opposed to EU law), as demonstrated in *Pickin v British Railways Board (1974)*, although it did show itself willing in *R* (1991) to ignore a word used in an Act of Parliament. Furthermore, Parliament is free to enact legislation nullifying a decision taken in the House of Lords, as it did in the **War Damage Act 1965** which followed the decision in *Burmah Oil Co v Lord Advocate (1965)*. Article 7 of the ECHR, now binding on all public authorities save Parliament under s 6(1) of the HRA, states: 'No one shall be held guilty of any criminal offence on account of any act or omission which did not constitute a criminal offence under national or international law at the time when it was committed.' This Article reinforces the protection against non-retroactivity in criminal law but, since it is incorporated through the HRA, could simply be overridden by Parliament and therefore makes no formal difference to the separation of powers.

The reluctance of the judiciary to depart from the will of Parliament flows from the doctrine of parliamentary sovereignty which – it should be acknowledged – is the most prominent feature of the UK Constitution in a way which marks it out from other constitutions. Parliament can legislate on any subject and therefore could pass laws severely curtailing civil liberties without facing the possibility that such legislation might be declared unconstitutional. The HRA 1998 specifically declares that the incompatibility of any legislation with the incorporated Convention rights will not render that legislation void or deprive it of effect (ss 3(2) and 4(6)). Parliament's full powers to invade civil rights are thus maintained, at least as a matter of law. This lack of legal restraint has both a positive and a negative aspect. It means that while Parliament can legislate on any subject, it cannot bind successive Parliaments. If it could, then obviously each successive Parliament would not be free to legislate on any matter. This aspect of sovereignty means that where there is inconsistency between a previous and a subsequent Act, the latter impliedly repeals the former to the extent of its inconsistency. Authority for this proposition derives from *Ellen Street Estates Ltd v Minister of Health (1934)*, although it may now no longer be true as regards implied repeal of 'constitutional statutes' (*Thoburn* (2002).[2]

However, it may be argued that parliamentary sovereignty has been weakened by Britain's membership of the EU. After the ruling of the European Court of Justice in *Factortame v Secretary of State for Transport (No 2) (1991)*, the House of Lords accepted that where Community law was clear, it must prevail over domestic law subsequent or previous, though it did not deal with the (still hypothetical) instance in which Parliament in a statute expressly instructed the courts to apply domestic law in preference to EU law. It re-affirmed this position in *Secretary of State for Employment ex p EOC (1994)*. Theoretically, Parliament could repeal s 2(4) of the European Communities Act 1972, which gives primacy to community law; in practice, it would almost certainly refrain from doing so, at least whilst the UK remains part of the EU.

It may be concluded that despite some diminution in the constitutional force of parliamentary sovereignty, it still is the dominant feature of the constitution, and therefore to an extent undermines the doctrine of the rule of law and of the separation of powers, although it is submitted that it does not render them wholly irrelevant. The HRA and the CRA have strengthened both these doctrines to a significant degree, but of course both remain subject to the doctrine of parliamentary sovereignty.

▌NOTES

1 Students could note that the HRA may paradoxically be said to undermine the rule of law by adding further uncertainty to the law. The Act requires all legislation to be read and given effect in such a way as to be compatible with the Convention rights 'so as is possible'. Potentially, therefore, all legislation which touches on ECHR issues is now open to re-interpretation; a considerable period of uncertainty will thus ensue. The case of *A (2001)* is a good example: the statutory provision in question, s 41 of the Youth Justice and Criminal Evidence Act was given a radically different meaning from that which appears on its face; it is difficult to know in advance which other statutory provisions might be thus judicially re-shaped, thus rendering their meaning uncertain until so determined.

2 Further support for this argument could be given, such as this statement from *Sir Robert Megarry VC in Manuel v Attorney General (1983)*: 'Once an instrument is recognised as being an Act of Parliament, no English court can refuse to obey it or question its validity.'

Question 4

'The legal limitation of parliamentary sovereignty by means of a codified constitution has now become essential due to the failure of traditional checks on government power and the refusal of the Labour government to give real teeth to its reforms in this area.'

Discuss.

Answer plan

This is a particularly topical question and is therefore likely to be quite popular with examiners. It is, however, quite demanding. It assumes that 'traditional checks' have failed; that it is desirable to limit parliamentary sovereignty; that the Labour reforms – principally the **Human Rights Act (HRA) 1998**, but also the **Constitutional Reform Act 2005 (CRA)** – have not properly addressed this problem; and that a codified constitution would be likely to provide such limitation. All these assumptions should be tested. As the question raises a large number of issues, care must be taken in planning in order to ensure that they all receive adequate coverage. It would be quite easy to devote most of the essay to the problem of entrenchment, for example. Note that there is some overlap between this area and the discussion in Chapter 9 concerning the adoption of a UK Bill of Rights. However, adoption of a Bill of Rights could take place without a new constitutional settlement and, indeed, whether it should do so is one of the main issues in the Bill of Rights debate.

The following issues should be addressed:

- Lord Hailsham's notion of an 'elective dictatorship';
- the role of the House of Lords in providing a check on the power of the Commons; the impact of reform so far and prospects for further reform;
- the role of the media in informing the public as to government actions;
- the impact of membership of the EU and the role of the European Convention on Human Rights (ECHR);
- the impact of the HRA, CRA and the Freedom of Information Act 2000;
- the benefits which might flow from a codified constitution;
- the difficulties of entrenching a new constitutional settlement: s 2(4) of the European Communities Act 1972 as a model.

Answer

Within the UK, there is no written constitution which has a higher status than the rest of the law. The body of rules relating to the structure, functions and powers of the organs of State, their relationship to one another and to the private citizen is to be derived from common law, statute and constitutional conventions. Therefore, the constitution does not impose limits on what may be done by ordinary legislation in the way that many constitutions do. The legislative competence of the UK

Parliament is unlimited save (perhaps) in the field of EU law. No Parliament may bind its successors or be bound by its predecessors, and the courts cannot question the validity of an Act of Parliament. Therefore, no formal mechanism exists ensuring that the rights of minorities and individual citizens are not infringed by Parliament. Instead, there has been an informal acceptance that such rights will be respected – that the legally unlimited power of Parliament will not be used to the full. This informal acceptance is reflected in the structure of the HRA. While it allows citizens to enforce their Convention rights against government and other public bodies, it expressly preserves the right of Parliament to pass legislation infringing upon the Convention rights and makes no attempt to entrench itself. Its enactment does not, therefore, fully answer the doubts which have been expressed as to the wisdom of placing reliance on such informal restraints. Similarly, the Freedom of Information Act 2000 which, for the first time, gives a basic right of access to government information, is a statute, like any other, subject to ordinary repeal. While devolution has given Scotland, Wales and Northern Ireland local administrations which are limited, *inter alia*, by the guarantees in the ECHR, Westminster retains full powers to legislate in the devolved areas, and to repeal the devolution legislation itself.

In 1976, Lord Hailsham put forward the view that the current constitutional arrangements amounted to an elective dictatorship for which the only remedy was a written constitution. This view has since been endorsed many times from the other end of the political spectrum. It arises due to a perception that the House of Commons has become subordinate to the government which controls it through the party machine. Lord Hailsham wrote that legislation of major importance was passed with wholly inadequate debate and that Parliament was being reduced to little more than a rubber stamp. He also considered that although absolute power was conferred on Parliament, those powers were concentrated in an executive government formed out of one party which, due to the electoral system, might not fairly represent the popular will.

When the government in power has a large majority, this problem is likely to be exacerbated as suggested by the use, in 1988, of a three-line whip against a Conservative back bencher's Private Members' Bill (Richard Shepherd's Bill in 1988, intended to reform s 2 of the Official Secrets Act 1911) and the guillotining of the parliamentary debate on the Official Secrets Bill 1989. The recent passage of quite draconian anti-terrorism legislation – the Anti-Terrorism, Crime and Security Act 2001 – in response to the September 11 attacks – further provides a startling example of how Parliament may readily renounce its scrutinising and checking function: the legislation, which ran into over 100 clauses, was passed through the Commons in only 16 hours, even though it clearly contained numerous provisions which had little or no relation to the threat from international terrorism. The House of Lords made a number of improvements to the Bill, but its harshest provisions, including the powers to detain without trial certain terrorist suspects, a provision which required the UK to derogate from Art 5 of the ECHR, were left basically intact. Very recently, the Commons has shown some willingness to reject or ameliorate particularly draconian provisions in government bills: the proposal in the Terrorism Act 2006 to extend the period for which police may detain terrorist suspects without charge to 90 days was rejected by the Commons, which allowed only an extension to 28 days; similarly, the Commons insisted (by one vote) upon certain liberalising amendments made by the House of Lords, but opposed by the Government, to the new offence of incitement to religious hatred in the Racial and Religious Hatred Bill 2005. Nevertheless, these are the only legislative defeats inflicted on the Blair government in 11 years, and this in the context of a government that has passed thousands of pages of legislation a year (3,500 in 2004 alone) and created over 3,000 new criminal offences since 1997.

Furthermore, the secrecy which cloaks the actions of ministers hampers the Opposition in scrutinising their actions. The corollary of government secrecy is misinformation: the case of *Ponting (1985)* testified to its extent. At the time of writing, the Freedom of Information Act 2000 has recently come into force (in 2005); however, while for the first time it gives UK citizens a basic legal right to government information and backs this up with impressive and independent enforcement mechanisms, it has been widely criticised for its numerous, very wide exemptions and the inclusion of a ministerial veto over the release on public interest grounds of certain classes of information held by central government (see, for example, the coruscating critique of R. Austin in Jowell and Oliver, *The Changing Constitution* (5th edn, 2004), chapter 16).

Other checks on governmental power are perceived as relatively weak. The House of Lords has had some successes, notably the incorporation into the Police and Criminal Evidence Act 1984 of a provision with great potential to safeguard the liberty of the citizen (s 78), its recent, repeated rejections of the Labour government's attempts to curtail the right to trial by jury, and the improvements it has made to successive Terrorism Bills in 2001, 2005 and 2006, as well as to the Legislative and Regulatory Reform Bill 2006. However, the Lords are not generally so bold; when they oppose a Bill sent up by the Commons, they tend to propose amendments at the Committee stage rather than vote against the second reading. The Lords will rarely insist on their amendments to a government Bill although, of course, they may do so when the government lacks an effective majority to ensure their rejection in the Commons. Under the Salisbury Convention, the Lords will not reject measures which were contained in the government's manifesto. However, this has not stopped the Lords making important amendments to such legislation, against strong government opposition. The European Elections Bill 1998 introduced proportional representation for elections to the European Parliament, in line with a promise in Labour's manifesto for the 1997 General Election. The Lords five times restored an amendment providing for an 'open' rather than a 'closed' list of candidates (something on which the manifesto had been silent) which had been repeatedly rejected by the Commons, eventually causing the Bill to be lost. Ultimately, the government can threaten to pass a Bill under the 1911 and 1949 Parliament Acts procedure if the Lords appear minded to oppose it, giving the Lords only a year's power of delay over most legislation, though the scarcity of its use (four times since 1949) illustrates the generally very self-restrained approach of the Lords (it was eventually used in relation to the European Elections Bill) . There is general agreement that the removal of most of the hereditary peers from the House in 1999 has given the House a greater sense of its own legitimacy, which has manifested itself in a more assertive stance *vis à vis* the government-dominated Commons. Nevertheless, as indicated above, the House ultimately gave way on most of the crucial issues relating to the protection of liberty raised by the Anti-Terrorism Bill 2001.

The Wakeham proposals for reform of the House of Lords were referred to a Joint Committee of both Houses for consideration, after the government's White Paper – which proposed a largely nominated House, with most of the safeguards for ensuring its independence proposed by Wakeham removed – was roundly rejected in 2002 by MPs and peers alike in a rare victory for parliamentary power over central government. However, when its report, giving various options for a fully appointed, fully elected or a hybrid house was debated by Parliament in 2003, the Commons voted down every option, once more effectively stalemating attempts at further reform. The 2006 Queen's Speech promised that the Government would bring forward proposals on Lords Reform, and a leaked report by Jack Straw, Leader of the House of Commons, calls for a mixed 50/50 elected/appointed House. A strong independent element of around 20% independent peers, preserving the House's traditional strengths in (partial) independence from party control and expertise would be retained. Whether this proposal for Lords Reform, unlike all others since 1999, will succeed remains to be seen. While such a reform would undoubtedly greatly increase the *de facto* power of the House – by giving it the confidence to use its formal, legal powers far more fully than it does at present – there appears to be no governmental support for giving the House greater legal powers over legislation than it currently possesses, if anything, the Government seems minded to try to *reduce* the Lords powers. Unlike nearly every second chamber in liberal democracies abroad, the House has no special powers over legislation altering the constitution, while the Salisbury Convention will doubtless remain in place in any future reform (see G. Phillipson, (2003) *Public Law* 32). The recent report by the Joint Committee on Conventions (1st Report, 2005–06) recommends the continuation of the Salsibury convention, and its codification in a resolution of the House of Lords.

Traditionally, the operation of a free and diverse press has offered a further check to government power; prior to the Freedom of Information Act 2000, the press was mainly dependent on a system of official and unofficial leaks, though there was evidence of increasing usage of the government's Code of Practice on Access to Information, policed by the Parliamentary Commissioner, whose recommendations on release of information were generally, though not invariably, complied with. The 2000 Act should improve matters, although the sweeping class exemption it contains for information relating to the formulation of government policy in s 35 will probably mean much information of great interest in this area will be disclosed, as at present only at the discretion of Ministers. When this lack of a really rigorous and transparent FOI regime is coupled, as it is at present, with the concentration of the press in a few hands, the quality of diversity is weakened, and when certain of the most powerful owners of the press are generally sympathetic to the government (as was the case during much of the Thatcher era), a loss of independence may follow. There is a danger that certain organs of the press will merely peddle the same government 'leaks' or press handouts dressed up in different forms to suit different markets.[1]

Although it may be true that traditional checks on government power are ineffective, it is arguable that newer ones will have an increasing impact. The EU, which will have a growing influence,[2] has already had an impact on parliamentary sovereignty, curbing government power in areas such as sex discrimination. Section 2(4) of the European Communities Act 1972 provides, in effect, that UK Acts of Parliament shall be construed and have effect subject to directly applicable Community law. In this respect, it is clear from judgments of the European Court of Justice (see *Costa v ENEL (1964)*) that Community law should prevail over national law, a principle broadly accepted by the UK courts in *Factortame Ltd and Others v Secretary of State for Transport (No 2) (1991)*.

The rulings of the European Court of Human Rights have, to an extent, acted as a substitute for a domestic Bill of Rights and have led to better protection of human rights in such areas as prisoners' rights *(Golder (1975))*, freedom of expression *(Sunday Times case (1979))* and privacy *(Malone (1985))*. The main problem was that the process of invoking the ECHR by 'going to Strasbourg' was extremely cumbersome, lengthy and expensive. This has now been addressed through the enactment of the HRA 1998. Litigants are now able to assert their Convention rights against any public authority in any UK court or tribunal. The HRA makes it unlawful for a public authority to perform an act that is incompatible with the Convention rights, unless legislation unambiguously mandates or authorises such actions (s 6). All legislation must now be read 'so far as . . . possible' to be compatible with the Convention rights (s 3). There is no doubt that this Act therefore represents a very real and substantial limitation upon Executive action. The decision in *Brind (1991)*, in which the House of Lords refused to impose a presumption that statutes granting wide ministerial discretion give no power to infringe Convention rights, has been unequivocally reversed. Moreover, ministers now have to make a statement when introducing legislation into Parliament that it does not infringe Convention rights or that it does, but they wish to proceed in any event (s 19). A statement that it did amount to an infringement would amount to a declaration that the UK was quite deliberately violating its Treaty obligations and breaching international law; this will therefore act as a powerful deterrent against the introduction of such legislation (although a minor instance of this has already arisen, in relation to a relatively contentious issue of interpretation of Art 10: the UK refuses to accept the correctness of the Strasbourg court's finding that a complete ban on political advertising in broadcasting is a violation of Art 10 and has maintained such a ban in the Communications Act 2003, making a negative (s 19) statement in relation to it when the Bill was introduced). It is likely, therefore, that clear and serious statutory infringements of the ECHR will become rare if not extinct phenomena, whilst the courts can deal with ambiguous statutory infringements by the robust interpretative approach specified in s 3. Cases such as *A (2001), Ghaidan v Mendoza (2004)* and *Offen (2001)* indicate the potency of that provision, though other decisions (such as *Re W and B (2002)*) are more cautious and it is safe to say that no definitive interpretation of s 3 has been judicially agreed upon. Nevertheless, the HRA clearly provides for a strong and concrete restraint upon Executive action and, in practice, will probably ensure that legislation infringing basic rights becomes a thing of the past, though the recent derogation from Art 5 of the ECHR following the September 11 attacks in 2001, in order to allow for the detention without trial of certain suspected international terrorists, indicates that the UK is very far from developing a strong culture of respect for the ECHR: whilst the Government did withdraw the derogation and allowed the legislation to lapse following the House of Lord's landmark decision in *A v Secretary of State (2001)*, it promptly introduced the Prevention of Terrorism Act 2005, containing draconian provisions for control orders, the operation of which the Court of Appeal has already found to violate Article 5 of the Convention. Repeal of the HRA itself, of course, remains a legal possibility; indeed at present it is official Conservative policy. It should be stressed again that Parliament's formal legal powers are not in any way restricted by the Act.

Judicial independence generally has been significantly boosted by the Constitutional Reform Act 2005, which reforms judicial appointments, bringing in a significant independent element in the Judicial Appointments Commission, and places a clear duty on Ministers of the Crown to uphold judicial independence and not seek to influence the outcome of any judgment (s 3). However, the statute itself remains subject to repeal, although this is politically unlikely. It may therefore be argued that there is a need for a further check on parliamentary power. A codified constitution might meet that need, at least theoretically, if it allowed the judiciary to act as a more effective check on Parliament through the ability to strike down legislation as unconstitutional, as in Canada, the US and South Africa. (At present, the judiciary will refuse to invalidate legislation which has been enacted by Parliament *(Pickin v British Railways Board (1974))*. In particular, if a Bill of Rights were entrenched within the constitution, basic civil rights might be more surely guaranteed to the UK citizens. Adoption of a written constitution might address other problems identified by Lord Hailsham, including over-centralisation and unfairness in the electoral system.

However, it has sometimes been doubted whether entrenchment of a written constitution is possible in our system. Entrenchment could be attempted by means of a provision that the constitution could be repealed or amended only by means of a referendum, or perhaps by a two-thirds majority of Parliament. If a later Parliament purported to repeal part of the constitution without a referendum, would the judges refuse to give effect to such legislation on the grounds that it was unconstitutional? Under the traditional doctrine of implied repeal, as exemplified in *Ellen Street Estates v Minister of Health (1934)*, judges would give effect to the later legislation. However, it might be possible to create artificially a discontinuity of power which would have the effect of modifying parliamentary sovereignty permanently, after which adoption of a written constitution might be possible. O Hood Phillips considered that this could occur if Parliament extinguished itself, transferring its powers to a new Constituent Assembly. Dicey took the view that it would be untenable to espouse 'the strange dogma sometimes put forward that a sovereign power, such as the Parliament of the UK, can never, by its own act, divest itself of authority' (*An Introduction to the Study of the Law of the Constitution*, 10th edn, 1959, p 68). On this view, the judges would accept the new constitutional settlement; possibly, as Wade suggests, the Judges' Oath should also be amended in order to make it clear that their allegiance had changed.

Moreover, as already mentioned, the judges have accepted at the very least a variant of the rules of implied repeal flowing from s 2(4) of the European Communities Act 1972. It appears to follow from *Macarthy's v Smith (1981)* and from *Factortame* that Parliament has succeeded in partially entrenching s 2(1) of the European Communities Act by means of s 2(4), due to the imposition of a requirement of form (express words) on future legislation designed to override Community law. This development lends more force to the argument that entrenchment of a written constitution is possible, although it is disputed by Laws LJ in *Thoburn*, who interprets *Factortame* and other judgments as simply providing, that by virtue of the common law, certain statutes may not be subject to implied repeal.

In conclusion, it may be argued that while many of the traditional means of curbing government power no longer seem to be effective, the HRA is likely to constitute a new and powerful guarantee against oppressive government; joined now by the Freedom of Information Act, a very substantial movement towards more open and limited government is be apparent. The objections to the un-entrenched UK Constitution will of course remain, though they may become less practically evident. They can only be fully addressed by a new constitutional settlement.

NOTES

1 It could also be pointed out here that the freedom of the media is, in any event, hampered by the laws of libel, contempt, official secrets, and particularly recently by the action for breach of confidence. The possibility of prior restraint via the use of an interim injunction to preserve confidentiality, combined with the extension of the law of contempt in *Attorney General v Newspaper Publishing plc (1987)*, supporting such an injunction, arguably represents the most worrying curb on media freedom since *Attorney General v Times Newspapers (1974)*.

2 Further developments in the influence of EU law could be considered at this point. The House of Lords in *Litster v Forth Dry Docks Ltd (1989)* determined that even where EU law is not directly effective, priority for EU law should be ensured by means of national law. The House of Lords was prepared to construe the domestic legislation contrary to its *prima facie* meaning, because it had been introduced expressly to implement the directive in question.

Question 5

How far has Scottish devolution affected the unitary nature of the UK and its 'unwritten' constitution?

Answer plan

Questions on devolution often focus upon the whole scheme, requiring comparison of the settlements for Scotland, Wales and Northern Ireland, and often requiring the candidate to comment on the asymmetric nature of the scheme. Another popular topic is the issue of the unresolved 'West Lothian' or 'English' question, whereby Scottish MPs continue to vote on matters solely affecting England, whereas English MPs now no longer vote on the broad swathe of areas devolved to Scotland. Where a more specific question is asked, it will often focus upon the constitutional implications of devolution to Scotland, the most significant of the schemes (at least while Northern Ireland devolution remains in abeyance as at the time of writing).

The following matters

Answer

A unitary constitution is one in which there is a central legislature, with competence to legislate for the whole of the state in all areas, without restrictions upon it deriving from the sharing of legislative power with provincial legislatures. The doctrine of Parliamentary sovereignty, still probably the central feature of the UK constitution, logically implies a unitary state; moreover, up until recently, the UK, unlike many other states, had no provincial legislative bodies, with power to make laws for particular regions of the state, such as those that exist in Canada, the US and Germany. The 'unwritten' – more properly, 'uncodified' – nature of the UK constitution means, at its most basic, that whilst reforms such as Scottish devolution are readily introduced through the ordinary legislative process, such constitutional provisions have no special status, and can be repealed, with none of the special procedures required for changes in the constitutions of other countries, such as referenda or two thirds majorities in the legislature. This question will consider how far, if at all Scottish devolution has affected these foundational constitutional characteristics. In doing so, it will go beyond analysis of the strict legal position, giving consideration also to the position as a matter of constitutional convention and/or political practice.

A unitary constitution can be contrasted with federalism as seen, for example, in the constitutions of the US, Canada and Germany. Federalism may be defined as having three key characteristics. First, there exist both federal and state or provincial legislatures, and, crucially, each have *exclusive* areas of competence: *both* are limited legislatures with a defined area of competence. Thus, typically, federal legislatures are competent to legislate on matters such as defence, macro-economic policy and national transport policy and regulation; provincial legislatures deal with matters such as education, health policy, and housing. Because both legislatures have independent areas of power, neither are competent to dissolve the other. Second, there must be a written constitution, which defines and limits the jurisdiction of both federal and provincial legislatures. Third, there must be a Supreme, or Constitutional Court which has the power to review the *vires* of Acts of both legislatures and annul them as unconstitutional if they have strayed into areas reserved for the other legislature.

Whilst the UK has always been a unitary state, it has also always recognised the special status of Scotland within the union. The Treaties of Union established full political and economic union between England and Scotland in 1707. These made the two countries one, setting up a new British Parliament as the supreme Parliament for the new country. However, it was agreed at that time, and written into the treaties as supposedly unchangeable principles, that Scotland should retain its separate legal system, its separate established Church – the Presbyterian Church of Scotland – and its separate education systems. While the Westminster Parliament was sovereign and thus legislated for Scotland, many bills were known as 'Scottish' bills, that is, concerned with Scottish affairs only. Before devolution, the Scottish Office, situated in Edinburgh, administered Scottish affairs. Scotland was allocated a block grant which the Secretary of State was at liberty to allocate in accordance with what were thought to be local needs and priorities. Scotland thus had quite a high degree of what can be referred to as executive devolution and has preserved its separate legal system, church, and education system.

The perceived problem was two-fold: first, this partially separate administration of Scotland could well be controlled by a political party which had been clearly rejected in the polls in Scotland itself. For example, throughout the 1980s and in the 1990s, up until the election of a Labour government in 1997, Scotland was governed, like the rest of the UK, by a Conservative administration. The problem was that Scotland had consistently voted Labour or Scottish Nationalist during that period. It was thus seen, with some justice, as a system which delivered unrepresentative government for Scotland. The other problem was that the system was seen as being neither sufficiently accountable nor as *locally* accountable. While the Scottish Office was situated in Edinburgh, it was not accountable to any Scottish body, but to the Westminster Parliament and it arguably received inadequate scrutiny there. As Munro notes:

> The Scottish Office's appearance on the parliamentary question rota once every three weeks was hardly commensurate with the scale of their activities, and more generally it was obvious that the House of Commons had insufficient time for scrutiny of Scottish administration. (Munro, *Studies in Constitutional Law* (2nd edn 1999, p 39)

Following a rising tide of opinion in favour of change, the Scottish Constitutional Convention, made up of representatives from the Labour Party, Liberal Democrats, trades union, churches and other small parties was formed. The Convention proposed a Parliament for Scotland which would exercise substantial legislative powers and this proposal was accepted by the incoming Labour Government. The legislation putting in place the Scottish Parliament (SP) was not passed until the proposal that there should be a Scottish Parliament had been put to the Scottish people in a referendum. The question of whether there should be such a Parliament and that it should have tax-raising powers was approved in a referendum by over 70 per cent of those who took part, on a reasonable turnout of 60 per cent. As discussed further below, this is of great political-conventional significance, though not relevant in strict law. Under the Scotland Act 1998 (SA), the Parliament has 129 members (known as MSPs), elected under a mixture of first-past-the-post and proportional representation electoral systems.

What then are the competencies of the Scottish Parliament? The first point to note is that the legislation is designed quite explicitly so as *not* to produce a federal system. The White Paper, *Scotland's Parliament* (Cm. 3658, 1997 para 4.2) stated: 'The United Kingdom Parliament is and will remain sovereign in all matters'. This intention is made plain in the Scotland Act; s 28(7) states, 'This section does not affect the power of the Parliament of the United Kingdom to make laws for Scotland.' This provision can only have been included for the sake of absolute certainty: as a matter of orthodox constitutional law, Parliament could not have restricted its own powers by giving them away to the new Scottish Parliament. Moreover, the SA makes it clear that the Scottish Parliament is, unlike, Westminster, a limited legislature. Section 29(1) states: 'An Act of the [SP] is not law so far as any provision of the Act is outside the legislative competence of the [SP].'

What then was the scheme chosen for the devolution of power to the SP? Instead of setting out the specific powers which were to be shared with Scotland, a different route was taken: those which powers which were not to be shared (known as 'reserved powers') are specified, so that anything not mentioned is deemed to be devolved. The competence of the SP is thus defined negatively – the Scottish Parliament may not legislate on 'reserved matters' (Scotland Act, Sched 5), which are retained at Westminster (contrast the Scotland Act 1978). The areas reserved to Westminster include UK constitutional issues; foreign and defence policy; fiscal, economic and monetary system (that is, macro-economic issues, including interest rates and the currency); common markets for UK goods and services; employment and social security and transport safety and regulation. The powers thus devolved include: all areas of education; local government; land development and environmental regulation; many aspects of transport policy; the Scottish NHS, the legal system (civil and criminal law (excepting areas covered by EU law and the ECHR); agriculture and fisheries; sports, arts and culture. Per 29 of the Act, the SP may not legislate contrary to EU law or the European Convention on Human Rights nor for the territory of another country and nor may it alter the terms of the Scotland Act itself (with a few minor exceptions). Clearly then the Scottish Parliament is not a legislature within a federal system: it has no legally exclusive competence, since the Westminster Parliament retains its ability to legislature for the whole of the UK, while the SP can be abolished by the Westminster Parliament.

In certain other respects, however, the SP *does* follow the model of a legislature in a federal system: the vires of its legislation can be raised either post or pre-enactment; at present, the final determinant of 'devolution issues' is the Judicial Committee of the Privy Council (JCPC), although this jurisdiction is given to the new Supreme Court by the CRA 2005, once it comes into being. Reed commented shortly after the scheme was set up that some within Scotland 'might regard it as ironical, to say the least, that the Scots having voted for self-government by a Scottish Parliament are now to be governed, in a sense, by judges' (Reed, 'Devolution and the Judiciary' in Cambridge Centre for Public Law, *Constitutional Reform in the United Kingdom: Practice and Principles* (1998), p 23). However, whilst this remains true in a theoretical sense, there have been no cases in which legislation of the Parliament has been annulled by the courts. A challenge was launched to the **Protection of Wild Mammals**

(Scotland) Act 2002, which banned hunting with hounds in Scotland, but in *Whaley v Lord Advocate (2004)* was held to disclose no argument that the SP had acted outside its powers in a judgment that stressed the wide area of discretion to be afforded to the Parliament in determining such issues, as a democratically elected body representing the Scottish people.

Having surveyed the legal position, which, as we have seen, firmly precludes the creation of any kind of federalism, it is necessary to examine the position as a matter of convention or political practice. As noted above, the SA expressly reserves to the Westminster Parliament the right to legislate on all matters, including those devolved to the SP. However, as Tam Dayell, MP remarked at the time of the passing of the Act, '[this] may conceivably be true in an arcane legal sense, but in the political reality of 1998 it is palpably misleading and about as true as it would be to say that the Queen can veto any legislation' (HC Deb vol 305, col 366 (28 January 1998).

The problem would arise if the Westminster Parliament wished to legislate in one of the devolved areas in order to overturn the policy of the Scottish Executive, or in opposition to its wishes. This would be unlikely to happen while, as at present, the UK Government is controlled by the same party as the Scottish Executive, but could well arise if the SE was formed from a different party. It would arise in its most acute form if the SNP controlled the Executive. If the SE threatened to resign if the Westminster Parliament passed the legislation in question, this would be likely to make the Government very reluctant to press forward with its legislation. This is because, while, as a matter of law, the UK Parliament retains the power to legislate even in the devolved areas, the perception of the Scots is that the devolved areas belong to the Scottish Parliament. Attempts by the UK Parliament to legislate in those areas without the consent of the SP would be very likely to precipitate a political crisis. If a Scottish Executive resigned in protest, precipitating an election, the fear by the UK government would be that such an action would ignite a wave of nationalist sentiment, making it likely that a new Scottish Parliament would be elected with a majority of nationalists and perhaps a mandate to seek independence from the UK. It is at this point that the strict legal position becomes far less important than political realities. As Bogdanor has put it 'In practice . . . sovereignty is being transferred and Westminster will not be able to recover it, except under pathological circumstances' ('Devolution – the Constitutional Aspects' in *Constitutional Reform*, op.cit. p 12).

There has indeed been express recognition of the de facto surrender by Westminster over the devolved areas by the UK Government. A memorandum of understanding signed between the UK Government and the SE states:

> . . . the UK Government will normally proceed in accordance with the convention that the UK Parliament would not normally legislate with regard to devolved matters except with the agreement of the devolved legislature.

This convention, known as the Sewell convention, has been faithfully followed by Westminster; whilst Westminster *has* passed legislation intruding into the devolved areas, this has only taken place with the consent of the SP. This indeed was the lesson from the experience of Northern Ireland devolution over 50 years: the UK Government, despite often being strongly opposed to measures enacted at Stormont, did not use the sovereignty of Parliament to overrule it, until the breakdown of law and order forced the resumption of direct rule.[1]

In the result, one may put forward an argument that what we have in the UK is now a form of quasi-Federalism. At this point, we must recall the three components of federalism defined above: they are (a) legislatures with separate and distinct areas of competence; (b) that those limits are fixed by the constitution and (c) that there is a Supreme Court with power to review the *vires of* legislation of each body. Given the existence and strength of the Sewell convention, we may say that, at the conventional level, (a) is satisfied – the SP Parliament legislates for Scottish, devolved matters, the UK Parliament for the reserved areas only (or with the permission of the SP, the devolved areas). As for point (b), the constitution for these purposes would be the Scotland Act. While it is clearly not "higher law" in the sense that it remains subject to ordinary express repeal, if it becomes impossible to repeal or amend it as a matter of political reality without the consent of the SP then it becomes a form of de facto higher law. In this respect, the fact that the SP was set up with the clear backing of the Scottish people as approved in a referendum is of great significance: it makes its abolition, or emasculation, without the consent of the Scottish people, virtually politically impossible. As for (c), the Supreme Court is at present the JCPC, soon to become the new UK Supreme Court. Of course, whilst this body has full powers to review and indeed strike down Acts of the SP that exceed its *vires*, it has no power to do so in relation to Acts of the Westminster Parliament. Nevertheless, it is plausible to assume that courts will develop an interpretative presumption to the effect that the latter does not intend to legislate in the devolved areas without the consent of the SP, as the Sewell Convention states. This could lead to a position in which courts are prepared to read Westminster legislation that *did* intrude into such matters without consent as narrowly as possible, so as to prevent such intrusion, as indeed, Loveland has suggested. While the formal *vires* of the UK Parliament would not be affected, this would amount to quite a strong de facto restriction upon its powers, as we have seen for example in relation to the ability of Parliament to enact effective ouster clauses (*Anisminic*).

In conclusion, then: it is clear law that devolution to Scotland has not altered the legal basis of the UK constitution. It remains a unitary system: the UK Parliament retains full legislative competence in relation to Scotland, so that no power has, strictly speaking, been 'transferred' to the Scottish Parliament; moreover the Scotland Act, whilst doubtless a 'constitutional statute' under the *Thoburn* doctrine, undoubtedly remains subject to express repeal at least, by Parliament. However, with the UK constitution, it is always necessary to view it through two perspectives – legal and political-conventional. In terms of the latter perspective, a marked change has come about. The UK Parliament, as a matter of expressly declared, and so far faithfully followed, constitutional convention is now a limited Parliament – it will not legislate in the areas devolved to Scotland without the consent of the Scottish Parliament. Further the Scotland Act plainly has a special status as a matter of political fact – it will be impossible to repeal it or modify it in a way that reduces the scope of devolution without the consent of the Scottish Parliament. Moreover, the Scottish people are living, in relation to many areas of government, under what is in effect a codified constitution – the Scotland Act itself, which delimits the power of their legislature and government and cannot be changed by them. Viewed through this second lens then, devolution to Scotland has introduced a convention of federalism and a marked degree of codification to the UK constitution.

▌NOTE

1 Students could expand on this point. Northern Irish devolution was established in 1922. However, it was not until 1967 that then Prime Minister Harold Wilson threatened to use Parliamentary Sovereignty to impose reforms on Stormont. However, the majority of Unionist MPs were not prepared to accept the reforms, so in the end the only alternative left to the UK was to resume direct rule in 1972. This however would be most unlikely to happen in Scotland; it happened in Northern Ireland first because the Unionists wanted fervently to remain part of the UK and second because the nationalist community perhaps had a perception that even direct rule was less bad than rule by their direct political opponents the Unionists. In Scotland, there would be no such feeling.

CHAPTER 2

PARLIAMENTARY SOVEREIGNTY, THE HUMAN RIGHTS ACT AND THE EUROPEAN UNION

INTRODUCTION

Textbooks on constitutional law often deal with parliamentary sovereignty and European Union (EU) law in separate chapters. However, exam questions on sovereignty will now often have explicit EU dimensions, and will, in any event, almost invariably require explanation of the impact of EU law on the traditional doctrine. Therefore, this chapter deals with the traditional view of parliamentary sovereignty and the impact of EU law together. The impact of the Human Rights Act (HRA) 1998 on sovereignty is also a very topical subject and we include a question specifically devoted to that complex issue, as well as including consideration of its significance in some of the other essays, where relevant. Thus, four main issues are covered in this chapter: the nature of parliamentary sovereignty and possible legal limitations on it; the impact of EU law on the traditional doctrine of parliamentary sovereignty; the means by which EU law can take effect in the UK (direct and indirect effect); and the impact of the HRA on sovereignty. Questions on sovereignty and on the applicability of EU law in the UK may be of the problem or essay type, though essays are probably more common. Both are included here.

Checklist

Students should be familiar with the following areas:

- the traditional doctrine of parliamentary sovereignty: the doctrine of implied repeal; possible authority for departure from the doctrine: *AG for New South Wales v Trethowan (1932)*;

- the main academic arguments surrounding the possible limitations on Parliament, including possible self-limitation;
- the effect of ss 2(1), 2(4) and 3(1) of the European Communities Act 1972;
- the primacy of Community law: *Costa v ENEL (1964)*;
- the direct and indirect effect of Community law; the *Francovich* principle;
- the purposive approach to domestic legislation supposed to implement an indirectly effective Community law;
- the partial entrenchment of s 2(1) of the European Communities Act: Macarthy's v Smith (1981); the *Factortame* litigation; *Secretary of State for Employment ex p EOC (1994)*;
- the alternative and broader explanation given for the above in the case of *Thoburn (2002)*
- the implications of the above for protection of a Bill of Rights;
- the extent of protection for the HRA – whether the normal doctrine of implied repeal will fully apply; recent case law under the Act.

Note in relation to the *Factortame* litigation: *Factortame (1990)* refers to the first decision of the House of Lords (HL), cited in the Tables as [1990] 2 AC 85; *Factortame (1990)* (ECJ) refers to the decision of the European Court of Justice (ECJ) on interim relief, cited in the Tables as [1990] 3 CMLR 1, ECJ; *Factortame (No 2) (1991)* refers to the second decision of the HL, cited in the Tables as [1991] 1 AC 603; *Factortame (No 3) (1992)* refers to the decision of the ECJ on the substantive issue, cited in the Tables as [1992] QB 680.

Question 6

Consider the validity of the following statement: '. . . once an instrument is recognised as being an Act of Parliament, no English court can refuse to obey it or question its validity' (*per Sir Robert Megarry VC in Manuel v AG (1983)*).

Answer plan

This is a fairly demanding question as it concerns two quite complex aspects of sovereignty: the ability of the courts to consider the validity of a statute and the effect of accession to the European Community.

The following matters should be considered (two aspects of the doctrine of parliamentary sovereignty arising from the statement):

- the validity of an Act of Parliament; the refusal of the courts to consider proceedings in Parliament; the 'enrolled Bill' rule and its modification in the case of *Jackson (2006)*
- the position under the Human Rights Act (HRA) 1998;
- compliance with statutory provisions; the relevance of the rule that no Parliament can bind its successors; the effect of the European Communities Act 1972 and the doctrine of the primacy of EU law – *Factortame* litigation;
- modification of the statement made by Sir Robert Megarry in order to take the primacy of EU law into account.

Answer

There are two aspects to this question: first, that the judges will not ask whether what appears to be an Act of Parliament is valid, in the sense that it has been passed in accordance with lawful procedure; second, that the judges will not refuse to obey it. Of course, it might be argued that the first aspect is embodied in the second; in other words, the lack of validity of a statute might merely be one ground among others which could be put forward as a reason for disapplying the provision in question. Nevertheless, the issues are distinguishable in that a negative answer to the first question will preclude the second, although a positive answer will still leave the second question open. In one instance, a court is confining itself to asking the narrow question: what is an Act of Parliament? In the other, a court may be accepting that there are circumstances in which an Act of Parliament accepted as valid will yet not be applied. The two aspects of this question will therefore be considered separately. It will be argued in relation to the first that the courts will in general decline jurisdiction to examine the authenticity of purported Acts of Parliament. In relation to the second, it will be argued that the traditional concept of parliamentary sovereignty as expressed in the statement must be modified due to the UK's membership of the European Community.

In determining whether the courts will question the validity of a statute, it is unhelpful to ask whether it has been recognised as such, because to say so begs the question as to what the recognition of an Act of Parliament involves. An Act of Parliament is an expression of the sovereign will of Parliament; if, however, Parliament is not constituted as Parliament, or does not function as Parliament within the meaning of the law, it would seem to follow that it cannot express its sovereign will in the form of an Act of Parliament. However, the courts have declined opportunities to declare an Act a nullity where it has been asserted that something which appears to be an Act of Parliament and which bears the customary words of enactment is not authentic. In *Edinburgh and Dalkeith Railway Co v Wauchope (1842)*, the court was asked to find that the legislation in question, a Private Act, had been improperly passed and was therefore invalid, in that Standing Orders had not been complied with. Lord Campbell said, *obiter*, that if, according to the Parliament Roll, an Act has passed both Houses of Parliament and has received the royal assent, a court can neither inquire into the manner in which it was introduced into Parliament nor into what passed in Parliament during its progress through the various parliamentary stages. This rule, now known as 'the enrolled Bill rule', was relied upon in *Pickin v British Railways Board (1974)*: Mr Pickin had sought to challenge a Private Act of 1836 on the basis that Parliament had been misled by fraud. The House of Lords held that he was not entitled to examine proceedings in Parliament to show that the Act had been passed due to fraud. That action therefore failed.[1]

Perhaps, after *Pickin's* case, the possibility still remains that a court might be prepared to take note of an assertion that a Bill had not obtained a majority at the final reading in the House of Commons, although this would risk collision with the privilege of the House not to have its internal proceedings investigated. Generally speaking, then, the courts will decline jurisdiction to declare an apparently authentic Act of Parliament a nullity.[2]

There are, however other circumstances in which a court might treat a purported statute as nugatory; a Bill to prolong the life of a Parliament beyond five years might be passed in the Commons but not in the Lords (such a Bill is explicitly excluded from the 1911 Parliament Act procedure) and receive the royal assent. It would state that it had been passed in accordance with the Parliament Acts; if so, a court might treat it as a nullity as 'bad on its face'; its defective nature would be apparent without needing to inquire into proceedings in Parliament. This has been taken further by the House of Lords in the recent decision in *Jackson* (2006). In this case, the Hunting Act was challenged on the basis that it had been passed without the consent of the House of Lords under the 1911 Parliament Act, as amended by the 1949 Act. It was argued that because the 1949 Act had used the very procedure for bypassing the Lords contained in the 1911 Act to modify the 1911 Act (by reducing the Lords power of delay from 2 to 1 years), it was not a valid Act of Parliament. Therefore the Hunting Act, passed under the 1949 Act, was not a valid Act either. This argument was rejected by the House of Lords. However, a clear majority of the Lords accepted that a Bill which used the 1949 Act to modify the 1911 Act in order to allow its use to pass a Bill extending the life of a Parliament beyond five years would not be a valid Act of Parliament. Such a Bill is explicitly excluded from the Parliament Acts procedure in the 1911 Act. To use that procedure first to repeal the prohibiting clause in the 1911 Act and then to pass a Bill under the Parliament Act procedure to extend the life of a Parliament, thus indirectly circumventing the provision designed to ensure that this could not happen without the consent of the Lords, would, the majority held, be contrary to the intention of the 1911 Act and would thus not be accepted by the courts as a valid Act of Parliament. This indicates something of a departure from the literalism of the enrolled Bill Rule and a determination to protect the public from the dangers of tyranny driven by a majority in the House of Commons.

If a court were asked to disapply a statute not because something in its background was alleged to render it invalid but due to other factors, it would, according to the traditional doctrine of parliamentary sovereignty, decline to do so except where the other factor consisted of incompatibility between the statute before it and a subsequent statute. This doctrine includes the notion that Parliament cannot bind its successors because the latest expression of Parliament's will must prevail.

In *Ellen Street Estates Ltd v Minister of Health (1934)*, it was argued that the Acquisition of Land (Assessment of Compensation) Act 1919 prescribed a certain manner for authorising the acquisition of land. It provided in s 7 that other statutes 'shall have effect subject to this Act'. If s 7 applied to subsequent enactments, provisions of the Housing Act 1925 which were inconsistent with the 1919 Act would have no effect. However, Maughan LJ held, *obiter*, that Parliament cannot bind itself as to the form of future enactments. Thus, the courts will not give effect to a statute which is in conflict with a later statute, on the basis that the earlier statute has been impliedly repealed to the extent of its inconsistency. However, in *AG for New South Wales v Trethowan (1932)*, the Privy Council upheld the requirement of a referendum before a Bill to abolish the Upper House was presented for the royal assent. Although, as a number of commentators have pointed out, this decision may be of limited application as involving a non-sovereign legislature, it does suggest that a class of legislation exists for which it may be appropriate to delineate the manner and form of any subsequent amendment or repeal.

However, although there may be instances in which the traditional doctrine of implied repeal might not be applied, can it be assumed that apart from those considered, the courts will obey a statute which constitutes the latest expression of Parliament's will? The doctrine of parliamentary sovereignty as explained by Dicey means that Parliament has the right to make, unmake or amend any of its Acts and that such power is not open to challenge by any outside body. Since 1688, the doctrine of the supremacy of Parliament has developed to the stage when, in *Pickin v British Railways Board* (1974), it appeared clearly settled that the notion of finding an Act of Parliament invalid could be said to be obsolete. This notion might be qualified today on the ground that if a word in an Act of Parliament is incapable of bearing a sensible meaning, it appears that the courts may be prepared to disregard it. The House of Lords so held in *R (1991)* on the basis that the word 'unlawful' in the Sexual Offences Act 1956 must be mere surplusage. The HRA contains no clause purporting to protect the Act from future repeal, in this respect following the pattern of the legislation creating the devolved institutions. But it also emphatically re-affirms the traditional doctrine of sovereignty by allowing the courts only to make declarations of incompatibility if they find statutes incompatible with the rights guaranteed by the ECHR. Section 4(6) of the Act states that such declarations have no effect on the 'Validity, continuing operation or enforcement' of the legislative provisions in respect of which they are made. However, s 3(1) of the Act, in which the courts are instructed to construe all legislation compatibly with the Convention rights 'if possible', is such a strong adjuration that it arguably enables courts to blur the line between 'interpretation' of an Act of Parliament and rewriting it, presenting at least a practical challenge to Parliament's ability to enforce its will through legislation. The case of *A (2001)*, in which words were read into a statute in such a way as to alter radically its *prima facie* meaning, is a vivid illustration of this, though it must be conceded that other cases, in particular *Re W and B (2002)*, indicate a more cautious approach.

Most importantly, a further qualification to the rule deriving from *Pickin* must be introduced due to the UK's membership of the European Union. Community Treaties and Community law capable of having direct effect in the UK were given such effect by the European Communities Act 1972 which, by s 2(1), incorporated all existing Community law into UK law. No express declaration of the supremacy of Community law is contained in the Act; the words intended to achieve this are contained in s 2(4) of the 1972 Act, which reads as follows: ' . . . any enactment passed or to be passed . . . shall be construed and have effect subject to the foregoing provisions of this section.' The words 'subject to' appear to suggest that the courts must allow Community law to prevail over a subsequent Act of Parliament. '[T]he foregoing' are those provisions referred to in s 2(1) giving the force of law to 'the enforceable Community rights' there defined.

The problem arises in respect of statutes passed after 1 January 1972. According to the traditional doctrine of parliamentary sovereignty, the later Act should prevail as representing the latest expression of Parliament's will, but the Community doctrine of the primacy of EU law and s 2(4) would require Community law to prevail. In this respect, it has become clear from the Treaty as interpreted by the ECJ (see *Costa v EN EL (1964)* and *Amministmzione delle Finanze dello Stato v Simmenthal SpA (1978)*) that it is an implied Community principle that Community law should prevail over national law.

In *Secretary of State for Transport ex p Factortame Ltd and Others (1990)*, the UK courts had to consider the question of direct conflict between domestic and European Community law. The applicants, who were unable to comply with the conditions imposed on them under the Merchant Shipping (Registration of Fishing Vessels) Regulations 1988 made under the Merchant Shipping Act 1988, sought a ruling by way of judicial review that the Regulations contravened the provisions of the EEC Treaty by depriving them of Community law rights. A ruling on the substantive questions of Community law was requested from the ECJ and pending that ruling, an order was made by way of interim relief, setting aside the relevant part of the 1988 Regulations.

This order was set aside by the Court of Appeal; Bingham LJ remarked, however, that where the law of the Community is clear:

> whether as a result of a ruling given on an Art 177 [now 234] reference or as a result of previous jurisprudence or on a straightforward interpretation of Community instruments, the duty of the national court is to give effect to it in all circumstance

To that extent, a UK statute is not as inviolable as it once was. The House of Lords upheld the ruling on the ground that no court had power to make an order conferring rights upon the applicants which were directly contrary to UK legislation. The result of these two rulings was clearly in accord with the traditional doctrine of parliamentary sovereignty as far as English law was concerned. However, their Lordships also accepted that Community law might impose other requirements which would be overriding. The Lords referred to the ECJ for a preliminary ruling on the question of whether Community law required that a national court should grant the interim relief sought.

The European Court of Justice held (*Secretary of State for Transport ex p Factortame Ltd (1990)* (ECJ)) that the force of Community law would be impaired if, when a judgment of the Court on Community law rights was pending, a national court was unable to grant interim relief which would ensure the full efficacy of the eventual judgment. Therefore, when the only obstacle to granting such relief was a rule of national law, that rule must be disapplied. In view of this judgment (*ex p Factortame Ltd (No 2) (1991)*), the House of Lords granted the relief sought by the vessel owners. The position taken by the House of Lords was re-affirmed in *Secretary of State for Employment ex p EOC (1994)*.

It follows from this decision that if it is clear that a statute is inconsistent with EU law, the domestic court would have to disapply it, in other words, refuse to give it effect. However a different explanation for the result in *Factortame* was given in *Thoburn (2002)*, which involved a challenge to EC regulations on the exclusive use of metric measurements by traders and retailers. Laws LJ held that Parliament could not bind itself in any way and had not done so in the 1972 Act. He declared:

> Parliament cannot bind its successors by stipulating against repeal, wholly or partly, of the ECA. It cannot stipulate as to the manner and form of any subsequent legislation. It cannot stipulate against implied repeal any more than it can stipulate against express repeal.

Rather the explanation for *Factortame* was that the *courts* had recognised the 1972 Act as but one example of what Laws LJ called 'a constitutional statute', essentially those which affected fundamental rights or 'the relationship between citizen and State in some general, overarching manner'. The legal consequence of recognising a statute as 'constitutional' was simple: 'Ordinary statutes may be impliedly repealed. Constitutional statutes may not.' It is too early to say whether this revised view of sovereignty has won general acceptance amongst the senior judiciary. If it does, and given our findings on *Factortame*, it is evident that the statement made by Sir Robert Megarry should be modified to read as follows: 'once an instrument is recognised as an Act of Parliament *and is compatible with any enforceable Community law*, no English court can refuse to obey it or question its validity, *although it may refuse to allow it to impliedly repeal a previous, "constitutional statute"*'.

NOTES

1 It could be pointed out here that challenges to the validity of an Act or part of an Act may be mounted on other grounds. In *Cheney v Conn (1968)*, a taxpayer appealed against an assessment of income tax made under the Finance Act 1964 on the basis that Parliament had acted unlawfully in making the statute; he argued that it was contrary to international law, as part of the money would be used for the construction of nuclear weapons. In response, it was held that the statute could not be unlawful because 'what the statute . . . provides is the law and the highest form of law that is known to this country'. Thus, the courts will not accept that Parliament had no power to make the statute in question.

2 Students could note that this point also receives some support from Slade LJ in *Manuel v AC* itself, although he did not finally resolve the issue. The question of whether the courts can determine the validity of a statute can ultimately only be resolved by the courts; the statement made by Megarry VC fails to take that factor into account and is, therefore, too simplistic. It could be explained here that this ruling was based on the Court's judgment in *Amministrazione delie Finanze dello Stato v Simmenthal SpA (1978)*, in which it had held that conflict between provisions of national law and directly applicable Community law must be resolved by rendering the national law inapplicable, and that any national provision or practice withholding from a national court the jurisdiction to apply Community law even temporarily was incompatible with the requirements of Community law.

Question 7

Would you agree that, under our current constitutional arrangements, a Bill of Rights could not be protected from repeal and that the Human Rights Act 1998 makes no attempt to so protect itself?

Answer plan

In answering this question, it should be borne in mind that a number of different forms of protection could be suggested for the Bill of Rights short of entrenchment. Essentially, the following matters should be considered:

- the doctrine of parliamentary sovereignty;
- the danger of erosion of the Human Rights Act (HRA) 1998 and of any Bill of Rights due to implied repeal by subsequent enactments;
- the attempt to prevent inadvertent implied repeal through ministerial statements of compatibility;
- the construction of subsequent enactments so as to avoid conflict with the HRA under s 3; a comparison with the approach of the courts to protecting EC legislation from repeal under s 2(4) of the European Communities Act 1972; an assessment of case law so far on s 3;
- the consequences of this approach – the partial protection of the Convention rights;
- the preclusion by the HRA of the possibility of the judiciary using the more radical approach taken in *Secretary of State for Transport ex p Factortame Ltd and Others (No 2) (1991)* to protect the Convention;
- the implications of *Thoburn (2002)*; dicta suggesting the possibility of limits to sovereignty in *Jackson (2006)*
- the possibility of entrenchment by means of a new constitutional settlement.

Answer

The adoption of a Bill of Rights intended to exist for all time is incompatible with the doctrine of parliamentary sovereignty: under that doctrine, a purported Bill of Rights would in fact have the same status as other enactments in that it would be vulnerable to express and (possibly) implied repeal. This, indeed, was the stance taken by the White Paper (Cm 3782) on incorporation of the European Convention on Human Rights (ECHR); the HRA makes no attempt to entrench the Convention into UK law, and indeed explicitly states that incompatibility between Convention rights and either future or past UK legislation will not affect the validity or continuing effect of that legislation. Under the doctrine of sovereignty, no Parliament may bind its successors or be bound by its predecessors, and the courts cannot question the validity of an Act of Parliament (see *Pickin v British*

Railways Board (1974)). It follows that Parliament can repeal or amend any statute and that where a later statute is incompatible with a former, it repeals the former to the extent of its incompatibility. Thus, the adoption of a Bill of Rights appears to include the unconstitutional notion of limiting the legislative competence of successive Parliaments.

Express repeal of all or part of the Bill of Rights might be undertaken by a subsequent Parliament out of sympathy with its aims, while implied repeal – which might at times be unintentional – could gradually and insidiously erode it. For example, a Bill which, in future, sought to *entrench* the provisions of the ECHR would contain a clause protecting the right to privacy – Art 8. If a subsequent enactment dealt with an aspect of privacy (such as the use of newly developed surveillance devices) in terms that clearly allowed for violations of the rights guaranteed by Art 8, this Act would prevail. The Bill of Rights might eventually become almost worthless – in fact, worse than worthless, because it could be used by government to cloak erosions of freedom while at the same time raising expectations it could not fulfil. This danger cannot be ruled out in relation to the HRA.

However, arguably, certain forms of protection for enactments, even amounting to a weak form of entrenchment, already exist in our constitution and are utilised by the HRA. (The word 'protection' is used as being wider than 'entrenchment'.) It is possible that a convention of respect for the Bill of Rights would grow up; this may well be the case with the HRA. It is a constitutional truism that Parliament never uses its power to the full; for example, it is inconceivable at present that Parliament would limit suffrage to those with incomes over a certain level. Similarly, the Bill of Rights, although enacted as an ordinary Act of Parliament, might acquire such prestige that although its express repeal remained theoretically possible, it would never be undertaken. This may represent the best protection for the HRA. However, this cannot be taken for granted: the derogation from Art 5 of the ECHR following the September 11 attacks in 2001 in order to allow for the detention without trial of certain suspected international terrorists indicates that the UK is very far from developing a strong culture of respect for the ECHR, although the acceptance by the UK Government that the legislation necessitating the derogation should be allowed to lapse once it had been found to unlawful by the House of Lords in *A v Secretary of State (2004)* is some evidence against this. Even outright repeal of the HRA cannot be ruled out: the present Government would not presumably undertake such a course, given that the Act was its own initiative, but David Cameron's Conservative party are presently committed to its repeal and replacement by exceedingly ill-defined 'British Bill of Rights'. Moreover, even if Parliament does prove reluctant to engage in express repeal, implied repeal would still remain a possibility.

The HRA deals with such a possibility in two ways. The first of these is the provision in s 19 that ministers, when introducing legislation subsequent to the enactment of the HRA, must make a statement as to whether the legislation is or is not compatible with the Convention rights. This is clearly designed to prevent governments from engaging in a stealthy erosion of rights; it should also help to guard against inadvertent erosion by focusing minds in Parliament and government on whether the legislation is indeed Convention compliant. Governments would be thought to be extremely reluctant openly to announce that they are introducing incompatible legislation, since this would amount to a declaration of an intent to breach the UK's Treaty obligations. However, an instance of this has already arisen, albeit in relation to a relatively contentious issue of interpretation of Art 10: the UK refuses to accept the correctness of the Strasbourg court's finding that a complete ban on political advertising in broadcasting is a violation of Art 10 and has maintained such a ban in the Communications Act 2003, making a negative s 19 statement in relation to it when the Bill was introduced. Of probably greater concern is the fact that governments may rely upon the inherent imprecision of many of the Convention rights and the possible consequential lack of legal certainty as to whether particular provisions are Convention compliant in order to argue that doubtful legislation is, in fact, compatible. Arguably, this occurred in relation to the Regulation of Investigatory Powers Act 2000, the Terrorism Act 2000, the Anti-Terrorism, Crime and Security Act 2001 and the Prevention of Terrorism Act 2005, all of which contain draconian powers of interference with Convention rights. Such cases of ambiguity may be dealt with by judges under the interpretative rule in s 3 of the HRA, to which we shall turn in a moment. However, the introduction of legislation which would very clearly have the effect of eroding Convention rights will become politically much more difficult, although, there is nothing to stop Parliament repealing s 19 itself.

Legislation which is of doubtful compatibility with the ECHR may be prevented from impliedly repealing the protected rights by virtue of s 3(1). This strongly worded section instructs the courts that in interpreting both previous and future legislation so far as is possible, they must read and give effect to it in such a way as to make it consistent with the Convention rights. This amounts to a form of protection which may be as strong as judges care to make it although, of course, s 3 could in future be expressly repealed or modified. Just how much protection can be afforded by such an approach can be illustrated by reference to the stance judges have taken in relation to the protection of EU law from implied repeal. The equivalent provision to s 3 of the HRA is s 2(4) of the European Communities Act 1972, which reads as follows: ' . . . any enactment passed or to be passed . . . shall be construed and have effect subject to the foregoing provisions of this section.' The words 'subject to' appear to suggest that the courts must allow Community law to prevail over a subsequent Act of Parliament.[1] The 'foregoing provisions' are those of s 2(1), importing Community law into national law.

The House of Lords in *Pickstone v Freemans (1988)* found that domestic legislation – the Equal Pay (Amendment) Regulations – made under s 2(2) of the

European Communities Act appeared to be inconsistent with Art 141 (ex 119). It held that despite this apparent conflict, a purposive interpretation of the domestic legislation would be adopted; in other words, the plain meaning of the provision in question would be ignored and an interpretation would be foisted upon it which was not in conflict with Art 141. This was done on the basis that Parliament must have intended to fulfil its EC obligations in passing the Amendment Regulations once it had been forced to do so by the ECJ.[2] The House of Lords followed a similar approach in *Litster v Forth Dry Dock Engineering (1989)*. These decisions provide authority for the proposition that Parliament cannot by plain words impliedly depart from the provisions of European Communities law (except by repealing part or all of the European Communities Act 1972). Probably, it could do so only by stating expressly that it was so acting. In *Macarthy's Ltd v Smith (1981)*, Lord Denning accepted that an express provision that the instrument in question should prevail over inconsistent Community law would be obeyed. Clearly, such a ruling involves a departure from the rule (deriving from the *dicta* of Maughan LJ in *Ellen Street Estates Ltd v Minister of Health (1934)*) that Parliament cannot bind itself as to the form of future enactments. Thus, partial entrenchment of s 2(1) of the 1972 Act has occurred.

There are some signs that this approach is indeed being followed, at least in some of the cases under the HRA. The House of Lords' decision in *A (2001)* concerned the interpretation to be given to s 41 of the Youth Justice and Criminal Evidence Act 1999, which forbade any evidence to be given in a rape trial of the woman's sexual history, including any previous sexual history with the alleged rapist, except in very limited circumstances. This was thought to raise an issue of compatibility with Art 6 of the ECHR which provides, *inter alia*, that: 'In the determination of . . . any criminal charge against him, everyone is entitled to a fair and public hearing within a reasonable time by an independent and impartial tribunal established by law.' Lords Steyn and Hutton were prepared to hold that given the very strong wording of s 3(1) and *Pepper v Hart (1992)* statements in Parliament to the effect that declarations of incompatibility (indicating that the attempt to ensure compatibility using s 3(1) had failed) were to be a remedy of last resort, the only way in which Parliament could legislate contrary to a Convention right would be by 'a clear limitation on Convention rights . . . stated in terms'. This approach led them simply to read into the relevant part of s 41 words which were not there, namely, that evidence was to be admitted where that was necessary to achieve a fair trial. It may be noted that Lord Hope considered that this approach went too far, crossing the line from interpretation to legislating. He considered, in what is certainly the more usual understanding of the word 'interpreting', that the judge's task was limited to identifying specific words which would otherwise lead to incompatibility and then re-interpreting those words, clearly not something which Lords Steyn and Hutton – and for that matter Lord Slynn – undertook. Lord Hope's approach arguably found more support from the House of Lords in *Re W and B (2002)*, in which their Lordships emphasised the importance of not stepping over the boundary from statutory interpretation to 'statutory amendment'. A more activist approach, arguably involving the re-writing, rather than the re-intepretation of legislation occurred in *Ghaidan v Mendoza (2004)*. However the decision *Bellinger v Bellinger (2003)* clearly indicated that the courts will sometimes refuse to engage even in relatively straightforward re-interpretation of legislation, in terms of linguistics, where it is felt that the change is complex and significant enough to require consideration by Parliament. In that case, the House of Lords refused to interpret the word 'female' in the Matrimonial Causes Act 1973 to reflect modern understandings of the protean nature of gender so that it included post-operative male to female transsexuals and would thus allow the applicant validly to marry a man. To change the meaning of a single word in this way was clearly therefore a 'possible' interpretation even under the most modest views of what that elusive word means. However, the interpretation was rejected and a declaration of incompatibility made instead. Nevertheless, if the approach in *A* and *Mendoza* is followed in even some areas of rights protection, the result will be that Parliament has, through s 3(1), succeeded in imposing a requirement of express words upon such of its successors that wish to legislate incompatibly with the Convention rights.

It should be noted, however, that the parallel with EU law must be treated with caution. In 1972, the UK was signing up to a legal order in which the supremacy of EU law had already been firmly established by the European Court of Justice (ECJ) (for example, in *Costa v ENEL (1964)*) and was arguably necessary if the purposes of the Community were to be achieved. No such situation applies in relation to the European Convention, and indeed the White Paper expressly disclaims any such comparison (para 2.12). In practice, many judges may not be prepared to go as far to protect the Convention as they have to protect the law of the Community as the case-law above indicates. Even if a *Litster*-style approach were to be generally adopted, the courts would at least occasionally be bound to come across provisions which are not capable of a compatible construction. In such a case, the incompatible statute would have to stand: the HRA expressly seeks to preclude judges from taking the further radical step of disapplying incompatible statutes, the step taken in the EC context in the case of *Secretary of State for Transport ex p Factortame (No 2) (1991)*.

The line of reasoning taken in *Thoburn* (2002) represents a possible alternative route to the protection of the HRA from implied repeal. In that decision, which involved a challenge to EC regulations on the exclusive use of metric measurements by traders and retailers, Laws LJ held that Parliament could not bind itself in any way and had not done so in the 1972 Act. Rather the explanation for *Factortame* was that the *courts* had recognised the 1972 Act as but one example of what he called 'a constitutional statute', essentially those which affected fundamental rights or 'the relationship between citizen and State in some general, overarching manner'. The legal consequence of recognising a statute as 'constitutional' was simple: 'Ordinary statutes may be impliedly repealed. Constitutional statutes may not.' Clearly, the

HRA is a 'constitutional statute' under this analysis, indeed, it was one of the examples instanced by the judge. It is too early to say whether this revised view of sovereignty has won general acceptance amongst the senior judiciary, but if it does, the HRA will have gained through common law the protection from implied repeal that Parliament refused to give it.

Depending then upon the approach of the judiciary, the incorporated ECHR may turn out to be at least partly protected from implied repeal, while its express repeal remains unlikely. The HRA may therefore, contrary to the assertion in the question, be said to endow the Convention rights with at least the *potential* for some protection against future repeal, though the Act appears to rule out expressly the wholesale suspension of implied repeal engineered in the area of EU law.

Although this is not an issue in relation to the HRA, there is, finally, the possibility that a future Bill of Rights could be given substantial procedural protection from repeal. Constitutions throughout the world adopt a number of different forms of entrenchment of codes of rights. The constitution of the USA can be amended only by a proposal which has been agreed by two-thirds of each House of Congress or by a convention summoned by Congress at the request of two-thirds of the States. The proposed amendment must then be ratified by three-quarters of the States' legislatures. The amendment procedure itself – Art V of the Constitution – can be amended only by the same method.

It is generally thought that if a Bill of Rights for the UK were enacted containing a provision that it could not be repealed except in accordance with some such procedure, the courts would not give effect to it. However, De Smith suggests that Parliament could redefine itself so as to preclude itself as ordinarily constituted from legislating on a certain matter. The argument is based on the redefinition of Parliament under the Parliament Acts of 1911 and 1949: if Parliament could make it easier for itself to legislate on certain matters, equally, it could make it harder, thereby entrenching certain legislation. However, this analogy has come under attack from Munro (*Studies in Constitutional Law*, 2nd edn, 1999) on the ground that the Parliament Act procedure introduces no limitation on parliamentary sovereignty. The only authorities which would support this proposition come from other constitutions; in *AG for New South Wales v Trethowan (1932)*, the Privy Council upheld the requirement of a referendum before a Bill to abolish the Upper House was presented for the royal assent. Although, as De Smith argues, this decision may be of limited application as involving a non-sovereign legislature, it does suggest that a class of legislation exists for which it may be appropriate to delineate the manner and form of any subsequent amendment or repeal. The South African case of *Harris v Minister of the Interior (1951)* is to similar effect. Thus, the point cannot be regarded as settled.

Therefore, a proposal that the Bill of Rights be fully entrenched would be constitutionally controversial and probably impossible without a written constitution. However, is it clear that the Bill of Rights could be entrenched within a written constitution? Dicey considered that it would be untenable to espouse 'the strange dogma, sometimes put forward, that a sovereign power such as the Parliament of the UK can never by its own act divest itself of authority' (*An Introduction to the Study of the Law of the Constitution*, 10th edn, 1959, p 68). On this view, judges would accept the new constitutional settlement; possibly, the Judges' Oath should also be amended so that they owed allegiance to the new settlement as opposed to a subsequent statute.

NOTES

1 It had been thought that membership of the Community did not represent any surrender of sovereignty: Lord Gardiner said in 1969: There is, in theory, no constitutional means available to us to make it certain that no future Parliament would enact legislation in conflict with Community law' (HL Deb, Cols 1202–04, 8 May 1969).

2 It could be noted that the Court of Appeal in *Pickstone v Freemans (1988)* went further: it treated Art 141 as having more authority than the Equal Pay (Amendment) Regulations and made a ruling consistent with Art 141.

Question 8

In March 2001, Parliament passes the Parental Leave Act, s 1 of which provides that men or women are entitled to five months' parental leave on 80 per cent of full pay after the birth of their baby. Section 2 provides that any employer who fails to provide the said parental leave shall be liable in damages which shall be equivalent to the salary which would have been paid. Section 3 provides that no Bill to amend or repeal the Act shall be laid before Parliament, unless the Equal Opportunities Commission (EOC) has approved the changes.

In 2002, a European Community Regulation is passed allowing men and women equal access to parental leave and making provision that an employer who refuses to grant such leave will be liable in damages.

In 2003, a Bill amending s 1 of the Parental Leave Act 2001, with the effect that men are no longer entitled to parental leave, is laid before Parliament without the approval of the EOC, and is enacted as the Parental Leave Amendment Act 2003.

Advise Mr B, who asks for parental leave in 2004 but is refused it by his employer.

Answer plan

A problem question is commonly set in this area which will usually involve conflict between two statutes, thereby requiring discussion of the doctrine of implied repeal. It will often also involve conflict between domestic law passed subsequently to directly enforceable European Community law. In many instances the statute in relation to which implied repeal is raised as an issue could be considered as a 'constitutional statute' under the *Thoburn* analysis, although this is not a possibility here.

Essentially, the following matters should be considered:

- an explanation of the traditional doctrine of implied repeal;
- a possible authority for departure from the doctrine: *AG for New South Wales v Trethowan (1932)*;
- a conclusion as to the lack of redress available to Mr B under domestic law;
- the effect of s 2(4) of the European Communities Act 1972;
- the partial entrenchment of s 2(1) of the European Communities Act: *Macarthy's v Smith (1981) and Secretary of State for Transport ex p Factortame (No 2) (1991)*.

Answer

In addressing this question, Mr B's position under domestic law will be considered first before examining the relevance of the 2002 EC Regulation.

Under the traditional doctrine of parliamentary sovereignty, Parliament is competent to legislate on any matter whatsoever and no court is competent to question the validity of an Act of Parliament. This lack of legal restraint has both a positive and a negative aspect. It means that while Parliament can legislate on any subject, it cannot bind successive Parliaments. If it could, then clearly each successive Parliament would not be free to legislate on any matter. That aspect of sovereignty means that where there is inconsistency between a previous and a subsequent statute, the latter impliedly repeals the former to the extent of its inconsistency. Authority for this proposition derives from *Ellen Street Estates Ltd v Minister of Health (1934)*, in which it was argued that the Acquisition of Land (Assessment of Compensation) Act 1919 prescribed a certain manner for authorising the acquisition of land. It provided in s 7 that other statutes 'shall have effect subject to this Act'. If s 7 applied to subsequent enactments, provisions of the Housing Act 1925 which were inconsistent with the 1919 Act would have no effect. However, Maughan LJ held that Parliament cannot bind itself as to the substance or form of future enactments.

If a court was prepared to consider whether Parliament had consulted the EOC, this would breach 'the enrolled Bill rule' expressed in *Edinburgh and Dalkeith Railway Co v Wauchope (1842)*. The court was asked to find that the legislation in question, a Private Act, had been improperly passed and was therefore invalid because Standing Orders had not been complied with. Lord Campbell said, *obiter*, that if according to the Parliament Roll, an Act has passed both Houses of Parliament and has received the royal assent, a court can inquire neither into the manner in which it was introduced into Parliament nor into what passed in Parliament during its progress through the various parliamentary stages. This rule was relied upon in *Pickin v British Railways Board (1974)*: Mr Pickin had sought to challenge a Private Act of 1836 on the basis that Parliament had been misled by fraud. The House of Lords held that he was not entitled to examine proceedings in Parliament to show that the Act had been passed due to fraud. That action therefore failed.

In the instant case, the 2003 Act expressly repeals s 1 of the 2001 Act and therefore, on the face of it, Mr B can claim no redress. Section 3 of the 2001 Act has not, however, been repealed and it could therefore be argued that the later Act is invalid as, in passing it, Parliament did not follow the correct consultative procedure as laid down in s 3. However, the doctrine of implied repeal set out above and, in particular, the *dicta* of Maughan LJ in *Ellen Street Estates v Minister of Health* would suggest that s 3 of the 2001 Act is impliedly repealed as inconsistent with the expression of Parliament's will in the 2003 Act.

Is there any authority on which Mr B could rely in order to escape the conclusion that the 2003 Act, although not enacted in accordance with s 3 of the 2001 Act, will nevertheless be followed? If any can be found, he could rely on s 1 of the 2001 Act in order to claim leave or damages from his employer. In this instance, it would not be possible to claim that the 2001 is a 'constitutional statute' and therefore, under the analysis of Laws LJ in *Thoburn*, immune from implied repeal. In *AG for New South Wales v Trethowan (1932)*, the Privy Council upheld the statutory requirement of a referendum before two Bills could be presented for the royal assent. Although, as commentators have argued, this decision may be of limited application as involving a non-sovereign legislature (a view in accordance with that of Lord Evershed MR in *Harper v Home Secretary (1955)*), it does suggest that a class of legislation *may* exist for which it may be appropriate to delineate the manner or form of any subsequent amendment or repeal. For example, s 1 of the Northern Ireland Act 1998 provides that Northern Ireland will not cease to be part of Her Majesty's dominions without conducting a poll in Northern Ireland. If a future Act of Parliament purported to revoke this guarantee without first conducting a poll in Northern Ireland, it is at least arguable that the courts would hold the later statute to be invalid, as occurred in the South African case of *Harris v Minister of the Interior (1951)*. This view receives some support from Slade LJ in *Manuel v AG (1983)*, although he did not finally resolve the issue. In a Canadian case, *Drybones (1970)*, the Canadian Supreme Court took the view, *obiter*, that it had the power to render inoperative statutes passed after the Bill of Rights 1960 which were incompatible with it.

However, these decisions are of doubtful persuasive authority when the attempt is made to apply them in the British constitutional context. In *Harris*, for example, the wording of the Speaker's certificate on the face of the instrument in question indicated that the specially prescribed procedure had not been followed; moreover, the ruling did not encompass the legal effect of a self-imposed procedural requirement.[1] It may, therefore, be determined that the weight of authority is against upholding a requirement that Parliament cannot legislate without first complying with a procedural requirement such as that laid down by s 3 of the 2001 Act. Therefore, under the doctrine of implied repeal, the 2003 Act will prevail; under domestic law, Mr B cannot seek redress from his employer. However, in 2002, the EC passed the regulation allowing men or women parental leave. Can Mr B rely on that regulation despite the 2003 Act?

Under s 2(4) of the European Communities Act 1972, 'any enactment passed or to be passed . . . shall be construed and have effect subject to the foregoing provisions of this section'. The words 'subject to' appear to suggest that the courts must allow Community law to prevail over a subsequent Act of Parliament. '[T]he foregoing' are those provisions referred to in s 2(1) giving the force of law to 'the enforceable Community rights' there defined. Section 3(1) provides that questions as to the meaning or effect of Community law are to be determined 'in accordance with the principles laid down by any relevant decision of the European Court'. Under Art 249 of the EC Treaty, regulations have direct applicability and are binding on all Member States without requiring implementation or adoption by national law. It is clear from judgments of the European Court of Justice (ECJ) (see *Costa v ENEL (1964)* and *Amministrazione delle Finanze dello State v Simmenthal SpA (1978)*) that Community law should prevail over national law in all circumstances. Thus, on the face of it, Mr B can rely on the 2002 Regulation. It does not matter that he is seeking to rely upon it in an action against a private body, his employer: regulations, unlike directives, have horizontal as well as vertical effect. However, there is clearly a direct conflict between it and the subsequent 2003 Act and, according to the doctrine of implied repeal, the 2003 Act should take precedence over the former instrument. When a conflict has arisen between Community law and a subsequent domestic enactment, the UK courts have where possible adopted what has been termed a 'purposive' approach. In *Pickstone v Freemans (1988)*, the House of Lords determined that the plain meaning of the domestic provision in question would be ignored and an interpretation would be placed upon it which avoided a conflict with Art 141 (ex 119) of the EC Treaty. However, there seems to be no means of resolving the conflict between the 2003 Act and the 2002 Regulation in this manner due to their complete incompatibility.[2]

In such a situation, it now seems to be clear, following the decision in *Secretary of State for Transport ex p Factortame Ltd (No 2) (1991)*, that the incompatible UK legislation should be set aside, or 'disapplied'. The House of Lords initially determined that as a matter of UK law, no domestic court had power to make an order conferring rights upon the applicants which were directly contrary to UK legislation. However, following a reference to the ECJ, the House of Lords accepted that the Community now imposes the requirement, accepted by Parliament when it passed the 1972 Act, that EU law should override inconsistent domestic legislation, whenever passed. It therefore made an order 'disapplying' the incompatible legislation. In *Secretary of State for Employment ex p EOC (1994)*, the House of Lords followed *Factortame* in finding that judicial review was available for the purpose of securing a declaration that UK primary legislation is incompatible with EU law. It was found that certain provisions of the Employment Protection (Consolidation) Act 1978 were indirectly discriminatory and were, therefore, in breach of Art 141 (ex 119) and the Equal Pay and Equal Treatment Directives.

It might appear to follow from *Factortame* and the EOC case that Parliament has effectively succeeded in partially entrenching s 2(1) of the European Communities Act by means of s 2(4), due to the imposition of a requirement of form (express words) on future legislation designed to override Community law. Thus, as no express words are used in the 2003 Act (such as 'these provisions are intended to take effect notwithstanding any contrary provision of Community law') and assuming that on a straightforward interpretation of its provisions, the meaning of the 2002 Regulation is clear, it would seem that it will prevail over the 2003 Act. If so, it will be the duty of the domestic court to give it effect according to the above decisions.

If the meaning of the 2002 Regulation is not sufficiently clear, a reference might be made to the ECJ under Art 234 in order to determine its effect. If so, it would appear that the Court would clearly rule in favour of the primacy of Community law relying on *Simmenthal SpA* and the ruling of the ECJ on the substantive issue in the *Factortame* litigation: *Secretary of State for Transport ex p Factortame (No 3) (1992)*; the only question to be determined would be the correct interpretation of the regulation. This question cannot be finally resolved without examining the provisions of the 2002 Regulation; however, on the face of it, the result would be in favour of the applicant.

It therefore appears that Mr B may rely upon the 2002 Regulation to claim redress from his employer either immediately before the domestic courts or after a reference to the ECJ.

▌NOTES

1 The views of academic writers on this issue could be considered at this point: Sir Ivor Jennings argues (*Constitutional Laws of the Commonwealth*, 1957) that a requirement to seek the approval of some outside body would constitute a change in the composition of Parliament and so be binding on the legislature. O Hood Phillips (*Constitutional and Administrative Law*, 7th edn, 1987, Chapter 4)

attacks this view on the basis that it would lead to an absurdity, as all the elements constituting Parliament would have to be summoned to Westminster to deliberate, vote and hear the royal assent.

2 The House of Lords felt able to adopt this approach because the regulations in question had been adopted with the express intention of giving effect to Community law. In the instant case, this argument could not be used. Thus, *Pickstone* may be of no assistance. In *Garland v British Rail Engineering (1983)*, the House of Lords adopted what has been termed a 'rule of construction' approach to s 2(4) in the context of a conflict similar to that in the instant case. Lord Diplock suggested (without resolving the issue) that even where the words of the domestic law were incompatible with the Community law in question, they should be construed so as to comply with it. This argument could be considered at this point as a means of avoiding a conflict with domestic law which would provide Mr B with the relief he seeks. The UK courts appear to have left open the possibility that a UK court might refuse to give effect to words expressly demonstrating an intention to legislate contrary to EU law.

Question 9

Article 141 of the Treaty Establishing the European Union provides: 'Each Member State shall, during the first stage, ensure and, subsequently, maintain the application of the principle that men and women should receive equal pay for equal work.'

In 2004, the UK government takes the view that the principle of equal pay for work of equal value is inappropriate in a free market economy and that, therefore, severe restrictions should be placed upon the ability to bring an equal value claim. The Equal Pay Amendment Bill 2004 is therefore laid before Parliament and duly passed as the Equal Pay Amendment Act 2004. Section 1 of the 2004 Act provides: 'In sub-s (2) of s 1 of the Equal Pay Act 1970 [equality clauses to be implied into contracts of employment], after the words "of equal value to that of a man in the same employment", there shall be inserted the following words: "and the claimant has been in the same employment for a minimum of five years".' Section 2 provides: 'It is hereby declared that in the event of a conflict between any provision of EU law and the provisions of this Act, the provisions of this Act shall prevail.'

(a) Would a UK judge give primacy to UK law if faced with a claimant employed for less than five years who wished to bring an equal value claim against her employer?

(b) Would it make any difference to your answer if Art 141 was not directly effective in UK law?

(Note: you are not asked to decide the likely outcome of the case or to consider the other provisions of the Equal Pay Act 1970.)

Answer plan

A problem question in this area usually concentrates on the issue of conflict between a post-accession domestic instrument and the previous directly effective Community law. The first part of this question consists of the type of question which is commonly set; it concerns the most direct conflict possible between Community law and domestic law, and is quite straightforward. It turns on the question of whether or not Community law is subject to the rule of express repeal. The second part concerning the issues raised by the concept of indirect effect is more demanding. However, it raises a very important constitutional issue which is likely to appear more frequently on constitutional law papers in future: the extent to which UK judges can and will implement an indirectly effective instrument through the vehicle of domestic legislation, regardless of the wording of the domestic instrument in question.

Essentially, the following matters should be considered:

(a)

- s 2(1) and (4) of the European Communities Act 1972;
- the traditional doctrine of parliamentary sovereignty;
- the primacy of Community law: *Costa v ENEL (1964)*;
- Art 141: direct effect;
- the purposive approach to domestic legislation supposed to implement Community law;
- the probable attitude of the UK courts to s 2 of the 2004 Act: *Macarthy's v Smith (1981); Garland v British Rail Engineering Ltd (1983); Secretary of State for Transport ex p Factortame (No 2) (1991)*;
- the implications of *Thoburn*.

(b)

- is the doctrine of the primacy of Community law inapplicable to indirectly effective instruments?;
- *Litster (1989)*: a domestic court must construe domestic legislation contrary to its *prima facie* meaning so as to implement the directive fully;
- *Marleasing (1990)*, as interpreted by *Faccini Dori (1994)* and *Webb*: the obligation on domestic courts to construe national law so far as possible as to conform with directives;
- conclusion: UK courts would give effect to s 2 of the 2004 Act.

Answer

(a)

Community Treaties and other Community law capable of having direct effect in the UK were given such effect by s 2(1) of the European Communities Act 1972. Section 2(4) provides that: ' . . . any enactment passed or to be passed . . . shall be construed and have effect subject to the foregoing provisions of this section.' The words 'subject to' appear to suggest that the courts must allow Community law to prevail over a subsequent Act of Parliament. '[T]he foregoing' are those provisions referred to in s 2(1) giving the force of law to 'the enforceable Community rights' there defined. Section 3(1) provides that questions as to the meaning or effect of Community law are to be determined 'in accordance with the principles laid down by any relevant decision of the European Court'.

However, under the traditional doctrine of parliamentary sovereignty, Parliament is competent to legislate on any matter whatsoever and no court is competent to question the validity of an Act of Parliament. This lack of legal restraint means that while Parliament can legislate on any subject and is free to amend or repeal any previous enactment, it cannot bind successive Parliaments. It follows that where there is inconsistency between a subsequent and a former statute, the later statute impliedly repeals the former to the extent of its inconsistency. Authority for this proposition derives from *Ellen Street Estates Ltd v Minister of Health (1934)* and *Vauxhall Estates Ltd v Liverpool Corp (1932)*.

On the other hand, s 2(4) of the 1972 Act and the Community doctrine of the primacy of EU law flowing from the Treaty and from judgments of the European Court of Justice (ECJ) (see *Costa v ENEL (1964)*) require that Community law should prevail over national law. In *Amministrazione delle Finanze dello Stato v Simmenthal SpA (1978)*, it was held that conflict between provisions of national law and directly applicable Community law must be resolved by rendering the national law inapplicable, and that any national provision or practice withholding from a national court the jurisdiction to apply Community law even temporarily was incompatible with the requirements of Community law. Furthermore, the ECJ made it clear in *Costa v ENEL (1964)* that Community law would prevail over both subsequent and previous domestic law. Thus, s 2(4) of the 1972 Act appears to import a departure from the traditional doctrine of parliamentary sovereignty, in that a limitation as to the subject matter of future legislation seems to have occurred.

In the instant case, it would seem clear, therefore, that under s 2(4) of the 1972 Act and in accordance with the doctrine of the primacy of Community law, s 1(2) of the Equal Pay Act 1970 as amended by the 2004 Act should take effect subject to Art 141, assuming that Art 141 is directly applicable in national law. It is clear from the ruling of the ECJ in *Defrenne v Sabena (1975)* that Art 141 is directly effective.[1] Therefore, on this basis, it would appear that the claimant would not be barred from proceeding: s 2 of the 2004 Act would be ineffective due to the doctrine of the primacy of EU law and therefore Art 141 would render ineffective the provisions of s 1(2) of the Equal Pay Act 1970 as amended by the 2004 Act. In other words, the claimant would purport to bring a claim under the Equal Pay Act which would then be barred due to the operation of s 1(2) as amended; she could then rely on Art 141.

Of course, under the traditional doctrine of express and implied repeal, the contrary result would be achieved. Since the 2004 Act is the later instrument, s 2(4) of the 1972 Act would be repealed to the extent of its inconsistency with s 2 of the 2004 Act, and Art 141 would take effect subject to s 1(2) of the 1970 Act as amended. However, the UK courts have, with some reluctance, accepted that the traditional understanding of parliamentary sovereignty has had to undergo a modification to deal with the implications of the UK's membership of the EC. When a conflict has arisen between Community law and a subsequent domestic enactment, the UK courts have, where possible, adopted what has been termed a 'purposive' approach. In *Pickstone v Freemans (1988)*, the House of Lords determined that the plain meaning of the domestic provision in question would be ignored and an interpretation would be imposed upon it which avoided a conflict with Art 141 of the EC Treaty. Similarly, in *Litster v Forth Dry Dock and Engineering Co Ltd (1989)*, the House of Lords interpreted certain UK regulations so as to give them the meaning required by the EC directive they purported to implement.

In the instant case, however, the object of s 1(2) of the 1970 Act as amended is clearly incompatible with the object of Art 141 which is to remove pay discrimination. Thus, it would seem impossible to interpret it in any way which could render it compatible with Art 141. Moreover, both *Litster* and *Pickstone* were concerned with inadequate implementation of a directive: the courts could claim to be fulfilling Parliament's will by adopting a purposive as opposed to a literal interpretation in order to ensure that the provision in question did the job it was intended to do. In the instant case, it is clear that the courts could not make such a claim, first, because the 2004 Act was not passed in order to implement a directive and, second, because Parliament's will is clearly expressed to be at variance with Community law in s 2 of the Act.

Had s 2 been omitted from the 2004 Act, *dicta* of Lord Denning in *Macarthy's v Smith (1981)* might have provided a means of resolving the conflict between s 1(2) of the 1970 Act as amended and Art 141:

> ... we are entitled to look to the Treaty ... not only as an aid but as an overriding force. If our legislation ... is inconsistent with Community law ... then it is our bounden duty to give priority to Community law.

However, he added:

> If . . . our Parliament deliberately passes an Act with the intention of repudiating the Treaty or any provision in it – or intentionally acting inconsistently with it – then I should have thought that it would be the duty of our courts to follow the statute.

In other words, the proposition put forward by Lord Denning was to the effect that s 2(4) of the European Communities Act had brought about a variant of the rules of implied repeal but that the rules of express repeal still applied. On this basis, in the instant case, the domestic court would have to apply s 1(2) of the 1970 Act as amended due to the express intention of s 2 of the 2004 Act to legislate contrary to Community law. This receives some support from *Garland v British Rail Engineering Ltd (1983).*[2]

However, in *Secretary of State for Transport ex p Factortame (1990)*, the House of Lords and the Court of Appeal may have gone further than Lord Denning in accepting that Community law might impose requirements which would override domestic law. In the Court of Appeal, Bingham LJ said that, where the law of the Community is clear (as arguably it was not in the instant case):

> . . . whether as a result of a ruling given on an Art 177 [now 234] reference or as a result of previous jurisprudence or on a straightforward interpretation of Community instruments, the duty of the national court is to give effect to it in all circumstances . . . To that extent, a UK statute is not as inviolable as it once was.

Therefore, once a ruling from the European Court had been obtained, Lord Bingham held that the Divisional Court would have to apply it even though this involved 'disapplying' an Act of Parliament. He did not expressly enter the caveat that effect would have to be given to express words used in the Merchant Shipping Act 1988 declaring that its provisions should prevail over those of Community law, although he did state: ' . . . any rule of domestic law which prevented the court from giving effect to directly enforceable rights established in Community law would be bad.'

Once the ruling by the ECJ on the issue of interim relief *was* obtained (*Factortame Ltd v Secretary of State for Transport (1990) (ECJ)*), the House of Lords applied it (*ex p Factortame (No 2)* (1991)). Thus, the issue of attempted express repeal of EU law was not clearly determined (any findings would have been *obiter* in any event), and therefore it is not certain what a UK court would do if faced with a provision such as s 2 of the 2004 Act. In *Secretary of State for Employment ex p EOC (1994)*, the House of Lords followed *Factortame* in finding that judicial review was available for the purpose of securing a declaration that UK primary legislation is incompatible with EU law. It was found that certain provisions of the Employment Protection (Consolidation) Act 1978 were indirectly discriminatory and were therefore in breach of Art 141 (ex 119) and the Equal Pay and Equal Treatment Directives.

However, it is at least arguable after *Factortame* that partial entrenchment of s 2(1) of the 1972 Act has been brought about on the basis of a requirement of manner rather than form: if a UK statute is to override Community law, s 2(4) (and, perhaps, s 3(1)) of the European Communities Act must first be repealed. On this argument, it seems that the judge in the instant case would ignore the express intention of Parliament and would refuse to give effect to s 2 of the 2004 Act. The claim would therefore be considered under Art 141, as opposed to s 2(1) of the Equal Pay Act as amended by the 2004 Act.

However, the alternative analysis of *Factortame* given in *Thoburn (2002)* must also be considered. The case involved a challenge to EC regulations on the exclusive use of metric measurements by traders and retailers. Laws LJ held that Parliament could not bind itself in any way and had not done so in the 1972 Act. He declared:

> Parliament cannot bind its successors by stipulating against repeal, wholly or partly, of the ECA. It cannot stipulate as to the manner and form of any subsequent legislation. It cannot stipulate against implied repeal any more than it can stipulate against express repeal.

Rather, the explanation for *Factortame* was that the *courts* had recognised the 1972 Act as but one example of what he called 'a constitutional statute', essentially those which affected fundamental rights or the relationship between citizen and State in some general, overarching manner. The legal consequence of recognising a statute as "constitutional" was simple: "Ordinary statutes may be impliedly repealed. Constitutional statutes may not." Under this line of reasoning, all that has happened is that the courts have recognised the 1972 Act as a 'constitutional statute', meaning that it cannot be impliedly repealed. However, it can still therefore be overridden by express words, making Parliament's meaning clear beyond doubt. Such a view would reinforce a court's probable disinclination to embark on the constitutional enormity of ignoring a clear expression of Parliament's will. It is perhaps more likely that a court would instead attempt to distinguish the instant case from *Factortame*. It would be possible to do so on the basis that there was some uncertainty as to compatibility between the Merchant Shipping Act 1988 and provisions of Community law and, therefore, it need not be assumed that Parliament intended to legislate contrary to Community law. The UK courts were therefore merely accepting that an outcome should be avoided which would be contrary to Parliament's presumed intention. In the instant case, where Parliament's intention is completely clear, the court might feel itself bound to give effect to it. Such an outcome would arguably be contrary to Lord Bingham's remarks; however, they would not be binding as they were *obiter*. On this argument, the court would not allow the claimant to rely on Art 141 and would consider the claim under the 2004 Act (in which case, it would fail). Alternatively, the court might seek a ruling from the ECJ as to how it should respond to such a dilemma.

(b)

In answering this question, it will be assumed that Art 141 can be treated as though it were an indirectly effective directive. If Art 141 were not directly effective, it would seem from *Duke v GEC Reliance Ltd (1988)* that it would not be given primacy over domestic law; the House of Lords held that s 2(4) of the 1972 Act applied only to directly effective law. However, in *Litster v Forth Dry Docks Ltd (1989)*, the House of Lords (without referring to *Duke v GEC*) determined that even where EU law is not directly effective, priority for EU law should be ensured by means of national law if possible. The House of Lords was prepared to construe the domestic legislation contrary to its *prima facie* meaning, because it had been introduced expressly to implement the directive in question.

However, in the instant case, the 2004 Act has been introduced explicitly in order to depart from Community law. In *Kolpinghuis Nijmegen (1986)*, the ECJ held that the obligation on domestic courts to interpret national law to comply with EU law was limited by the general principles of legal certainty and non-retroactivity. At one point, it seemed as if the ruling in *Marleasing SA v La Commercial Internacional de Alimentation SA (1990)* required domestic courts, faced with legislation which ran directly counter to the terms of an indirectly effective directive, to give effect to the directive regardless of the terms of the national legislation. However, in *Faccini Dori v Recreb (1994)*, the ECJ made it clear (at para 26) that the obligation on the domestic court was only to ensure such compatibility where the wording of the national law made this possible. The House of Lords in *Webb v Emo Cargo (1993)* had made it clear that for its part, it could not accept the absolutist interpretation of *Marleasing*. In the instant case, if the court bore in mind *Duke v GEC* and the need for legal certainty, the decision might be influenced by the legitimate expectation of the claimant's employer (arising from s 1(2) of the Equal Pay Act as amended by the 2004 Act) that no action could be brought by the claimant until she had been employed by him for five years; if so, the court would refuse to give Art 141 primacy and would give effect, instead, to the 2004 Act. Such an outcome would be in conformity with the *Faccini Dori* position, since it is clearly not possible to construe the 2004 Act into conformity with Art 141.

NOTES

1 It may be noted that Art 141 is both horizontally and vertically effective; in other words, although it is addressed to States, it is directly applicable against individuals and against State bodies. Therefore, in the case for consideration, it would be irrelevant that the judge was faced with a claimant bringing a claim against a private employer as opposed to an emanation of the State: the same issues in respect of Community law would arise in either case.

2 Lord Diplock suggested in *Garland v British Rail Engineering Ltd (1983)* that national courts must strive to make domestic law conform to Community law however wide a departure from the *prima facie* meaning may be needed to achieve consistency'. However, he added that they should do so only while it appeared that Parliament wished to comply with EU law.

Question 10

How far has the principle of parliamentary sovereignty survived the *Factortame* litigation?

Answer plan

The *Factortame* litigation is a popular subject for examiners and, therefore, a question on these lines is commonly set. Such a question is reasonably straightforward, assuming that the examinee is familiar with the convoluted *Factortame* saga.

Essentially, the following matters should be considered:

- the traditional doctrine of parliamentary sovereignty;
- s 2(1) and (4) of the European Communities Act 1972: the primacy of Community law (*Costa v ENEL (1964)*);
- the implications of *Secretary of State for Transport ex p Factortame (1990)* (*ECJ*): the issue of interim relief; the doctrine of express repeal;
- *Secretary of State for Transport ex p Factortame Ltd and Others (No 2) (1991)*: the substantive issue;
- the implications of the *Thoburn* (2002) analysis
- conclusion: sovereignty in abeyance?

Answer

The doctrine of parliamentary sovereignty as explained by Dicey means that Parliament has the right to make, unmake or amend any Act of Parliament, and that such power is not open to challenge by any outside body. Since 1688, the doctrine of the supremacy of Parliament has developed to the stage when, in *Pickin v British Railways Board (1974)*, it appeared clearly settled that the notion of finding an Act of Parliament invalid could be said to be obsolete. This lack of legal restraint has both a positive and a negative aspect. It means that while Parliament can legislate on any subject, it cannot bind successive Parliaments. If it could, then clearly each successive Parliament would not be free to legislate on any matter. Thus, where there is inconsistency between a subsequent and a former statute, the later statute impliedly repeals the earlier one to the extent of its inconsistency with the former. Authority for this proposition derives from *Ellen Street Estates Ltd v Minister of Health (1934)*.

However, a qualification to the rule deriving from *Pickin* must be introduced due to the UK's membership of the EC. As the UK is a dualist State, Community law had to be given effect by domestic legislation. This was achieved by the European Communities Act 1972 which, by s 2(1), incorporated all existing Community law capable of having direct effect into UK law. No express declaration of the supremacy of Community law is contained in the Act; the words intended to achieve this are contained in s 2(4) of the Act 1972, which reads as follows: '. . . any enactment passed or to be passed . . . shall be construed and have effect subject to the foregoing provisions of this section.' The words 'subject to' appear to suggest that the courts must allow Community law to prevail over subsequent Acts of Parliament. '[T]he foregoing' are those provisions referred to in s 2(1) giving the force of law to 'the enforceable Community rights' there defined. Section 2(4) would therefore seem to have protected s 2(1) against implied repeal, thereby running contrary to the traditional view of parliamentary sovereignty.

According to that view, post-accession statutes should prevail over Community law incorporated under the 1972 Act as representing the latest expression of Parliament's will, but the Community doctrine of primacy of EU law and s 2(4) would require Community law to prevail. In this respect, it was clear from the judgments of the ECJ (see *Costa v ENEL* (1964), *Amministrazione delle Finanze dello Stato v Simmenthal SpA (1978)* and *Marleasing SA v La Commercial Internacional de Alimentacion SA (1990)*) that Community law should prevail over both subsequent and previous national law. *Secretary of State for Transport ex p Factortame* (1990) made a contribution to the question of the primacy of EU law because the UK courts had to confront directly the question of conflict between EU law and domestic law.

Under the Merchant Shipping (Registration of Fishing Vessels) Regulations 1988 made under the Merchant Shipping Act 1988, British fishing vessels were required to re-register on a new register from 1 March 1988. Vessels could qualify for entry onto the new register only if their owners or, in the case of companies, their shareholders were either British citizens or were domiciled in Britain. The applicants were unable to comply with these conditions and consequently could not qualify for entry. The applicants sought a ruling by way of judicial review that the legislation contravened provisions of the EEC Treaty by depriving them of Community law rights. These included the prohibition of discrimination on grounds of nationality, the prohibition of restrictions on exports between Member States, the provision for the free movement of workers and the requirement that nationals of Member States are to be treated equally with respect to participation in the capital of companies established in the EC. A ruling on the substantive questions of Community law was requested from the ECJ and, pending that ruling, which could not be expected for another two years, the Divisional Court made an order by way of interim relief, setting aside the relevant part of the 1988 Regulations and allowing the applicants to continue to operate their vessels as if they were British-registered.

This order was set aside by the Court of Appeal. Bingham LJ said, however, that where the law of the Community is clear:

> . . . whether as a result of a ruling given on an Art 177 [now 234] reference or as a result of previous jurisprudence or on a straightforward interpretation of Community instruments, the duty of the national court is to give effect to it in all circumstances . . . To that extent, a UK statute is not as inviolable as it once was.

In the instant case, it had not yet been established that the statute was inconsistent with Community law and, in those circumstances, it was held that the court had no power to declare a statute void.

The applicants appealed to the House of Lords, which upheld the ruling of the Court of Appeal and referred to the ECJ for a preliminary ruling on the question of whether Community law required that a national court should grant the interim relief sought. Lord Bridge said that if it appeared after the ECJ had ruled on the substantive issue that domestic law was incompatible with the Community provisions in question, Community law would prevail.

The European Commission then successfully sought a ruling in the ECJ that the nationality requirement of s 14 of the Merchant Shipping Act be suspended (*Re Nationality of Fishermen: EC Commission v UK (1989)*) pending the delivery of the judgment in the action for a declaration. This decision was given effect in the UK by means of the Merchant Shipping Act 1988 (Amendment) Order 1989. The ECJ then ruled on the question of interim relief, relying on *Amministrazione delle Finanze dello Stato v Simmenthal SpA (1978)*. Predictably, it found that a national court must set aside national legislative provisions if that were necessary to give interim relief in a case concerning Community rights (*Factortame Ltd v Secretary of State for*

Transport (1990) (ECJ)). The House of Lords then granted the interim relief sought, thus applying Community law in preference to UK law (*ex p Factortame (No 2) (1991)*).

Now that the issue as to the question of interim relief is resolved, it appears that the UK courts have accepted that where Community law is certain, it should be applied in preference to domestic law. Where it is unclear, and the applicants who wish to rely on Community law have a seriously arguable case, the domestic law should be disapplied if that is necessary to give interim relief pending a ruling on the issue from the European Court. Thus, the courts clearly have the power to refuse to obey an Act of Parliament and Parliament is therefore effectively constrained in its freedom to legislate on any subject. If it does legislate inconsistently with Community law, its legislation may be disapplied. If it wishes to avoid this restraint, it will have to use express words demonstrating its intention. Thus, Parliament has succeeded in partially entrenching s 2(1) of the European Communities Act by means of s 2(4) which imposes a requirement of form (express words) on future legislation designed to override Community law. As in practice, such express words would almost certainly not be used, it appears to be impossible for Parliament to depart from the principle of the primacy of directly effective Community law,[1] unless it decided to withdraw from the Community.

However, the alternative analysis of *Factortame* given in *Thoburn (2002)*, which directly challenges the above account, must also be considered. The case involved a challenge to EC regulations on the exclusive use of metric measurements by traders and retailers. Laws LJ held that Parliament could not bind itself in any way and had not done so in the 1972 Act. He declared:

> Parliament cannot bind its successors by stipulating against repeal, wholly or partly, of the ECA. It cannot stipulate as to the manner and form of any subsequent legislation. It cannot stipulate against implied repeal any more than it can stipulate against express repeal.

Rather the explanation for *Factortame* was that the *courts* had recognised the 1972 Act as but one example of what he called 'a constitutional statute', essentially those which affected fundamental rights or 'the relationship between citizen and State in some general, overarching manner'. The legal consequence of recognising a statute as 'constitutional' was simple: 'Ordinary statutes may be impliedly repealed. Constitutional statutes may not.' Under this line of reasoning, all that has happened is that the courts have recognised the 1972 Act as a 'constitutional statute' meaning that it cannot be impliedly repealed. However, it can still therefore be overridden by express words, making Parliament's meaning clear beyond doubt. This analysis suggests therefore that the ECA is protected only from implied repeal.

Can it further be argued that even if express words were used, a UK court would not give them effect? If so, sovereignty would be at least suspended in the area affected by Community law, unless and until Parliament repealed the European Communities Act 1972. In contrast to *dicta* of Lord Denning in *Macarthy's v Smith (1981)* to the effect that a domestic court would give regard to express words in a statute requiring it to override Community law, and to those of Laws LJ noted above, Lord Bingham in *Factortame* did not enter a caveat that effect would have been given to express words used in the Merchant Shipping Act 1988 declaring that its provisions should prevail over those of Community law. He came close to suggesting that effect would not be given to such words in observing: ' . . . any rule of domestic law which prevented the court from giving effect to directly enforceable rights established in Community law would be bad.' Perhaps, therefore, one could go so far as to suggest that entrenchment of s 2(1) of the 1972 Act has been brought about on the basis of a requirement of 'manner' rather than 'form': if a UK statute is to override Community law, s 2(4) of the European Communities Act must first be repealed. However, this is a bold assumption as the point has not yet been determined.

In *Secretary of State for Transport ex p Factortame Ltd (No 3) (1992)*, the ECJ had to consider the substantive issue. It ruled that while, at present, competence to determine the conditions governing the nationality of ships was vested in the Member States, such competence must be exercised consistently with Community law. The Court then determined that Part II of the Merchant Shipping Act 1988 was discriminatory on the grounds of nationality contrary to Art 43 (ex 52) and, therefore, did not so conform. This ruling means that the UK courts will have to apply Community law in preference to the Merchant Shipping Act 1988, which must be disapplied. Thus, the case seems to have dispelled doubts as to the supremacy of Community law.

The final result of the *Factortame* litigation seems to be an acceptance of the primacy of Community law by the British courts and the consequent fettering of the legislative competence of the UK Parliament. *Factortame* represents a departure from the 'rule of construction' approach to s 2(4) of the 1972 Act, as exemplified in *Macarthy's* and in *Garland v British Rail Engineering (1983)*, which arguably left sovereignty intact in that such an approach was applied only where it was clear that Parliament intended to comply with Community law.

Statements made as to the nature of parliamentary sovereignty must now undergo some modification; for example, it might now be said that 'once an instrument is recognised as an Act of Parliament *and is compatible with any enforceable Community law*, no English court can refuse to obey it or question its validity' (a modification of a statement made by Sir Robert Megarry in *Manuel v AG (1983)*). However, it must be remembered that the outcome of *Factortame* is merely consistent with the probable intention of Parliament as expressed in s 2(4) of the European Communities Act 1972; arguably, the case has merely brought about full acceptance of the implications of that provision by the judiciary.[2] Moreover, although the doctrine of parliamentary sovereignty has been greatly affected, it is arguable that it would revive in its original form if the UK withdrew from the Community.

NOTES

1   In *Litster v Forth Dry Docks Ltd (1989)*, the House of Lords determined that even where EU law is not directly effective, priority for EU law should be ensured by means of national law, even if this meant construing the domestic legislation contrary to its *prima facie* meaning. It was prepared to do this because the relevant national legislation had been introduced expressly to implement the directive in question. However, where domestic legislation bore on its face express words demonstrating that Parliament had intended to avoid implementing the indirectly effective instrument, it is arguable that the court would give them effect.

2   The change in attitude of the UK judiciary could be considered further. Like the judiciary in the other Member States, the UK judiciary has gradually come to a full realisation of the need to achieve a uniform application of Community law throughout the Member States. However, this has taken some time, as can be seen by comparing a case such as *HP Bulmer Ltd v J Bollinger SA (1974)* with *Factortame*. The *Bulmer* case is in this sense similar to a German case: *Internationale Handelsgesellschaft mbH (1974)*.

Question 11

'Parliament in 1972 accomplished the impossible and (to a degree) bound its successors' (TRS Allan). Do you agree?

Answer plan

This is a very popular question on constitutional law papers. It may take the form of the question: 'Would you agree that parliamentary sovereignty has suffered a severe trammeling due to obligations arising from membership of the EC?' The instant question is not as wide ranging as that, but concentrates on the specific issue of partial entrenchment. It should be noted that the assumption made as to the impossibility of entrenchment aside from Community obligations should be attacked, albeit briefly.

The following issues should be addressed:
- the traditional doctrine of parliamentary sovereignty: Parliament cannot bind its successors;
- the possible limitation of this doctrine;
- the provisions of s 2(1) and (4) of the European Communities Act 1972;
- the doctrine of the primacy of Community law as put forward by the European Court of Justice (ECJ);
- the 'purposive' approach to conflict between UK and Community law;
- the partial entrenchment of s 2(1) by means of a requirement of 'form' – express words;
- the analysis of *Thoburn* (2002);
- the partial entrenchment by means of a requirement of 'manner'?

Answer

The traditional doctrine of parliamentary sovereignty as put forward by Dicey includes the notion that the legislative competence of the UK Parliament is unlimited, in the sense that its powers to make laws on any subject, to unmake or amend any Act of Parliament, are not open to challenge. It follows that Parliament may not be bound by its predecessors; it would otherwise suffer a limitation of its power. The statement made by Allan assumes that apart from the effect of accession to the European Communities, no departure from this traditional doctrine is possible. This assumption will be considered briefly before examining the wider issue as to the impact of the European Communities Act 1972 on the traditional doctrine of parliamentary sovereignty.

In *Ellen Street Estates Ltd v Minister of Health (1934)*, it was argued that the Acquisition of Land (Assessment of Compensation) Act 1919 prescribed a certain manner for authorising the acquisition of land. It provided in s 7 that other statutes 'shall have effect subject to this Act'. If s 7 applied to subsequent enactments, provisions of the Housing Act 1925 which were inconsistent with the 1919 Act would have no effect. However, Maughan LJ held that Parliament cannot bind itself as to the form of future enactments. Thus, it appears that the courts will not give effect to a statute which is in conflict with a later statute on the basis that the earlier statute has been impliedly repealed to the extent of its inconsistency. However, in *AG for New South Wales v Trethowan (1932)*, the Privy Council upheld the requirement of a referendum before a Bill to abolish the Upper House was presented for the royal assent. Although, as a number of commentators have argued, this decision may be of limited application as involving a non-sovereign legislature, it does suggest that a class of legislation exists for which it may be appropriate to delineate the manner and form of any subsequent amendment or repeal.

For example, s 1 of the Northern Ireland Act 1998 provides that Northern Ireland will not cease to be part of Her Majesty's dominions without conducting a poll in Northern Ireland. If a future Act of Parliament purported to revoke this guarantee without first conducting a poll in Northern Ireland, it is at least arguable that the courts would hold the later statute to be invalid, as had occurred in the South African case of *Harris v Minister of the Interior (1951)*. This view also receives some support from Slade LJ in *Manuel v AG (1983)*, although he did not finally resolve the issue. Thus, although Allan's assumption is broadly correct as to the traditional impossibility of entrenchment, it is at least worth testing. What then has been the impact of the European Communities Act 1972 on this doctrine?

The UK became a member of the European Community with effect from 1 January 1973 by virtue of the Treaty of Accession 1972. Treaties and Community law capable of having direct effect in the UK were given such effect by s 2(1) of the European Communities Act 1972, which incorporated all existing directly effective Community law into UK law. No express declaration of the supremacy of Community law is contained in the Act; the words intended to achieve this are contained in s 2(4), which reads as follows: ' . . . any enactment passed or to be passed . . . shall be construed and have effect subject to the foregoing provisions of this section.' The words 'subject to' appear to suggest that the courts must allow Community law to prevail over subsequent Acts of Parliament. '[T]he foregoing' are those provisions referred to in s 2(1) giving the force of law to 'the enforceable Community rights' there defined. Section 3(1) provides that questions as to the meaning or effect of Community law are to be determined 'in accordance with the principles laid down by any relevant decision of the European Court'.

The problem arises in respect of statutes passed after 1 January 1973.[1] According to the traditional doctrine of parliamentary sovereignty, the later Act should prevail as representing the latest expression of Parliament's will, but the Community doctrine of the primacy of EU law and s 2(4) would require Community law to prevail. In this respect, it is clear from judgments of the ECJ (see *Costa v ENEL (1964)*) that Community law should prevail over national law. In *Amministrazione delle Finanze dello Stato v Simmenthal SpA (1978)*, it was held that conflict between provisions of national law and directly applicable Community law must be resolved by rendering the national law inapplicable, and that any national provision or practice withholding from a national court the jurisdiction to apply Community law even temporarily was incompatible with the requirements of Community law.

How have the UK courts approached this conflict?[2] In *Felixstowe Dock and Railway Co v British Transport Docks Board (1976)*, Lord Denning MR dismissed a challenge to UK law on the basis that 'once a Bill is passed by Parliament and becomes a statute, that will dispose of all discussion about the Treaty. These courts will have to abide by the statute without regard to the Treaty at all'. This was the traditional approach; however, it then gave way to what has been termed a 'rule of construction' approach to s 2(4). In *Garland v British Rail Engineering (1983)*, Lord Diplock suggested (without resolving the issue) that even where the words of the domestic law were incompatible with the Community law in question, they should be construed so as to comply with it. This approach was applied in *Pickstone v Freemans (1988)* in the House of Lords, although not in the Court of Appeal. The Court of Appeal ruled that domestic legislation – the Equal Pay (Amendment) Regulations 1983 made under s 2(2) of the European Communities Act – was inconsistent with Art 141 (ex 119) of the EC Treaty. It then treated Art 141 as having more authority than the Amendment and made a ruling consistent with Art 141.

The House of Lords avoided this controversial approach but, by a less overtly contentious route, achieved the same result. It held that although the two provisions appeared to be in conflict, a purposive interpretation of the domestic legislation would be adopted; in other words, the plain meaning of the provision in question would be ignored and an interpretation would be imposed upon it which was not in conflict with Art 141. In order to achieve this, the plain meaning of the words 'which, not being work in relation to which para (a) or (b) above applies' in s 1(2)(c) of the Equal Pay Act 1970 as amended had to be ignored. This was done on the basis that Parliament must have intended to fulfil its EC obligations in passing the Amendment Regulations once it had been forced to do so by the ECJ. The House of Lords followed a similar approach in *Litster v Forth Dry Dock Engineering (1989)*.[3] These decisions provide authority for the proposition that plain words in a statute will not be given effect if to do so would involve a departure from the provisions of European Community law.

It might appear to follow that Parliament has succeeded in partially entrenching s 2(1) of the European Communities Act by means of s 2(4) by imposing a requirement of form (express words) on future legislation designed to override Community law. However, the House of Lords in both *Litster* and *Pickstone* cloaked its disregard of statutory words by the finding that they were reasonably capable of bearing a meaning compatible with Community obligations. *Dicta* of Lord Denning in *Macarthy's v Smith (1981)* do, however, suggest more clearly that partial entrenchment of s 2(1) of the 1972 Act has occurred:

> . . . we are entitled to look to the Treaty . . . not only as an aid but as an overriding force. If . . . our legislation . . . is inconsistent with Community law . . . then it is our bounden duty to give priority to Community law.

Further support for Lord Denning's view comes from the *Factortame* litigation; indeed, support might even be found for the inference that words in a statute, although expressly requiring a court to do so, could not override Community obligations.

Secretary of State for Transport ex p Factortame (1990) concerned the Merchant Shipping (Registration of Fishing Vessels) Regulations 1988 made under the Merchant Shipping Act 1988, whereby British fishing vessels were required to re-register on a new register. The applicants, who were unable to comply with the conditions for registration, sought a ruling by way of judicial review that they contravened the provisions of the EC Treaty by depriving them of Community law rights. A ruling on the substantive questions of Community law was requested from the ECJ and, pending that ruling, an order was made by way of interim relief, setting aside the relevant part of the 1988 Regulations. This order was set aside by the Court of Appeal and the applicants appealed to the House of Lords which upheld the Court of Appeal ruling on the ground that no court had power to make an order conferring rights upon the applicants which were directly contrary to UK legislation. The result of these two rulings was clearly in accord with the traditional doctrine of parliamentary sovereignty as far as English law was concerned. However, the rulings also accepted that Community law might impose requirements which would be overriding.

In the Court of Appeal, Bingham LJ said that where the law of the Community is clear:

> . . . whether as a result of a ruling given on an Art 177 [now 234] reference or as a result of previous jurisprudence or on a straightforward interpretation of Community instruments, the duty of the national court is to give effect to it in all circumstances . . . To that extent, a UK statute is not as inviolable as it once was.

Lord Bingham did not enter the caveat that effect would have been given to express words used in the Merchant Shipping Act 1988 declaring that its provisions should prevail over those of Community law. It could therefore be suggested that entrenchment of s 2(1) of the 1972 Act has been brought about on the basis of a requirement of manner rather than form: if a UK statute is to override Community law, the European Communities Act must first be repealed.

The House of Lords referred to the ECJ for a preliminary ruling on the question of whether Community law required that a national court should grant the interim relief sought. The European Court held that the force of Community law would be impaired if, when a judgment of the Court on Community law rights was pending, a national court was unable to grant interim relief which would ensure the full efficacy of the eventual judgment. Therefore, when the only obstacle to granting such relief was a rule of national law, that rule must be disapplied (*Secretary of State for Transport ex p Factortame Ltd (1990)* (ECJ)). The House of Lords then applied this ruling, granting the interim relief sought (*ex p Factortame (No 2) (1991)*). In *Secretary of State for Employment ex p EOC (1994)*, the House of Lords followed *Factortame* in finding that judicial review was available for the purpose of securing a declaration that UK primary legislation is incompatible with EU law. It was found that certain provisions of the Employment Protection (Consolidation) Act 1978 were indirectly discriminatory and were therefore in breach of Art 141 (ex 119) and the Equal Pay and Equal Treatment Directives.

It follows from the decisions of the House of Lords and the Court of Appeal that if it is clear that a statute is inconsistent with EU law which is directly enforceable, the domestic court would have to disapply it. Lord Bingham's words referred to above were *obiter*, but nevertheless support the view that partial entrenchment of s 2(1) of the 1972 Act has indeed occurred, but only where Community law is clear and directly enforceable. In so arguing, it should be borne in mind that the House of Lords has not yet struck down an Act of Parliament. It has therefore accepted the possibility of partial entrenchment of s 2(1) of the 1972 Act by means of a requirement of 'form' or arguably 'manner', but has not yet put it into practice.

However, the alternative analysis of *Factortame* given in *Thoburn (2002)* must finally be considered. The case involved a challenge to EC regulations on the exclusive use of metric measurements by traders and retailers. Laws LJ held that Parliament could not bind itself in any way and had not done so in the 1972 Act. He declared:

> Parliament cannot bind its successors by stipulating against repeal, wholly or partly, of the ECA. It cannot stipulate as to the manner and form of any subsequent legislation. It cannot stipulate against implied repeal any more than it can stipulate against express repeal.

Rather the explanation for *Factortame* was that the *courts* had recognised the 1972 Act as but one example of what he called 'a constitutional statute', essentially those which affected fundamental rights or the 'relationship between citizen and State in some general, overarching manner'. The legal consequence of recognising a statute as 'constitutional' was simple: 'Ordinary statutes may be impliedly repealed. Constitutional statutes may not.' Under this line of reasoning, all that has happened is that the courts have recognised the 1972 Act as a 'constitutional statute' meaning that it cannot be impliedly repealed. However, it can still therefore be overridden by express words, making Parliament's meaning clear beyond doubt. More importantly, this interpretation flatly contradicts the view of TRS Allan given in the question: Parliament has not succeeded in entrenching the 1972 Act and thus bound its successors: the courts have simply modified the doctrine of implied repeal in order to give some limited protection to constitutional statutes, of which the 1972 is but one example.

NOTES

1 Clearly, any Community law will prevail over UK legislation enacted before 1 January 1973. Authority for this can be found in rulings such as those in *Henn (1980)* and *Goldstein (1983)*. This is uncontroversial and merely accords with the ordinary operation of the doctrine of parliamentary sovereignty.

2 The difference between indirectly and directly effective instruments could be considered at this point. Some Community law has direct effect in the UK. This will apply in respect of regulations, treaties and some directives (if certain conditions are fulfilled as laid down in *Van Duyn v The Home Office (1974)*). If an instrument is not directly effective, domestic legislation must be introduced to implement it.

3 *Litster*, it could be pointed out, was concerned with an indirectly effective directive. Nevertheless, the approach of the House of Lords suggested that where legislation had been introduced specifically to implement a directive, UK courts must interpret it so as to conform with the directive 'supplying the necessary words by implication' in order to achieve such conformity. Thus, primacy of even indirectly effective instruments was assured, except in instances where no domestic legislation had been introduced to implement them.

Question 12

Has the Human Rights Act 1998 had any effect on the sovereignty of Parliament?

Answer plan

This is a very topical question, given the recent, important House of Lords case law on s 3(1) of the Human Rights Act (HRA) 1998. It is a tricky question because, on its face, the simple answer to the question is 'no', it being clear that the HRA has, formally speaking, carefully preserved the traditional doctrine of parliamentary sovereignty; however a good answer would go considerably further than simply explaining this.

The following issues should be addressed:

• the traditional doctrine of parliamentary sovereignty: Parliament cannot bind its successors;

• the ways in which the HRA preserves this: ss 4(6) and 3(2);

- the evidence that Parliament can apparently limit itself at least as to form: the courts' response to the European Communities Act 1972; the contrary analysis of *Thoburn* (2002);
- the argument that s 3 of the HRA, as interpreted, can amount to the suspension of implied repeal;
- the significance of s 19 in avoiding legislative infringements of the Convention;
- conclusion.

Answer

The traditional doctrine of parliamentary sovereignty as put forward by Dicey includes the notion that the legislative competence of the UK Parliament is unlimited, in the sense that its powers to make laws on any subject, to unmake or amend any Act of Parliament, are not open to challenge. It follows that Parliament may not be bound by its predecessors; it would otherwise suffer a limitation of its power. Any statute passed by Parliament is subject either to express repeal or to implied repeal, whereby a later inconsistent statute impliedly repeals any earlier statutes to the extent of their inconsistency with it. It will be argued in this essay that the HRA purports to preserve in full the above, traditional Diceyan doctrine of sovereignty, but that a closer look at certain aspects of the Act and recent case law thereon, together with insights derived from the courts' treatment of the European Communities Act, reveals that the true picture is rather more complex and nuanced.

The White Paper *Bringing Rights Home* (Cm 3782), which preceded the Human Rights Bill, made it clear that the Act would make no attempt to entrench itself against either express or implied repeal. This was explained to be due to the importance the government attached to the doctrine of parliamentary sovereignty. Thus, the legislation incorporating the European Convention on Human Rights (ECHR) was to follow the traditional British constitutional method: it would be no different in status from legislation regulating dog licensing. The Act contains no statement that it is intended to last 'for all time forth' in the manner of the Union legislation which merged Scotland with England and then Great Britain with Northern Ireland. Nor does it seek to lay down any requirements of manner or form with which future legislation curtailing Convention rights or repealing the HRA itself would have to comply to be valid, as does, for example, the Northern Ireland Act 1998. Most importantly, it provides that if any statutes contain provisions that are found to be inconsistent with any of the Convention rights, such statutes will remain valid and of full effect (ss 3(2)(b) and 4(6)). Section 4 states that a 'a declaration of incompatibility' – made if the court cannot interpret legislation so as to be compatible with the Convention rights – 'does not affect the validity, continuing operation or enforcement of the provision in respect of which it is given'. In part, the Act in effect simply confirms the orthodox constitutional position that later statutes override previous inconsistent ones. In this respect, the HRA is of the same status as any other Act of Parliament, although it introduces the innovation of the formal judicial declaration of incompatibility under ss 4 and 10, which can trigger the parliamentary 'fast track' procedure to amend the offending legislation by means of secondary legislation which, however, leaves Parliament entirely free as to whether to remedy the incompatibility which the courts have found to exist.

However, in relation to statutes passed *prior* to the HRA, the Act provides for a departure from orthodoxy. Under the doctrine of implied repeal just mentioned, one would expect that where it was found that a provision in a statute *pre-dating* the HRA was incompatible with one or more of the Convention rights, that provision would be thereby impliedly repealed. However, ss 3(2)(b) and 4(6) do not take this route: by stating that the provisions of *any* statute found to be incompatible with Convention rights remain valid and in force, they have the effect that, in a departure from normal doctrine, the doctrine of implied repeal will not apply. In other words, where a provision of an *earlier* statute is found to be incompatible with a Convention right, it will nevertheless remain in force. In this respect, then, the HRA makes a quite clear alteration to the normal rules of parliamentary sovereignty; already, therefore, it is possible to conclude that the bald assertion in the title of this essay requires modification at least in this respect.

The HRA may, however, make a further and more important alteration to the traditional understanding of sovereignty. Section 3(1) of the Act provides: 'So far as is possible to do so, primary legislation and subordinate legislation must be read and given effect in a way which is compatible with the Convention rights.' This amounts to an attempt to impose a particular interpretative approach on all future statutes, and as such, amounts to a form of protection for the Convention rights which may be as strong as judges care to make it. Since what is 'possible' in statutory interpretation is not defined in the Act and is open to argument, one reading of s 3(1) would see it as giving a mandate to judges to treat *all* legislation as Convention compliant, unless it contains express statements of its incompatibility, using techniques such as reading words into legislation, ignoring words which imply incompatibility, adopting strained linguistic techniques and so on (see *Young* [2002] *CLJ* 53). Just how much protection can be afforded in this way can be illustrated by reference to the approach judges have taken in relation to the protection of EU law from implied repeal. The equivalent provision to s 3 of the HRA is s 2(4) of the European Communities Act 1972, which reads as follows: '. . . any enactment passed or to be passed . . . shall be construed and have effect subject to the foregoing provisions of this section.' The words 'subject to' appear to suggest that the courts must allow Community law to prevail over a subsequent Act of Parliament. The 'foregoing provisions' are those of s 2(1) importing Community law into national law.

The House of Lords in *Pickstone v Freemans (1988)* found that domestic legislation – the Equal Pay (Amendment) Regulations – made under s 2(2) of the European Communities Act appeared to be inconsistent with Art 141 (ex 119). It held that despite this apparent conflict, a purposive interpretation of the domestic legislation would be adopted; in other words, the plain meaning of the provision in question would be ignored and an interpretation would be foisted upon it which was not in conflict with Art 141. This was done on the basis that Parliament must have intended to fulfil its EC obligations in passing the Amendment Regulations once it had been forced to do so by the ECJ. The House of Lords followed a similar approach in *Litster v Forth Dry Dock Engineering (1989)*.

It might of course be objected that the argument being made here is that Parliament has by ordinary statute (the HRA) altered the rules of parliamentary sovereignty itself, precisely what the orthodox doctrine will not allow. But it is submitted that the literature in this area tends to rule out the possibility of Parliament being able to bind itself as to 'manner and form', as if the two types of restrictions may readily be lumped together. In fact, they are very distinct: there is now clear evidence that Parliament can bind itself at least as to the *form* of future legislation; there is no such evidence in relation to restrictions as to *manner*: cases from the Commonwealth, such as *AG for New South Wales v Trethowan (1932)*, are inconclusive.

What then is the evidence that Parliament may now restrict itself as to the form of future legislation? The clearest example relates to the European Communities Act 1972 again and its interpretation in the case of *Secretary of State for Transport ex p Factortame (No 2) (1991)*. The case is well known but, in brief, s 2(4) of the European Communities Act 1972 amounted to an attempt of some kind by the Parliament of 1972 to fetter its successors. As noted above, s 2(4) states that: 'any enactment passed *or to be passed* shall be construed and have effect subject to the foregoing provisions of this section' (emphasis added). The 'foregoing provisions' were those that made Community law enforceable in the UK. By saying that any enactment *to be passed*, that is, any future enactment, must take effect 'subject to' the provisions of this Act, Parliament appeared to be suggesting that the courts must allow Community law to prevail over subsequent Acts of Parliament. This was clearly an attempt to suspend the normal doctrine of implied repeal. Instead of any later statute which conflicted with EU law impliedly repealing it, such a later statute would have to either be 'construed', that is, interpreted so that it did not conflict with EU law, or if it could not be so interpreted, it would have to be deprived of effect insofar as it conflicted with Community law, that is, given effect 'subject to' EU law.

Parliament was quite evidently, therefore, trying to alter the rule of parliamentary sovereignty itself and the decision in *Factortame (No 2)* appears to indicate that the courts are quite willing to allow it to do so, quite contrary to Wade's view that 'this rule is ultimate and unalterable by any legal authority' ('The basis of legal sovereignty' [1955] CLJ 189). The case arose because the Merchant Shipping Act 1988 placed restrictions on the abilities of non-British fishermen to fish in British waters. As such, it was in clear conflict with the non-discrimination principle of EU law. The House of Lords held that notwithstanding that the Merchant Shipping Act (MSA) post-dated the European Communities Act, the former would prevail: the MSA must be disapplied to the extent of its inconsistency with EU law.

The clear finding of law to be drawn from the decision is that if Parliament wishes to legislate contrary to EU law, it must use express words, either instructing the court to disregard EU law when applying the particular statute, or possibly by repealing the European Communities Act first. In any event, it is clear that the courts accepted that Parliament could change the law of sovereignty. As Lord Bridge remarked, the decision was not 'a novel and dangerous invasion by a Community institution of the sovereignty of Parliament', because Parliament had 'voluntarily accepted' a diminution of its sovereignty by passing the European Communities Act in 1972. The courts' view at least (and it is the courts which ultimately determine the parameters of the sovereignty doctrine) seems to be that Parliament can, in principle, alter the application of the doctrine of sovereignty to particular statutes. The question is whether they will use s 3(1) of the HRA in order to effect such a change.

Just how potent s 3(1) is can be seen by the decision of the House of Lords in *A* (2001). The case concerned the interpretation to be given to s 41 of the Youth Justice and Criminal Evidence Act 1999, which forbade any evidence to be given in a rape trial of the woman's sexual history, including any previous sexual history with the alleged rapist, except in very limited circumstances. This was thought to raise an issue of compatibility with Art 6 of the ECHR, which provides, *inter alia*, that: 'In the determination of . . . any criminal charge against him, everyone is entitled to a fair and public hearing within a reasonable time by an independent and impartial tribunal established by law.' Lords Steyn and Hutton were prepared to hold that, given the very strong wording of s 3(1) and *Pepper v Hart* statements in Parliament to the effect that declarations of incompatibility were to be a remedy of last resort, the only way in which Parliament could legislate contrary to a Convention right would be by 'a clear limitation on Convention rights . . . *stated in terms*' (emphasis added). This approach led them simply to read into the relevant part of s 41 words which were not there, namely that evidence was to be admitted where that was necessary to achieve a fair trial. It may be noted that Lord Hope, in contrast, considered that this approach went too far, crossing the line from interpretation to legislating. He considered, in what is certainly the more usual understanding of the word 'interpreting', that the judge's task was limited to identifying specific words which would otherwise lead to incompatibility and then re-interpreting those words, clearly not something which Lords Steyn and Hutton – and for that matter Lord Slynn – undertook. Lord Hope's approach arguably found more support from the House of Lords in *Re W and B (2002)*, in which their Lordships emphasised the importance of not stepping over the boundary from statutory interpretation to 'statutory amendment'.[1] A more activist approach, arguably involving the re-writing, rather than the re-intepretation of legislation occurred in *Ghaidan v Mendoza (2004)*. However the decision *Bellinger v Bellinger (2003)* clearly indicated that the courts will sometimes refuse to engage even in relatively straightforward re-interpretation of legislation, in terms of linguistics, where it is felt that the change is complex and significant enough to require consideration by Parliament. In that case, the House of Lords refused to interpret the word 'female' in the Matrimonial Causes Act 1973 to reflect modern understandings of the protean nature of gender so that it included post-operative male to female transsexuals and would thus allow the applicant to validly marry a man. To change the meaning of a single word in this way was clearly therefore a 'possible' interpretation even under the most modest views of what that elusive word means. However, the interpretation was rejected and a declaration of incompatibility made instead. Nevertheless, if the approach in *A* and *Mendoza* is followed in even some areas of rights protection, the result will be that Parliament has, through s 3(1), succeeded in imposing a requirement of express words upon such of its successors that wish to legislate incompatibly with the Convention rights.

It may be further suggested that there is a more subtle way in which while as a matter of law, the Act represents no threat to sovereignty, it may nevertheless amount to a kind of *de facto* 'higher law', not in reality of the same status as other Acts of Parliament. In this respect, the duty of ministers introducing legislation under s 19 of the HRA is of relevance. Under that section, ministers must make a statement when introducing legislation into Parliament that it does not infringe Convention rights, or that they believe it does, but they wish to proceed in any event. Statements of the latter kind would amount to a declaration that the UK intended deliberately to violate its Treaty obligations and to breach international law. The necessity of making such statements, which would cause immediate international condemnation, will inevitably act as a powerful deterrent against the introduction of such clearly incompatible legislation. However, an instance of this has already arisen, albeit in relation to a relatively contentious issue of interpretation of Art 10: the UK refuses to accept the correctness of the Strasbourg court's finding that a complete ban on political advertising in broadcasting is a violation of Art 10 and has maintained such a ban in the Communications Act 2003, making a negative s 19 statement in relation to it when the Bill was introduced. Nevertheless, it remains the case that open infringements of the

Convention are likely in future to be highly unlikely (unless of course s 19 is itself repealed). At the same time, the possibility of *inadvertent* legislative infringements should be removed, since Parliamentary Counsel will have to scrutinise any Bill prior to its introduction into Parliament to ensure its compatibility with the Convention, so that the minister responsible can make the statement of compatibility to Parliament under s 19. What is likely to slip through both these safeguards is ambiguously worded legislation, which *may* infringe Convention rights, depending upon how it is interpreted by the courts. Governments may indeed rely upon the inherent imprecision of many of the Convention rights and the possible consequential lack of legal certainty as to whether particular provisions are Convention compliant in order to argue that doubtful legislation is, in fact, compatible. Arguably, this occurred in relation to the Regulation of Investigatory Powers Act 2000, the Terrorism Act 2000, the Anti-Terrorism, Crime and Security Act 2001 and the Prevention of Terrorism Act 2005, all of which contain draconian powers of interference with Convention rights. Such legislation should, however, be dealt with by the courts under s 3(1) of the Act: that provision should ensure that *ambiguous* legislation is always interpreted compatibly with Convention rights. Thus, since openly incompatible legislation is most unlikely to be introduced by any government, inadvertent incompatibilities weeded out prior to parliamentary scrutiny, and ambiguities resolved in favour of the Convention by the courts, the effect may be that in practice, Parliament no longer passes legislation which, once interpreted, infringes Convention rights.

All this could of course theoretically be removed simply by repeal of the HRA. Whether this happens or not depends upon whether some convention of respect develops in relation to that Act. At present, it seems clear that at least amongst Conservative politicians, such a convention is so far from developing that they have recently been urging its repeal upon the Labour government, and pledging to do some themselves, if elected, replacing it with an (ill-defined) British Bill of Rights.[2]

In conclusion, it is clear that the HRA alters the doctrine of sovereignty by suspending the doctrine of implied repeal in relation to statutes passed prior to the HRA itself. It is arguable that s 3(1) of the HRA can be used by the judges as a vehicle to safeguard Convention rights against implied repeal: *A* is an example of this, though the radical approach of this case has not been used consistently. Moreover, the broader politico-constitutional picture reveals that it is naïve and crude simply to take the HRA on its face as an 'ordinary' statute: it is not a Bill of Rights, but it does have a different status from other Acts of Parliament.

▌NOTES

1 Students could explore here some of the other decisions on s 3(1). Lord Nicholl's *dicta* in *Re W and B* that a reading of legislation under s 3(1) should not 'depart substantially from a fundamental feature of an Act of Parliament' find support in

the *dicta* of Woolf CJ in *Poplar Housing (2001)* and of Lord Hope in *Lambert (2001)*; *Offen (2001)* is an activist decision more akin to that of *A*.

2 Students could also draw attention to the apparent lack of respect for the Convention displayed in the hasty decision to derogate from Art 5 of the ECHR following the September 11 attacks in 2001, in order to allow for the detention without trial of certain suspected international terrorists although the acceptance by the UK Government that the legislation necessitating the derogation should be allowed to lapse once it had been found to be unlawful by the House of Lords in *A v Secretary of State (2004)* is some evidence against this.

CHAPTER 3

THE HOUSE OF COMMONS

INTRODUCTION

This chapter brings together a number of rather disparate topics. The three areas commonly examined are: parliamentary privilege, scrutiny of legislation and the Executive, and delegated legislation.

Parliamentary privilege is a reasonably straightforward and discrete topic and most students find it fairly easy to master the basic and clearly established principles. It is, however, an area replete with unresolved questions and students should ensure that they are aware of the conflicting authorities and views on these questions, are able to offer a sensible evaluation of them, and can formulate their own opinions. Students need to be familiar with the main thrust of the report of the Nolan Committee on parliamentary regulation of Members' outside interests, the rules and mechanisms for their enforcement, including the Commons vote in May 2002 to relax the rules regarding their outside interests. In the area of Members' freedom of speech, the Defamation Act 1996 has introduced a significant change. Both these matters are covered here, as is the possible impact of the Human Rights Act 1998 on both areas of privilege. Finally, students should have some awareness of the reforms proposed by the Joint Committee on Parliamentary Privilege which reported in 1999. It should be noted that the privileges of the Lords and the Commons are basically identical, but that the area almost invariably arises both in practice and in exams in relation to the Commons. The topic lends itself equally well to either essay or problem questions, though the latter seem to be more common in practice.

Scrutiny of legislation and administration is examined by essay questions, which are invariably evaluative in approach. It should be noted that in some syllabuses, particularly on GDL courses, the House of Lords will probably be examined together with the Commons in one question. If a question requires discussion of 'Parliament', this means, of course, both Houses. The two areas of legislation and administration can be examined separately, as in this chapter, or combined together in one question. The basic arguments in the area are fairly easy to grasp, so in order to produce a better than average answer, students should try to marshal original examples for their arguments from cases and materials books, and current events. Particular note should be taken of the ongoing reforms to the Select Committee system being suggested by various select Committees, including the Modernisation, Public Administration and Liaison Committees of the House of Commons, and also the ongoing controversy over the system for selecting the membership of Select Committees, culminating in a Commons vote in May 2002 which approved some other changes designed to strengthen the Select Committees, but rejected a proposed mechanism for ensuring their independence.

Delegated legislation is an unusually versatile topic for examination purposes. The topic can merely be an area which should be brought into other essays (note that any essay about parliamentary scrutiny of legislation should include a section on delegated legislation), or it can be examined in a separate essay question, which will generally centre around the justifications for delegated legislation and its disadvantages. Alternatively, the topic may appear in the form of a problem question revolving around the legal effects of non-compliance with laying and publishing requirements, with perhaps the addition of an aspect of judicial review. Therefore, to be confident in handling this topic in a problem, students should have a working knowledge of judicial review, for which see Chapter 7.

Checklist

Students should be familiar with the following:

Parliamentary privilege:

- a list of all the privileges, including those virtually defunct, with greater awareness of the important ones;

- the area of freedom of speech: the controversy over what amounts to 'proceedings in Parliament'; the status of written accounts and broadcasts of debates, proceedings of committees, etc; the meaning of 'impeached or questioned' as interpreted by the courts and the impact of the Defamation Act 1996; the decisions in *Prebble (1994)* and *Hamilton v Al Fayed (2001)* and the possible impact of the Human Rights Act 1998 through Art 6 of the European Convention on Human Rights, but the difficulties of using the Act against Parliament; the recommendations of the Joint Committee on Privileges;

- the right of the House of Commons to regulate its own composition and proceedings, with particular reference to the new rules on registration and declaration of Members' interests;

- the ban on paid advocacy and the mechanisms for enforcing these rules, including the Parliamentary Commissioner for Standards and Privileges; criticisms of the weaknesses of these mechanisms and the possibility of party interest weakening the authority of the Standards Committee; the May 2002 changes to the rules; the possible impact of the Human Rights Act 1998 as above; the concepts of 'contempt' and 'breach of privilege'; conflicts between the House and the judiciary over which body has the right to determine the extent and interpretation of privileges, and the House's right to punish for breach of them.

Scrutiny of administration/legislation including delegated legislation:

- the basic rationale behind the perceived need for effective scrutiny – derived from the separation of powers;
- questions to ministers including limitations on topics and opportunities for short debates; Westminster Hall;
- Select Committees: remit, powers, limitations and effectiveness; recent examples; the partial implementation in May 2002 of reforms suggested by the Select Committee on the Modernisation of the House of Commons; the Osmotherly rules – revised in 2005;
- scrutiny of national finance, the Public Accounts Committee, the Comptroller and Auditor General;
- the argument whether over the Commons' role in relation to legislation: for publicity, etc, or acting as a genuine separate legislative body;
- illustrations of government omnipotence: statistics on the number of government Bills which become law; whips and the legislative process;
- an analysis of efficacy in the field of publicity: curtailment of scrutiny by guillotine, closure; the use of timetabling of Bills; the effect on pre-legislative process of the anticipated response of the House;
- the partial implementation of reforms suggested by the Select Committee on the Modernisation of the House of Commons;
- scrutiny of delegated legislation: the Joint Committee on Statutory Instruments, the effectiveness of negative/positive resolution procedure and requirements under the Statutory Instruments Act 1946 and the legal effect thereof; judicial review; the benefits and detriments of delegated legislation.

Note that the Joint Committee's Report is HLP 43–41 (1998–99).

Question 13

During a House of Commons debate on a Private Members' Bill to legalise cannabis, Heather MP accuses Laurence MP, an Opposition MP who has spoken in favour of the Bill, of being 'bribed' to speak in favour of, and move an amendment to it, by Stoned UK, a group which campaigns for the legalisation of cannabis. She says that this information was given to her in a letter from one of her constituents, Mrs Spod, and that she has passed the letter on to a group of MPs campaigning for legalisation, known as Members for Free Weed (MFW). Heather also says that Laurence has an agreement with Stoned UK to provide it with advice and information on parliamentary feeling on possible legalisation and any relevant legislative proposals, and that he makes use of a research assistant, funded by the group. Laurence responds by accusing Heather (truthfully) of supplying cannabis to other MPs to smoke in the Members' Tea Room.

Laurence approaches the Speaker after the debate and admits that the second part of Heather's accusation, as to his agreement with Stoned UK and the research assistant, is true. He says that he has received a number of letters from members of the group urging him to do all he can in Parliament to support the current Bill, and saying that they hope he will give the group 'a good return in this respect' for its investment in his research assistant.

It subsequently emerges that Mrs Spod blames Laurence for the fact that one of her children has recently started smoking cannabis, a matter about which she is very bitter. The child saw Laurence speaking in a debate and found him very persuasive.

Discuss the parliamentary and legal consequences of the above.

Answer plan

This is a fairly typical question in that it requires students to discuss the protection given to verbal and written statements by the privilege of freedom of speech in a wide range of situations, while throwing in a number of possible infringements of the rules relating to Members' interests and also a criminal offence committed in the House. (This often appears as an assault by an MP on another Member/the Speaker or the damaging of the mace.) The status of the words spoken in the House and the letter from Mrs Spod are fairly uncontroversial, so the answer should devote more time to the letter to MFW and the central problem which it raises of whether such a letter amounts to a 'proceeding in Parliament' – an issue which will virtually always need discussion in answers on this topic. It is important to consider Laurence's possible violation of the rules relating to Members' interests from the perspective of possible contempts committed by both him *and* Stoned UK. When dealing with any given event, students must always bear in mind the possibility of both legal *and* parliamentary consequences, and the fact that 'legal consequences' can include both civil and criminal liability.

The following matters should be discussed:

- defamatory words spoken in debate: Art 9 of the Bill of Rights confers absolute privilege. Is there a possible breach of privilege by Heather? Does the Human Rights Act (HRA) 1998 have an impact here?;
- the letter from Mrs Spod: is this qualified privilege *but* defeated by malice?;
- the letter to MFW: is it a proceeding in Parliament and therefore absolutely privileged? If not, then is this qualified privilege *but* defeated by malice?;
- whether Laurence may be in breach of the rules governing registration of interests; the production of employment agreements and a declaration of interests by virtue of his association with Stoned UK;
- whether Laurence has breached the 'advocacy' rule by his actions in debate;
- whether Stoned UK has committed a contempt of Parliament by trying to limit Laurence's freedom of action;
- the drug selling by Heather: serious contempt of the House; whether courts have jurisdiction – likely outcomes.

Answer

This question raises the following broad issues: whether actions by Laurence in defamation against Heather and Mrs Spod would succeed; whether Laurence's association with Stoned UK would be viewed by the House as a contempt of Parliament for breach of registration requirements and of the advocacy rules; and what criminal and/or parliamentary consequences would flow from Heather's drug selling activities.

The allegations of Laurence's bribe-taking are *prima facie* defamatory (any possible defence of justification will not be considered in relation to the defaming of Laurence). The words spoken by Heather in debate would be covered by absolute privilege under Art 9 of the Bill of Rights 1688; *Wason v Walter (1868)* confirmed that Art 9 provides complete civil and criminal immunity for Members in respect of words spoken by them during proceedings in Parliament, and this position was re-affirmed by the Privy Council in *Prebble v Television New Zealand (1994)*. Thus, no cause of action would lie for slander. It is possible that at some future point, the European Court of Human Rights might find this absolute bar a violation of the Art 6 right to a fair trial of those such as Laurence, who have no possible means of having the alleged injury to their reputation adjudicated upon in court. In *A v UK (2002)*, the European Court of Human Rights heard a complaint from a woman who claimed to have been defamed during proceedings in the UK Parliament, which had been reported in the press. She argued that her inability to bring proceedings in court violated both her right to privacy under Art 8 and her right to a fair trial under Art 6 and to a remedy under Art 13. The Court found no violation: the privilege which blocked her action was necessary to protect free speech in Parliament and was narrower in scope than the comparable rules existing in other European countries. Whilst Parliament is specifically excluded from the definition of those 'public authorities' which are bound to respect Convention rights (s 6(3) of the HRA), the point could be raised in legal proceedings for defamation, relying on the courts' duty as a public authority itself (s 6(3)) to act compatibly with Convention rights under s 6(1). Nevertheless, given the decision in *A v UK* considered above, it seems highly likely that UK courts would rule against any such claim. In terms of the parliamentary consequences of this matter, the House might regard Heather's repetition of the accusations as a misuse of privilege and therefore a contempt, particularly if she had made no attempt to verify the contents of the letter.[1]

A libel action against Mrs Spod would have a much better chance of success. The letter from Mrs Spod will not be covered by absolute privilege, since it clearly does not amount to a proceeding in Parliament; it may be protected by qualified privilege provided it is in the public interest and there is an absence of malice (*Rule* (1937)). The letter is clearly on a matter of public concern, but the facts suggest that absence of malice may be difficult to establish, since the allegation is substantially untrue and hostility towards Laurence is presumably a motive; therefore, qualified privilege would probably not be available to Mrs Spod as a defence against Laurence.

By sending a copy of the letter to MFW, Heather has re-published the libel therein contained. It is uncertain whether the sending of a letter in this way would amount to a proceeding in Parliament and thus be covered by absolute privilege. The case of *GR Strauss* (1958), in which the MP concerned wrote a letter to the Paymaster General on possible misconduct by the London Electricity Board, is applicable but not conclusive. The Committee of Privileges held that the writing of such a letter was a 'proceeding in Parliament', and thus covered by absolute privilege, but the Commons narrowly rejected this finding on a vote. However, decisions by the Commons on matters of privilege set no binding precedent. Furthermore, subsequent events have suggested that the matter would now be differently decided. In 1967, the Select Committee on Parliamentary Privilege strongly recommended that legislation be enacted to reverse the Commons' decision in *Strauss;* in 1970, the Joint Committee on Publication of Proceedings in

Parliament proposed a definition of 'proceedings in Parliament', which included letters exchanged between MPs for the purpose of allowing them to carry out their duties. (Their proposed definition was subsequently approved by the Faulks Committee on Defamation 1975 and the Committee of Privileges 1976–77.) However, the recent report of the Joint Committee on Parliamentary Privilege in 1999 strongly recommended that such correspondence should *not* attract absolute privilege, the Committee deeming such protection unnecessary, given the effectiveness of the qualified privilege defence in protecting MPs over recent years.

In the case of *Rost v Edwards (1990)*, the plaintiff wished to adduce evidence contained in a letter alleging the failure of another Member to register an interest from an MP to the Speaker, to be given in court to support a libel action. Popplewell J was of the opinion that the letter added nothing to the evidence in the case but added, *obiter*, that he had 'no hesitation' in stating that he thought the letter was covered by (absolute) privilege. He cited no authorities in support of this view, but presumably regarded the letter as a 'proceeding in Parliament' which could not be questioned outside Parliament under Art 9 of the Bill of Rights. It is hard to say now whether the weight of authority and expert opinion is still in favour of such letters being afforded absolute privilege. However, in the instant case, since the accusations in the letter were directly relevant to an issue then being debated by the Commons, Heather could perhaps hope for a reversal of the *Strauss* verdict.

If such a decision was made, then any attempt by Laurence to continue the action in respect of Heather's re-publishing of the libel could amount to a breach of privilege as the Committee of Privileges considered the Electricity Board's action against Strauss to be.

Turning to the possibility that the letter would not attract absolute privilege, then following *Beach v Freeson (1972)*, it should at least be deemed to enjoy qualified privilege since Heather and the recipients, MFW, have a common, legitimate interest in the contents; if Heather can then additionally show that she was not actuated by malice, Laurence cannot succeed. Since, however, 'malice' can mean merely lack of belief in the statements made in the relevant material, Heather would have difficulty in proving lack of malice if the letter had mentioned Mrs Spod's grievance against Laurence, thus giving Heather a reason to doubt the former's good faith.

The possible consequences of Laurence's association with Stoned UK now fall to be considered. Laurence's position raises a number of issues (the possible *responses* of the House will be discussed once Laurence's possible breaches of the rules have been considered). First of all, it is clear that his agreement to provide advice to Stoned UK for which he receives a material benefit, namely, a paid research assistant, is an interest which should have been entered on the Register of Members' Interests. Laurence's association with Stoned UK clearly falls into Category 3 of the

Register: ' . . . any provision to clients of services which depend essentially upon, or arise out of, the Member's position as a Member of Parliament.' (*The Guide to the Rules Relating to the Conduct of Members*, para 22; hereafter, *The Guide*.)

Laurence's obligations go further than mere registration: his agreement with Stoned UK clearly amounts to what a Resolution of the House has described as 'an agreement which involves the provision of services in his capacity as a Member of Parliament' (Resolution of 6 November 1995; see *The Guide*, paragraphs on 'Agreements for the Provision of Services', following para 48). Therefore, according to that Resolution of the Commons, the agreement must be put into writing and the amount of benefit obtained must be declared by reference to the bands specified in the Resolution. The agreement must then be lodged with the Parliamentary Commissioner for Standards (hereafter, 'the Commissioner'). It is irrelevant that Laurence's agreement may be a verbal one only – it must be placed in written form and lodged with the Commissioner regardless (*The Guide*, para 48).

In addition to being placed in formal written form, there is the issue of declaration. The House's Resolution of 22 May 1974 states that 'In any debate or proceeding of the House or its Committees . . . [each Member] shall disclose any relevant pecuniary interest or benefit . . . he may have.' Plainly, an agreement to provide parliamentary services for a group campaigning for the legalisation of cannabis, in return for a funded research assistant, amounts to a pecuniary benefit relevant to the debate of a Bill to legalise cannabis. Laurence should have declared his interest at the beginning of his remarks in debate. Paragraph 78 of the Guide States that 'The Committee on Standards and Privileges has made it clear that it would regard it as a very serious breach of the rules if a Member failed to register or declare an interest which was relevant to a proceeding he had initiated.' Unfortunately for Laurence, he has moved an amendment, something which clearly amounts to 'initiating a proceeding' and thus a breach of the rules (see the definition of 'initiating' a proceeding in para 78). He has therefore committed a very serious breach.

The rules of the House go further than mere disclosure and declaration: Laurence may also have fallen foul of the so called 'advocacy rule'. The relevant Resolution of the Commons states that 'no Member . . . shall, on consideration of any remuneration . . . or reward or benefit in kind . . . advocate or initiate any cause or matter on behalf of any outside body or individual . . . by means of any speech, Question, Motion, introduction of a Bill, or Amendment to a Motion or a Bill' (extract from a Resolution of the House of 15 July 1947, as amended on 6 November 1995; reproduced in *The Guide*, para 71). As guidance provided by the Committee on Standards and Privileges, now forming part of the Guide, makes clear, this prohibits either initiating or participating in parliamentary proceedings in a way that 'seek[s] directly to confer a benefit *exclusively* upon a body' from which the Member receives the payment (*The Guide*, para 76). Although Laurence has both initiated and participated in proceedings, and spoken in favour of a cause which Stoned UK supports, his actions could not be said to have sought to confer a benefit 'exclusively' on Stoned UK. It is suggested that these words would refer to a speech in a debate which, for example, asked for a special tax concession to be given to the particular organisation in question.

In conclusion, therefore, Laurence has failed to register his interest in Stoned UK and has failed to deposit his agreement with the Commissioner as required; in any event, he has failed to declare his interest in debate, although he has not breached the advocacy rule. The above omissions would be investigated, if complaint was made, by the Commissioner and, if he found a *prima facie* case, considered by the Committee on Standards and Privileges. The sanctions they could demand on finding a breach of the rules range from requiring Laurence to apologise to the House at the lowest end to expulsion from the House at the highest.

In relation to the position of Stoned UK, it is clear that if, as in the *Yorkshire NUM case (1975)*, the sponsoring organisation threatens to withdraw financial support in the event of the MP not voting (or abstaining) as desired, there is no doubt that such threats would be viewed as a serious contempt. Here, the threat is not explicit as in the *NUM* case, but Stoned UK's letters clearly amount to an attempt to apply pressure in respect of a specific matter – the Bill to legalise cannabis – and therefore amount to an attempt to 'control or limit the Member's complete independence and freedom of action' as forbidden by the 1947 Resolution; as such, it would certainly be unacceptable to the House. It is likely that Stoned UK would at the least be required immediately to repudiate the letters, and to make no further attempts to restrict Laurence's freedom of action.

Finally, the probable consequences of Heather's drug selling activities must be examined. The selling of cannabis within the House would certainly amount to a serious contempt, and expulsion might well be considered appropriate. Heather has also committed a criminal offence, which raises the issue of whether the courts would regard themselves as having jurisdiction over an offence such as this committed within the confines of the House. In *Bradlaugh v Gossett (1884)*, Stephen J stated that he knew of 'no authority for the proposition that an ordinary crime committed in the . . . Commons would be withdrawn from the ordinary course of criminal justice'. However, both *Sir John Eliot's Case (1668)*, in which the Lords were loath to decide whether an assault on the Speaker was covered by privilege, and the more recent case of *Graham-Campbell ex p Herbert (1935)*, in which the High Court considered that a magistrate lacked jurisdiction to prosecute Members for selling alcohol without a licence in the Members' Bar, suggest that the courts are unsure of their right to try such cases in the normal way. The Joint Committee was highly critical of any idea that the simple fact that events happened within the physical premises of Parliament should exempt them from criminal liability, commenting: 'This privilege does not embrace and protect activities of individuals, whether Members or non-Members, simply because they take place within the precincts of Parliament . . . A criminal offence committed in the precincts is triable in the courts.'

In a matter as serious as drug dealing, it seems clear that the House would not seek to resist the matter being dealt with in the ordinary way by the courts, for it does not have adequate powers to deal with ordinary crime. In any event, Parliament would be anxious to avoid the unfavourable publicity that would undoubtedly ensue from an attempt to protect such an offender through an assertion of immunity by virtue of privilege.

▌NOTE

1 The likely response of the House to this possible contempt could be explored. Mention could be made of the *Colonel 'B'* case in 1978, in which Parliament took no action against MPs who had used their privilege of freedom of speech to break the *sub judice* rule and thus commit a clear contempt of court with impunity. In 1984, a Member committed a breach of the privilege of freedom of speech in seeking to limit the freedom of action of other Members by words spoken in debate (*Bank's case (1984)*). The Committee of Privileges recommended that no action be taken against the Member. It would seem unlikely, therefore, that Heather would be punished, even if a finding of breach of privilege were made. It could also be noted that in *Strauss*, the vote on whether the Electricity Board had committed a breach of privilege, which went against Strauss, divided substantially along party lines – Strauss being an Opposition MP. Since Laurence is also a Member of the Opposition, if party allegiance was given more weight than expert opinion in the vote, Laurence could likewise receive a verdict that the libel action against him did not constitute a breach of privilege.

Question 14

' . . . the House [of Commons] ought to relinquish its jurisdiction over breaches of privilege and contempts to the courts . . .' (De Smith). Discuss with particular reference to the privilege of freedom of speech.

Answer plan

This is a fairly straightforward question in that it gives the student the chance to range quite widely through the topic, rather than requiring an answer which focuses on a specific area, such as the conflict between the judiciary and Parliament over the right to determine the scope of privilege. That conflict should be examined, and can be used as an argument for De Smith's contention, but students should cast their net more widely. It should be noted that a verdict on De Smith's opinion should be given in concluding the essay. Although it would be safe to agree with the proposition, the more ambitious student should aim to question whether jurisdiction over *all* contempts should be handed over to the courts, and might perhaps conclude with a modified version of the original statement.

The following areas should be covered:

- the conflict between the judiciary and the Commons over freedom of speech – uncertainty over the resolution of this;
- the uncertainty of the extent of freedom of speech caused by the above conflict;
- the unsatisfactory nature of the Commons as arbitrating body: it sets no precedents, uncertainty results and party considerations may intrude;
- the criticisms of the Committee on Standards and Privileges, in particular, the possibility that its proceedings would violate Art 6 of the European Convention on Human Rights (ECHR); the problems with using the Human Rights Act (HRA) 1998 directly against it;
- is the solution the handover of jurisdiction to the courts or perhaps a partial handover?;
- the views of the Joint Committee on the above.

Answer

The contention by De Smith which is the subject of this question could be understood as relating only to the House's power to deal as it sees fit with a person who commits a breach of privilege or contempt once it has been established that a breach or contempt has taken place. For the purposes of this discussion, however, he will be taken to be arguing that the decision as to whether a particular action amounts to a contempt should also be taken by the judiciary rather than Parliament. Such a change would have the result that the judiciary would, in some cases, have to define the boundaries of privilege in order to ascertain whether any breach had actually occurred. De Smith's proposal, if put into effect, would thus amount to quite a radical change. The discussion below will examine the various difficulties inherent in the present situation, and attempt to establish whether they justify such radical reform.

Not all questions of breach of privilege have caused difficulties; those which affect only Members of Parliament in their capacity as MPs, such as the disciplining of MPs who misuse the parliamentary platform to insult or defame other Members, have been agreed by Parliament and the courts to be under the sole jurisdiction of Parliament. Parliament's handling of these privileges has been relatively unproblematic, though it seems that public dissatisfaction with the Commons' system of self-regulation is growing. This is compounded by a belief that since 1997, the Labour-dominated Committee on Standards and Privileges has at times been over-lenient with prominent Labour MPs (including Keith Vaz and Geoffrey Robinson) accused of breaches of the rules governing Members' interests, and by the widespread belief that Elizabeth Filkin, the former Standards Commissioner, was in effect forced out in 2002 for being over-diligent in investigating breaches of the rules.

It is those privileges which in their exercise can affect the legal rights of those outside Parliament which have caused difficulties. The first problem considered will be the conflict between Parliament and the judiciary, which has resulted from Parliament's self-asserted jurisdiction over this type of privilege.

The privilege of freedom of speech has been the most controversial. The exercise of this privilege can give rise to two possible breaches or contempts: the first is its misuse in the House by MPs which, as has been said, is unproblematic. The second can occur where a litigant sues in defamation in respect of words which Parliament has deemed to be absolutely privileged, that is, immune from civil or criminal proceedings. When this happens, Parliament can regard the action as a contempt and attempt to prevent the litigant from exercising his legal right to sue and enforce the judgment of the court.

This was illustrated in 1839 in the case of *Stockdale v Hansard*. Stockdale brought an action in respect of allegedly defamatory words in a report of prison inspectors published by *Hansard*, by order of the Commons. When the action was tried, the court decided that *Hansard*'s reports were not covered by absolute privilege, so that Stockdale could proceed. The court further adjudged that the House did not 'have the power to declare what its privileges are', while the House passed a resolution affirming that it was the sole judge of its own privileges. The House showed its readiness to back up its resolution with force by imprisoning the Sheriff of Middlesex for contempt when he attempted to enforce the court's judgment in favour of Stockdale by levying execution upon *Hansard*'s property; the courts backed away from confrontation by refusing to grant the Sheriff a writ of habeas corpus. The court stated that it refused the writ because the Speaker's warrant did not state the facts which allegedly constituted the contempt, and it would not be seemly for them to enquire further since, as De Smith puts it, although 'the House of Commons was not a superior court . . . it was entitled to as much respect as if it were'.[1]

It is not certain that the matter could again be resolved as it was in *Stockdale*. Calvert considers it uncertain 'that a court of law would meekly accept a general return to a writ' in similar circumstances (*Introduction to British Constitutional Law*, 1985, p 115). Keir and Lawson, in contrast, take the view that the courts 'yielded the key to the fortress' by refusing to question the legality of imprisonment for contempt where no reason is given, implying that a precedent has been set (*Cases in Constitutional Law*, 6th edn, 1979, p 225). Further, if the *Lords* was asked to grant a writ of habeas corpus, it could not avoid questioning the Commons' actions on the grounds that the Commons was a superior court. An appeal was in fact made to the Lords in *Paty's* case (1704), but the counsel preparing it was promptly imprisoned by the Commons. However, in *Prebble v Television New Zealand (1994)*, the Privy Council appeared to accept that parliamentary privileges could not be questioned in court except in exceptional circumstances. The whole area may therefore still be said to be encased in a web of ambiguity; conflicts could arise in the future because two different bodies may claim competing jurisdictions over the ambit of privilege. No precedent has been set as to how to resolve these conflicts other than the frustrating by Parliament of the powers of the courts by imprisoning its officers, which in fact is not a resolution but merely a stalemate; further, it is not even certain whether such an outcome would be repeated if the issue arose again.

It is possible that at some future point, the European Court of Human Rights might hold that the prevention by Parliament of the trial of matters raising privilege constitutes a violation of the Art 6 right to a fair trial of those defamed by MPs who have no possible means of having the alleged injury to their reputation adjudicated upon in court. In *A v UK (2002)*, the European Court of Human Rights heard a complaint from a woman who claimed to have been defamed during proceedings in the UK Parliament, which had been reported in the press. She argued that her inability to bring proceedings in court violated both her right to privacy under Art 8 and her right to a fair trial under Art 6 and to a remedy under Art 13. The Court found no violation: the privilege which blocked her action was necessary to protect free speech in Parliament and was narrower in scope than the comparable rules existing in other European countries. Whilst Parliament is specifically excluded from the definition of those 'public authorities' which are bound to respect Convention rights (s 6(3) of the HRA), the point could be raised in legal proceedings for defamation, relying on the courts' duty as a public authority itself (s 6(3)) to respect Convention rights under s 6(1). Nevertheless, given the decision in *A v UK* considered above, it seems highly likely that UK courts would rule against any such claim.

Thus, the present competition for jurisdiction over those privileges which affect persons outside the House clearly gives rise to great difficulties. As stated in the resolution of the Commons in *Stockdale*, Parliament not only reserves the right to punish contemners, but claims to be solely entitled to determine how far privilege extends. This claim, and its denial by the courts, has given rise to a second major problem with the present state of affairs, namely, a real uncertainty as to the *extent* of certain privileges, particularly freedom of speech. Absolute privilege attaches to words spoken in the course of debates or proceedings in Parliament by virtue of Art 9 of the Bill of Rights 1688. The ambiguous words here are 'proceedings in Parliament', and the interpretation to be given to these words is at present shrouded in uncertainty.

This uncertainty can be attributed first to the fact that both the courts and Parliament claim to be entitled to interpret these words. Should conflict flow from them reaching different results, the outcome remains uncertain, as discussed above. The case of *Rost v Edwards (1990)*, in which it was said that in dealing with grey areas of privilege, the court should not be astute to see its jurisdiction ousted, shows that the judiciary is in no way retreating from its historic insistence on its duty to interpret privilege according to the common law. As noted above, if an issue is raised regarding the compatibility of the parliamentary privilege of freedom of speech with the Art 6 right to a fair trial of those defamed in Parliament, UK courts might be forced to determine the matter, though the exclusion of Parliament from the definition of 'public authority' might provide the courts with a means of avoiding the issue.

The second reason for uncertainty lies in the nature of the House of Commons as a decision-making body. If a question of privilege arises, the Committee on Standards and Privileges (CSP) will consider the matter and make a recommendation to the Commons. Unfortunately, the Commons does not always follow the Committee's recommendations, nor is it bound by its previous decisions. Both of these drawbacks are illustrated by the case of *GR Strauss (1958)*. Strauss MP wrote a letter to the Paymaster General on possible misconduct by the London Electricity Board. The Committee of Privileges held that the writing of such a letter *was* a proceeding in Parliament, and thus covered by absolute privilege, but the Commons narrowly rejected this finding on a vote. If the situation were to recur, this finding could be changed, and indeed, subsequent reports by various parliamentary committees suggest that the matter should now be decided differently.[2] However, the fact remains that the House would be free to reject this weight of learned opinion and the *obiter* comments of Popplewell J in *Rost v Edwards (1990)* to the effect that letters between MPs and the Speaker were covered by privilege. This possibility is lent credence by the suggestion from *Strauss* that the Commons, being a party-political animal, may not always be capable of excluding party considerations from its decisions. The decision to reject the recommendation of the Committee on Strauss' letter split broadly along party lines which, since Strauss was an Opposition MP, meant an unfavourable verdict. One could envisage party considerations intruding themselves, for example, in the case of a senior government figure sued for libel; in determining whether the minister's publishing of the libel was covered by privilege, government MPs might well be more concerned with possible embarrassment for the government than with following expert recommendation.

Thus, the Commons is not ideally suited to make the final decisions on matters of privilege, but the CSP has itself been subject to criticisms as a forum for trying issues which at least theoretically could result in the imprisonment of those it finds to have been in breach of privilege or to have committed contempts. First, it is nominated in proportion to party strengths; it is unusual for it to divide along party lines, but it did so in the *WJ Brown* case *(1947)*, in delivering a verdict which favoured the government MP concerned. Second, in denying alleged contemners the right to legal representation, and on occasion condemning them without giving them the opportunity to put their case (the Electricity Board was condemned unheard in *Strauss*), the Committee is open to the charge of breaching the rules of natural justice. The justice of this second criticism was recognised by the 1967 Select Committee on Parliamentary Privilege, which recommended a number of procedural changes aimed at giving those at risk of condemnation a right to put their case in a proper manner. The Committee's proposals have not yet been enacted.

It might be thought that changes to this unsatisfactory position could be forced on Parliament by an aggrieved MP taking action under the HRA for a declaration that proceedings of the CSP amounted to a breach of Art 6 of the ECHR, and possibly claiming damages; however, it is submitted that this is a remote prospect. Although it is true that in extreme cases, the sanctions recommended by the Committee could, through expulsion of a Member, lead to loss of his livelihood (making the consequences of an adverse judgment more grave than those of many a criminal conviction), nevertheless, Art 6 refers to 'the determination of [a citizen's] civil rights and obligations or . . . any criminal charge against him', a wording which would not appear to be apt to cover the Committee's remit. Furthermore, even if it could be argued that the Committee's activities were *prima facie* covered by Art 6, it appears that no action could be brought under the HRA, quite apart from the fact that one would expect a court to be minded to refuse jurisdiction in a matter affecting Parliament's regulation of its own affairs. This is because the Act: makes it 'unlawful for a *public authority* to act in a way which is incompatible with a Convention right' (s 6); provides that proceedings may be brought in respect of such an act (s 7); and provides that damages or other remedies may be awarded to the aggrieved claimant (s 8). However, s 6(3) specifically states that neither House of Parliament nor 'a person exercising functions in connection with proceedings in Parliament' count as 'public authorities' for the purposes of the Act. No action could therefore be brought against either the Committee or the House itself by an aggrieved Member. If the action were struck out, or simply lost, the claimant could of course still take his case to the European Court of Human Rights under the right of individual petition enshrined in the Convention, provided that all domestic avenues had been exhausted.

It may further be argued that Parliament's jurisdiction over breaches of privilege is unsatisfactory, since its effect can be to prevent the court from giving adequate weight to freedom of expression and the interests of justice. In *Prebble v Television New Zealand Ltd (1994)*, the Privy Council evaded the possibility of a conflict with Parliament in considering an instance in which a litigant wished to rely on words spoken in Parliament in order to raise the defence of justification in defamation proceedings. Certain of the particulars of the justifications relied on statements and actions which took place in Parliament. The plaintiff applied to strike out those particulars which concerned matters taking place in the House and which were, therefore, under Art 9 of the Bill of Rights 1688, subject to parliamentary privilege. The defendant argued that Art 9 only operated in legal proceedings so as to prevent questioning of statements made in the House when those proceedings sought to assert legal consequences against the maker of the statement, or alternatively that Art 9 did not extend to prevent challenges to the truth of statements made in Parliament when the maker of the statements himself initiated them.

However, it was found that Art 9 could not be limited in this way, bearing in mind the wider principle (of which Art 9 was said to be but one manifestation) that the courts and Parliament recognise their respective constitutional roles, and the courts will not allow any challenge to be made by evidence led in court to actions or statements in Parliament in performance of its legislative functions or in protection of its privileges. It was recently confirmed by the House of Lords in *Hamilton v Al Fayed (2001)* that Art 9 'precludes any challenge in court, whether by evidence, cross-examination or submission, to the veracity or propriety of anything done in the course of parliamentary proceedings' (*per* Lord Browne-Wilkinson). In *Prebble*, the Privy Council went on to say that in very special circumstances, where it was impossible to determine the matter at issue between the parties, a stay might be ordered so that Parliament could determine whether it wished to waive privilege in the interests of justice. Libel actions in which most of the matters of justification were covered by privilege might fall within that special rule. However, in the present case, in which the defendant would still be able to put forward most of the matters relied on in justification, that exceptional procedure should not be followed. While it may be argued that this decision – and *Al Fayed* – avoided addressing the fundamental issue at stake, namely, whether the courts should assert a right to jurisdiction in such matters where fundamental rights of the citizen – the right to a fair trial – are at issue, deviation from it is unlikely for so long as Parliament claims to be able to determine whether privilege should be waived in a given case. The HRA may require the courts to reassess the balance they strike between the importance of access to justice (guaranteed by Art 6 of the Convention) and parliamentary privilege, which is not a right protected *per se* under the Convention. However, the practice of ordering a stay on trials where the ability of the defendant to adduce his case is seriously handicapped by parliamentary privilege may well satisfy the requirements of Art 6.

It may be noted that following the enactment of the Defamation Act 1996, a claimant MP, suing in respect of allegations relating to his parliamentary conduct, may, if he finds it necessary for his case, waive privilege, allowing both parties to refer to proceedings in Parliament; the action can therefore proceed. This indeed occurred in *Al Fayed*, and the House of Lords confirmed that the choice lies with the individual MP concerned. Where, however, the defendant *alone* wishes to refer to parliamentary proceedings to defend itself, as in *Prebble*, it has no ability to waive privilege, a position which may be regarded as yet another unfair and undesirable consequence arising from Parliament's – now individual MPs' – claim alone to decide when privilege may be waived and when enforced. A more serious criticism of the change brought about by the Act was made by Lord Lester during the Bill's passage: The immunities written into Art 9 were not included simply for the personal . . . benefit of Members . . . but to protect the integrity of individual legislators.' ((1996) NLJ, 17 May, p 719.) It can therefore be argued that if the system whereby Parliament *as a whole* regulated the area of privilege was unsatisfactory, the new position, whereby one individual MP can in the pursuit of his own interests decide whether privilege should apply, is 10 times worse. This criticism was accepted by the Joint Committee on Parliamentary Privilege, which was highly critical of the unfairness represented by s 13 of the Defamation Act 1996; its 1999 report suggested that the power to waive privilege be given instead to each House of Parliament.

If it is accepted that Parliament's control over those privileges which affect the rights of those outside Parliament is manifestly unsatisfactory on a number of grounds, two questions naturally arise. First, would the problems be solved by handing over the jurisdiction to the courts as De Smith suggests, and second, if this is in general terms an acceptable solution, should control over punishment for *all* contempts be handed over?

The first question, it is submitted, is easily answered. The only one of the above problems which could be readily solved while leaving Parliament in control is the want of natural justice in the CSP. The remainder of the problems are inherent in the nature of the Commons and the attitude of the judiciary. For example, it has been suggested that Parliament could pass an Act defining 'parliamentary proceedings'. To pass such an Act would not, however, solve the problem as to whether Parliament's or the courts' interpretation of the Act would be binding. A complete, rather than a partial solution to the unsatisfactory nature of the current situation can only be achieved, it is submitted, by a handover of jurisdiction to the judiciary.

In relation to the second question, it is hard to believe that De Smith is advocating a handover of control over all contempts to the courts. In any event, this would be impracticable in the case of instant disciplining of MPs who, for example, grossly abuse each other in debate. A sensible line to draw would be that drawn by the courts themselves when they have considered the issue of privilege; punishment for contempts and breaches which affect only Members of the House could properly remain within the exclusive purveyance of Parliament, though MPs should not, it is submitted, be sheltered from the criminal law as they were in *Graham Campbell ex p*

Herbert (1935). However, where the rights of ordinary citizens are affected, the courts should be the sole arbiters.

NOTES

1 Students could note that in giving a return which did not state the facts upon which the allegation of contempt was based, Parliament had clearly learnt from *Paty's case (1704)*, in which the Speaker gave the grounds for the finding of contempt: one of the judges (Holt CJ), hearing the application for habeas corpus, dissented from the finding that the writ could not be granted, stating that where the reasons given could not amount in law to a breach of privilege or contempt, habeas corpus ought to be granted.

2 These include reports by the 1967 Select Committee on Parliamentary Privilege, the 1970 Joint Committee on Publication of Proceedings in Parliament, the Faulks Committee on Defamation 1975 and the Committee of Privileges (1976–77).

Question 15

'Before the formally dramatic part of the legislative process even begins, almost all the terms of almost all (government) Bills are settled' (Calvert). Would you agree that the House of Commons is redundant as a legislative body?

Answer plan

This question demands a critical assessment of the effectiveness of the House of Commons in its role as a legislative body. This is the type of question which is most commonly asked. It should be emphasised again that in some examinations, the question will refer to 'Parliament' not 'the Commons', so that any answer would have to include the role of the Lords, which is considered separately in Chapter 4. This answer should confine itself to the Commons' control over legislation; scrutiny of the Executive through, for example, Select Committees is not relevant here. Students should note that there is an implied presumption behind the question, namely, that if the House cannot often alter government Bills, it may be 'redundant'. This presumption must be challenged by the student because it is of rather more interest to discuss what the House should be aiming to achieve rather than what it actually does achieve, although an analysis of the latter is clearly crucial in the answer.

Essentially, the following areas should be covered:

- a brief discussion of the doctrine of the separation of powers and the basic charge against the Commons of failure to control legislation;

- illustrations of government omnipotence and an explanation of how this is achieved: whips and government majority coupled with an indication of the legislative process; examples from the Blair government;

- the argument that the Commons' role lies in scrutiny; the issue of publicity;

- an analysis of effectiveness in this field; the curtailment of scrutiny by guillotine, closure and programming; the effect on the pre-legislative process of the anticipated response of the House; scrutiny of delegated legislation; the greater recent use of pre-legislative scrutiny;

- a brief discussion of the ways in which the Commons could improve its current performance, in particular, those suggested by the Modernisation, Liaison and Public Administration Committees;

- conclusion: does the Commons perform an important function?

Answer

The doctrine of the separation of powers first postulated by John Locke in 1690 and expanded by Montesquieu in the eighteenth century required, *inter alia*, that a body separate from the Executive should be vested with legislative power in order to guard against the amassing of disproportionate power in the Executive arm of the State. Parliament has never been a legislative body entirely free from the influence of the Executive, but the increasing dominance of the government of the day through organised political parties has led constitutional observers to view the Commons as having lost its role as legislator, becoming instead a body which merely serves to legitimise government legislation. In what follows, the accuracy of this view will be assessed, alternative views of the role of the Commons will be explored, and a verdict on the continuing importance of the Commons will be offered.

If the role of the Commons is seen as being to provide independent assessment of the merit of government Bills and to make numerous amendments and rejections, then there can be little doubt that it is not fulfilling this role. The role of settling the aims and content of legislation is now assumed by the Legislation

Committee of the Cabinet. Government Bills are drafted by Parliamentary Counsel on receipt of a memorandum of instructions from the sponsoring department. Thus, as Calvert puts it, 'the substantial task of legislating will have been largely discharged before the Bill is . . . read . . . in the House' (*Introduction to British Constitutional Law*, 1985, p 84).

Throughout debate, the system of whipping will operate to subordinate the judgment of individual MPs to personal ambition and party loyalty. Considerable pressures can be brought to bear on potential rebels, and the efficiency of the party whips, together with the overall majority with which the first-past-the-post system is likely to endow the government, will ensure that the vast majority of government Bills will reach the statute books. In the 1985–86 parliamentary session, out of 50 government Bills, 48 became law. The Blair government has not lost any Bills in the House of Commons; it has however very recently lost a handful of votes on particular clauses in committee. It was defeated in its attempt to have overturned certain Lords amendments to the Racial and Religious Hatred Bill 2005 designed to restrict the ambit of the new offence of incitement to religious hatred, and protect free speech; it was also defeated in the Commons on its proposal to extend the time for which terrorism suspects can be held without charge for questioning. The Government's proposed 90-day time limit was defeated and a compromise, of an extension to only 28 days, was passed instead. Nevertheless, these are the only legislative defeats inflicted on the Blair government in 11 years, and this in the context of a government that has passed thousands of pages of legislation a year (3,500 in 2004 alone) and created over 3,000 new criminal offences since 1997. Thus, the generally very compliant position of the House of Commons stands in strong contrast to the position in the much more independent House of Lords, which has imposed numerous important legislative reversals on the government.

The committee stage is often perceived as a time in which party loyalties are less strong and more constructive debate may take place. Unfortunately, MPs are often simply lacking in the expertise required to challenge increasingly complex government legislation from a position of sufficient knowledge. Further, as the Modernisation Committee has put it, the committee stage 'which is meant to be the occasion when the details of the legislation are scrutinised, has often tended to be devoted to political partisan debate rather than constructive and systematic scrutiny', a style which is particularly unsuited to examining the factual and technical background to a Bill (Select Committee on the Modernisation of the House of Commons, First Report (HC 190, 1997–98)). The Standing Committee stage for the Poll Tax legislation – a hugely controversial change to local government finance, which eventually had to be scrapped, at a total cost of £1.5 billion – has been described as 'a futile marathon . . . mostly a matter of posturing . . . scrutiny by slogan and sound bite' (Butler, *Failure in British Government*, quoted HC Deb, Col 1098, 13 November 1997).

Thus, in general, the committee stage results in the acceptance of government amendments only because, as Griffiths' examination of standing committees found, 'party discipline is largely maintained' ('Standing Committees in the House of Commons', in Walkland and Ryle, *The Commons Today*, 1981, p 130). Further, many Opposition amendments are designed not to increase the effectiveness of the Bill, but to embarrass the government or simply to apply time pressure: the political role of Opposition MPs may prevent them undertaking *constructive* criticism. The Hansard Society has commented that standing committees 'fail to deliver genuine and analytical scrutiny of [bills], their political functions are neutered, dominated almost exclusively by government . . . , they fail to engage with the public and the media (in contrast to select committees) and they do not adequately utilise the evidence of experts or interested parties'. (Quoted in Select Committee on Modernisation of the House of Commons First Report, 1995–06, HC 1097 para 50.)

Should one conclude from the above that the Commons is redundant? It is suggested that this would be premature. Apart from the fact that the Commons still acts as a constitutional safeguard against the unfettered power of the Executive, so that governments are aware that they may not be able to rely on their members to pass legislation which would, for example, threaten the basic liberties of citizens, it may be argued that the view which sees the Commons as redundant because it is largely powerless to amend or reverse the government's programme is wrongheaded. In fact, it can be contended that the Commons would be undermining democratic accountability if it substantially changed government Bills, since the legislative programme which attracted the greatest proportion of votes should be enacted in accordance with the voters' presumed wishes. This argument was undoubtedly what Professor Crick had in mind when he wrote 'the phrase "parliamentary control" should not mislead anyone into asking for a situation in which governments can have their legislation changed or defeated . . .' . (*The Reform of Parliament, 1964*, p 80).

Such a point of view is clearly open to a number of objections: it can be plausibly argued that many people vote not after a careful assessment of which legislative programme they would like to see enacted, but on the basis of traditional loyalty, misinformation, misunderstanding or their reaction to politicians' perceived personalities. Further, it is undoubtedly true that people may vote for a party even though they may object to some of its specific legislative proposals. Finally, the accountability argument in favour of a strong Executive would not apply to non-manifesto government Bills introduced in response to circumstances which have changed since the time of the last General Election. In spite of these arguments, it is submitted that the accountability argument remains attractive as a basic principle, the root of which is not touched by the above objections which are arguably endemic in any party democracy: the United States' political system, which clearly embodies an actual as opposed to a formal separation of powers, is still open to these objections.

The second argument against the supposed redundancy of the Commons points out that it is simply unrealistic to expect the House of Commons to subject government Bills to *independent* scrutiny. The government is the government precisely because it is the party with an overall majority in the Commons. Therefore, by definition, the majority of MPs in the House will be predisposed to support legislation introduced by the government. It is thus built into the nature of parliamentary government that most MPs will not be impartially minded.

If it is accepted, then, that the role of the Commons is not to reverse or drastically amend the government's manifesto programme, then what useful function does it play other than that of a mainly theoretical constitutional safeguard? It is suggested that four main functions may be identified. The first is the education of both government and electorate through the publicising effects of debate in the Commons: the electorate will become aware of the issues surrounding a Bill, whilst the reaction of newspapers, commentators and the public to debates on the proposed legislation will help keep the government informed of the drift of public opinion. The second is the influence on the pre-legislative process which both back benchers and Opposition MPs may have, and the third is the limited amount of improvement and amendment which, despite the partisan nature of the Commons, still does take place. The fourth is clarification of the meaning of a Bill which may take place as governments explain and defend their legislation during debate. It is clear that in relation to all of these functions, the amount of time and resources which Members have available to them to devote to scrutiny of legislation will be crucial; the importance of the second and third will be closely tied to the size of the government's majority.

If a voter is to exercise his choice in a meaningful way, it is clearly vital that he should have a basic grasp of current political issues. Parliamentary debate, it is submitted, plays a vital role in disseminating an awareness of the issues surrounding a given piece of legislation. The Opposition has a vested interest in putting forward and publicising every possible argument against a piece of government legislation. Similarly, the government will wish to explain the principles behind the legislation and present the arguments in its favour. It is conceded that other bodies (such as pressure groups and the media) can and do carry out these roles, but parliamentary debate has the advantage of being rather more dramatic and consequently more newsworthy than, for example, a report on a government Bill by an interested body.

The opportunity for debate in the Commons may also have some effect on the pre-legislative stage. The Commons acts as a forum in which the Opposition can express criticisms of legislation from many sources in society, including pressure groups and those who would be directly affected by the proposals. Government spokesmen will wish to know what these criticisms will be in order to be able to deploy counter-arguments. This desire encourages the government to engage in consultation with these relevant groups; there is a general practice that a department will not introduce a Bill affecting a major organisation without prior consultation with that organisation. Further, the government must take into account the likely response of its own back benchers to legislation, as ascertained by the whips. If back benchers are aware of widespread public discontent at proposed legislation, this will be relayed to the government which will wish to avoid the embarrassment of hearing its own supporters expressing public dissent – dissent which, as P Norton remarks, 'provides good copy for the press' (*The Commons in Perspective*, 1981, p 119). The effect of this anticipated response may be to force the government into modifying its proposals; this was dramatically exemplified in the Labour government's abandonment of its proposed industrial relations legislation in 1969, when it realised that its own MPs did not support the measure. Similarly, in October 1992, John Major's government was forced to abandon its plans for immediate closure of 31 coal pits in order to avoid near certain defeat by Conservative back benchers. The present government, cushioned by a succession of large majorities, is far more likely to feel strong enough to disregard such threatened rebellions; indeed, it did so shortly after taking power when it forced through a cut in single parent benefit despite a threatened back bench revolt which, when it duly appeared, generated considerable adverse publicity for the government and the measure in question.[1] On other occasions, however, the threat of rebellion did force concessions from government: a recent example relates to legislation on asylum proposed by the Blair government in 1999, as Cowley notes ((2001) Parlt Aff 815). Sixty-one Labour MPs signed an Early Day Motion opposing the proposals, and there was speculation in the press that the government faced potential defeat. Concessions were duly granted by the Home Secretary, buying off most of the rebels. Since the 2005 election, in which the Government's majority was cut to around 60, it has had to engage far more in such pre-legislative negotiation with potential rebels.

The opportunities of both back benchers and the Opposition to exert pre-legislative influence on Bills are markedly increased when the government publishes Bills in draft, to allow more detailed comment on them from Select Committees and other interested bodies. This practice was welcomed by the Modernisation Committee, which commented that such practice would provide 'a real chance for the House to exercise its powers of pre-legislative scrutiny in an effective way' (HC 382, 2000–01, para 19). Important examples have included Bills on the Food Standards Agency, Freedom of Information, Tobacco Advertising, Financial Services and Anti-Terrorism; in a number of cases, amendments proposed by Select Committees were accepted by the government. It has been commented that this process is 'far less partisan and far more open to analysis and debate, and, as a consequence, makes, where it is possible, for far better law'. (HC Deb, 26 June 2006, col 43).The Joint Committee on Human Rights now plays a particularly significant role in advising the government and parliament as to whether proposed Bills are compatible with the European Convention on Human Rights: on occasions, its reports have resulted in pre-legislative concessions from the Government. The practice of publishing Bills in draft is being used more frequently: 18 were treated this way in the five years between 1992 and 1997; 39 between 2000 and 2005.

It is submitted that the influence of the Commons in these areas does give it a useful role to play. It must be noted, however, that the government can, to a certain extent, muzzle the publicising role of the Commons and reduce the Opposition's chance to embarrass it by curtailing the time available for debate. The use of the 'closure' allows debate to be simply cut off at the instance of government whips (if supported on a vote)[2] while the 'guillotine', in which a set amount of time is allocated by the government for each stage of debate, has been increasingly used in the past 20 years. Six government Bills were guillotined in the 1987–88 session. Both of these devices undoubtedly inhibit the Commons in its scrutinising function. The present government has made much greater use of what is known as the programming' of Bills: that is, the setting of an agreed timetable, giving reasonable opportunity for debate, in advance, rather than in response to short term time pressures. However, the experiment has been highly controversial. Many commentators view the result of programming all Bills as simply having been to entrench the reduction in scrutiny and remove from the Opposition its power of delay. In one notorious incident, detailed by a dissenting report, set out in the Appendix of a Modernisation Committee Report (HC 382, 2000–01), the time allowed for debate of an important Bill, the Criminal Justice and Police Bill, 'simply proved inadequate. When the guillotine fell at 7 pm in Standing Committee, the Committee had only reached Clause 90 out of 132'. In addition, the whole of Part III of the Bill had not been considered. In an unprecedented move, the government tabled a motion 'deeming' that the Bill had been reported 'as if' consideration of it had been completed by the Committee. The dissenting report concluded: 'The proposition that Opposition parties and back benchers will get greater opportunities to debate and vote on the issues of most concern to them simply has not been borne out by experience in this session of the experiment of systematic guillotining of all Bills. Similarly the evidence of this session is that the House has not scrutinised legislation better.' It remains to be seen whether the experiment of programming all government Bills will be continued.

The argument that the Commons plays a valuable role in the scrutiny of legislation is far weaker in relation to delegated legislation. Clearly, as with primary legislation, the Commons only rarely defeats government Bills; however, the publicising and deterrent effects of the Commons' scrutiny are widely regarded as having become of only negligible value. The Select Committee on Procedure (1977–78) warned that 'the system provides only vestigial control of statutory instruments and is in need of complete reform'. Fundamentally, the problem is that instruments subject to negative affirmation are increasingly becoming law without ever having been debated by the Commons: in 1978–79, 71.7 per cent of prayers for annulment were debated; in the 1985–86 session, this percentage had dropped to 30.6 per cent. In practice, it is the government which determines how much time shall be made available for consideration of statutory instruments; it can thus limit scrutiny to negligible proportions.[3]

The third suggested function for the Commons was its ability to achieve a limited amount of amendment and improvement to Bills in Committee. This does happen on occasion, though generally only when the government's majority is small or the measure is not one of party controversy. There are perhaps two main reasons why this does not happen more: first, as the Modernisation Committee put it, 'There has been a distinct culture prevalent throughout Whitehall that the standing and reputation of ministers have been dependent on their Bills getting through largely unchanged' (HC 382, 2000–01, para 7). Second, MPs suffer from a lack of resources and therefore lack the expertise necessary to expose often highly technical legislation to constructive criticism. As Griffith and Ryle comment, 'the Opposition has no back up comparable to that of the minister's Departmental Staff' (*Parliament: Functions, Practice and Procedures*, 1989, p 317). Norton, whilst noting that MPs' resources have increased dramatically since 1960, remarks that 'By international standards, [their] office, secretarial and research facilities remain poor' (*Does Parliament Matter?*, 1993, p 20). Further, the *ad hoc* nature of the Committees means that they are unable to build up much expertise in a particular area.

An alternative procedure allows Bills to go to Special Standing Committees, which can hold Select Committee-like meetings at which oral evidence can be taken from expert witnesses and ministers and relevant documentation examined. The Committee is thus given the time and resources to build up its expertise on the area covered by the legislation in question, before going on to the usual clause by clause examination of the Bill and amendments. This procedure was followed during the passing of the Criminal Attempts Act 1981 and substantial changes were made during the committee stage. The Modernisation Committee has recommended that this or similar alternative procedures should be followed more often: it has been used only 9 times since 1980 to date, most recently for the Adoption and Children Bill in 2001–02. Again, whether more Bills actually follow such a route and the impact which this would have remains to be seen.

Finally, clarification as to the meaning and implementation of a Bill was instanced earlier in this essay as a useful product of parliamentary debate: the recent passage of the Prevention of Terrorism (Additional Powers) Act 1996 is instructive in this respect. Despite the fact that the Bill was guillotined, a few important points emerged from the Home Secretary's speeches during the debate. The most controversial provision in the Bill allowed for the police to stop and search persons for items related to terrorist offences, without any reasonable suspicion. In response to numerous questions during the debate about the safeguards balancing the new power, two key points were made: first, guidance as to the operation of the powers will be issued by the Home Secretary to the police; second, and more specifically, the Home Secretary will instruct the police to apply the Police and Criminal Evidence Act (PACE) 1984 Code for Stop and Search to all searches under the new power (HC Deb, Col 265, 2 April 1996). The second point is particularly important and, given the silence of the new Act itself as to the applicability of the Code, may enable the courts to decide, through perusal of *Hansard* under the *Pepper v Hart* rule, that Parliament's intention was that the Code should be applied. Thus, significant legal consequences could flow from this assurance.

In conclusion, therefore, it has been suggested that the Commons performs a number of useful functions, albeit with varying results, depending on the size of the government's majority. It is thus far from being a redundant body. However, it is clear that it could achieve far more through the use of more varied procedure, particularly in Committee, far greater use of pre-legislative scrutiny by expert Select Committees, something which has already had some impact, the provision of greater resources for members and a shift away from a culture based heavily on confrontation and defence. Its inefficacy in dealing with delegated legislation is a very serious shortcoming which is being exacerbated as such legislation increases in bulk and significance; reform is thus urgently needed if the Commons is not to become redundant in relation to this very important method of law-making.

▌NOTES

1   It could be added here that the government will, of course, expect the Opposition to oppose its Bill, but if it is anticipated that Opposition criticism will have popular support, the government may reconsider its proposals. As Ronald Butt puts it: 'If [the government] suspects that the Opposition will have an attractive case, it will do its best, within broad limits, to make that case less attractive, or to steal and adapt the Opposition's clothes' (*The Power of Parliament*, 2nd edn, 1969, p 317). Butt instances the extensive amending of the capital gains provisions of the 1964 Labour government by the Chancellor produced, he argues, by the exposure of weak elements in the Labour proposals by the Opposition. Again, of course, this influence will tend to be greater when the government's majority is not secure.

2   The Speaker's discretion to refuse to put the matter to a vote could be noted; he or she may not allow a vote, if to allow it would amount to an abuse of the rules of the House or an infringement of the rights of the minority. The motion must then be passed with at least 100 Members in favour.

3   The scrutiny provided by the Joint Committee on Statutory Instruments could be explained here. The Committee has a duty to consider all delegated legislation laid before the House and must draw attention to legislation which is defective or unacceptable in some way, for example, it imposes a tax or makes unexpected use of the power granted by the parent Act. It should be noted that an adverse report by

the Committee has no automatic effect. The Committee itself has recommended that a report by it should automatically render an instrument subject to affirmative resolution. This would guarantee debate on it and would be a substantial improvement on the Commons' scrutiny of delegated legislation.

Question 16

How far is it true to say that House of Commons' scrutiny of the government 'illustrates again the unequal struggle between MPs and the Executive'? (Hunt, *Open Government.*)

Answer plan

This is a straightforward question, demanding an evaluative description of the various methods deployed by the Commons to scrutinise administration of policy and financial matters. Students should be careful not to stray into the Commons' role in the legislative process except in passing. It is essential for each method to be evaluated in terms of Hunt's quotation – students must not fall into the trap of a mere recitation of methods of scrutiny.

Essentially, the following areas should be covered:

- the rationale behind the perceived necessity for effective parliamentary scrutiny;
- questions to ministers: limitations on topics and evaluation;
- opportunities for short debates: lack of publicity; impact of Westminster Hall;
- Select Committees: remit, powers, limitations and effectiveness; recent reforms;
- scrutiny of national finance: the Public Accounts Committee, the Comptroller and Auditor General;
- concluding evaluation.

Answer

The concern expressed in Hunt's comment arises from the notion that thorough scrutiny of the Executive arm of the State is vital to a democratic system. It is an important convention, essential to the idea of responsible government, that the

Executive should be held accountable to Parliament. The convention owes something to the rationale behind the doctrine of the separation of powers as expounded by Montesquieu, namely, that each organ of the State should act as a check on the powers of the others. The aim of this discussion will be to explore the extent to which Commons' scrutiny of the Executive amounts to effective control over central government. At the outset, it is conceded that the House of Commons in its non-legislative function is not one of the three arms of government in the classical sense; however, it will be argued that it fulfils the rationale behind this classical notion because it acts as a check on central government.

The most obvious forum for scrutiny is the floor of the House of Commons, though it is here that scrutiny can be at its most ineffective. For example, Adjournment Debates are often poorly attended, thus achieving little publicity and requests for Emergency Debates are seldom granted. Early Day Motions were previously only rarely debated; however, the setting up of Westminster Hall as a separate chamber of the Commons has improved this position. Far more publicity is given to the questioning of ministers on the floor of the House. Some 45–50 minutes are set aside every day, except Friday, for oral answers to be given to Members' questions. Nearly 50,000 questions were put down by MPs in 2003–04, the large majority of which, of course, are answered in writing. The oral answering of questions is now often afforded live television coverage. Oral questions and their supplementaries tend to be used as an opportunity to probe ministers' grasp of their portfolios or to attack government policy. They thus have some effect in ensuring that ministers are kept up to the mark and provide an opportunity for weak elements in government policy to be publicly exposed. They are one of the few times in which ordinary back benchers can raise matters directly with Cabinet ministers.

However, the ability of Members to put down really probing questions is reduced by the lack of information and support staff available to back benchers. Ministers, by contrast, have the aid of a skilled team of civil servants who provide them with answers to the tabled questions and undertake research into the questioner's known interests and concerns in an attempt to anticipate and prepare the minister for possible supplementaries. This inequality has led some observers to call for the establishment of a Department of the Opposition to improve the efficiency of Opposition MPs by giving them a staff of civil servants which would go some way to redressing the imbalance between ministers and MPs. Needless to say, no such department has yet been created.[1] As a method of obtaining information, questions requesting written answers are far more effective. However, as Tomkin has noted, 'An answer to a question cannot be insisted upon if the answer is refused by the minister; the Speaker has refused to allow supplementary questions in these circumstances' ((1996) 16(1) LS 63, p 81). Furthermore, there are a large number of matters on which a minister will refuse to answer. These excluded areas have been cut down a little – ministers may no longer withhold information on the basis of 'established parliamentary convention', but instead only 'when disclosure would not be in the public interest which should be decided in accordance with the relevant statutes and the Freedom of Information Act 2000' (see the (non-statutory) *Ministerial Code*). However, the 2000 Act on access to information specifies very large areas where information should not be given, wider than those in the previous Code, in the view of some commentators. In particular, there is a class exemption in s 35 in relation to all information relating to 'the formulation or development of government policy'. The only limitation to this astonishingly broad exemption – which is not subject to any burden on ministers to prove that any harm would be caused by releasing the information in question – is that statistical information relating to a decision is no longer exempted once the decision is made. But, for example, evidence of other policy options considered, and the reasons for rejecting them, would be covered by the exemption. Other excluded areas include information that would prejudice defence, national security or international relations, or where it would involve disclosing commercial confidences; unreasonable, voluminous or vexatious requests (ss 12 and 14); and information which would harm the 'effective conduct of public affairs' (s 36) – this exception, in particular, being very wide and vague. In addition, a minister may refuse to answer any question which would be likely to cost more than a certain amount (currently £600) to research. The Speaker will also not allow questions which do not relate to the minister's area of responsibility and may refuse questions on a number of other grounds, including that they do not fulfil the traditional purpose of a question – to ask for information or press for action. Recently answered questions will also be disallowed.

There is no suggestion by parliamentary commentators that factual answers to parliamentary questions are routinely untruthful. There are, however, persistent complaints from MPs, monitored and publicised by reports from the Public Administration Committee, that answers are often partial, that they disregard parts of the question, or that they are given late. The Freedom of Information Act 2000 for the first time introduces a general right of access to government information, policed by an independent Information Commissioner and which is ultimately enforceable through the contempt jurisdiction of the High Court (s 52), and MPs will of course be able to make as much use of the Act as anyone. It will therefore deal with the basic problem that ministers cannot at present ultimately be compelled to release information. However, the Act is riddled with the extremely wide ranging exemptions discussed above – broader even than those in the Code, in the view of some commentators. The Information Commissioner can ultimately order release of the information concerned; however, where the information relates to a central government department, and its release is ordered on public interest grounds, its release can ultimately be vetoed by a Cabinet minister (s 53).

Leaving aside the issue of veracity, ministers' questions may have a more hidden but arguably very important result, as postulated by Sir Norman Chester in his 'Questions in the House' (quoted in Walkland and Ryle, *The Commons Today, 1981,* pp 189–199). He points out that many decisions in a department will be taken at a low level without the minister's actual accord or knowledge. The tabling of a question which queries this decision and the subsequent investigation by the minister and senior members of the department will bring the decision to the minister's attention. The minister will then either have to justify it which will bring the decision to public attention, or modify departmental policy if it becomes apparent that it is evolving in a manner which was not originally intended. However, as mentioned above, for such questions to have this effect, back benchers must have the means of gaining information about the day-to-day running of departments.

It was precisely to give back benchers more in-depth knowledge of government departments that the Select Committees were set up in 1979, covering between them each of the major government departments with the exception of the Law Officers Department and the Lord Chancellor's Department, which were brought within the system in 1991. The Select Committees have three main advantages as a method of scrutiny over questions or debate on the floor of the House. First, since MPs tend to commit themselves to a Committee for a considerable period, they have time to build up a reasonable level of expertise on their area of concern (an ability enhanced by their power to send for papers and records), which clearly enables them to probe more deeply into departmental affairs. Second, the Committees tend to be more non-partisan than almost any other Commons organisation; however, members of the Committee of Selection which nominates the MPs to the Committees are themselves chosen by the whips, so that the government can still exercise partial control in an attempt to keep known outspoken and independently minded MPs off the Committees. A recent attempt to reform this system, as proposed by the Liaison and Modernisation Committees, was rejected by the Commons in May 2002, though an incident in July 2001 indicates that, occasionally, back bench MPs may revolt in the face of blatant attempts by government whips to keep known independently minded and critical MPs off Select Committees. Following the June 2001 General Election, the government sought to remove two chairs of Select Committees who it saw as being particularly critical of government policy: Gwyneth Dunwoody, previously chair of the Transport Committee and Donald Anderson, former chair of the Foreign Affairs Committee. The motion was rejected in a large rebellion by Labour MPs. Moreover, it remains true that most Committee reports are unanimous and many are critical of government policy. The Social Services Committee, for example, brought out a report which was critical of the government-introduced Social Fund shortly before the 1992 General Election. More recently, despite its Labour-dominated ranks, the Transport Committee has brought out a number of trenchant, critical reports. Its most important was a forensic dissection of the government's Ten Year Transport Plan – its master-plan for tackling the hugely difficult issue of cutting down car usage and improving public transport as an alternative. The Report (HC 558–1, 2001–02) was widely viewed in the media as sounding the death knell for the plan as originally conceived by John Prescott, while some viewed it as partly responsible for the resignation, in June 2002, of the then Transport Secretary, Stephen Byers. The ability of the Committees to operate in a non-partisan fashion marks their work out particularly clearly from the general character of proceedings in the House, described by one back bench MP as 'government and Opposition, locked into a permanent election campaign' (HC Deb, Col 1099,13 November 1997).

The third advantage of the Committees is their ability to send for civil servants and ministers for questioning which is far more systematic and searching than anything that could take place in the Commons Chamber. This power to question members of the Executive is clearly crucial to the efficacy of the Committees, and not surprisingly has caused controversy. In 1979, the Leader of the House pledged that 'every minister . . . will do all in his or her power to co-operate with the new system of Committees' (HC Deb, Col 425, 25 June 1979). On the whole, this promise and its necessary concomitant of ensuring civil service co-operation has been honoured. A study of the Select Committees by Nevil Johnson found that 'the new Committees have, as a rule, gained a satisfactory degree of co-operation from . . . both ministers and officials' (see 'Departmental Select Committees', in Ryle and Richards, *The Commons Under Scrutiny*, 3rd edn, 1988, pp 166–70). However, the Committees have sometimes found themselves frustrated when investigating areas of acute sensitivity by the refusal of certain key witnesses to attend. For example, in 1984, the government would not allow the Director of Government Communications Headquarters to give evidence to the Select Committee on Employment which was enquiring into the trade union ban at GCHQ. A long-standing problem has been the refusal of ministers in the previous and present governments to allow their Special Advisers, thought by many to exercise more power than many ministers, to appear before any Select Committees, despite the revision of the 'Osmotherly rules' in 2005 to provide for their attendance, and assurances given to the Liaision Committee in 2004 that Special Advisor would now be allowed to give such evidence (Minutes of Evidence, HC 1180–i, Q 26). The Public Administration Select Committee found in 2005 that there was still a marked reluctance by Ministers, notably the Prime Minister, to allow the questioning of Special Advisers by Select Committees (1st Special Report, 2005–06). For example, the Transport Committee recently published a report bitterly condemning the refusal of Treasury ministers to attend its inquiry into the PPP scheme for the London Underground, despite the fact that the Treasury was clearly the moving force behind the scheme (see HC 771, 2001–02). Moreover, the basic principle remains that it is for Ministers to decide which civil servants and Advisors should attend on their behalf (evidence to Liaison Committee, ibid).

If a Committee is seriously dissatisfied with a refusal to disclose information, the matter could be put forward for debate in the House and a finding of contempt of Parliament would then be possible. Indeed, in 1981, the Leader of the House gave a 'formal undertaking' that if such refusal to attend or to divulge information caused widespread concern in the House, the government would 'seek' to find time to allow such a debate. Committees have, however, showed themselves unwilling to evoke contempt proceedings, leaving bad publicity from a refusal to attend as the main persuasive sanction. As the Liaison Committee noted, in its 1997 Report (HC 323–1, 1996–97, para 12), the Standards and Privileges Committee now has power to order the attendance of any Member – and indeed to require that specific documents or records in the possession of a Member relating to its inquiries be laid before the Committee. The Liaison Committee recommended that this power should be given to the departmental Select Committees.

An important step forward in accountability was unexpectedly agreed between the Committees and the government in 2002. Up until then, a convention prevented the Select Committees from questioning the most important member of the Executive – the Prime Minister. However, in April 2002, perhaps in an attempt to deflect criticism that Mr Blair's administration had little respect for Parliament, it was announced that the Prime Minister would make himself available for questioning, once a year, by the Liaison Committee, a Select Committee composed of the chairs of the departmental Select Committees. The first session took place in July 2002 and they are generally agreed to have gleaned important insights in particular into Blair's views on the internal running of his government.

To some extent, different problems arise in the case of civil servants. Having secured their attendance, the Committee may then find itself hampered by their refusal to divulge certain information on the basis that to do so would contravene the advice given in the so-called 'Osmotherly rules', governing the conduct of civil servants before Select Committees (now entitled *Departmental Evidence and Response to Select Committees (2005)*), which sets out matters about which they should not give evidence; the basic rule is that civil servants should give evidence 'on behalf of the minister and under his instructions.' This applies even to the chief executives of the semiautonomous 'Next Steps' Agencies, who have considerable areas of devolved responsibilities, and is thought to be particularly unsatisfactory in their case. On the whole, however, Committees have not found Civil Service recalcitrance a serious handicap; for example, the Select Committee on Trade and Industry stated in its second report of 1985–86: 'In the vast majority of previous . . . Committees, no serious problem has arisen.'

However, the record of the Committees in obtaining the government records they require is less reassuring: in the words of the 1997 Liaison Committee report, 'It is in [this area] that most difficulties have arisen' (para 14). The Committee found that governmental promises to make time for a Commons debate on a refusal to provide requested documentation have not been properly honoured: 'There have been a significant number of cases where Committees have been refused specific documents but the government has not provided time for the subject to be debated.' The Committee recommended that 'the onus should be shifted onto the government to defend in the House its refusal to disclose information to a Select

Committee' (para 16).[2] In general, however, it should be conceded that both the restrictions on the divulging of information and the refusal of persons to attend are likely to hamper the Committees in exposing major government embarrassments, but interfere little with their day-to-day scrutiny of the relevant departments.

A package of proposals to strengthen Select Committees was recently agreed between the Liaison and Modernisation Committees, and most of the key recommendations were accepted by the Commons in May 2002. The key elements include: greater resources for Select Committees, including making available assistance by the National Audit Office and more support staff; the encouragement of an alternative career structure in Select Committees, intended to enhance their prestige by payment for their Chairpersons; greater coordination between Committees and clarification of their tasks, which now include much greater involvement in pre-legislative scrutiny as well as an informal role in scrutinising appointments to Next Steps Agencies and other key quangos.

Clearly, scrutiny over the national finances is a vital link in the chain of the Commons' control of the Executive; it is, however, patchy. As Colin Turpin comments, government borrowing 'largely escapes scrutiny', while detailed parliamentary examination of departmental supply expenditure 'was abandoned long ago' (*British Government and the Constitution, 1990*, p 482). However, in the area of verifying the authorisation of expenditure and ascertaining that value for money has been obtained, the Public Accounts Committee has been notably effective. It is, as De Smith notes, 'scrupulously non-partisan', while the value of its investigations is greatly enhanced by the fact that the Comptroller and Auditor General (an officer of the House and therefore independent from the government and assisted by a staff of several hundred) sits with it.

The Committee seeks to achieve proper accountability by asking for clear objectives to be set, for proper monitoring of programmes to be established from their outset, and by comparing achievement with expectation. In the early 1980s, it exposed the inadequate notice given to the House of the spiralling costs of the Polaris Enhancement Project which had reached £1,000m from an initial estimate of £175m. The Committee revealed how such information was being concealed from the Commons and won the significant promise from the government that the Committee would in future be supplied with adequate financial information about defence costs. A more recent report received a great deal of attention, being concerned with the controversial issue of the effectiveness of the Private Finance Initiative (PFI) (HC 460, 2001–02).

Overall, it is clear that the efficacy of the Commons' scrutiny of the Executive is uneven. Supplementaries asked in the House may expose a weak area or force a ministerial investigation into a departmental decision, but on the other hand, they may have been foreseen by a minister's civil servants who will have briefed the minister thoroughly beforehand. Moreover, Select Committees' investigations may be hampered by the refusal of crucial witnesses to attend. Clearly, enhancement of the Select Committees' powers to enforce attendance – as recommended by the Modernisation Committee in 2001 and accepted for consideration by the House in May 2002 – would improve their effectiveness. In general, the key to effective scrutiny is undoubtedly sufficient information. Where MPs do not possess it, their questions will often miss the mark. Where, like the Public Accounts Committee, they have access to an abundance of detail, penetrating criticisms can be made – criticisms which can force the government into greater accountability in future. While the Executive is possessed of far more information than the Commons, the struggle to call it effectively to account must remain an unequal one. However, the Select Committees have undoubtedly achieved some small but significant redress of the imbalance of power because they have endowed at least some MPs with a measure of expertise.

NOTES

1 Students could point out the disadvantages that could result from such a reform. Douglas Wass, in a lecture proposing a Department of the Opposition, conceded that there were fears that the department might inhibit the emergence of new parties, and that the department's civil servants might 'capture the minds' of the Opposition front bench, encouraging a drift to the middle ground commonly presumed to be favoured by the Civil Service (quoted in Turpin, *British Government and the Constitution,* 1990, p 451).

2 A recent example deriving from the arms to Sierra Leone affair could be given here. Problems arose between the Foreign Affairs Committee and the Foreign Secretary Robin Cook during the Committee's investigation into the affair, in which it appeared that Foreign Office officials had been aware that arms shipments from the UK breached a UN embargo on the export of arms to Sierra Leone. The minister refused to provide the Committee with a number of key telegrams from the UK's High Commissioner in Sierra Leone to the Foreign Office; the objection was the usual one of the need to preserve confidences. A compromise formula, that a summary of the telegrams would be made available to the Committee and members of it would be able to visit the Foreign Office to examine the actual documents to verify the accuracy of the summaries, was eventually reached (see the Committee's reports (HC 760 and 1057–1, 1997–98)).

Question 17

Discuss the following views of the role of Select Committees: 'They are intended to redress the balance of power between Parliament and the Executive'; 'they are an institution which is expected to stay on the sidelines.'

Answer plan

This question is quite demanding because it requires detailed knowledge of the operation of Select Committees. It is also topical due to the growing perception that Select Committees provide a surer means of scrutinising the Executive than procedures on the floor of the Commons, the recent package of reforms agreed by the Commons in May 2002 and the increased scope of the Committees' work. The following matters should be considered:

- the concept of government responsibility to Parliament;
- the role of Select Committees in scrutinising the actions of the Executive; their independence and non-partisan approach;
- the impact of their reports on policy-making;
- the difficulties faced by the Committees in obtaining the persons and papers they need;
- the restrictions on the types of questions which civil servants will be prepared to answer;
- the efficacy of the Public Accounts Committee;
- the recent reform proposals agreed.

Answer

The statements taken together imply that expectations of the constitutional change which would be brought about by the Select Committees were high in some quarters, but that in others, it was always assumed that the new Committees were not intended to fulfil them due to various limitations. It should be noted that the phrase 'stay on the sidelines' may be taken to mean both that the input of the Committees into the policy-making process is bound to be marginal, and also that the Committees' powers, in terms of their ability to gather evidence, are inherently limited and that they are therefore expected to be non-intrusive institutions. Both interpretations will be addressed.

It is clear that the new Select Committees were set up in 1979 due to widespread dissatisfaction with procedures on the floor of the House of Commons as a means of scrutinising the workings of government, and a consequent perception that the balance of power between the Executive and Parliament was not being maintained under the then current arrangements. While written answers to parliamentary questions are a useful source of information, it is widely accepted that oral questioning of ministers on the floor of the House can never be a very effective scrutinising tool, for two reasons. First, there is simply insufficient time for in-depth scrutiny. Second, the *culture* surrounding the institution of Question Time is in general that of an adversarial party system: the key conflict is between the Opposition and the government, rather than between parliamentarians and the Executive. The new Committees were intended to provide opportunities for more in-depth and impartial scrutiny. They were better equipped and organised than their predecessors, set up in the 1966–70 Parliament. Their function was expressed to be 'to examine the expenditure, administration and policy of the principal government departments'. The Committees allow officials and ministers to be questioned in a systematic and searching manner not possible on the floor of the House of Commons. Furthermore, the members of the Committees are (within limits to be discussed) well informed and can call on the assistance of expert advisers. The published reports of Committees constitute a very significant and valuable source of information about the workings of government. The Committees show an impartiality remarkable in the contentious atmosphere of the Commons; they conduct their business in an inquisitorial as opposed to an adversarial manner dictated by party lines. This can be partly explained by the fact that the Committees' members are chosen from the back benches: no front bench spokesmen are appointed to them, although former ministers may be. The members of the Committee of Selection which nominates the MPs to the Committees are themselves chosen by the whips, so that the government can still exercise partial control in an attempt to keep known outspoken and independently minded MPs off the Committees; it means that the whips also control both the filling of vacancies on Committees and, more importantly, at what point in a new Parliament they are set up. As the Liaison Committee complained in an influential report, *Shifting the Balance* (HC 300, 1999–2000), there have as a result sometimes been 'long delays' before the Committees are established: the government is thus able to escape scrutiny for sustained periods. A recent attempt to reform this system, as proposed by the Liaison and Modernisation Committees, was rejected by the Commons in May 2002, though an incident in July 2001 indicates that occasionally, back bench MPs may revolt in the face of blatant attempts by government whips to keep known independently-minded and critical MPs off Select Committees. Following the June 2001 General Election, the government sought to remove two chairs of Select Committees who it saw as being particularly critical of its policy: Gwyneth Dunwoody, previously chair of the Transport Committee, and Donald Anderson, former chair of the Foreign Affairs Committee. The motion was rejected in a large rebellion by Labour MPs.

It can be difficult to assess the impact of the Committees on departmental policy-making, because Committee reports may merely contribute to debate which was already occurring. However, an example of a concrete result flowing from a Select Committee report can be seen in the positive response of the Labour government to the report of the Home Affairs Select Committee on police complaints and the disciplinary procedure for officers accused of misconduct (HC

258–1, 1997–98; the government's response appears as HC 683). A large number of the Committee's findings and recommendations were accepted by the government, including the broad thrust of the Committee's findings that the present procedures of the Police Complaints Authority were inadequate and that significant reform was required to strengthen the complaints system. There is no doubt that a number of very recent Select Committee reports which were critical of government policy have had a marked impact, receiving extensive publicity in the media, thus always forcing government further to explain and defend its policies from the criticisms made and, on occasion, causing it to reconsider its policies.[1] More recently, the Liaison Committee, in its Annual Report for 2004, noted that: 'The Culture, Media and Sport Committee's inquiry into the Government's plans for reform of the national lottery concluded that multiple licences were a recipe for disaster and identified a number of other ways for encouraging effective competition for a single operating licence.' As a result, 'The Government reconsidered its policy and subsequently published the National Lottery Bill, which provided for a "clear and firm presumption" for a single licence, awarded by competition'. The Secretary of State subsequently wrote to the Committee stating that 'The work the Government undertook . . . was hugely influenced by the work of the Committee.'

Although the role of the Select Committees is probably significantly more valuable than that played by debate in the Commons as a means of subjecting ministers to scrutiny, the Committees are subject to important limitations in terms of time and information available to them (although there has been some marked improvement in some of these areas of late and further reforms were agreed in May 2002). Committees may need to appoint sub-committees in order to discharge their function adequately; up until recently, only three of the Committees have been empowered to set up one sub-committee each. All Committees now have this ability. They have the formal power to send for 'persons, papers, and records', but this power is rarely invoked; they prefer to act by invitation. In any event, Committees cannot compel MPs or ministers to attend before them: an order would have to made by the House, a largely theoretical possibility only. Committees have experienced difficulty at times in acquiring information or interviewing the minister or official they wish to question. For example, in 1984, the government would not allow the Director of Government Communications Headquarters to give evidence to the Select Committee on Employment which was inquiring into the trade union ban at GCHQ. In 1988, the Agriculture Select Committee wished to interview Edwina Currie after the salmonella-in-eggs affair and she was requested to attend its inquiry. When she refused, the Committee reiterated its request and stated its view that it was for the Committee to determine whether or not her evidence was relevant. Eventually, she did attend, but did not accept that the Committee had power to compel her attendance. A long-standing problem has been the refusal of ministers in the previous and present governments to allow their

Special Advisers, thought by many to exercise more power than many ministers, to appear before any Select Committees, despite the revision of the 'Osmotherly rules' in 2005 to provide for their attendance, and assurances given to the Liaision Committee in 2004 that Special Advisor would now be allowed to give such evidence (Minutes of Evidence, HC 1180–118i, Q 26). The Public Administration Select Committee found in 2005 that that there was still a marked reluctance by Ministers, notably the Prime Minister, to allow the questioning of Special Advisers by Select Committees (1st Special Report, 2005–06). For example, the Transport Committee recently published a report bitterly condemning the refusal of Treasury ministers to attend its inquiry into the PPP scheme for the London Underground, despite the fact that the Treasury was clearly the moving force behind the scheme (see HC 771, 2001–02). Moreover, the basic principle remains that it is for Ministers to decide which civil servants and Advisors should attend on their behalf (evidence to Liaison Committee, ibid).

The record of the Committees in obtaining the government records they require gives rise to more concern: in the words of the 1997 Liaison Committee report, 'It is in [this area] that most difficulties have arisen' (para 14). The Committee found that governmental promises to make time for a Commons debate on a refusal to provide requested documentation have not been honoured: 'There have been a significant number of cases where Committees have been refused specific documents but the government has not provided time for the subject to be debated.' The reference to a debate is to the House's formal power to make a finding that a refusal to supply requested documents – or indeed a refusal to attend a Committee at all – represented a contempt of Parliament. Such a finding could only be made after a debate, and the Committee recommended that 'The onus should be shifted onto the government to defend in the House its refusal to disclose information to a Select Committee' (para 16) and that the power of the Privileges Committee 'to require that specific documents or records in the possession of a member relating to its inquiries be laid before the Committee' be extended to all Committees.

Not only are the powers of Committees to require the attendance of ministers and officials and the production of documents rather weak and uncertain, the areas about which they may interrogate civil servants and the chief executives of 'Next Steps' Agencies are subject to quite basic restrictions. Under the so called 'Osmotherly rules', governing the conduct of civil servants before Select Committees (now entitled *Departmental Evidence and Response to Select Committees (2005)*), there are a number of matters about which civil servants may not give evidence. The basic rule is that civil servants should give evidence 'on behalf of' the minister and under his instructions. This applies even to the chief executives of the semi-autonomous Next Steps Agencies, who have considerable areas of devolved responsibilities, and is thought to be particularly unsatisfactory in their case. As a number of parliamentary and academic commentators have observed, this restriction can hamper the ability of Select Committees to uncover instances where operational failures attributed by ministers to mistakes by officials or chief executives are in reality the result of ministerial interference, or matters for which the minister is clearly responsible, such as resources or overall policy guidelines. On the whole, however, Committees have not found Civil Service recalcitrance a serious handicap; for example, the Select Committee on Trade and Industry stated in its second report of 1985–86: 'In the vast majority of previous . . . Committees, no serious problem has arisen.'

Assessment of the Select Committees' efficacy must beware of generalisations; some Committees are perceived as more rigorous in their criticism of government than others. The Public Accounts Committee, set up in 1861, is sometimes viewed as the most successful Select Committee in terms of its efficacy as a means of scrutinising the effects of government policy. It engages in the monitoring of extravagant government spending and imprudent contractual transactions. The Committee seeks to achieve proper accountability by asking for clear objectives to be set, for proper monitoring of programmes to be established from the outset and by comparing achievement with expectation. The value of its investigations is greatly enhanced by the fact that the Comptroller and Auditor General (an officer of the House and therefore independent from the government who is assisted by a staff of several hundred) sits with it.

It is difficult to ascertain the effect of such criticism, though it is generally thought that the Committee's reports are treated with respect by the Civil Service. Further, the Committee has on occasions exacted concessions from the government over the availability of financial information to the House; in the early 1980s, its embarrassing revelations of government non-disclosure of the spiralling costs of the Polaris Enhancement Programme were followed by a government pledge to keep the Committee better informed of defence expenditure.[2]

A package of proposals to strengthen Select Committees was agreed between the Liaison and Modernisation Committees in 2002 and most of the key recommendations were accepted by the Commons in May of that year. The key elements include: greater resources for Select Committees, including making available assistance by the National Audit Office, and more support staff; the encouragement of an alternative career structure in Select Committees intended to enhance their prestige by payment for their chairs; greater coordination between Committees and clarification of their tasks, which now include much greater involvement in pre-legislative scrutiny, as well as an informal role in scrutinising appointments to Next Steps Agencies and other key quangos.

While only time will tell how far these reforms will enhance the quality and effectiveness of the work of Select Committees, in general it is apparent that, certainly at present, the Committees are somewhat hampered in their scrutinising function. Therefore, although they can go some of the way towards redressing the balance of power between Parliament and the Executive, their power and influence in this respect are limited. It is generally accepted that significant constitutional changes cannot be effected by procedural reform and this was probably recognised at the time when the Committees were set up. The Committees do operate on the sidelines both in the sense that – as G Drewry puts it – they 'are in the business of scrutiny and exposure, not government' (*The New Select Committees, 1989*) and because even their abilities in this respect are curtailed. Their contribution to parliamentary accountability, especially in terms of the information they glean and their ability to subject ministers and officials to sustained, non-partisan scrutiny, has undoubtedly improved the ability of the House to investigate and scrutinise government in some depth.

▌NOTES

1 Students could give a further example at this point: the scathing report of the Culture, Media and Sport Committee on the failure to build a new national stadium at Pickett's Lock at which to hold the National Athletics Championship. A widely quoted paragraph in the Committee's report found that there had been 'a scandalously inept treatment of public money' (HC 264, 2001–02).

2 It might be useful at this point before arriving at the conclusion to draw a brief comparison between the work of the Commons' Select Committees and those of the Lords. In some respects, the Lords' Select Committees may be more valuable in this context than those of the Commons. Their work has changed in nature and increased enormously since 1972. Before that time, they tended to be concerned with the administration and procedure of the House. Since then, a number of Select Committees, such as the European Communities Committee, have been set up in response to specific needs. The Lords' Select Committees tend to have more time to receive evidence than those of the Commons, and may therefore produce more considered reports. They may also have wider terms of reference than those in the Commons. For example, the European Communities Committee was able to consider the merits of legislation, unlike the corresponding Committee in the Commons. Moreover, in contrast to the Commons' Select Committee Reports, the Lords' Reports will always be debated.

CHAPTER 4

THE HOUSE OF LORDS

▌INTRODUCTION

This is a reasonably straightforward area which is examined by means of essay questions. Traditionally, questions tended to focus on the paradox of the House of Lords as an anachronism which yet seemed to play a valuable constitutional role. Recently, however, the Lords has become the focus of the Blair government's constitutional reform programme, with the removal of most of the hereditary peers from the House of Lords in 1999, the Wakeham Report on long term reform, the government's almost universally derided White Paper in response, the influential report of the Public Administration Committee with its counter-proposals for a far more democratic and assertive House, the recent votes on reform by both Houses in 2003 on the proposals of the Joint Committee on Lord Reform, which resulted in no agreement, and the Government's latest push for further reform, mentioned in the November 2006 Queen's Speech. Recent indications from the Government that it believes the powers of the Lords should be reduced, and the report on the Salisbury and other conventions by the Joint Committee on Conventions (2006) should also be noted. Examination questions are therefore very likely to appear on this highly topical area, and are almost bound to focus on one or more of the above elements of reform. Students, however, need to place their knowledge of the various reform proposals within the context of a solid base of knowledge about the current composition and powers of the Lords, the conventional restraints upon the House, the party balance and the nature and distinctive value of the work it does.

Checklist

Students should be familiar with the following areas:

- the limits on the powers of the Lords under the Parliament Acts 1911 and 1949;
- the conventions on the use of the Lords' powers, including recent examples;

- the role of the Lords in relation to legislation emanating in the Commons, including recent examples;
- the scrutiny of delegated legislation of the Executive and of European legislation;
- the Lords' role in initiating legislation; Private Members' Bills emanating in the Lords;
- the composition of the Lords; note that the current composition, including the balance between the different types of peers and the Lords' party make-up, can easily be checked on the Parliament's website at www.publications.parliament.uk;
- the removal of the hereditary peers and its consequences;
- further proposals for reform: Wakeham; the White Paper, the Fifth Report of the Public Administration Committee; the Joint Committee's Report in 2002 and the subsequent votes; indications of the Government's latest plans for reform; the report of the Joint Committee on Conventions.

Note the following references: those to the Public Administration Committee are to its Fifth Report (HC 494, 2001–02); to Wakeham are to the report, *A House for the Future* (Cm 4534); and to the government's White Paper are to *The House of Lords: Completing the Reform* (Cmd 5291).

Question 18

'Although the House of Lords has some value, it is an anomaly in a democracy and should be abolished or radically reformed; the removal of the hereditary peers is no substitute for this.'

Discuss.

Answer plan

This is quite a straightforward example of a question likely to be asked on the House of Lords, since it asks for an evaluation of the Lords as it still is. While the recent reform proposals by Wakeham, etc, are not specifically mentioned, they should be discussed, albeit briefly in the answer, bearing in mind that the question focuses on whether reform is needed, not specifically on what form that reform should take. Students do not therefore need to consider the details of proposed reforms, but merely their broad outlines. The removal of the hereditaries must of course be specifically considered. The discussion of reform *must* be related to the strengths and weaknesses of the House identified earlier in the essay.

Essentially, the following matters should be discussed:

- the anomalous composition of the Lords;
- the role of the Lords in relation to legislation emanating in the Commons; its value and recent examples;
- the value of the Lords' scrutiny of European legislation;
- the limits on the powers of the Lords under the Parliament Acts 1911 and 1949 and by convention;
- The Wakeham, government and Public Administration Committee proposals for reform with a view to improving democratic accountability; the factors arguing against reform;
- the merits and demerits of the removal of the hereditaries.

Answer

The anomalous position of the House of Lords in a modern democracy is perhaps its most remarkable feature: not one member of the UK Parliament's second chamber is elected. All hold their positions either through birth, appointment or the office they hold. There are still these three main groups in the Lords, although following the House of Lords Act 1999, the balance between the life and hereditary peers has swung dramatically in the former's favour. Prior to that Act, by far the largest group, constituting 750 out of a total of 1,273 in 1998, were the hereditary peers, who inherit their title through birth and pass it on from generation to generation. The second largest group was the life peers, 488 strong; the third, 26 Bishops and 26 Law Lords. The position following the 1999 Act is now somewhat different, though no more democratic. As at end November 2006, the House numbered 750 peers, of whom 606 are life peers and only 92 hereditaries, those selected for retention by a vote of the hereditary peers only. The Bishops and Law Lords remain. Not only is the House thus wholly undemocratic, it is also unrepresentative of women. In 1998, there were only 96 female peers out of 1,273, that is, less than 10 per cent. That was largely due to the fact that the vast majority of hereditary peerages descend only to male issue. This has now improved to 142 women out of a total of 750, or nearly 19 per cent.

The House's second major affront to democracy formerly lay in the fact that one party, the Conservatives, historically had a permanent strong predominance; the position here has undergone a more marked improvement. In January 1998, out of a total of 1,146 peers, 495 were Conservatives, 322 Cross-Benchers (independent peers), 157 Labour and 68 Liberal Democrat. Conservative peers thus outnumbered Labour Lords by around 4:1. The hereditaries, as one would expect, were overwhelmingly Conservative-leaning: 319 took the Conservative whip, compared to only 16 Labour peers. A more useful guide to party influence can be gained by examining the allegiance of those who attended more than 50 per cent of the sessions – only about one-third of peers. The figures for the 1996–97 session showed that out of a total of 399, the Conservatives had 195, or 49 per cent; the Cross-Benchers and Labour both had 83, or 21 per cent; while the Liberal Democrats had 37, or 9 per cent.

Following the removal of the bulk of the hereditaries and a deliberate and successful attempt by Mr Blair to rebalance the Lords through his appointment of large numbers of life peers, the position has undergone a significant change. As at end November 2006, Labour is now the largest single party, but only by a handful of peers: Labour has 212 seats, the Conservatives 207, while the Liberal Democrats have increased their number of seats notably to 78. Very importantly, there are now 201 Cross-Bench peers, who now represent 27 per cent of the total. While the Conservatives are still over-represented, given that they came well behind Labour in the popular vote in the last three General Elections, their preponderance has been substantially reduced, and in practice all legislation requires cross-party support to pass. Peers taking a party whip are appointed by the Queen on the advice of the Prime Minister; new cross-bench peers are nominated by the (non-statutory) Appointments Commission.

Despite its undemocratic and unrepresentative nature, most commentators accept that the House of Lords has a valuable part to play in the British constitutional process. Perhaps its most important role lies in scrutinising public Bills passed by the House of Commons, on which it spends around half of its time.[1] The House passes a large amount of amendments to such Bills: in the 1987–90 sessions, the average number of amendments passed was over 2,600. The vast majority of these were subsequently accepted by government (2,038 out of 2,056 in the 1992–93 session), reflecting the fact that most are introduced by government and are technical in nature. But the House is not simply a forum in which government can correct its own mistakes. Barnett's conclusion is that 'the Lords is both very active in relation to legislation, and makes a substantial impact on many legislative proposals' (*Constitutional and Administrative Law*, 4th edn, 2002, p 532). A significant number of its amendments represent changes of principle of a minor or major nature. To an extent, therefore, the Lords can compensate for the inadequate scrutiny bestowed by the Commons, scrutiny which is widely perceived as consisting merely of an endless party battle, rather than a rigorous assessment of the merits of legislative proposals. It can therefore provide a much needed check on the government-dominated Commons, a check which is particularly valuable when, as has been the case since 1997, the government in power has a large majority, thereby rendering the Opposition largely ineffective. The Lords may delay controversial or unpopular legislation or it may be able to procure the acceptance of amendments which are unwelcome to the government. It has done both on a number of occasions in the last two decades, during times when Oppositions have been wholly unable to do likewise.

For example, during the 1980s, due to the nature of the parliamentary process, the Labour party was helpless in the face of the large Conservative majority. In contrast, the Lords inflicted 173 defeats on the government between 1979 and 1991, some of them relating to important and controversial measures. For example, the House passed a wrecking amendment to the Local Government (Interim Provisions) Bill in 1984, with the result that the Conservative government had to reconsider its plans to retroactively nullify the result of the 1984 elections to the Greater London Council. In February 1996, the Lords inflicted a major defeat on the government's Broadcasting Bill by voting to deny Sky Television exclusive rights to the eight most important sporting events of the year, including Wimbledon and the Olympic Games, ensuring that the majority of viewers who did not have Sky would be able to view the events on BBC or ITV. The government was forced to accept the change, described at the time as 'the biggest government upset in the Lords since 1988' ((1996) *The Independent*, 7 February). The defeat undoubtedly represented a blow to the government's free market policy on broadcasting, and thus marked a clear rebuff by the Lords of a central and politically contentious strand of government policy.[2] The Lords has also defied the present government which, with its decisive majority, can steamroller opposition in the Commons in a similar manner. Thus, the Lords thrice rejected a provision in the Teaching and Higher Education Bill 1998 which waived the payment of fees for the fourth year of a degree taken at a Scottish university for Scottish students, but not those from the rest of the UK, a provision which had attracted widespread opposition outside Parliament. The government was eventually forced to promise an independent review of the system within six months of its establishment, an important concession. The Lords also broken with a (contested) convention in 2000 by rejecting a piece of secondary legislation – the Greater London Authority (Election Expenses) Order 2000 – which dealt with the nuts and bolts of the London mayoral and assembly elections, in particular, the amount of electoral expenditure which candidates would be allowed to incur; the Order required only negative approval, that is, it would go through automatically unless voted against. It appears that the Lords only in fact rejected secondary legislation once in the 20th century (see Brazier, *Constitutional Practice*, 2nd edn, 1994, p 254, footnote 119), in 1968, in relation to a sanctions order against Rhodesia. That in fact was an order requiring positive approval from the Lords: Erskine May reveals that it had never voted down orders requiring only the negative approval procedure. Nevertheless, the Lords, to the consternation of the government, threw the Order out and, in so doing, quite clearly relied upon their newly reformed status. The Joint Committee on Conventions, reporting in 2006, rejected the Government's view that it was a breach of convention for the House to reject statutory instruments, though it conceded that the power to do so should be used only in exceptional circumstances. In 2000, the Lords inflicted a further major defeat on the government over its Criminal Justice (Mode of Trial) Bill. The heart of the controversial legislation was cl 1, which removed the right of defendants to choose jury trial in 'either way' offences, such as theft and burglary. The crucial part of the debate took part in Committee stage and only got as far as cl 1. The very first amendment put down restored the right of the defendant to be tried by a jury in such cases at his election, and thus ripped the heart out of the Bill. It was therefore what is commonly referred to as a 'wrecking amendment', since it altered the fundamental principle of the legislation.

The Lords is often seen as having a particularly important role to play in the protection of civil liberties, an issue to which the Commons may often show little sensitivity when both main parties feel obliged to show their 'toughness' on law and order issues. The Lords inserted an important amendment to the Police and Criminal Evidence Bill 1984, allowing evidence unfairly obtained to be excluded; this eventually prompted the government to put forward its own amendment which became s 78 of the Act. The War Crimes Bill 1990 was rejected outright by the Lords, on the grounds that the convictions of former Nazi war criminals, which it aimed to facilitate, would be inherently unsafe.

Similarly, in January 1997, the Lords defeated the government to procure an important amendment of principle to the Police Act 1997. As originally conceived, the Bill gave police officers the power to enter premises to plant listening devices to assist in the detection of crime. Authorisation was to be given by the Chief Constable; by contrast, when the police want to tap phones, they must obtain a warrant from the Home Secretary. There was also no exception in relation to bugging premises where conversations involving legal professional privilege might take place – listening devices could therefore have been planted at lawyers' offices. The Lords inserted an amendment to compel the police to seek prior judicial approval before installing listening devices, forcing the government to bring forward its own, similar proposals. Similarly, in 2001, their Lordships imposed a series of major defeats on the government, including a record five in one session in relation to its Anti-Terrorism, Crime and Security Bill 2001 which *inter alia* allowed for the detention without trial for an indefinite period of suspected international terrorists. As is apparent from any reading of the debates, this was done in no narrow partisan spirit – imposing defeats on a governing party just because they are the other side – but out of genuine concern for basic liberties. In the result, the Lords forced some important concessions from the government, a pattern that was repeated in relation to the Prevention of Terrorism Act 2005 and the Racial and Religious Hatred Bill. Notably, the Lords succeeded in imposing important liberalising amendments to the proposed new offence of incitement to religious hatred which, in a rare rebellion, were accepted by the House of Commons against the will of the Government.

It is first worth asking why the Lords works so much better as a revising Chamber than the Commons (a view widely accepted by commentators). Philip Norton (in Jones (ed), *Politics UK*, 1994, p 354) has suggested three main features of the House of Lords which render it 'particularly suitable' for the task of detailed consideration of legislation. First, as an unelected body, it cannot claim legitimacy to reject the principle of measures agreed by the elected House; thus, by default, it has to concentrate on the detail. Second, its membership includes people who have distinguished themselves in particular fields – law, education, industry, industrial relations – so that it can look at relevant legislation from the point of view of practitioners in the field rather than of professional politicians. Thus, for example, when considering the Criminal Justice Bill 1997, major speakers included former Secretaries, the Master of the Rolls and the Lord Chief Justice. Bogdanor also stresses this factor in relation to the scrutiny of EC legislation. Third, because the House does not consider money Bills, it has more time than the Commons to debate non-money Bills; furthermore, there is no provision for guillotines or closures to be imposed on debate, so that all amendments are discussed unless withdrawn.

It should be pointed out that two of the positive attributes which Norton identifies arise from the fact that the House is not elected. Its lack of legitimacy means it cannot reject the principle of Bills; the fact that it does not consider money Bills is also a reflection of its lower, because undemocratic, status. The paradoxical notion that much of the value which commentators perceive in the Lords is attributable to the one characteristic which most lays it open to attack – its unelected status – is a recurring theme in the literature on the subject.

To this can be added the relative political independence of the Lords. First of all, the large contingent of cross-bench peers ensures a strong input of non-party opinion and analysis. That around 27 per cent of peers are now independents compares strikingly to the single independent MP in the Commons at the present time – himself a rarity. Furthermore, the Lords are not as susceptible to party pressure exerted by the whips as are MPs; most have no political future to safeguard, and so are not as vulnerable to threats or promises. These conclusions are borne out by evidence as to how the Lords behaves in practice: defeats of governments of both political complexions are far more frequent than in the Commons, in which, at least if the government has a workable overall majority, they are almost unheard of. The Blair Government has so far suffered 2 defeats in the Commons on legislation (on the Terrorism Act 2006 and the Racial and Religious Hatred Bill) in nine years, during which an average of around 3,000 pages of primary legislation has been passed every year (3,500 in 2004); the Lords has inflicted numerous reversals – 219 between 1998 and 2004 alone. However, any claim that the House of Lords defies its own composition to the extent that it is actually even-handed as between the parties would be going too far. As Jack Straw noted in the Queen's Speech debate in 1998, 'In an average session when the Conservatives have been in power, there have been 13 defeats of government business in [the Lords]. In an average session when Labour has been in power, the figure has been five times that – on average, 60 defeats (HC Deb, Cols 573–574, 30 November 1998). Despite this, it is incontestable that the Lords shows far greater political independence than does the Commons. Moreover, its bias towards Conservative legislation seems to have decreased now that the parties are far more balanced.

However, while the above factors may facilitate the valuable work the House performs, its unelected and partisan make-up has led it to impose certain conventional restraints on the exercise of its own powers, which essentially mean that it is generally unwilling to impose its will upon the government-dominated Commons. These include the Salisbury Convention, that the Lords should neither vote down the principle of legislation promised in a manifesto nor pass what are known as 'wrecking amendments' to it. Under the legal restrictions on the powers of the Lords introduced by the Parliament Acts, the Lords may only in the end delay a non-money Bill for one year, provided that it has been passed by the Commons in two successive sessions and twice rejected by the Lords. Its powers over money Bills (those which relate exclusively to central government taxation, expenditure or loans) were effectively removed altogether: such Bills can be presented for the royal assent within one month, unless passed unamended by the Lords. Again, these limitations reflect the lower status of the unelected House.

Turning to the issue of reform, it is suggested that in principle, some balance needs to be struck between preserving at least some of those qualities which allow the House to perform its current valuable work – in particular, its expertise across a range of areas, its willingness to examine in detail and a relatively weak degree of party control – and remedying the basic problem of the House's undemocratic and unrepresentative nature. It is the fact that the House's undemocratic nature is strongly linked to the current value of its work that has made the problem of its reform so intractable.

As an initial point, it is suggested that mere abolition is not the answer: such a move would leave the whole problem of elective dictatorship via the Executive-controlled Commons untouched, and would mean the loss of the valuable work which the Lords undertakes in relation to government and European legislation. Moreover, the Commons would become hopelessly overworked. Turning then to proposals for a reformed second chamber, as Brigid Hadfield has pointed out ('Whither or whether the House of Lords' (1984) 35(4) NILQ 313), changing the *composition* of the Lords presents a basic problem. If the members were elected, the chamber could become simply a rival to the Commons, resulting in political impasse. Alternatively, if both chambers were dominated by the same party and the new chamber was as easily dominated by the government as the Commons, it might become redundant. Electing the second chamber might well also jeopardise the current value of its work, since the appointed independent experts who contribute so much to the value of the Lords' work would be lost, replaced by professional politicians. It was these arguments which led both Wakeham and the government in its White Paper to reject a wholly elected Lords. However, a non-elected House would also pose difficulties, both in terms of arguments over the selection procedure (though any system would seem preferable to having the Prime Minister select peers) and because of the fact that a non-elected senate would have no mandate to assert its will against the elected House of Commons. It was the lack of legitimacy of an appointed Lords, as well as its political unpopularity – clearly seen in the press response to the Wakeham and government proposals – that fatally undermined those proposals. Clearly, some balance is needed: the Lords must have greater democratic legitimacy or it will continue to be a second-class sidelined body, unwilling to assert its will even when it has a strong argument. On the other hand, making it wholly elected would risk impasse with the Commons, and perhaps more importantly jeopardise precisely those qualities of the Lords – expertise, relative independence from a party – which, it is currently agreed, make its work most worthwhile. It is therefore suggested that the way forward for the Lords is to build on the positive aspects of the Wakeham proposals – an independent statutory Commission to make appointments for the non-elected members, and determine the percentage of party peers nominated, in order to remove the unacceptable patronage of the Prime Minister of the day, the duty to achieve greater representation in terms of race, sex and regionalism, the retention of a strong independent body of peers, and introducing a strong proportion of elected peers – 50 per cent or 60 per cent as suggested by the Public Administration Committee. Recent Government statements appear to indicate a softening of its previous stance of hostility towards a mixed elected/appointed House, and the latest proposal from Jack Straw, the Leader of the Commons, is for a 50:50 mix.

The removal of the hereditary peers has had a number of beneficial effects, discussed above, including re-balancing the House, giving it more meritocratic legitimacy and thus a greater willingness to use its powers, and substantially ameliorating its most unacceptable feature. However, it is accepted that this reform is no substitute for the more radical reform suggested above, which should preserve the best features of the existing Lords, whilst giving it the legitimacy to use its powers far more extensively than at present.

NOTES

1 Students could note that the Lords also initiates a fair amount of legislation: around one-sixth of its time is spent initiating Bills which tend to concern either law reform measures, international Acts, Acts relating solely to Northern Ireland

or Scotland, and matters which are not party-politically controversial. For example, the Human Rights Act 1998 was introduced into the Lords. In this respect, the fact that the Lords does not have any constituents can be valuable: its members can safely propose and debate legislation on contentious moral issues without fearing a backlash of opinion against them; for example, the initiative to relax the prohibition against homosexual activity came from the Lords.

2 It could be noted at this point that another major area of valuable work undertaken by the House is its scrutiny of EC legislation, a task of great importance, given the ever-growing impact of such legislation on the UK. The main responsibility for this area of the Lords' work lies with the House of Lords Select Committee on the European Communities. The Committee takes evidence from a wide variety of sources; it is not hamstrung, and neither is the whole House when debating its reports, by the battle between Euro-sceptics and Europhiles which is waged interminably in the Commons, but can bring to bear a more rational analysis. Bogdanor states that 'there is widespread agreement that the scrutiny procedures adopted by the Lords are amongst the most effective in the Community' (in *The Changing Constitution*, Jowell and Oliver (eds), 3rd edn, 1994, p 12).

Question 19

'The valuable legislative function of the House of Lords is impaired because such powers as it possesses are not often used to their full effect.' Do you agree? How far, if at all, has the removal of most of the hereditary peers affected this position?

Answer plan

This is a somewhat tricky version of a typical House of Lords question. Its assumption that the House of Lords does have a valuable legislative function must be questioned, as must the implication that its role is quite severely circumscribed. Clearly, it is vital to address in detail the issue of the removal of the hereditary peers.

Essentially, the following matters should be considered:

• the formal limits on the powers of the Lords under the Parliament Acts 1911 and 1949;

• the conventions on the use of the Lords' powers; changes in the Salisbury convention since 1999 and the report of the Joint Committee on Conventions in 2006;

- the importance of conventions as compared to formal limitations;
- the role of the Lords in scrutinising legislation, particularly legislation affecting civil liberties;
- the Private Members' Bills emanating from the Lords;
- the scrutiny of delegated legislation; a convention of restraint?;
- the impact of the removal of the hereditary peers and re-balancing of the political composition of the Lords on the above; how further reform might affect the behaviour of the Lords.

Answer

This question implies that the legislative function of the House of Lords is quite severely circumscribed. Before considering the effect of such circumscription, it should first be determined how far the Lords may be said to refrain from full use of its powers and how far it is restrained from doing so by legislation.

The Lords has the same right to initiate and revise legislation as the Commons, subject to the provisions of the Parliament Acts 1911 and 1949. The Acts allow the House of Commons to assert political supremacy over the Lords in two very important instances. First, when a Bill has been passed by the Commons in two successive sessions and it is rejected for a second time by the Lords, it can be presented on its second rejection for the royal assent. One year must elapse between the second reading of the Bill in the Commons at the first session and its passing in the Commons in the second.

Second, if a Bill is a money Bill, as defined in s 1(2) of the Parliament Act 1911 (a measure which relates exclusively to central government taxation, loans or expenditure) and is passed by the Commons but not passed by the Lords without amendment within one month after it receives it, it may be presented to the Queen for the royal assent and become an Act of Parliament. This provision was brought forward after the Lords had rejected the Finance Bill 1909; essentially, it means that the Lords has no powers at all over money Bills.

However, the limits on the Lords' power under the Parliament Acts are not as significant as may at first appear. First, not all Bills are subject to the Parliament Acts. Exemption extends to private Bills, statutory instruments, Bills to extend the life of a Parliament and Bills originating in the House of Lords — a fair proportion of government legislation. Second, in practice, the government will not want to wait for over a year before securing the passage of its legislation and so will be prepared to accept compromise amendments. The Parliament Acts procedure has in fact only been used six times since 1911, indicating that the conventional limitations upon the Lords' power – together with the willingness of governments to accept amendments rather than face delay – on the whole preclude the need for the *legal* assertion of the Commons' supremacy.

Perhaps the most important, and certainly the most clearly established, convention of self-restraint has been termed the 'doctrine of the mandate' or the 'Salisbury Convention'. This doctrine was explained by Lord Salisbury in 1964 as a guiding principle that where legislation had been promised in the governing party's manifesto, the Lords would not block it on the ground that it should be regarded as having been approved by the British people. The Salisbury Convention is taken very seriously by the Lords; there has been no clear instance where the Lords has flatly rejected a manifesto Bill since the Second World War, although the Liberal Democrats have recently indicated that they no longer support the Convention.

The application of the Convention to amendments to manifesto Bills is less clear. Logically, it should preclude the Lords from amending a Bill in such a way as to remove from it some element which was promised in the manifesto or, in general, changing it so radically that it is no longer recognisable as an implementation of the manifesto pledge. But the Lords has not allowed the government of the day to be the sole judge as to whether a given amendment has this effect: thus, it has, on four occasions in the last 50 years, caused Bills to be lost by insisting on what the Labour governments of the day saw as 'wrecking amendments', thus causing a Bill to run out of time and be lost. The House of Commons (Redistribution of Seats) Bill in 1968–69 was one example. A more recent display of the Lords' activism was provoked by the European Parliamentary Elections Bill 1998, a controversial example, because the Bill itself clearly fulfilled a manifesto pledge – to introduce proportional representation for elections for the European Parliament. As passed by the Commons, the Bill provided that the voting system to be used would see MEPs elected on a 'closed' list system, whereby votes would be cast for a party only, so that the party, not the voter, would select the actual candidates who were elected. The Lords inserted an amendment which would have changed it to an 'open' list system, and then repeatedly re-inserted this amendment upon its repeated rejection by the Commons. Following the Lords' fifth restoration of the amendment, it was clear that the Bill had run out of time and the government announced that it was lost. Defending itself against the charge that its insistence on the amendment breached the Convention, Lord Mackay cited the relevant manifesto pledge: 'We have long supported a proportional voting system for election to the European Parliament', and pointed out there was 'no mention' of the electoral system to be used. The Joint Committee on Conventions reported in 2006, finding that the Salisbury Convention now included three components: first the House of Lords should not vote down a manifesto Bill on 2nd Reading; second, that the Lords will not pass 'wrecking amendments' to it, and third, that it will be passed and returned back to the Commons for consideration of any Lords amendments.

In relation to non-manifesto Bills, there is more of a general practice of self-restraint than a clear convention. The Lords very rarely reject government Bills outright; indeed, the rejection of the War Crimes Bill 1990 and the Parliament Bill 1947 represent the only occasions when this happened in 50 years. The Lords is also reluctant, in practice, to restore amendments to any Bill which the government has had overturned in the Commons. Indeed, O Hood Phillips has suggested (*Constitutional and Administrative Law*, 7th edn, 1987, p 148) that there is almost a convention that the Lords will not return a government Bill to the Commons for reconsideration more than once. That this is indeed not a firm convention, but merely a general description of practice has been vividly illustrated by events surrounding the European Elections Bill, in which, as noted, the Lords restored its rejected amendment no less then five times. It took a similarly assertive stance over the Teaching and Higher Education Bill 1998: a provision in the Bill which waived the payment of fees for the fourth year of a degree taken at a Scottish university for Scottish students, but not those from the rest of the UK, led the Lords to restore on three occasions an amendment rejected by the Commons which equalised the position for students from all parts of the UK. The government was eventually forced to promise an independent review of the system within six months of its establishment, an important concession.

In 2000, following the reform of the Lords removing most of the hereditary peers – a matter considered further below – the House took a still more assertive stance in its response to a controversial piece of *primary* legislation, which would have restricted the right of a defendant to choose trial by jury. The heart of the government's Criminal Justice (Mode of Trial) Bill was cl 1, which removed the right of defendants to choose jury trial in 'either way' offences, such as theft and burglary. The crucial part of the debate took part in Committee stage and only got as far as cl 1. The very first amendment put down restored the right of the defendant to be tried by a jury in such cases at his election, and thus ripped the heart out of the Bill. It was therefore what is commonly referred to as a 'wrecking amendment', since it altered the fundamental principle of the legislation. This amendment was carried in the Lords by a large majority. The government spokeswoman, Baroness Jay, immediately announced that since the Bill 'no longer represented government policy', it would be withdrawn. It is important to note that the Bill started life in the Lords, not the Commons. Therefore, by effectively throwing out the Bill, the Lords had prevented the Commons being able even to see it. A report in *The Times* remarked that this was the 'first time in memory' that 'a mainstream Bill' had been 'killed . . . before it had reached the elected House'. The House of Lords also insisted on amendments to the Terrorism Acts of 2001 and 2005, although giving way on a number of others (see Phillipson (2004) PL 352).

Although the House of Lords is generally reluctant to engage in a head-on collision with the Commons and therefore uses its powers circumspectly, this does not mean that it has no value as a means of keeping a check on the activities of the other chamber. Indeed, most commentators accept that the House of Lords has a valuable part to play in the British constitutional process. Perhaps its most important role lies in scrutinising public Bills passed by the House of Commons, on which it spends around half of its time. The House passes a large amount of amendments to such Bills: in the 1987–90 sessions, the average number of amendments passed was over 2,600. The vast majority of these were subsequently accepted by government (2,038 out of 2,056 in the 1992–93 session), reflecting the fact that most are introduced by government and are technical in nature. However, the Lords is not simply a forum in which a government can correct its own mistakes. Barnett's conclusion is that 'the Lords is both very active in relation to legislation, and makes a substantial impact on many legislative proposals' (*Constitutional and Administrative Law*, 4th edn, 2002, p 532). A significant number of its amendments represent changes of principle of a minor or major nature. To an extent, therefore, the Lords can compensate for the inadequate scrutiny bestowed by the Commons, scrutiny which is widely perceived as consisting merely of a party battle, rather than a rigorous assessment of the merits of legislative proposals. It can therefore provide a much needed check on the government-dominated Commons, a check which is particularly valuable when, as present, the government in power has a large majority, thereby rendering the Opposition largely ineffective. The Lords may delay controversial or unpopular legislation, or it may be able to procure the acceptance of amendments which are unwelcome to the government. It has done both on a number of occasions during the 1980s and 1990s, at a time when Oppositions have been wholly unable to do likewise.

Thus, during the 1980s, due to the nature of the parliamentary process, the Labour party in the Commons was helpless in the face of the large Conservative majority. In contrast, the Lords inflicted 173 defeats on the government between 1979 and 1991, some of them relating to important and controversial measures.[1] The Lords has also, as noted above, defied the present government which, with its decisive majority, can steamroller opposition in the Commons.

The Lords is often seen as having a particularly important role to play in the protection of civil liberties, an issue to which the Commons may often show little sensitivity when both parties feel obliged to show their 'toughness' on law and order issues. For example, in January 1997, the Lords defeated the government to procure an important amendment of principle to the Police Act 1997. As originally conceived, the Bill gave police officers the power to enter premises to plant listening devices to assist in the detection of crime. Authorisation was to be given by the Chief Constable; by contrast, when the police want to tap phones, they must obtain a warrant from the Home Secretary. There was also no exception in relation to bugging premises where conversations involving legal professional privilege might take place – listening devices could therefore have been planted at the offices of lawyers. The Lords inserted an amendment to compel the police to seek prior judicial approval before installing listening devices, forcing the government to bring forward its own, similar proposals.

Where, however, civil liberties clash with the fight against terrorism, historically, the Lords has sometimes fared no better than the Commons in forcing governments to reconsider sometimes draconian measures. Indeed, it has often offered no resistance at all to the rushing through of legislation, often in response to particular atrocities, refusing to exercise even to a small degree its powers to debate legislation at length. Thus, the Lords offered no resistance in 1974 to the first Prevention of Terrorism Bill, passed through both Houses in a single day, following the outrage generated by the Birmingham pub bombings. The Prevention of Terrorism (Additional Powers) Bill 1996 was likewise passed in one day, as was the Criminal Justice (Terrorism and Conspiracy) Bill 1998, which passed through the Lords in a few hours, despite its far-reaching implications for civil liberties (it allows a conviction of membership of a proscribed organisation to be obtained on the combination of the word of a senior police officer and inferences from silence). Despite expressions of deep unease that were heard from numerous peers, the Lords felt that it would be 'irresponsible' to delay the Bill. Such instances represent particularly marked refusals by the Lords to use its powers.

Again, however, it appears that the removal of the hereditary peers has had some effect here. The Anti-Terrorism, Crime and Security Bill 2001, introduced into Parliament in response to the perceived greater threat from international terrorism following the attacks on America on September 11 2001, represented a significant test for the Lords. The Bill was a long one: 126 clauses and eight lengthy Schedules. The most controversial part of the Bill allowed for the indefinite detention of suspected international terrorists, albeit with some judicial oversight, which required the UK to derogate from Art 5 of the European Convention on Human Rights. However, much of the Bill did not in fact deal with specific anti-terrorism measures. It included a new offence of incitement to religious hatred which, in itself, would clearly provide no assistance in the fight against terrorism, new police powers extending to all criminal suspects – not just suspected terrorists, and measures to put in place a new Code of Practice on retention of communications data – websites visited, mobile phone calls made and so on. The approach of the Lords may be contrasted with that of the Commons, which first of all accepted a timetable of only 16 hours in which to scrutinise a Bill 124 pages long, and then imposed not a single amendment on the government. By contrast, their Lordships imposed a series of major defeats on the government, including a record five in one session and, as is apparent from any reading of the debates, this was done in no narrow partisan spirit – imposing defeats on a governing party just because they are the other side – but out of genuine concern for basic liberties. On some points, the government was forced to accept complete defeat: the proposed creation of an offence of incitement to religious hatred was repeatedly rejected by the Lords and eventually dropped from the Bill altogether. The Lords also procured the insertion of 'sunset' clauses against government resistance, whereby the more draconian aspects of the legislation would automatically lapse after a specified period. However, the House did eventually accept compromises from the government on other issues, including on the exclusion of judicial review in relation to the detention of suspected terrorists and on the controversial information-sharing provisions. This compromise in particular – it did not restrict the scope of the information-sharing provision to terrorist-related offences, as the Lords had wanted – seems to illustrate clearly the point that the House's lack of perceived legitimacy as an undemocratic body in the end crucially weakens its resolve to resist proposals approved by the elected Commons. The Lords took a similarly activist stance in relation to the anti-terrorism legislation of 2005 and 2006, as well as the Racial and Religious Hatred Bill 2005. The Lords amendments passed to that Bill not only ensured that the offence could only be committed with specific intent, but also contained an important saving clause, designed to ensure a very robust degree of protection for freedom of speech in relation to the discussion of religious matters. Their insistence upon these amendments eventually resulted in the Commons accepting them, in a very rare legislative rebellion against the government.

It should of course be remembered that the Lords' value does not only lie in its ability to amend or delay legislation: Bills which are not seen as contentious in party-political terms, such as the National Heritage Bill (1980–81 session), are regularly introduced into the Lords, thus relieving pressure in the Commons. Private Members' Bills may also be put down by peers.[2]

The Lords also performs a valuable service by contributing to the scrutiny of delegated legislation. Its powers in this respect are the same as those of the House of Commons, as they were not curbed by the Parliament Acts. For example, on occasion, a point raised in debate in the Lords may lead the government to withdraw the legislation in question with a view to amending it. However, a very clear picture of self-restraint emerges in this area also: up until 2000, the Lords had only once since 1945 thrown out a piece of delegated legislation, and that was the highly controversial Southern Rhodesia Order 1968. Indeed, some observers were of the view that there was in fact a convention that the Lords would not reject delegated legislation at all. The Wakeham Report appeared to act on this assumption, in recommending that the Lords' unused veto power should be replaced by a short power of delay; this was in spite of the fact that when, in 1994, it was suggested to the House that a convention had come into being that the Lords would not vote down items of subordinate legislation, their Lordships' response was bullish: a motion by Lord Simon of Glaisdale to the effect that the House had unfettered freedom to vote on any subordinate legislation before it was overwhelmingly approved in October of that year.

In this area, the removal of the hereditary peers seems to have had a particularly clear effect. The Lords in 2000 was unhappy with the refusal of the government, in its legislation governing the London mayor and assembly, to give candidates a free 'mail shot' to the electorate. The Lords chose to express its discontent on the matter in a novel way: it voted on a piece of secondary legislation – the Greater London Authority (Election Expenses) Order 2000, which dealt with the nuts and bolts of the London mayoral and assembly elections, in particular, the amount of electoral expenditure which candidates would be allowed to incur; the Order required only negative approval, that is, it would go through automatically unless voted against. Erskine May reveals that the House has *never* voted down orders requiring only the negative approval procedure. Nevertheless, the Lords, to the consternation of the government, threw the Order out and in so doing, quite clearly relied upon its newly reformed status. During the debate, there was some disagreement about whether the practice of the Lords not to reject secondary legislation had achieved the status of a constitutional convention. Some peers certainly took this view, while others firmly rejected such a notion, pointing to the House's resolution of October 1994 cited above. Others, such as Lord Cranbourne for the Conservatives, still appeared to believe that while there may have been a convention that the House would not reject such legislation, it would not apply now, the House being a reformed chamber, which was not necessarily bound by the conventions of the unreformed House. In general, there was strong support for a more assertive attitude on the part of the new House. The Government's evidence to the Joint Committee on Conventions took the view that it was a breach of convention for the Lords to reject statutory instruments; the Committee in its 2006 report clearly rejected this view, concluding that this was not so, but that the power to reject should be exercised only in exceptional circumstances, including in particular in relation to delegated legislation which altered primary legislation and where the statutory instrument deals with matters normally found in primary legislation.

On the whole, however, the general picture is clear: the House of Lords, which is in a weaker position to resist government Bills (both legally and by convention) than the Commons, in fact utilises its ability to improve Bills in matters of detail, to introduce important changes of principle and to force the government to reconsider far more than the theoretically omnipotent Commons. Thus, the criticism outlined in the question applies in fact less to the second chamber than the first.

It may therefore be argued that the Lords has managed to create a delicate balance between appearing as a superfluous body which merely rubber stamps the Commons' decisions, and as an undemocratic and anachronistic body which interferes too far in the legislative function of the elected part of Parliament. It is clear that the removal of the hereditary peers has already resulted in a more assertive attitude from their Lordships. However, given that the core reason for their restraint – their undemocratic status – has not been touched by the removal of the hereditaries – it is unlikely that either the Salisbury Convention or the House's nuanced convention of general restraint will disappear until more comprehensive, democratic reform gives the House unquestionable legitimacy.

NOTES

1 Students could give the example of the Lords' response to the government's highly contentious policy of restricting the appeal and social security rights of asylum seekers in the UK, as set out in the Asylum Bill 1996. The basic policy of the Bill is to draw up a 'white list' of countries considered safe; asylum seekers from these countries would face a presumption against their admittance and a 'fast track' procedure for determining their application which would limit their rights of appeal. The amendment carried in the Lords (on 23 April 1996) would exempt from the 'white list' category applicants 'who can show a reasonable claim that [they] have been a victim of torture' in their own country and those 'claiming to fear persecution in a country which has a recently documented record of torture' and would therefore considerably restrict the amount of applicants subject to the new provisions. The amendment thus represents a significant attack on the policy behind the Bill.

2 Students could expand on this point by noting that Private Members' Bills introduced in the Lords may not receive the royal assent, but may be valuable for raising debate and stimulating interest. For example, the Anti-Discrimination (No 2) Bill 1972–73 raised interest when being discussed by the Lords' Select Committee. This led to espousal of the Bill first by back benchers and then by the government. The eventual result was the Sex Discrimination Act 1975. It may also be pointed out that as the Lords has no constituents to whom it is accountable, it may feel free to bring forward Private Members' Bills on emotive and contentious subjects, such as homosexuality and abortion. The initiative for relaxing the law relating to homosexual conduct, which eventually resulted in the passing of the Sexual Offences Act 1967, came from the Lords, not the Commons.

Question 20

In the light of the current nature and work of the House of Lords and its value, evaluate the recent proposals for reform of the House of Lords including those of The Royal Commission under Lord Wakeham and the Public Administration Committee (PAC) in their Fifth Report (HC 494, 2001–02). What in your view is the best way forward for comprehensive reform?

Answer plan

This question, or something similar to it, is almost bound to appear on examination papers over the next few years until concrete plans differing from those of Wakeham are brought forward in the form of draft legislation. The version given here is quite tricky, as it requires specific comparisons to be made with the proposals of the Public Administration Committee (PAC). The answer requires evaluation in the light of the value of the current work of the Lords, so specific examples of that work should be given, and an explanation produced as to why that work is valuable and how far different reform proposals might risk jeopardising it in the search for a more legitimate and representative House.

Essentially, the following matters should be considered:

- a brief outline of what is valuable in the current work of the Lords, and how that relates to its composition;
- an outline of the Wakeham proposals, with indications of how the Government's White Paper differed;
- the criticisms of Wakeham and of the White Paper;
- the counter-proposals of the PAC;
- the limited area of consensus;
- the argument for a wholly elected House;
- conclusion.

Answer

In tackling the above question, the following approach will be taken. In order to set the context for analysis of the value of the current House, a brief outline of its composition will first be given. Second, the essay will seek to discuss briefly what is generally agreed to be of value about the current House of Lords and how this is related to its current composition. Third, it will outline the proposals of Wakeham and the White Paper and indicate the main criticisms of them. Finally, the essay will contrast these with the reforms suggested by the PAC, and explain why it is argued that these represent a better compromise between the competing aims of reforming this most unusual second chamber.

It is necessary first to describe briefly the current House of Lords. There are still three main groups in the Lords, although following the House of Lords Act 1999, the balance between the life and hereditary peers has swung dramatically in the former's favour. As at end November 2006, the House numbered 750 peers, of whom 606 are life peers and only 92 hereditaries, those selected for retention by a vote of the hereditary peers only. The Bishops and Law Lords remain. Not only is the House thus wholly undemocratic, it is also unrepresentative of women. In 1998, there were only 96 female peers out of 1,273, that is, less than 10 per cent. That was largely due to the fact that the vast majority of hereditary peerages descend only to male issue. This has now improved to 142 women out of a total of 750, or nearly 19 per cent.

The House's second major affront to democracy formerly lay in the fact that one party, the Conservatives, historically had a permanent strong predominance; the position here has undergone a more marked improvement. In January 1998, out of a total of 1,146 peers, 495 were Conservatives, 322 cross-benchers (independent peers), 157 Labour and 68 Liberal Democrat. Conservative peers thus outnumbered Labour Lords by around 4:1. The hereditaries, as one would expect, were overwhelmingly Conservative-leaning: 319 took the Conservative whip, compared to only 16 Labour peers. A more useful guide to party influence can be gained by examining the allegiance of those who attended more than 50 per cent of the sessions – only about one-third of peers. The figures for the 1996–97 session showed that out of a total of 399, the Conservatives had 195, or 49 per cent; the cross-benchers and Labour both had 83, or 21 per cent; while the Liberal Democrats had 37, or 9 per cent.

Following the removal of the bulk of the hereditaries and a deliberate and successful attempt by Mr Blair to rebalance the Lords through his appointment of large numbers of life peers, the position has undergone a significant change. As at end November 2006, Labour is now the largest single party, but only by a handful of peers: Labour has 212 seats, the Conservatives 207, while the Liberal Democrats have increased their seats notably to 78. Very importantly, there are now 201 cross-bench peers, who now represent 27 per cent of the total. While the Conservatives are still over-represented, given that they came well behind Labour in the popular vote in the last three General Elections, their preponderance has been substantially reduced, and in practice all legislation requires cross-party support to pass. Peers taking a party whip are appointed by the Queen on the advice of the Prime Minister; new cross-bench peers are nominated by the (non-statutory) Appointments Commission and appointed by the Queen.

Thus, in practice, all legislation requires cross-party support to pass. This provides a marked contrast to the position in the House of Commons, where the electoral system generally gives one party an overall majority, and often a large one, as recently under Blair, even though that party has not gained a majority of the popular vote.

It may now be asked, what is thought to be of value about the current House and its work, and how is this related to its composition? Answering this question will enable us to take some first steps towards evaluating the various reform packages mentioned in the question. The value of the current House can perhaps be summed up as being: relative independence from party and government control; expertise; and readiness to consider and amend legislation in detail. These points will now be expanded upon.

Despite its undemocratic and unrepresentative nature, most commentators accept that the House of Lords has a valuable part to play in the British constitutional process. Perhaps its most important role lies in scrutinising public Bills passed by the House of Commons, on which it spends around half of its time. The House passes a large amount of amendments to such Bills: in the 1987–90 sessions, the average number of amendments passed was over 2,600. The vast majority of these were subsequently accepted by government, reflecting the fact that most are introduced by government and are technical in nature. However, the Lords is not simply a forum in which government can correct its own mistakes. Barnett's conclusion is that 'the Lords is both very active in relation to legislation, and makes a substantial impact on many legislative proposals' (*Constitutional and Administrative Law*, 4th edn, 2002, p 532). A significant number of its amendments represent changes of principle of a minor or major nature. To an extent, therefore, the Lords can compensate for the inadequate scrutiny bestowed by the Commons, providing a much needed check on the government, a check which is particularly valuable when, as at present, the government in power has a large majority, thereby rendering the Opposition largely ineffective. The Lords may delay controversial or unpopular legislation, or it may be able to procure the acceptance of amendments which are unwelcome to the government. It has done both on a number of occasions in the last two decades, during times when Oppositions have been wholly unable to do likewise.

Recently, for example, the Lords broke with a (contested) convention in 2000 by rejecting a a piece of secondary legislation – the Greater London Authority (Election Expenses) Order 2000 – which dealt with the nuts and bolts of the London mayoral and assembly elections.[1] The Lords has also provided protection for a fundamental right: the right to jury trial. In 2000, the House inflicted a major defeat on the government over its Criminal Justice (Mode of Trial) Bill, which removed the right of defendants to choose jury trial in 'either way' offences, such as theft and burglary. As in this instance, the Lords is often seen as having a particularly important role to play in the protection of civil liberties, an issue to which the Commons may show little sensitivity when both main parties feel obliged to show their 'toughness' on law and order issues. Examples include the amendment inserted by the Lords to the Police and Criminal Evidence Bill 1984 allowing evidence unfairly obtained to be excluded, which eventually prompted the government to put forward its own amendment, which became s 78 of the Act, the rejection of the War Crimes Bill 1990 and the amendment made to the Police Act 1997 to ensure prior judicial approval before the police could install listening devices. Similarly, in 2001, their Lordships imposed a series of major defeats on the government, including a record five in one session in relation to its Anti-Terrorism, Crime and Security Bill 2001, which *inter alia* allowed for the detention without trial for an indefinite period of suspected international terrorists. The Lords forced some important concessions from the government, a pattern that was repeated in relation to the Prevention of Terrorism Act 2005 and the Racial and Religious Hatred Bill. Notably, the Lords succeeded in imposing important liberalising amendments to the proposed new offence of incitement to religious hatred which, in a rare rebellion, were accepted by the House of Commons against the will of the Government.

Why then does the Lords work so much better as a revising chamber than the Commons (a view widely accepted by commentators)? Philip Norton (in Jones (ed.), *Politics UK*, 1994, p 354) has suggested three main features of the House of Lords which render it 'particularly suitable' for the task of detailed consideration of legislation. First, as an unelected body, it cannot claim legitimacy to reject the principle of measures agreed by the elected House; thus, by default, it has to concentrate on the detail. Second, its membership includes people who have distinguished themselves in particular fields – law, education, industry and industrial relations – so that it can look at relevant legislation from the point of view of practitioners in the field rather than of professional politicians. Third, because the House does not consider money Bills, it has more time than the Commons to debate non-money Bills; furthermore, there is no provision for guillotines or closures to be imposed on debate, so that all amendments are discussed unless withdrawn.

It should be pointed out that two of the positive attributes which Norton identifies arise from the fact that the House is not elected. Its lack of legitimacy means it cannot reject the principle of Bills; the fact that it does not consider money Bills is also a reflection of its lower, because undemocratic, status. The paradoxical notion that much of the value which commentators perceive in the Lords is attributable to the one characteristic which most lays it open to attack – its unelected status – is a recurring theme in the literature on the subject.

To this can be added the relative political independence of the Lords. Whilst, as noted above, the Conservatives are still over-represented given their defeats in the last three General Elections, the House is overall, now quite balanced. First of all, the large contingent of cross-bench peers ensures a strong input of non-party opinion and analysis. That around 27 per cent of peers are now independent compares strikingly to the single independent MP in the Commons at the present time – himself a rarity. Furthermore, the Lords are not as susceptible to party pressure exerted by the whips as are MPs; most have no political future to safeguard, and so are not as vulnerable to threats or promises. These conclusions are borne out by evidence as to how the Lords behaves in practice: defeats of governments of both political complexions are far more frequent than in the Commons, in which, at least if the government has a workable overall majority, they are almost unheard of. The Blair Government has so far suffered 2 defeats in the Commons on legislation (on the Terrorism Act 2006 and the Racial and Religious Hatred Bill) in nine years, during which an average of around 3,000 pages of primary legislation has been passed every year (3,500 in 2004); the Lords has inflicted numerous reversals: 219 between 1998 and 2004 alone.

However, while the above factors may facilitate the valuable work the House performs, its unelected and partisan make-up has led it to impose certain conventional restraints on the exercise of its own powers, which essentially means that it is generally unwilling to impose its will upon the government-dominated Commons. These restraints include the Salisbury Convention, that the Lords should neither vote down the principle of legislation promised in a manifesto nor pass what are known as 'wrecking amendments' to it.[2]

In the light of the above, we may now turn to a basic outline of the reforms suggested by Wakeham and others and an evaluation of them. Wakeham's proposals can be briefly stated: the *powers* of the new chamber will be broadly comparable with those of the present Lords, though the report does suggest changes to its powers over delegated legislation; indeed, all the proposals cited in the question broadly leave the powers of the Lords unchanged. They have thus rejected the suggestion, favoured by the Liberal Democrats (amongst others) that the new chamber should have powers to delay a Bill certified by the Speaker as affecting human rights or important constitutional matters for the life of a Parliament, leaving the House markedly out of step with nearly all other second chambers in liberal democracies, which universally have special powers over constitutional legislation, as Russell's research establishes (*Reforming the Lords: Lessons from Overseas*, 2000).

It is Wakeham's proposals on composition that have proved most controversial. The report suggests a mainly appointed House of 550, with a minority of elected members to represent the regions. Unable to agree on an appropriate size for the democratic element, it instead put forward three options: option A, 65 members; option B, 87 members; and option C, 195 elected peers, which would be a substantial element at over one-third of the total membership. These first two options are clearly somewhat tokenistic in nature. The remainder of the House would be appointed by a statutory, independent Appointments Committee, which would scrutinise proposals put forward by the parties for new members of the House. It would be under a statutory duty to maintain an independent element of 20 per cent in the House, to ensure that at least 30 per cent of new members were women and that ethnic minorities were represented in numbers at least proportionate to their representation in the total population. It would also aim to ensure that the parties were represented roughly in proportion to the votes cast in the most recent General Election, thus removing the long standing permanent domination of the House by one party: the Conservatives. The powers of the Prime Minister in this area would be wholly removed: the Committee would have sole jurisdiction over appointments and be under no obligation to accept any nominations put to it.

The White Paper accepted the fundamentals of the Wakeham proposals. The key controversial changes which it proposed in relation to composition were as follows: first, it suggested leaving the parties to nominate the political non-elected members (Wakeham had proposed that the Appointments Commission should do this); second, the government proposed allowing both nominated and elected members to stand again; third, it suggested reducing the 15 year terms for members proposed by Wakeham. These changes are controversial, because taken together, their effect would be radically to increase party control over both the selection of members and their likely behaviour – since the threat of not being re-selected for membership could be used to enforce obedience to the whips. Shorter terms would make the threat of de-selection a more pressing one. It was these changes that led the parliamentary members of the Royal Commission to refuse to support the White Paper.

In terms of moving towards evaluation of the Wakeham/government proposals, Russell's work is the leading study in this area, in terms of identifying, through comparative analysis, the crucial factors which make for an effective second chamber. As summarised by the PAC, the reformed Lords should have the following qualities: (i) *distinct composition* – it is important that the House maintains a different make-up from the Commons, as at present; otherwise, it will not make any distinctive contribution to the legislative process. In particular, it is important to maintain its qualities of relative independence and expertise. It is also vital to ensure that the party balance in the chamber is different and more proportional from that in the Commons, to prevent one-party domination, giving the House an alternative and more broadly based perspective on the development of public policy; (ii) *adequate powers* – if the new Upper House is to make a significant impact, it will need to at least maintain its present, moderate powers; (iii) *perceived legitimacy* – in order to use its powers to the full, the new chamber (unlike the existing House of Lords) will need to be seen to have legitimacy, and be able to carry public support.

The Wakeham proposals clearly fulfil the first of these, in that the membership will be distinct from that of the Commons, in particular, because of the 20 per cent proportion of independent members; just as significantly, party balance in the Lords will form a strong contrast to the position in the Commons, since neither the government nor any other party in the Lords will have an overall majority. The current *powers* of the Lords are recognisably at the moderate end of the international spectrum, as Russell finds, though the proposed removal of the absolute veto over delegated legislation would amount to a significant weakening. The case for this change has now also arguably been lost, given that the Lords is now clearly prepared to use its veto power, as with the delegated legislation relating to the London assembly in 2000. The Joint Committee on Conventions, reporting in

2006, clearly rejected the notion that it was a breach of convention for the Lords to use this power, although it recommended that this should be done only sparingly. It is in relation to the third factor that Wakeham and *a fortiori* the White Paper fall down. Certainly, the general response to Wakeham and particularly to the White Paper in the press and elsewhere suggests that it would not be seen as sufficiently legitimate. The PAC's view was that the public were simply not prepared to support or even tolerate the continuation of such extensive patronage, certainly not from the political parties, but probably not even from an independent Appointments Commission.

The proposals of the PAC back Wakeham over the Appointments Commission, the 20 per cent proportion of independent members (who should be picked for their expertise and authority in their fields, especially human rights and constitutional matters), and the targets for making the House more representative in terms of gender, race, etc; they aim in essence to preserve the House's independence and expertise; to give it far greater legitimacy by increasing the elected element to a majority of the House' members. The PAC suggested 60 per cent, a figure which they thought represented the 'centre of gravity' amongst MPs.

Before reaching a conclusion on the above proposals, the obvious and seemingly more radical and democratic alternative – a fully elected House – should be considered. Such a House commands considerable public support, according to polls, and is the long standing policy of the Liberal Democrats. However, it is suggested that calls for such a House are simplistic and misguided. As noted above, most commentators on the current House agree that much of its value flows precisely from the fact that it is *not* elected. Amongst other things, its unelected nature leads to its relative political independence, its freedom from populist pressures, and in particular the presence of experts in various fields, which gives its scrutiny of legislation a mastery of important points of detail generally lacking in the Commons. The most common objection to a wholly elected House is that it would become simply a rival to the Commons, resulting in political impasse. It is suggested that this objection is somewhat simplistic, as it fails to take account of the fact that the new chamber could, via legislation, be given a clearly subordinate role and a different purpose from the Commons (that is, to act at present as a scrutinising and revising House, rather than one which challenges the Commons on matters of basic principle). The argument also does not take into account the legal limitations on the House represented by the Parliament Acts.

It is submitted that the real objection to a fully elected chamber is, as with all elections, that it would be practically impossible for anyone, save perhaps a few well known mavericks, to win a seat without standing as a member of one of the main political parties. Thus, the new chamber would be far more dominated than now by whipped party members. When both chambers were dominated by the same party, as would generally be the case, the second chamber would be most unlikely to offer any distinctive voice in the legislative process. This problem would be particularly acute if the Lords were, like the Commons, elected using the first-past-the-post system, which tends to over-represent the largest parties and under-represent the smaller. Electing the second chamber might well also jeopardise the current value of its work, in that its expertise and the presence within it of a range of viewpoints beyond party orthodoxies would be wholly lost.

If, for these reasons, it is accepted that the new chamber should have a mixture of party politicians and independents within it, then the PAC proposals begin to look the most attractive of those considered here. The strong elected element would give the House a hugely increased sense of legitimacy and would encourage it to use its powers to make the government think again, particularly where issues of basic human rights, the protection of unpopular minorities and/or constitutional change are at stake, as with the Anti-Terrorism Bill 2001. By contrast, a House based on the Wakeham, or worse, the government's blueprint, could ultimately be brushed aside as being dominated by party appointees. As Russell observes, the Canadian Senate is ultimately an ineffectual House, despite its very strong formal powers, precisely because of its lack of legitimacy as an appointed body. A 20 per cent elected element, as the government suggests (a slight increase on Wakeham's model B proposal), would simply not be enough to give the House enough self-belief to confront the government repeatedly and make it think again. For these reasons, it is concluded that the proposals of the PAC would combine the existing strengths of the House with the legitimacy to make it a far more influential voice in the political process, and are thus most worthy of support. In this respect, recent Government indications that it may be prepared to back such a reform are to be welcomed.

▎NOTES

1 A further example could be given: the Lords thrice rejected a provision in the Teaching and Higher Education Bill 1998 which waived the payment of fees for the fourth year of a degree taken at a Scottish university for Scottish students, but not for those from the rest of the UK, a provision which had attracted widespread opposition outside Parliament. The government was eventually forced to promise an independent review of the system within six months of its establishment, an important concession.

2 Students could make the point that this sense of its own lack of legitimacy was, perhaps, the factor that led the House to compromise so markedly in finally accepting many provisions of the Anti-Terrorism Bill 2001 (above) which it had initially rejected.

CHAPTER 5

PREROGATIVE POWERS

█ INTRODUCTION

Essay questions, as opposed to problems, tend to be set in this area and will usually concentrate on the extent to which courts can control the exercise of prerogative power. Interest may, however, start to focus more on the prerogatives relating to the appointment of a Prime Minister and the power to dissolve Parliament, if it seems that proportional representation (much more likely to produce uncertain situations in this respect) is likely to be adopted. Nevertheless, although this area can be tricky, partly due to the difficulty of defining terms such as 'the royal prerogative', students will probably find it fairly straightforward to revise because they do not need to cover an enormous amount of material. The impact of the Human Rights Act 1998 should also be considered, though at the time of writing, there is little significant case law specifically on its effect on the prerogative. Recent parliamentary support for a significant increase in parliamentary controls over the prerogative, either by way of legislation, or by the creation of a new constitutional convention, should also be considered.

Checklist

Students should be familiar with the following areas:

- the nature of prerogative powers;
- the more important prerogatives: the power to dissolve Parliament, to assent to Bills, to declare war, to dismiss and appoint ministers; the personal prerogative of the monarch: various immunities such as the Queen's personal immunity from suit or prosecution and property rights;
- the ambiguities surrounding the right to dissolve Parliament or to refuse a dissolution, etc;

- the matters which the courts have traditionally considered in relation to the prerogative: its existence and extent, its relationship with statute and the duty of the Crown to compensate citizens affected by prerogative powers;
- *Council of Civil Service Unions v Minister for the Civil Service* (the *GCHQ* case) (1984): powers exercised under the prerogative may be open to review; excluded categories of prerogative power and how they have been cut down since GCHQ; the impact of the Human Rights Act 1998 on review of the prerogative;
- the current near-absence of parliamentary controls over the exercise of the prerogative, particularly in relation to the use of armed force, and proposals for reform.

Question 21

How far do you think it is true to say that the role of judges in relation to the exercise of the royal prerogative may now prevent arbitrary Executive action?

Answer plan

This question is often asked in one form or another and is reasonably straightforward. Students should not spend much of their essay rehearsing legal history by outlining the 'old' position; rather, the emphasis should be on the *GCHQ* case and how the 'excluded categories' have fared since then. Discussion of of the impact of the Human Rights Act (HRA) 1998 will also gain marks.

Essentially, the following matters should be discussed:

- a definition of the prerogative;
- the historic willingness of the courts to determine whether a claimed power existed in law;
- the relationship of the prerogative with statute;
- a brief mention of the 'old' position on review of the exercise of the prerogative; the *GCHQ* case: powers exercised under the prerogative may be open to review; the excluded categories of prerogative powers, and subsequent case law which has whittled them away;
- the impact of the HRA.

Answer

In his *Commentaries on the Laws of England*, Blackstone wrote that the prerogative is 'that special pre-eminence which the King has, over and above all other persons, and out of the ordinary course of the common law, in right of his royal dignity'. The term 'prerogative', then, refers to powers which the sovereign has by common law as opposed to statute. One of the pre-eminent features of British constitutional history has been the gradual transfer of the exercise of these prerogatives from the monarch to ministers, and today, the vast majority are, in practice, exercised by the Prime Minister, the Cabinet or individual ministers. The prerogative includes most key matters relating to foreign affairs, such as the making of treaties, recognition of States and the use of force, and on the domestic front the power to dissolve Parliament, to assent to Bills, to award honours, to pardon criminals, to establish universities, to regulate the Civil Service and to dismiss and appoint ministers. The personal prerogative of the monarch includes various immunities, such as the Queen's personal immunity from suit or prosecution, and property rights. As to judicial control of the prerogative, three broad questions arise. First, who has the power to determine whether a claimed prerogative power exists in law? Second, and relatedly, how do the courts police the situation whereby there appears to be a clash between prerogative and statute? Third, are the courts prepared to review the manner in which a prerogative, recognised to exist, has been exercised and if so, what are the limitations upon this review?

The courts have long asserted that it is for them to determine whether a particular prerogative power actually exists and whether the decision taken falls within its scope. The famous *Case of Proclamations (1611)* made the seminal declaration that 'the King hath no prerogative, but that which the law of the land allows him.' The courts will not allow new prerogatives to be created by Executive *fiat*. In *BBC v Johns (1965)*, the BBC claimed that a new prerogative had come into existence; in response, Diplock LJ said: 'It is 350 years and a civil war too late for the Queen's courts to broaden the prerogative. The limits within which the Executive government may impose obligations or restraints on the citizens of the United Kingdom without any statutory authority are now well settled and incapable of extension.' However, the courts have, on occasions, been prepared to allow a recognised prerogative to broaden in adapting itself to new situations: in *Malone v Metropolitan Police Commissioner (1979)*, the assertion that a prerogative power existed to authorise telephone tapping was based on the argument that no new power was being created, although an old one was being extended to a new situation.

Also disturbing in this respect was the decision in *Secretary of State for the Home Department ex p Northumbria Police Authority (1989)*. The case will be considered further below; the key issue for present purposes was whether there was a hitherto largely unrecognised prerogative power to keep the peace, under which the Home Secretary could lawfully offer to supply CS gas and plastic baton rounds to any Chief Constable whose police authority would not supply him with such equipment. The court found that there was a general prerogative to keep the Queen's peace; while the judges conceded that there was virtually no authority for such a power existing, they used the ingenious argument that the 'scarcity of references in the books to the prerogative of keeping the peace within the realm does not disprove that it exists. Rather, it may point to an unspoken assumption that it does'. It was further said that there was no need to demonstrate the existence of a prerogative to equip or supply the police force. Rather, the power under which the Home Secretary wished to act in supplying CS gas and plastic bullets could be brought under the general umbrella of the prerogative to do all that was reasonably necessary to keep the peace. This rather accommodating approach by the courts to the existence and scope of prerogative powers seems plainly incompatible with the basic notion, derived from *Entick v Carrington (1765)*, that any act infringing on liberty must be justified by some positive piece of law. *Entick* had found that specific legal authority to justify government action must be found in the law books, and that if the books were silent, then that was judgment against the government. The court in *Northumbria Police* adopted the opposite view, offering little reassurance that doubtful claims of seemingly novel prerogative powers will be closely scrutinised by a judiciary vigilant to guard against arbitrary power.

The question whether a claimed prerogative power exists in law is often complicated by the existence of a statute which covers the same or similar legal terrain, but without expressly abolishing the prerogative. Given the doctrine of the supremacy of Parliament, one would expect the statute to prevail in such a situation and, indeed, this has been the position adopted by the courts. Thus, if a statute conflicts with the prerogative without expressly abolishing it, the courts will give effect to the statute on the ground that the prerogative must be treated as in abeyance, although it is not abolished. Thus, in *AG v De Keyser's Royal Hotel (1920)*, Lord Atkinson said: ' . . . when a statute is passed . . . it abridges the royal prerogative while it is in force to this extent: that the Crown can only do the particular thing under, and in accordance with, the statutory provisions.' This basic position was affirmed, *obiter*, by the House of Lords in *Secretary of State for the Home Department ex p Fire Brigades Union (1995)*, a case which will be returned to below. However, in the *Northumbria Police* case, the issue as to whether the Home Secretary had power under prerogative to supply riot equipment directly to Chief Constables required the Court of Appeal to consider whether this power had been abridged by provisions of the then Police Act 1964, which allowed the supply of such equipment but only with the consent of the relevant police authority. It was argued that since the Home Secretary had an undoubted power under the statute to supply equipment, subject to certain requirements, he could not claim a parallel prerogative power to supply such equipment without any safeguards. The court rejected this argument on the basis that the statute did not expressly state that equipment was not to be supplied under any other power, a finding which appeared to come close to stating that statute will only oust the prerogative if it uses express words in doing so.[1] This finding, which allowed decisions in what was an area with some significance for freedom of assembly to be made under a very vaguely defined prerogative power, instead of being subject to the safeguards laid down in the area by Parliament, smacks rather of a judicial abeyance of responsibility than a determination to prevent the exercise of arbitrary power.

However, the subsequent decision of the House of Lords in *Secretary of State for the Home Department ex p Fire Brigades Union* (1995) restores some confidence in the will of the judiciary to hold the Executive to the intention of Parliament, as expressed in statute. It was held that while a statute which has been passed but not yet brought into force cannot have the effect of displacing prerogative powers in the same area, nevertheless, whilst such a statute is in force, ministers may not set up a radically alternative scheme in reliance on the prerogative, as the Home Secretary had purported to do.

Turning to the issue of the propriety of the exercise of prerogatives admitted to exist, again, an increased determination of the judiciary to ensure the legal accountability of the Executive may be discerned. The traditional view of the courts was that where the Executive acted under an admitted prerogative power, the exercise of that power was not subject to review as it would have been had the minister acted under statute (see, for example, *Burmah Oil Co v Lord Advocate (1965)* and *AG v De Keyser's Royal Hotel (1920)*). However, in *Laker Airways v Department of Trade (1977)*, Lord Denning remarked: 'Seeing that the prerogative is a discretionary power to be exercised for the public good, it follows that its exercise can be examined by the courts just as any other discretionary power which is vested in the Executive.'

This approach was approved in the landmark case of *Council of Civil Service Unions v Minister for the Civil Service (the GCHQ case) (1984)*. The House of Lords had to consider a challenge to an Instruction issued by the Prime Minister under Art 4 of the Civil Service Order in Council, which prevented staff at GCHQ belonging to national trade unions. It had first to be determined whether the decision was open to judicial review at all. In general, a person affected by a decision concerning public law matters made under statutory powers may challenge it by way of judicial review under the heads (as classified in the case) of illegality, irrationality and procedural impropriety or breach of natural justice. The House of Lords determined that the mere fact of the power deriving from the prerogative as opposed to statute was not a sufficient reason to exclude it from review. The controlling factor determining whether a particular exercise of powers under the prerogative should be open to review was held to be the subject matter of the decision, rather than the source of the power. Lord Roskill suggested a number of prerogative powers which, by virtue of their nature and subject matter, were not amenable to the judicial process; these included the making of treaties, the disposal of the armed forces, the defence of the realm, the dissolution of Parliament, the prerogative of mercy, the granting of honours and the appointment of ministers. He termed these prerogative powers 'excluded categories', and found no reason why the power to regulate the Home Civil Service should fall into such a category. Having determined that decisions taken under prerogative powers were open to review, the House of Lords then found that the decision-making process had in fact been conducted unfairly, but that this was outweighed by the national security considerations in play.

In a number of cases since *GCHQ*, the courts have begun to whittle away Lord Roskill's excluded categories, suggesting a readiness in principle to review all prerogatives other than those which relate to matters at the heart of the political process, such as the dissolution of Parliament, the appointment and dismissal of ministers and matters of high foreign policy or defence: *Secretary of State for the Foreign Office ex p Rees Mogg (1994)* confirmed that the courts would not entertain challenges to the prerogative power to conclude treaties, in this case, the Treaty of Maastricht. It should be noted, of course, that Lord Roskill's list of excluded categories does not and never did represent an authoritative statement of the law; it was an *obiter* suggestion only.

Thus, in *Secretary of State for Foreign and Commonwealth Affairs ex p Everett (1989)*, it was held that the courts were competent to review the exercise of the prerogative power of the Secretary of State to issue passports, although the power was related to foreign affairs and had traditionally been regarded as unreviewable. A further inroad into the excluded areas was made by the decision in *Secretary of State for the Home Department ex p Bentley (1993)*, a case which fell squarely within one of Lord Roskill's excluded categories, namely, the prerogative of mercy. The issue was whether the Home Secretary's refusal to recommend a posthumous pardon for Derek Bentley, executed in 1953 for the murder of a policeman, was subject to judicial review. The court held that while the criteria to be used by the Home Secretary in making his decision were 'probably a matter of policy [and so] not justiciable', the Secretary had failed to consider the different types of pardon he could grant in the situation. Declining to make any order, the court 'invited' the Secretary to reconsider the case.

A more generalised attack on the scope of the excluded categories was made in the case of *Ministry of Defence ex p Smith and Others (1996)*. A number of homosexual servicemen and women challenged the policy of the armed forces to exclude homosexuals from service. The government argued that the case involved governmental policy in relation to the armed forces, and hence amounted to a challenge to 'the exercise of a prerogative in an area – the defence of the realm – recognised by the courts to be unsuitable for judicial review'. Both the High Court and the Court of Appeal firmly rejected this argument and held the decision to be susceptible to review, although, on the facts, the challenge did not succeed. Smith

LJ took the opportunity to put down a more general pointer, commenting that in his view, 'only the rarest cases' would be non-justiciable, those which involved 'national security properly so called and where in addition, the courts really do lack the expertise or material to form a judgment on the point at issue'. The remark was not confirmed by the Court of Appeal, but was not repudiated by it either.

The most recent cases are *R (on the Application of Abbasi & Anor) v Secretary of State for Foreign and Commonwealth Affairs & Secretary of State for the Home Department (2003)* and *CND v The Prime Minister of the United Kingdom and others (2002)*, which together confirm the courts' strong disinclination to review powers exercised in relation to foreign affairs and the use of armed force. In the former, a British national detained at Guantenamo bay argued that, since he was being subject, in effect, to arbitrary detention, in violation of habeus corpus, the Foreign Office had a duty either to make representations on his behalf to the US Government, or at the least, to explain why they had in fact taken no action in relation to his case. The Court's finding was that the mere fact that the prerogative power in relation to foreign affairs was in issue was not enough to oust the jurisdiction of the court – it was the particular subject matter that was determinative. Moreover, in an extreme case where the Foreign Office appeared to be refusing even to consider making representations to the US Government about someone in the position of the applicant, judicial review would lie; however, such consideration had been given in this case, and there was no question of the court ordering the Government to make representations. In the latter decision, CND requested the court to determine the correct legal interpretation of UNSC Resolution 1441, which gave Iraq a final chance to comply with previous resolutions as to disarmament and threatened serious consequences if it did not. It was of course not in dispute that the court did not have the lawful power to prevent the UK Government from commencing hostilities against Iraq by way of injunction or a quashing order: the question was whether the court could declare whether the Resolution did, or did not give the UK Government lawful grounds, as a matter of international law, to take such action, in the event of non-compliance by the Iraqi Government. The court in this case firmly disclaimed the invitation to enter upon any such determination on a number of grounds. In terms of the issues discussed here, the key reason was that any declaration by the court would be damaging to the UK's national interest in terms of international relations and defence, since it could embarrass or tie the hands of the UK Government. It was therefore non-justiciable. This finding was unsurprising, since it would have involved the court entering directly into a highly sensitive issue of international relations. The *Abbasi* decision is more interesting: it exemplifies the contemporary approach of the courts that it is not the broad area under consideration that determines justiciability, but rather whether the particular issues raised by the challenge involve questions unsuited to judicial determination. To that extent, the relatively crude 'list' approach of Lord Roskill in *GCHQ* has been quite substantially modified. It certainly seems that the position has moved on markedly since 1987, when Munro suggested that 'the propriety of *most* exercises of prerogative power will still continue to be unsusceptible to challenge in the courts' *(Studies in Constitutional Law*, 1987, p 182, emphasis added).[2]

The impact of the HRA on this area should also be briefly mentioned. As with other areas of judicial review, the Act adds a fresh, substantive ground of review against which the courts must consider the lawfulness of action taken under the prerogative, where a European Convention right is in issue. Section 6 of the Act states that it is 'unlawful for a public authority to act in a way which is incompatible with a Convention right'. This will have at least one important effect. Section 6(1) impliedly overrules the *dicta* in *GCHQ* about there being some areas of the prerogative which are still non-justiciable. Actions taken by government ministers under the prerogative will clearly be actions of a 'public authority'. They will therefore be unlawful if they breach Convention rights, according to s 6(1) of the HRA. Whether they fall into a category previously immune from judicial scrutiny will clearly be irrelevant. There will therefore be no areas excluded *per se* from judicial scrutiny where a Convention right is in issue.

Neither of the two recent case just discussed raised issues under the HRA. However, it is clear that the courts will continue to take a cautious line when reviewing decisions with implications for national security – a matter specified as a legitimate ground for curtailing Convention rights in a number of Convention Articles. Decisions under the HRA have already recognised the concept of an 'area of discretionary judgment', a phrase used in *DPP ex p Kebilene (1999)*, meaning essentially that in areas such as national security, the courts will tend to defer to the opinion of the Executive as to what is necessary to protect the State. This tendency has been apparent in a number of important decisions under the HRA, including *Secretary of State for the Environment, Transport and the Regions ex p Alconbury Developments Ltd (2001)* and *Brown v Stott (2001)*. Moreover, many of the excluded areas (treaty-making, appointment of ministers, granting of honours, etc) will not generally raise human rights issues. Furthermore, it should be noted that the HRA specifically protects acts of the prerogative from being annulled by the courts where they are expressed as Orders in Council. This is because such Orders are included within the definition of 'primary legislation' (s 21(1)) which, by virtue of s 3(2)(b) and (6), may not be struck down by the courts if found to be incompatible with Convention rights. Whether Orders in Council made under the prerogative may at present be struck down by the courts appears to be a matter of doubt; what is clear is that the HRA will insulate acts of prerogative power made in this way from successful assault on Convention grounds. While the courts may make a purely declaratory finding that the Order in question is in breach of the Convention, the sections cited provide that such a declaration will not affect the Order's continuing effect and validity.

But what will be the effect where the Convention does apply, and the decision challenged is not in the form of an Order in Council? In some such cases, it will be enough to show simply that a Convention right has been violated by the decision (because no, or no relevant, exceptions are applicable). In others, where the government can establish that a recognised exception to the right was in play (this is more likely to happen in those challenges relying on Arts 8–11), the applicant may have to establish that the decision assigned a disproportionately low level to the affected right. In both cases, the applicant will have a far less onerous task than the present one of having to show that the decision was wholly irrational, a hurdle the applicants could not cross in *Smith*.

In conclusion, with the exception of a few doubtful decisions such as *Malone* and *Northumbria*, a general movement first of all to bring the exercise of the prerogative within the remit of judicial review, and then to gradually extend the remit of that review to cover areas previously thought to be immune can be discerned. While a number of important areas remain largely immune from review, overall there has been a significant extension of the scope of the legal accountability of the Executive and hence a sharp restriction on the capacity of government for arbitrary action.

▌NOTES

1   Students could mention here that a number of commentators have pointed out that this principle, if correct, would make it actually harder to abolish parts of the prerogative than to repeal previous Acts of Parliament, since previous Acts can be impliedly repealed. This would seem to elevate the status of the prerogative over Acts of Parliament, in direct opposition to the basic principle that statute is the highest form of law known in this country.

2   The point could be made here that while the areas excluded from review may be shrinking, it is noticeable that the approach of the courts in a number of the key cases (*GCHQ; Smith; Bentley*) has been very cautious, the applicant failing in two of them and achieving only a partial victory in the third. If this approach prevails, the extension of review in these areas may turn out to be a symbolic rather than a real increase in legal accountability. Much may depend on how the courts apply the HRA in practice. The signs from the cases mentioned in the body of the essay indicate that a deferential approach under the HRA can amount to a level of scrutiny not greatly more exacting than that under *Wednesbury* (1948), though different in reasoning.

Question 22

Would you agree that the Royal Prerogative amounts to a substantially uncontrolled power in the hands of the Executive, particularly in relation to the power to take military action, and that therefore urgent reform is needed?

Answer plan

This question is much broader in scope than the previous one; it does not confine itself to asking the student to assess the extent of judicial control, but clearly also brings into play the controversial issue of the lack of formal parliamentary controls, much discussed recently, in the aftermath of the Iraq war. In addressing the latter issue, both the legal and the conventional position need to be considered, something which holds true also for the issue of possible reform.

The following matters should be considered.

- a definition of the prerogative;
- the historic willingness of the courts to determine whether a claimed power existed in law; the *GCHQ* case: powers exercised under the prerogative may be open to review;
- the excluded categories of prerogative powers, and subsequent case law which has whittled them away;
- the impact of the HRA;
- the absence of any legal control by Parliament over the prerogative and the conventional position;
- options for reform to give greater Parliamentary control;
- conclusions: statutory reform as the preferred option; a new Convention at the least.

Answer

The term 'prerogative' refers to powers which the sovereign has by common law as opposed to statute. One of the pre-eminent features of British constitutional history has been the gradual transfer of the exercise of these prerogatives from the monarch to ministers, and today, the vast majority are, in practice, exercised by the Prime Minister, the Cabinet or individual ministers. The prerogative includes most key matters relating to foreign affairs, such as the making of treaties, recognition of States and the use of force, and on the domestic front the power to dissolve Parliament, to assent to Bills, to award honours, to pardon criminals, to establish universities, to regulate the Civil Service and to dismiss and appoint ministers. The personal prerogative of the monarch includes various immunities, such as the Queen's personal immunity from suit or prosecution, and property rights. The concern lying at the heart of the statement in this question is that it is one of the unique and disturbing features of the UK Constitution that, by means of this historical relic, it allows powers of such great breadth, magnitude and importance to be wielded by the Executive alone: as a Labour Party paper of 1993 commented: 'It is where power is exercised by government under the cover of royal prerogative that our concerns are greatest . . . Massive power is exercised by executive decree without accountability to Parliament' (Labour Party, *A New Agenda for Democracy* (1993), p 33). Ironically enough, this area, which most concerned Labour in 1993, has remained entirely untouched by the great wave of constitutional reform enacted by the Blair administration from 1997 on, save for the impact of the Human Rights Act 1998 on judicial control of the prerogative. This essay will consider how far it is true to say still that the exercise of the prerogative remains largely unaccountable, particularly in terms of Parliamentary oversight, and whether, as suggested, there is a strong case for reform.

In terms of judicial accountability, the courts have long asserted that it is for them to determine whether a particular prerogative power actually exists and whether the decision taken falls within its scope. The courts will not allow new prerogatives to be created by Executive *fiat* (*BBC v Johns* (1965)). However, the courts have, on occasions, been prepared to allow a recognised prerogative to broaden in adapting itself to new situations: in *Malone v Metropolitan Police Commissioner* (1979), the assertion that a prerogative power existed to authorise telephone tapping was based on the argument that no new power was being created, although an old one was being extended to a new situation. Also disturbing in this respect was the decision in *Secretary of State for the Home Department ex p Northumbria Police Authority* (1989). The case will be considered further below; the key issue for present purposes was whether there was a hitherto largely unrecognised prerogative power to keep the peace, under which the Home Secretary could lawfully offer to supply CS gas and plastic baton rounds to any Chief Constable whose police authority would not supply him with such equipment. The court found that there was a general prerogative to keep the Queen's peace; while the judges conceded that there was virtually no authority for such a power existing, they used the ingenious argument that the 'scarcity of references in the books to the prerogative of keeping the peace within the realm does not disprove that it exists. Rather, it may point to an unspoken assumption that it does'. It was further said that there was no need to demonstrate the existence of a prerogative to equip or supply the police force. Rather, the power under which the Home Secretary wished to act in supplying CS gas and plastic bullets could be brought under the general umbrella of the prerogative to do all that was reasonably necessary to keep the peace. This rather accommodating approach by the courts to the existence and scope of prerogative powers seems plainly incompatible with the basic notion, derived from *Entick v Carrington* (1765), that any act infringing on liberty must be justified by some positive piece of law. *Entick* had found that specific legal authority to justify government action must be found in the law

163

books, and that if the books were silent, then that was judgment against the government. The court in *Northumbria Police* adopted the opposite view, offering little reassurance that doubtful claims of seemingly novel prerogative powers will be closely scrutinised by a judiciary vigilant to guard against arbitrary power.

Turning to the issue of the propriety of the exercise of prerogatives admitted to exist, again, an increased determination of the judiciary to ensure the legal accountability of the Executive may be discerned. The traditional view of the courts was that where the Executive acted under an admitted prerogative power, the exercise of that power was not subject to review as it would have been had the minister acted under statute (see, for example, *Burmah Oil Co v Lord Advocate (1965)* and *AG v De Keyser's Royal Hotel (1920)*). However, in *Laker Airways v Department of Trade (1977)*, Lord Denning remarked: 'Seeing that the prerogative is a discretionary power to be exercised for the public good, it follows that its exercise can be examined by the courts just as any other discretionary power which is vested in the Executive.'

This approach was approved in the landmark case of *Council of Civil Service Unions v Minister for the Civil Service (the GCHQ case) (1984)*, in which the House of Lords held that the mere fact of the power deriving from the prerogative as opposed to statute was not a sufficient reason to exclude it from review. The controlling factor determining whether a particular exercise of powers under the prerogative should be open to review was held to be the subject matter of the decision, rather than the source of the power. Lord Roskill suggested a number of prerogative powers which, by virtue of their nature and subject matter, were not amenable to the judicial process; these included the making of treaties, the disposal of the armed forces, the defence of the realm, the dissolution of Parliament, the prerogative of mercy, the granting of honours and the appointment of ministers. He termed these prerogative powers 'excluded categories', and found no reason why the power to regulate the Home Civil Service should fall into such a category. Having determined that decisions taken under prerogative powers were open to review, the House of Lords then found that the decision-making process had in fact been conducted unfairly, but that this was outweighed by the national security considerations in play.

In a number of cases since *GCHQ*, the courts have begun to whittle away Lord Roskill's excluded categories, suggesting a readiness in principle to review all prerogatives other than those which relate to matters at the heart of the political process, such as the dissolution of Parliament, the appointment and dismissal of ministers and matters of high foreign policy or defence: *Secretary of State for the Foreign Office ex p Rees Mogg (1994)* confirmed that the courts would not entertain challenges to the prerogative power to conclude treaties, in this case, the Treaty of Maastricht. It should be noted, of course, that Lord Roskill's list of excluded categories does not and never did represent an authoritative statement of the law; it was an *obiter* suggestion only.

Thus, in *Secretary of State for Foreign and Commonwealth Affairs ex p Everett (1989)*, it was held that the courts were competent to review the exercise of the prerogative power of the Secretary of State to issue passports, although the power was related to foreign affairs and had traditionally been regarded as unreviewable. A further inroad into the excluded areas was made by the decision in *Secretary of State for the Home Department ex p Bentley (1993)*, a case which fell squarely within one of Lord Roskill's excluded categories, namely, the prerogative of mercy. The issue was whether the Home Secretary's refusal to recommend a posthumous pardon for Derek Bentley, executed in 1953 for the murder of a policeman, was subject to judicial review. The court held that while the criteria to be used by the Home Secretary in making his decision were 'probably a matter of policy [and so] not justiciable', the Secretary had failed to consider the different types of pardon he could grant in the situation. Declining to make any order, the court 'invited' the Secretary to reconsider the case.

A more generalised attack on the scope of the excluded categories was made in the case of *Ministry of Defence ex p Smith and Others (1996)*. A number of homosexual servicemen and women challenged the policy of the armed forces to exclude homosexuals from service. The government argued that the case involved governmental policy in relation to the armed forces, and hence amounted to a challenge to 'the exercise of a prerogative in an area – the defence of the realm – recognised by the courts to be unsuitable for judicial review'. Both the High Court and the Court of Appeal firmly rejected this argument and held the decision to be susceptible to review, although, on the facts, the challenge did not succeed. Smith LJ took the opportunity to put down a more general pointer, commenting that in his view, 'only the rarest cases' would be non-justiciable, those which involved 'national security properly so called and where in addition, the courts really do lack the expertise or material to form a judgment on the point at issue'. The remark was not confirmed by the Court of Appeal, but was not repudiated by it either.

The most recent cases are *R (on the Application of Abbasi & Anor) v Secretary of State for Foreign and Commonwealth Affairs & Secretary of State for the Home Department (2003)* and *CND v The Prime Minister of the United Kingdom and others (2002)*, which together confirm the courts' strong disinclination to review powers exercised in relation to foreign affairs and the use of armed force. In the former, a British national detained at Guantenamo bay argued that, since he was being subject, in effect, to arbitrary detention, in violation of habeus corpus, the Foreign Office had a duty either to make representations on his behalf to the US Government, or at the least, to explain why they had in fact taken no action in relation to his case. The Court's finding was that the mere fact that the prerogative power in relation to foreign affairs was in issue was not enough to oust the jurisdiction of the court – it was the particular subject matter that was determinative. Moreover, in an extreme case where the Foreign Office appeared to be refusing even to consider making representations to the US Government about someone in the position of the applicant, judicial review would lie; however, such consideration had been given in this case, and there was no question of the court ordering the Government to make representations. In the latter decision, CND requested the court to determine the correct legal interpretation of UNSC Resolution 1441, which gave Iraq a final chance to comply with previous resolutions as to disarmament and threatened serious consequences if it did not. It was of course not in dispute that the court did not have the lawful power to prevent the UK Government from commencing hostilities against Iraq by way of injunction or a quashing order: the question was whether the court could declare whether the Resolution did, or did not give the UK Government lawful grounds, as a matter of international law, to take such action, in the event of non-compliance by the Iraqi Government. The court in this case firmly disclaimed the invitation to enter upon any such determination on a number of grounds. In terms of the issues discussed here, the key reason was that any declaration by the court would be damaging to the UK's national interest in terms of international relations and defence, since it could embarrass or tie the hands of the UK Government. It was therefore non-justiciable. This finding was unsurprising, since it would have involved the court entering directly into a highly sensitive issue of international relations. The *Abbasi* decision is more interesting: it exemplifies the contemporary approach of the courts that it is not the broad area under consideration that determines justiciability, but rather whether the particular issues raised by the challenge involve questions unsuited to judicial determination. To that extent, the relatively crude 'list' approach of Lord Roskill in *GCHQ* has been quite substantially modified. It certainly seems that the position has moved on markedly since 1987, when Munro suggested that 'the propriety of *most* exercises of prerogative power will still continue to be unsusceptible to challenge in the courts' (*Studies in Constitutional Law*, 1987, p 182, emphasis added).[1]

The impact of the HRA on this area should also be briefly mentioned. As with other areas of judicial review, the Act adds a fresh, substantive ground of review against which the courts must consider the lawfulness of action taken under the prerogative, where a European Convention right is in issue. Section 6 of the Act states that it is 'unlawful for a public authority to act in a way which is incompatible with a Convention right'. This will have at least one important effect. Section 6(1) impliedly overrules the *dicta* in *GCHQ* about there being some areas of the prerogative which are still non-justiciable. Actions taken by government ministers under the prerogative will clearly be actions of a 'public authority'. They will therefore be unlawful if they breach Convention rights, according to s 6(1) of the HRA. Whether they fall into a category previously immune from judicial scrutiny will clearly be irrelevant. There will therefore be no areas excluded *per se* from judicial scrutiny where a Convention right is in issue.

Neither of the two recent case just discussed raised issues under the HRA. However, it is clear that the courts will doubtless continue to take a cautious line when reviewing decisions with implications for national security – a matter specified as a legitimate ground for curtailing Convention rights in a number of Convention Articles. Decisions under the HRA have already recognised the concept of an 'area of discretionary judgment', a phrase used in DPP *ex p Kebilene (1999)*, meaning essentially that in areas such as national security, the courts will tend to defer to the opinion of the Executive as to what is necessary to protect the State. This tendency has been apparent in a number of important decisions under the HRA, including *Secretary of State for the Environment, Transport and the Regions ex p Alconbury Developments Ltd (2001)* and *Brown v Stott (2001)*. Moreover, many of the excluded areas (treaty-making, appointment of ministers, granting of honours, etc) will not generally raise human rights issues.[2]

But what will be the effect where the ECHR does apply? In some such cases, it will be enough to show simply that a Convention right has been violated by the decision (because no, or no relevant, exceptions are applicable). In others, where the government can establish that a recognised exception to the right was in play (this is more likely to happen in those challenges relying on Arts 8–11), the applicant may have to establish that the decision assigned a disproportionately low level to the affected right. In both cases, the applicant will have a far less onerous task than the present one of having to show that the decision was wholly irrational, a hurdle the applicants could not cross in *Smith*.

While a number of important areas remain largely immune from review, then, overall there has been a significant extension of the scope of the legal accountability of the Executive and hence a sharp restriction on the capacity of government for arbitrary action.

However, when we turn to the issue of Parliamentary accountability, we see a very different picture: there has been no matching increase in scrutiny, either as a matter of law or convention. One of the most remarkable features of the prerogative, to foreign observers, must be the way in which it allows 'almost the whole terrain of foreign policy in the UK [to be] carried on by the government . . . [without] the need to secure any formal [parliamentary] approval to its diplomatic agreements and executive decisions' (Blackburn, 'The House of Lords', in Blackburn and Plant (eds), *Constitutional Reform: The Labour Government's Constitutional Reform Agenda* (1999), p 33). Perhaps the most remarkable aspect of this situation is the complete absence of any formal parliamentary control over two of the most important types of decision which government may make: the signing of treaties, and the deployment of the armed forces abroad. As to the former, Blackburn notes: 'The UK now has the only Parliament in the European Union that lacks any formal mechanism for securing scrutiny and approval to treaties. The 1924 Ponsonby "Rule" – now a Foreign Office circular – is clearly inadequate as a basis for effective scrutiny. It involves the voluntary practice of governments laying treaties signed by the UK before Parliament as Command Papers after their entry into force, and in the case of treaties requiring legal ratification a copy being placed on the Table of the house 21 days beforehand.' He notes the complaint of the Labour Party, when in opposition: 'Treaty after treaty is concluded without the formal consent of Parliament. Indeed foreign policy as a whole is an area virtually free from democratic control and accountability.' (Labour Party, ibid).

The lack of any necessity to seek approval from, or even consult with Parliament before committing the country's armed forces to battle abroad, whether in a formal state of war or not, is perhaps the other most remarkable feature of the use of the prerogative. As Brazier comments:

> How odd – perhaps bizarre – it is that the approval of both Houses of Parliament is required for pieces of technical, and often trivial, subordinate legislation, whereas it is not needed at all before men and women can be committed to the possibility of disfigurement or death (R Brazier, *Constitutional Reform*, 2nd edn (1999), p 123).

Brazier notes that in the cases of Suez, the Falklands, and the Gulf War of 1991, no attempt was made to seek formal Parliamentary approval before committing forces to war. To these can be added the deployment and use of the RAF in Bosnia in the 1990s by the Major Government, and the prolonged campaign of air-strikes against the targets in Kuwait and Serbia authorised by the Blair Government, neither of which were the subject of formal parliamentary approval. It was in fact not until the Iraq war in 2003 that the Government decided that a formal vote should be held in Parliament before committing troops to battle, and this was done more as a matter of political necessity than out of a sense of constitutional *obligation*. Nevertheless, this dramatic parliamentary debate, which saw the resignation of Robin Cook from the Government, and a massive Labour rebellion, is now being seen as a model for the future.

There are two basic options for reform. First, at least some of the prerogatives could be replaced by legislation, such as a War Powers Act, setting out the lawful powers of the government to use armed force, and the procedures to be followed. These could include a requirement that a vote be held in Parliament to be held prior to the commencement of hostilities, unless necessity precluded it, in which case, such a vote would have to be held within, say, seven days. There have been a number of attempts to achieve such reform by Private Members Bill, most recently in one put forward by Lord Lester. The Public Administration Select Committee recently stated that:

> any decision to engage in armed conflict should be approved by Parliament, if not before military action then as soon as possible afterwards. A mere convention is not enough when lives are at stake (4th Report (2003–04).

It recommended a public consultation exercise on legislation to give effect to this proposal. The Select Committee on the Constitution (15th Report, 2005–06) recently took a different stance, arguing that the fear of exposing members of the armed forces to prosecution for taking part in what could be found an illegal war and the possibility of judicial review, once the power to use force was placed on a statutory footing, both pointed strongly away from a statutory solution. The Committee argued instead for a parliamentary convention whereby governments would be required to seek parliamentary approval before committing forces to actual or potential armed conflict. The concerns of the Constitution Committee are, it is suggested, overstated. First of all, there is already the possibility of legal consequences for waging unlawful war under the jurisdiction of the International Criminal Court. Second, if in future the UK government were only to use armed force when it was certain that it could justify such action as lawful, many would see this, following the Iraq war, as a positive rather than a negative result. It is suggested therefore that an overwhelming case can be made for legislative reform in this area.

In conclusion, there has been a marked increase in judicial control of the prerogative in the cases following *GCHQ*; nonetheless, the excluded, or non-justiciable areas remain of enormous significance. As Birkinshaw notes, '. . . it is ironic to realise that the exercise of some of the most important prerogatives is devoid of any control save political rebellion or insurrection – declaration of war for instance or the appointment of a Prime Minister' ('Decision-Making and its Control' in McEldowney and McAuslan, *Law, Legitimacy and the Constitution* (1985), p 152). Some of the most important prerogatives remain virtually free from judicial control, while there has yet to be established even a constitutional convention that Parliament be consulted over the exercise of the prerogative, even where hostilities are contemplated. Both Gordon Brown and David Cameron have recently expressed the view that there is a strong case for legislation in this area, although, as we have seen, parties have been much keener to promote such policies in opposition than in government. The reform suggested by the Public Administration committee is very long overdue, and it is to be hoped that it will be enacted in the near future.

▌NOTES

1 The point could be made here that while the areas excluded from review may be shrinking, it is noticeable that the approach of the courts in a number of the key cases (*GCHQ; Smith; Bentley*) has been very cautious, the applicant failing in two of them and achieving only a partial victory in the third. If this approach prevails, the extension of review in these areas may turn out to be a symbolic rather than a real increase in legal accountability. Much may depend on how the courts apply the HRA in practice. The signs from the cases mentioned in the body of the essay indicate that a deferential approach under the HRA can amount to a level of scrutiny not greatly more exacting than that under *Wednesbury* (1948), though different in reasoning.

2 Students could note here that the HRA specifically protects acts of the prerogative from being annulled by the courts where they are expressed as Orders in Council. This is because such Orders are included within the definition of 'primary

legislation' (s 21(1)) which, by virtue of s 3(2)(b) and (6), may not be struck down by the courts if found to be incompatible with Convention rights. Whether Orders in Council made under the prerogative may at present be struck down by the courts appears to be a matter of doubt; what is clear is that the HRA will insulate acts of prerogative power made in this way from successful assault on Convention grounds. While the courts may make a purely declaratory finding that the Order in question is in breach of the Convention, the sections cited provide that such a declaration will not affect the Order's continuing effect and validity.

CHAPTER 6

THE EXECUTIVE

INTRODUCTION

The Executive includes the government, the monarchy, the Civil Service, local government, the armed forces and the police. The areas examined within this topic tend to vary, and students should be guided in their revision by their own courses. For example, some courses include material on local government and central–local government relationships; others look at the issue of regulation and quangos in some details. The Royal Prerogative is a major part of any study of the Executive; it is considered in the previous chapter. This chapter will concentrate on the operation of central government, which includes consideration of the role of the Cabinet and the relationship between ministers, their departments and civil servants. Questions in this area tend to concern the relationship between the Prime Minister and the Cabinet and the extent to which individual ministers and government in general are responsible to Parliament. The latter topic has recently taken on greater importance following the Scott Report and the continuing concern about ministerial responsibility and accountability. Questions on the difficulties and confusions thrown up by the new approach to responsibility and, in particular, the issues raised by the Next Steps Agencies are very likely to be set. Clearly, government and Parliament are closely interlocked: government is part of the Executive but also dominates the legislative body – Parliament – and therefore there is some overlap between this area and Chapter 3 on the House of Commons. Chapter 3 is, however, concerned with the efficacy of scrutinising procedures in the House of Commons whereas, although such matters are touched on in this chapter, its emphasis is on the principle of ministerial responsibility.

Checklist

Students should be familiar with the following areas:

- Conventions relating to Cabinet government: collective Cabinet decision-making; the concept of collective government responsibility to Parliament;

- the basic concept of individual ministerial responsibility to Parliament; the distinction between 'accountability' and 'responsibility'; the difficulties with the distinction;

- the differing types of accountability of civil servants, chief executives of Next Steps Agencies and ministers;

- the obligation on ministers to accept blame/resign for mistakes of 'policy';

- Ministerial resignation in practice including recent examples;

- the extent of the obligation to account to Parliament; *The Ministerial Code;* the limitations on the types of questions that must be answered as set out in the Freedom of Information Act (a basic awareness of the position under the previous Code of Practice on access to government information (2nd edn, 1997) is also needed);

- the findings of the Scott Report; the giving of incomplete information; the concept of 'knowingly' misleading Parliament; the absence of resignations over information given to Parliament over WMD and Iraq;

- the Freedom of Information Act 2000, particularly the exemption in s 35 covering information relating to the development of government policy.

Note that references to Woodhouse are to D Woodhouse, 'Ministerial responsibility: something old, something new' [1997] PL 262; references to 'the Scott Report' are to Sir Richard Scott, *Inquiry into Exports of Defence Equipment and Dual-Use Goods to Iraq and Related Prosecutions* (HC 115–1, 1995–96); and references to the Public Service Committee are to its second Report (HC 231, 1995–96), unless otherwise stated.

Question 23

'The conventions of collective Cabinet decision-making and collective and individual ministerial responsibility to Parliament are more honoured in the breach than in the observance; the result has been a movement towards Prime Ministerial government and a consequent diminution of government accountability.'

Discuss.

Answer plan

A question concerning the conventions and the reality of Cabinet government is commonly set and is reasonably straightforward. This question requires a consideration of the operation of the three conventions together and their relationship with each other. It is therefore very wide ranging and it will not be possible to cover one area in depth if a proper essay structure is to be maintained.

The following matters should be considered:

- the convention of collective Cabinet decision-making; the dilution of the power of the Cabinet; the influence of Mrs Thatcher 1979–90 and the continuing influence of Mr Blair;
- the concept of collective Cabinet responsibility to Parliament; procedures on the floor of the House of Commons;
- the relationship between collective ministerial responsibility and individual ministerial responsibility;
- the notion of accepting personal fault for 'policy' only; the difficulties with this;
- the operation of the three conventions and Prime Ministerial government.

Answer

Bagehot, writing in 1867, called the Cabinet 'the most powerful body in the nation' (*The English Constitution*, 1963) and considered that collective responsibility meant that every member of the Cabinet had the right to take part in Cabinet discussion but was bound by the decision eventually reached. In contrast, in 1977, John Mackintosh (*The British Cabinet*, 1977) wrote: ' . . . the principal policies of a government may not be and often are not originated in Cabinet.' Michael Heseltine, in the aftermath of the Westland affair in 1986, said that there had been a 'breakdown of constitutional government', in that the Prime Minister had frustrated collective consideration of the Westland issue and many see Blair's administration as exemplifying a system of Presidential, rather than Cabinet, or collegial government.

These suggestions that conventions governing Cabinet government are in decline bear out the statement to be considered. The convention of collective decision-making clearly underpins collective responsibility: the obligation placed upon ministers by the convention of collective responsibility is most readily justified if government decisions are reached collectively. Thus, it will first be considered whether there has indeed been a diminution in the importance of collective decision-making.

The Cabinet is composed of around 22 ministers who agree to pursue a common policy; some ministers will be outside the Cabinet and it may include some whose offices involve few or no departmental responsibilities. The function of the Cabinet is, in theory, to determine finally the policy to be submitted to Parliament and to co-ordinate and control administrative action. However, a number of writers, including Richard Crossman, have considered that Cabinet government is developing into Prime Ministerial government and that therefore collective decision-making has suffered. Crossman wrote that the power of the Prime Minister to sack ministers, to determine the Cabinet agenda and the existence and membership of Cabinet committees meant that his control over the Cabinet was the most important force within it. Under Mrs Thatcher, who was Prime Minister between 1979 and 1990, the importance of this force became more apparent, not because she increased the power of the Prime Minister, but because she used the available power to the full. In particular, she displaced important decision-making to small informal groups of ministers convened by herself, and exercised the Prime Minister's exclusive right to appoint and reshuffle ministers in order to reshape the Cabinet in accordance with her own ideological outlook. For example, she managed, during the first two years of her administration, to move no less then five out of the seven 'moderates' or 'wets' out of the Cabinet. It seems fairly apparent that Mr Blair makes little use of full Cabinet; key decisions are taken by Cabinet Committees or small groups of ministers. For example, the crucial decision in May 1997 to give the Bank of England independence and the power to set interest rates was apparently taken by the Prime Minister and the Chancellor of the Exchequer, in consultation with their Special Advisers. Other members of the Cabinet were not even consulted. Many commentators see a marked centralisation of power under Mr Blair, with himself and Gordon Brown, the Chancellor, exerting great influence over the decisions and priorities of other departments. Richard Butler, the former Cabinet Secretary, who conducted a review on the intelligence used to justify the decision to launch the invasion of Iraq, has been highly critical of the Blair Government's style of decision-making. He has commented that 'the government reaches conclusions in rather small groups of people who are not necessarily representative of all the groups of interests in government' and that 'the Cabinet now . . . does not make decisions' (*Guardian* 10 December 2004).

However, in diluting and fragmenting the power of the Cabinet in this fashion, it might be argued that Thatcher and Blair were merely taking further a process which had already begun. The use of gatherings other than Cabinet to make decisions – inner Cabinets, Cabinet committees, ministerial meetings – had been growing for the last 30 years, and had arguably undermined the Cabinet as a decision-making body.[1] The general view of constitutional writers seems to be (see

Peter Hennessey, *Cabinet*, 1986) that although Mrs Thatcher flouted the spirit of Cabinet government, she did not destroy it. It is arguable that when John Major became Prime Minister in November 1990, the spirit revived, albeit in a form which Bagehot might not recognise. However, the Blair style of governing perhaps takes the process of marginalising Cabinet even further than did Thatcher. It seems clear that Mr Blair wishes to increase central control over the actions of government departments. The appointment in 1998 of Jack Cunningham as a Cabinet minister without portfolio, but charged with the task of overseeing the implementation of agreed government policy across the departments, is a concrete indicator of this.

If the Cabinet as an institution has suffered a decline along with the doctrine of *primus inter pares*, it might appear that the basis of the doctrine of collective ministerial responsibility will also have been undermined. It could also be argued that it has been undermined by the failure of accountability of the Cabinet to Parliament. Theoretically, a check is kept on the Executive through the operation of the convention of collective ministerial responsibility to Parliament. The convention means that ministers are collectively responsible to Parliament for their actions in governing the country, and therefore should be in accord on any major question. As all ministers are accountable to Parliament for government policy, no minister can disclaim his responsibility on the basis of disagreement with it. He should resign if in disagreement with the policy of the Cabinet on any major question. Examples of such resignations include Sir Anthony Eden's in 1938 over Chamberlain's policy towards Mussolini and arguably Michael Heseltine's in 1986 due to disagreement with government policy in respect of Westland plc and the requirement to submit statements on the subject to the Cabinet Office for prior clearance. Robin Cook's resignation, on the eve of the Iraq war in 2003, on the grounds that he could not agree with the decision to take military action, is a particularly clear and principled example.

It appears to follow from this convention that a government should resign after being defeated on a vote of no confidence in the House. On the face of it, unless Parliament can express its disapproval of government decisions and policy in this way, it might seem that it can have little impact on government action. However, only two governments, both in a minority in the Commons, have lost the confidence of the House since 1924. In 1924, Ramsay MacDonald's first Labour government was deserted by its Liberal allies, while in 1976, the Labour government lost its small majority, partly through by-election defeats, and was defeated on a Conservative vote of no confidence in 1979. Apart from these examples, governments which lose in the House on particular issues have managed to muster their majorities and procure a reversal of the vote. For example, in July 1992, the Major government suffered a defeat due to a back-bench rebellion in a vote relating to the Maastricht Treaty. However, the Prime Minister put down a motion of confidence the following day, and secured a majority.

However, the government's need to ensure its majority in the Commons means that it must retain the support of back benchers. It can use sanctions such as guillotining or whipping to ensure party solidarity, but a government which has to resort to such sanctions may become unpopular with the electorate. The ultimate sanction of withdrawal of the whip may be counterproductive, partly because it underlines disunity in the party and partly because MPs who have lost the whip may vote against the government. This was clearly seen in 1994 and 1995 after nine 'Euro-sceptic' Conservative MPs lost the whip. Thus, the need to retain the support of the parliamentary party has some impact on government policy. Such impact was clearly evident in the modification of the decision to close 31 coal mines without holding an inquiry in October 1992. The abandonment of the White Paper (Cmd 5291 (2001)) on completing reform of the House of Lords, setting out the government's concrete proposals for reform in response to the Wakeham Report (Cm 4534 (2000)) in the face of virtually unanimous opposition from the parliamentary Labour party, is another example. However, this sanction underpinning collective cabinet responsibility can only operate if the procedures available to Parliament in order to ensure supervision of government are effective. Such procedures, including debates and questions, are of value not merely because the possibility of defeat in the Commons or the adverse publicity resulting from a reduced majority affects government policy, but also because they are part of the continuous parliamentary scrutiny of the government, forcing it to explain and justify its actions.

However, there are important limitations on the efficacy of certain procedures. Questions to ministers are of limited value, because a minister cannot be compelled to answer any question and there are a large number of matters – now defined by large number of exemptions in the Freedom of Information Act 2000 – on which a minister will refuse to answer. Moreover, even matters which can be legitimately raised may be evaded by the use of various tactics, such as answering questions only in part, or providing only partial explanations in response to the parts that are answered. Due in part to the use of such evasion, some questions to ministers have to an extent ceased to be genuine requests for information, and have become an excuse for generating a short debate. However, a minister who is questioned about a departmental decision which was theoretically taken in apparent accord with his departmental policy will then have to consider the decision in detail. It may be that in consequence, he will make modifications to departmental policy if it becomes apparent that it is evolving in a manner which was not originally intended. Questions put down for reply by written answer are a much more effective way for MPs to simply obtain information.

Collective responsibility may further be undermined, it is suggested, by the doctrine of individual ministerial responsibility. If a decision announced by a minister has been taken in the Cabinet, it is arguable that the whole Cabinet should accept responsibility for it. Nevertheless, a minister may sometimes be held individually responsible in order to divert the adverse consequences arising from a strict application of collective responsibility. The resignation of the Secretary for Trade and Industry, Mr Brittan, in 1986 during the Westland affair could be characterised as such an instance; his acceptance of responsibility deflected demands for the resignation of the Prime Minister herself. It was arguable that the same thing happened over the resignation of Peter Mandelson in January 2001 in relation to the Hinduja passports affair. While the decision to grant the Hinduja brothers passports in an expedited manner was almost certainly not a decision made by the Cabinet, there was a strong sense amongst commentators that Mandelson's resignation was forced in order to keep the affair from damaging the Prime Minister himself (see, for example, Rawnsley, *Servants of the People: the Inside Story of New Labour* (2nd edn, 2001)). In other words, individual responsibility may at times act as a proxy for collective responsibility. Conversely, the convention of collective responsibility can prevent individual Ministers from having to take responsibility: no-one has been forced to resign either over the misleading information given to Parliament on Iraq's alleged WMD, or over the disastrous aftermath of the Iraq war, partly because, as Robin Butler's inquiry into the intelligence and presentational failings found, the errors made were collective ones. In this instance, collective responsibility has in effect shielded Mr Blair from taking individual responsibility for the decision to go to war which, it now appears fairly clear, was to a large extent driven by him personally.

The convention of individual ministerial responsibility means that ministers are responsible to Parliament for the conduct of the Executive, and therefore that for every branch of government business, there is a minister to explain and account for decisions. If a minister is personally blameworthy, he might be expected to resign depending on the nature of the misbehaviour. Conduct unbecoming a minister of the Crown, whether of a private or public nature, would probably lead to resignation (as with the resignation of Ron Davies in October 1998, after an indiscretion of some sort took place on Clapham Common), although the minister might be reinstated when it was thought that his misconduct had expiated itself. The prime example is the reinstatement of Peter Mandelson to the Cabinet less than two years after he had resigned in December 1998 following the revelation that he had been lent a very large sum of money from a fellow government minister, Geoffrey Robinson, and concealed the loan from the Prime Minister. Breach of the Ministerial Code or misuse of public office to do a personal favour may also force a resignation – as in the two resignations of David Blunkett. His first resignation from the Government, in December 2004, appears to have been over a mixture of embarrassment to the government over his personal life, and alleged misuse of his office to fast-track a visa application for his ex-lover's nanny. His position had also been weakened after he published a book which contained numerous attacks upon fellow Ministers. His second resignation, from the post of Work and Pensions Secretary, in November 2005, came after he was accused of breaking the Ministerial

Code by taking paid work while he was out of the Cabinet, without seeking advice from the relevant watchdog.

When departmental maladministration has occurred, matters are less clear cut. It seems that there is no expectation that a minister will accept responsibility, in the sense of personal blame, for every mistake occurring in his department. Although this was sometimes seen as the traditional view of ministerial responsibility, exemplified by the statement of Sir Thomas Dugdale following the Crichel Down affair (1958), researchers have concluded that there has never been an accepted convention that ministers will resign, or even accept blame, for every mistake occurring in their departments. The current trend, as exemplified by many episodes involving the previous Conservative administrations, in particular, the response of Michael Howard to the Learmont Report, and in the present administration of Robin Cook to the Sandline affair, is that ministers will only resign if it can be clearly shown that the fault for what has gone wrong rests with ministerial policy decisions, rather than the decisions of civil servants in their department.[2] A difficult case to classify, perhaps, is the resignation in May 2002 of the Secretary of State for Trade and Industry, Stephen Byers. Byers was forced out after months of hostile press coverage, particularly surrounding the circumstances of the dismissal of Byers' former press officer, Martin Sixsmith, and his refusal to sack another press adviser, Jo Moore, over her notorious 'good day to bury bad news' memo of September 11 2001. It is not clear that serious problems in his department's *policy* can be laid at his door, though there was extreme discontent in various quarters over his decision to place Railtrack in administration and his plans for its replacement, as well as the state of the railways generally. Moreover he had, through inept presentation (in particular, by apparently misleading Parliament and the public over exactly when Sixsmith had been dismissed), lost the trust of the general public – principally by relentless media attacks upon him – and so had become a liability to the government. In that sense, Byers' resignation simply reflects the 'realist' interpretation of ministerial 'responsibility': that ministers will be forced to resign only when, on a hard-headed political calculation, their staying on will cause more damage to the governing party than their resignation.

Suspicion has been voiced by various commentators that the split between 'operational matters' – for which the minister must account to Parliament, but need not accept personal responsibility – and matters of policy, for which he must both give an account and accept responsibility, is blurred and open to manipulation by the government of the day. In particular, commentators saw a tendency during the last administration to narrow down the areas of 'policy' for which ministers conceded they were personally responsible to 'high government policy and overall political strategy' (Woodhouse, p 269). The suspicion that the area of departmental activity for which ministers will accept responsibility is an ever-shrinking one is, to an extent, borne out by events during the 18 years of the previous Conservative administration. Although there were a number of major failings in government policy, including the arms to Iraq affair, the BSE crisis, the Poll Tax and the Pergau Dam affair, only one minister, Lord Carrington, actually accepted responsibility for error in his department (the Foreign Office) and resigned; this took place in the wholly exceptional circumstance of the actual loss of British territory – the Falkland Islands – by an armed invasion. Other than this, the only examples of the areas for which ministers will take responsibility are negative ones: where the particular problems that had occurred in the department were found by the minister *not* to be ones which would engage his responsibility.[3] Most resignations in fact occur either over sexual or financial misconduct or indiscreet and damaging remarks which embarrass the government, such as Edwina Currie's pronouncement over the infection of British eggs by salmonella. As noted above, Ron Davies' resignation fits this mould neatly. Woodhouse, writing in 2002, observed that 'in the second half of the 20th century, only the resignations of Dugdale (1954), Carrington (1982) and Brittan (1986) can, with any degree of certainty, be attributed to departmental fault' ([2002] PL 73). Estelle Morris's resignation as Education Secretary in October 2002 appeared to come about partly as a result of major administrative problems over the marking of A and A/S levels and the vetting of new teachers and at first sight might therefore appear to be a rare instance of a Minister taking responsibility for problems within her department or Agency. However, it is not a clear-cut instance, because Morris did not acknowledge that the mistakes made impelled her resignation; rather – and very unusually – her stated grounds for quitting her post were that she thought she did not have the political and strategic skills to do it as well as she would like. Woodhouse, however, sees recognition by Cook (in relation to the Sandline affair in 1998) and Straw (in relation to the passports crisis of 1999) of the principle of what she calls 'explanatory and amendatory responsibility', in that both ministers provided a full account of what had gone wrong (though Cook is criticised for some initial obstruction of the investigation by the Foreign Affairs Select Committee) and put in place remedial action which, in turn, they invited Parliament to scrutinise, thus 'completing the accountability cycle'.

It may perhaps be concluded that the responsibility of the Cabinet to Parliament has real force only when the government has a small majority. Otherwise, although Parliament may have some influence, it appears to be of an indeterminate and inadequate nature. Furthermore, it might be suggested that the current operation of the three conventions considered merely provides a cloak for Prime Ministerial power without accountability. The Prime Minister can present policies as though they were the product of Cabinet discussion, and can expect ministers who have not participated in such discussion to defend them. If such policies miscarry, ministers may be able to disclaim responsibility, perhaps on the basis that officials have erred, but eventually, if the only alternative is a demand for the resignation of the Prime Minister, an individual minister may be prepared to resign and the Prime Minister may be able to distance himself from what has occurred.

NOTES

1 Although this view may be generally acceptable, it could be pointed out that other Committees meeting before Cabinet convenes can strengthen rather than weaken it as an institution. The previous meetings can deal with the non-contentious points, so that Cabinet time is reserved for the really important policy issues.

2 It might be noted at this point that theoretically, a motion of censure may result in the dismissal of a minister but, in practice, such motions can always be defeated by a majority government.

3 Students could give the example of the Child Support Agency. As Woodhouse has pointed out, the CSA had a disastrous first year (1993): performance targets had not been met by a long way and there were countless cases of bad administration. Ministers blamed all the problems on bad management and the chief executive of the Agency resigned. Ministers refused to accept any personal responsibility for the problems despite the fact that, as Woodhouse puts it, 'the ministers' failure to ensure that the Agency was properly established, staffed and resourced directly affected the ability of the Agency to operate effectively' ('Ministerial responsibility', pp 269–270).

Question 24

'The doctrine of individual ministerial responsibility as currently understood fails to provide a clear and satisfactory framework for the division of responsibility and accountability as between ministers, civil servants and, in particular, the chief executives of Next Steps Agencies; consequently, it allows ministers to evade and displace responsibility for departmental failings and thus fails to provide a firm basis for accountable government.'

Discuss.

Answer plan

This is a much more focused question which requires more detailed knowledge of the subject area, in particular, the problems thrown up by the creation of the Next Steps Agencies. The subject of the question is not the extent of the obligation to give an account (for example, areas excluded from questioning), but rather the issue of responsibility for departmental errors and the allocation of accountability between ministers and officials. Recent examples should be used where possible to illustrate the student's ability to apply the general principles discussed to contemporary political activity.

The following matters should be considered:

- the distinctions between providing an account, being held to account and the acceptance of blame for errors;
- the current position on the acceptance of blame only for 'policy'; difficulties of 'hidden' policy problems and the ability of government to manipulate the concept of 'policy';
- examples of the effects of this difficulty in practice in relation to the prison service and the Child Support Agency (CSA);
- an explanation of how officials may be accountable to Parliament;
- the limitations on this by the Osmotherly rules and the difficulties thrown up by these limitations;
- the particular problems in relation to the Next Steps Agencies;
- the implications of the above difficulties regarding accountability for the problem of locating responsibility and overcoming ministerial evasion of responsibility;
- the possible impact of the Freedom of Information Act 2000.

Answer

The doctrine of individual ministerial responsibility has recently been the subject of much controversy: the doctrine itself and its efficacy were subject to a rigorous analysis in the Scott Report and the analysis continued, in the light of Scott's findings, by the Public Service Committee's inquiry into ministerial responsibility and accountability. The at least partial misleading of Parliament which took place in relation to the intelligence on Iraq and WMD has kept the controversy alive. The question suggests that the above review has not resulted in satisfactory solutions to the problems of dividing responsibility and accountability between ministers and officials. In what follows, the particular criticisms contained in the question will be addressed and an assessment made as to whether the charges of ministerial evasion and lack of proper accountability are made out.

It should be asked, first of all, what the notion of responsibility entails. Broadly speaking, two notions are involved: first, that for every area of government policy, there should be a minister who is prepared to explain and justify government policy either personally or via his officials; second, that in the case of failings within the department, someone will be prepared to take responsibility for that failure. The doctrine therefore requires both that there be some *obligation* on ministers to give an account of their actions and policies to Parliament, and that if fault is revealed, there must be some means for Parliament to exact some kind of redress. This can broadly be of two types: punitive, in the sense that the minister is 'punished' by being forced to resign; and rectificatory, or amendatory, whereby a minister must promise and execute action to correct the problems and then report back to Parliament on the success of that action, a response which may be more important in practice than whether any resignations are produced. Formally, Parliament does possess the power effectively to get rid of ministers by passing motions of no confidence or censure; it may also pass motions calling for changes in existing policy. In practice, as we shall see, this penal power is virtually never used, though the threat of its use can be important.

This basic distinction between the provision of an account and the reaction to it seems clear enough. However, the terminology that has been suggested and which appears to have been accepted by governments of both political persuasions is somewhat different, though it deploys the same basic concept. Here, a distinction is drawn between the duty to provide an account ('accountability') and the obligation to accept personal responsibility when things go wrong ('responsibility'). In this version, the duty to provide an account extends to answering criticisms, to defending the record of the department in question, even to what was termed above 'rectificatory' redress, namely, promising investigation and remedial action if necessary. So, 'accountability' goes far beyond the mere transmission of information: it means not only 'giving an account', but also 'being held to account', with the proviso that this does not include the acceptance of personal fault by the minister. Acceptance of such fault means acceptance of 'responsibility' and resignation may become an issue. The distinction may be illustrated by the example of a complaint about the poor quality of food in Brixton prison. The Home Secretary may be asked questions about this, may have to put in hand an investigation as to what has gone wrong and report back to Parliament on remedial action and whether this has worked. However, no one would realistically expect that the minister should be seen as personally at fault for this problem. As Jack Straw said when he became Home Secretary in 1997, he could not be blamed every time a prison officer accidentally left a cell door open.

Therefore, the first issue to be addressed is whether this distinction between 'responsibility' and 'accountability' works satisfactorily, or whether it provides a means for ministers to avoid accepting responsibility when they should. Whether there was ever a time when ministers accepted personal blame for every shortcoming in their department is highly doubtful; it now seems well established that ministers will only accept personal fault if it can clearly be shown that the fault for what has gone wrong rests with ministerial policy decisions rather than with the implementation of that policy by their officials.

There are two possible problems with the responsibility/accountability distinction: first, it has been suggested that the distinction between policy on the one hand and its implementation on the other is not a coherent one, and that drawing a sharp distinction simply obscures ministerial responsibility for the overall record of the department. This is because, as Professor Hennessey pointed out in evidence before the Public Service Committee: 'There is not actually a proper division between [policy and operations] . . . These are seamless garments. If, operationally, you hit real trouble, it is usually because the policy is flawed.' In other words, the day to day problems which occur in a department may in actuality be attributable to overall – but hidden – policy problems, such as insufficient funding. So, policy mistakes may be *inferred* from widespread operational difficulties. Government has, however, tended to take the opposite line, relying on a 'bright line' distinction between the two which serves in practice to exonerate ministers from blame after departmental failings have come to light. In fact, save for the resignation of Lord Carrington following the invasion of the Falkland Islands, it is virtually impossible to find any example of ministers admitting that responsibility for major departmental errors or failings lies with them. Thus, ministers have repeatedly denied responsibility for failings in the prison service: following breakouts by IRA prisoners in 1983, James Prior refused to accept blame; again, in 1984, after two IRA prisoners escaped from Brixton, Kenneth Baker refused to resign. More importantly, when the highly critical Learmont Report on the state of Britain's prisons came out, Michael Howard found that all the problems identified were due not to his policies, but to the way they had been put into practice by the head of the prison service, Derek Lewis, who he promptly sacked. The reaction of ministers to the appalling performance in its first year of the CSA is also instructive, as Woodhouse points out ('Ministerial responsibility', pp 169–170). Ministers refused to take any blame for the Agency's failure to meet its performance targets and its already long record of maladministration, despite the fact that as Woodhouse argues, 'the ministers' failure to ensure that the Agency was properly established, staffed and resourced directly affected the ability of the Agency to operate effectively'. No Labour Minister has taken personal responsibility for the continuing, disastrous record of the Agency, which, the Government recently announced, was to be fundamentally re-thought (an instance, instead of 'rectificatory accountability', though, arguably, somewhat overdue). Similarly, Cook, in relation to the Sandline affair in 1998, and Straw, in relation to the passports crisis of 1999, both stated that essentially operational decisions were to blame for the problems that arose in their departments, assertions which to be fair to them have been largely accepted by independent commentators (see, for example, Woodhouse [2002] PL 73). Cook did recognise systemic and cultural problems with the Foreign Office, but given that he had been Foreign Secretary for less than a year, could not reasonably be expected to take personal responsibility for these. At first sight, Estelle Morris's resignation as Education Secretary in October 2002 might appear to provide a counter-example, as it appeared to come about partly as a result of major administrative problems over the marking of A and A/S levels and the vetting of new teachers; it might therefore appear to be a rare instance of a Minister taking responsibility for problems within her department or Agency. However, it is not a clear-cut instance of taking such responsibility, because Ms Morris did not acknowledge that the mistakes made impelled her resignation; rather – and very unusually – her stated grounds for quitting her post were that she thought she did not have the political and strategic skills to do it as well as she would like.

The second related problem is that not only may operational problems be really attributable to hidden policy mistakes, but the notion of 'policy' itself is vague and subject to manipulation by government. Ministers in the Conservative administrations of the 1980s and 1990s showed a tendency to narrow down the areas definable as 'policy', thus making the minister responsible – in the sense of having to take the blame – for an ever-shrinking area. Thus, as Woodhouse points out ('Ministerial responsibility', pp 268–269), after the Brixton prison escapes in 1991, the Home Secretary, when called upon to resign, announced that 'policy' was confined to matters of overall strategy or high government policy, whilst departmental policies, which gave effect to the political preferences, were absorbed into 'administration'; a viewpoint also relied upon by Michael Howard following the Learmont Report in 1995, and described by him as having been accepted for 'years, even generations'.

The focus thus far has been on how well the division between responsibility and accountability works; the above analysis would appear to suggest that not only is the distinction unclear and unsatisfactory, but that the charge in the question that it allows ministerial evasion of their responsibilities appears to have some substance. We will now examine the operation of accountability, whether it enables Parliament to gain the information it needs or whether it contributes to the problems outlined above.

As a matter of common sense, clearly, a minister will not be able to give an account of everything going on within a large and complex government department in which hundreds of decisions may be taken every day. In practice, the minister will often either have to find out what has happened and report back to Parliament, or Parliament will have to question civil servants about the matter directly. The ability of Select Committees to subject civil servants and the heads of Next Steps Agencies ('Agencies') to sustained questioning, in order to obtain first hand information on the workings of the departments under their remit, is generally seen as being one of their main strengths. Additionally, it may be noted that heads of Agencies – with the exception of the head of the prison service – also give written answers to parliamentary questions on operational matters, which appear in *Hansard*. Thus the system does allow first hand questioning of officials, an important ingredient in effective information gathering and hence in ensuring accountability.

However, there are two major restrictions on this ability to engage in first hand questioning. First, ministers continue to assert the right – contested by Select Committees – to choose which particular civil servants appear in front of the Committees, though in practice they have usually acceded to Committee requests in this respect.[1] A particular problem of late has been the refusal of ministers in the Blair government to allow their Special Advisers, thought by many to exercise more power than many ministers, to appear before any Select Committees, despite the revision of the 'Osmotherly rules' in 2005 to provide for their attendance, and assurances given to the Liaision Committee in 2004 that Special Advisor would now be allowed to give such evidence (Minutes of Evidence, HC 1180-i, Q 26). The Public Administration Select Committee found in 2005 that that there was still a marked reluctance by Ministers, notably the Prime Minister, to allow the questioning of Special Advisers by Select Committees (1st Special Report, 2005–06), while the basic principle remains that it is for Ministers to decide which civil servants and Advisors should attend on their behalf (evidence to Liaison Committee, ibid). Perhaps more importantly, the basic principle of the Osmotherly rules is that both heads of Agencies and civil servants answer questions 'on behalf of ministers' (para 40); that is, they remain under ministerial instructions as to how to answer questions at all times. The Blair government has given this doctrine its full backing.

In practical terms, this restriction means that while an official may give his own account of factual matters, when it comes to providing explanations and justifications of departmental policy, he will provide only the government's view, without criticising it in any way, or suggesting alternatives – a restriction said to be justified by the need to retain Civil Service neutrality. Thus, in giving factual information, civil servants will have to avoid any suggestion that government policy may be flawed in any way. They will therefore give only a limited account. The application of this rule to the Chief Executives of Agencies is seen as particularly problematic, because it does not match the fact that the executives have full responsibility for operational matters delegated to them under their framework documents with an ability to give to Parliament a full account of the areas *within* that responsibility. The ability of the chief executives to manage their Agencies properly will, of course, be heavily dependent upon policy decisions on which they are forbidden to comment. This is unsatisfactory both for the chief executive and for Parliament. In effect, by instructing civil servants to take a particular line with a Committee, ministers can, to an extent, control the flow of information about the very incident in relation to which s/he stands accused of possible fault.

A further aspect of the doctrine which has attracted criticism is the fact that ministers still retain the duty to give an account of operational matters within Agencies, although responsibility for these matters is fully delegated to the chief executives. The whole point of the Agencies is that they are supposed to operate with a large degree of independence from ministers, so that they can be run on much more business-like lines and can be free from constant political interference. Additionally, the idea was that the clear demarcation of responsibility between ministers and chief executives would make the lines of responsibilities stronger and more transparent – it would be clear to Parliament and the public who was responsible for what. Given that this is the whole point of the changes, it seems futile and illogical to continue to maintain that the minister is accountable for everything going on in the Agencies.[2]

The final problem with the Osmotherly rules is as follows: we have noted above a tendency by ministers to attribute failures within a department to the mistakes of certain civil servants rather than to their own policy, thus freeing ministers from personal responsibility and any risk of forced resignation. However, Parliament may wish not simply to take the minister's word on this. It might like to get the other side of the story from the civil servants who are being forced to take the blame. The Osmotherly rules prevent this, giving rise to a situation in which Parliament has no way of independently ascertaining whether the minister's account is correct because civil servants and chief executives are only able to parrot the ministerial line, absolving policy – and thus the minister – of any blame. Thus, if ministers are concealing the fact that policy and not its implementation is responsible for the mistakes, Parliament is unlikely to be able to ascertain this by questioning civil servants. While the Freedom of Information Act 2000 in theory gives both MPs and the public a means of ascertaining the truth, there is a class exemption in s 35 in relation to all information relating to 'the formulation or development of government policy'. The only limitation to this astonishingly broad exemption – which is not subject to a burden on ministers to prove that harm would be caused by releasing the information in question – is that statistical information relating to a decision may be released once the decision is made. But, for example, evidence of other policy options considered and the reasons for rejecting them would not be. While the Information Commissioner can order release of the information concerned if satisfied (*per s* 2) that the public interest in withholding information does not outweigh the interest in its reception, its release can ultimately be vetoed by a Cabinet minister (s 53), because the information relates to a central government department. It remains to be seen whether the veto will be much used in practice; the fact that this Government has defied recommendations from the Parliamentary Ombudsman to disclose information under the previous Code of Practice on Access to Government Information does not bode well in this respect.

In conclusion, it may be argued that the present understanding of ministerial responsibility relies upon a series of distinctions which are open to manipulation and abuse by government, and that Parliament appears to be currently deprived of the ability to challenge such manipulation and make its own determination as to where responsibility should be located from a position of comprehensive knowledge, due to the restrictions represented by the Osmotherly rules. It may be further contended that the dogmatic application of these rules to chief executives and the continued accountability of ministers for the workings of the Next Steps Agencies seems illogical and likely to undermine the demarcation of duties between ministers and officials, which the Agencies are supposed to follow and uphold.

NOTES

1 Students could give a number of examples here of instances where Select Committees investigating areas of acute sensitivity to the government have found that key witnesses have been withheld from them. Thus, in 1984, the government would not allow the Director of *GCHQ* to give evidence to the Select Committee on Employment which was investigating the banning of trade unions at that organisation. Similarly, in 1986, the Defence Committee in the course of its inquiries into the Westland affair wished to interview certain named officials; the government minister in question would not allow them to attend. More recently, Robin Cook would not allow certain civil servants to appear before the Foreign Affairs Committee when it was investigating the Sandline affair in 1999.

2 Students could make the further point that the continued accountability of ministers for the day-to-day running of the Agencies encourages them to interfere with day-to-day decision-making in order to ensure outcomes that will be more politically acceptable. Thus, the supposed independence of the Agencies from political interference may be undermined by the continued political accountability of ministers for their actions, detracting from their basic *raison d'être*.

Question 25

'The obligation on ministers to give a full and frank account to Parliament of the actions of their departments is limited, uncertain and unsatisfactory in scope and does not in practice prevent Parliament from being misled or, at the least, under-informed.'

Discuss.

Answer plan

This is a fairly straightforward question on the scope of the duty to give an account to Parliament and one which is likely to be popular with examiners, given the findings of the Scott Report and the continued academic and parliamentary interest in accountability. Students should make sure that their answer includes practical examples – the findings of Scott provide the best source – of apparently unsatisfactory answers to parliamentary questions or letters. Answers must now indicate the possible impact of the Freedom of Information Act 2000 in this area

The following matters should be covered:

- the formulation of the obligation in *The Ministerial Code;* the status of the Code;
- the exceptions to the general duty of openness, as previously set out in the *Information Code* and now under the Freedom of Information Act 2000;
- the permissibility of making untrue statements in Parliament;
- the problem of the giving of incomplete or impartial information to Parliament, which may mislead it;
- the findings of the Scott Report on the above and the implications of the Iraq WMD fiasco;
- the problems with the fact that the Ministerial Code only prohibits the 'knowing' misleading of Parliament.

Answer

While Parliament has finally passed a Freedom of Information Act in 2000 (FOI 2000), it has only very recently come into force, and its impact upon Ministerial accountability to Parliament remains unclear at present. The obligation of ministers to account to Parliament for the actions and decisions of their departments remains one of the most important guarantees of a reasonable degree of transparency in government. The obligation has received unprecedented attention in the last few years; Lord Justice Scott made a series of findings on how far ministers had satisfactorily discharged their duty of 'explanatory accountability' (to use Marshall's phrase) in the particular context of the Arms to Iraq affair, though he also made some more general findings. The Public Service Committee undertook a comprehensive review of this area in 1995–97; one of the last actions of the Parliament of 1992–97 was to pass a resolution on ministerial accountability (on 20 March 1997) which became the basis of the governmental view of the extent of the obligation of accountability, set out in what was once *Questions of Procedure for Ministers* and is now, under the Blair administration, renamed *The Ministerial Code*. The at least partial misleading of Parliament which took place in relation to intelligence on Iraq's alleged WMD in the run up to the Iraq war has kept this subject firmly in the forefront of political debate. The question suggests that the convention is still unsatisfactory in formulation and not properly adhered to in practice. Both these assertions will be tested in order to arrive at a considered conclusion.

The obligation, as formulated by the present government, reads:

> It is of paramount importance that Ministers give accurate and truthful information to Parliament, correcting any inadvertent error at the earliest opportunity. Ministers who knowingly mislead Parliament will be expected to offer their resignation to the Prime Minister. Ministers should be as open as possible with Parliament and the public, refusing to provide information only when disclosure would not be in the public interest which should be decided in accordance with the relevant statutes and the Freedom of Information Act 2000.
>
> (Para 1.5, Ministerial Code (Cabinet Office, 2005))

This formulation follows more or less word for word the version put forward by the previous government which was approved by the House of Commons on 20 March 1997,[1] though it has been updated to take account of the advent of the FOI 2000. The wording of the obligation in the Code is important because the experience of the previous administrations suggests that it is this, the only authoritative formulation of the obligation we have, that will be relied upon by ministers accused of misleading Parliament, and so will set the parameters for debate.

The exceptions to the general duty to give information set out in *The Ministerial Code* itself must first be examined. The excluded categories of information still include all of those set out in the Official Secrets legislation and, more significantly, the very broad exemptions set out in the FOI 2000. These include:

- law enforcement and legal proceedings (ss 30 and 31);
- information which would violate the Data Protection Act (s 40) or be a breach of confidence (s 41);
- information which might harm national security, defence, the economy, international affairs or relations between UK Administrations;
- information relating to the formulation or development of government policy, including all advice relating to internal discussion and advice, for example, advice from civil servants to ministers or internal consultation and information relating to rejected policy options (s 35);
- unreasonable, voluminous or overly costly requests (ss 12 and 14);
- information which would harm the 'effective conduct of public affairs' (s 36) – this exception, in particular, being very wide and vague;

- finally, information relating to advice on the giving of honours is also excluded, so that, for example, the process by which a candidate is recommended and accepted for a life peerage remains secret.

It should be noted that some of the most significant of these exclusionary categories do not require a harm test: that is, in these categories, it does not even have to be shown that release of the information would cause any harm before the minister can refuse to supply it. This is the case in relation to the astonishingly broad exemption in s 35 noted above. The only limitation to this exemption is that statistical information relating to a decision is no longer exempted once the decision is made. But, for example, evidence of other policy options considered, and the reasons for rejecting them, would be covered by the exemption. The Information Commissioner can order release of the information concerned if satisfied (*per* s 2) that the public interest in withholding information does not outweigh the interest in its reception; however, because the information relates to a central government department, its release can ultimately be vetoed by a Cabinet minister (s 53).

While *The Ministerial Code* sets out areas in which answers may be refused, it also makes it clear that ministers must always be truthful with Parliament, 'correcting any inadvertent errors at the earliest opportunity'. However, are there then any circumstances in which it is permissible to tell a direct lie to Parliament? The answer appears to be that this would be acceptable only in the most extreme circumstances: examples mentioned by Scott and the Public Service Committee indicate that such a lie might be permissible if it was necessary in order to conceal an imminent devaluation of the currency, where disclosure would be economically catastrophic, or where an untruth was necessary in order to save the life of British citizens: the example has been given of a British MI6 agent arrested in a hostile country where, in order to save the person's life, it might be necessary for ministers to assure Parliament that the person was not working for the intelligence services. It seems to be generally accepted that only in the most extreme circumstances would such an action be permissible.

The more problematic question is whether, and if so when, it is legitimate to give incomplete answers to Parliament. It may be noted here that the version of the obligation to account to Parliament put forward by the Public Service Committee after its exhaustive inquiry included the requirement that ministers must take 'special care' to give information which is 'full and accurate' to Parliament, and that they must conduct themselves 'frankly and with candour' (see Annex 1 of the Report).

Such phrases strongly imply that information given by ministers should be comprehensive, and that ministers should make it clear if only partial information is being given, for whatever reason. The version which appears in *The Ministerial Code*, however, carefully eschews such phrases, using only the adjective 'truthful', not 'full', and saying nothing of 'frankness' or 'candour'. These omissions appear to leave the door open to the view that giving incomplete information is not necessarily misleading – the 'half a picture can be true' thesis put forward by two very senior civil servants, Sir Gore Booth and Sir Robin Butler, and a minister, William Waldegrave, during the Scott Inquiry. Waldegrave made his view explicit to the Public Service Committee: 'There are plenty of cases . . . where the minister will not mislead the House . . . but may not display everything he knows about the subject' (HC 27, 1993–94, para 125). The fact that this notion was given such authoritative support during the Scott Inquiry and afterwards suggests that it is one which commands quite widespread acceptance in government. Indeed, a senior civil servant in evidence to the Public Service Committee commented that

there is a commonly accepted culture that the function of [an answer to a PQ] is to give no more information than the minister thinks will be helpful to him or her, the minister, in the process of political debate in the House [HC 313, 1995–96, 20 March 1996, Q 21].

The objection to the 'half the picture' thesis is obvious, and was expressed forcefully in the Scott Report: the problem, Scott commented, is that the person getting the information will not know that the information is only partial. They are therefore 'almost bound . . . to be misled' (Scott Report, para D4.55). Scott suggested that the information given should, in the absence of compelling public interest reasons, be at the least a 'fair summary of the full picture'. There is nothing in *The Ministerial Code* which expressly deals with this institutionalised problem. This failure may be seen to be a further unsatisfactory aspect of the convention of accountability.

The fear that these deficiencies in the convention itself may lead to the misleading, or at least the under-informing of Parliament is, to an extent, substantiated by the quotes noted above. Further evidence may be found in the Scott Report. For present purposes, Scott's overall conclusion may be cited:

Government statements made in 1989 and 1990 about policy on defence exports to Iraq consistently failed . . . to comply with the standard set by [the earlier version of *The Ministerial Code* (QPM)] and, more importantly, failed to discharge the obligations imposed by the constitutional principle of ministerial accountability.

(para D4.63)

No such finding has been authoritatively made in relation to what has arguably been one of the gravest foreign policy disasters of recent times – the invasion of Iraq. In essence, Parliament was given information – that Iraq had WMD, in particular weapons that could be used within 45 minutes of the order to launch being given – which turned out to be comprehensively false. Despite the widespread popular perception that the Government, in particular Mr Blair, simply lied about the issue, it appears that the more accurate view is that the evidence rather was heavily 'spun' and that much of the fault lay with the intelligence services, and the failure of the Joint Intelligence Committee to scrutinise the raw data more sceptically and rigorously. In terms of presentation, Sir Robin Butler's Report found that at times caveats and doubts over specific claims were not passed onto Parliament. Thus the impression was given that the intelligence supporting the claims about Iraq's WMD threat was 'firmer and fuller' than it actually was. But Butler – to widespread skepticism – found that there had been 'no deliberate distortion' of the available information. This allowed Blair and his Government largely to escape Parliamentary censure for misleading it, although there is overwhelming evidence that the public has rejected Butler's findings and believes that Blair was disingenuous.

Returning to the Scott Report, the *practice* of governmental accountability to Parliament was found to be deeply unsatisfactory by the most comprehensive public and independent inquiry into the subject undertaken during the twentieth century. It is worth noting one of the government's defences to the claims that any of the responsible ministers, in particular, Mr Waldegrave, should resign, because it illustrates another important weakness with the current formulation of the convention of accountability. This was that Mr Waldegrave had not, contrary to the provision in QPM, 'knowingly' misled Parliament at all in saying that the guidelines on arms exports to Iran & Iraq had not changed, because his personal belief was that they had not. As Scott put it:

> Mr Waldegrave strenuously . . . asserted his belief, in the face of a volume of . . . overwhelming evidence to the contrary, that policy on defence sales to Iraq had indeed remained unchanged.

Mr Waldegrave argued that all that had happened was that the old guidelines (which were more restrictive in terms of allowing arms sales) were being applied 'flexibly', using the new guidelines as 'an interpretative gloss' on the old ones. Scott described this viewpoint as one 'that does not seem to me to correspond with reality' and added, 'The description of [the new policy] as merely a flexible interpretation of the guidelines . . . [was] bound to be misleading'. Nevertheless, he also said, 'I did not receive any impression of any insincerity on Mr Waldegrave's part' and that 'Mr Waldegrave . . . did not have any duplicitous intent' in putting forward this explanation.

This latter finding was repeatedly relied upon by the government to refute any argument that Waldegrave should resign: since he had not meant to deceive, it was argued, he had not 'knowingly' misled Parliament and therefore had not broken the rules. The problem with this approach is that it allows a minister who holds an honest but manifestly unreasonable – even bizarre – view that government policy has not changed simply to tell Parliament that there has been no change, even though he clearly ought to have realised that others might not share this view and thus be misled as to what had actually happened. The present position allows ministers to claim that they have adhered to their duty not to mislead Parliament, provided that it is not manifest beyond all possible argument that the particular interpretation of events they gave to Parliament was untrue. Blair and other Ministers have used exactly the same defence: whilst the statements made to Parliament on Iraqi WMD turned out to be false, they argued that they honestly believed them to be true at the time. It is suggested that the duty on ministers ought, in cases where the matter is arguable, to be not just to give their view – for example, 'the guidelines have not changed' – but to give full factual information as to what has occurred, and allow Parliament to draw its own conclusions. The convention, as set out in the Code, does not appear to require this at present. Very recently, Stephen Byers sought to rely on the defence that he had not 'knowingly' misled Parliament when he had wrongly announced in February 2002 that his former press officer, Martin Sixsmith, had resigned, when in fact this had not been agreed. Byers' story, seemingly accepted by Labour colleagues during a Commons debate in May 2002, was that this had been his genuine, though mistaken, understanding at the time from discussions with his permanent secretary. Byers refused to resign, or even apologise, stating that at all times he had acted in good faith, representing to Parliament – and to the public – the position as he believed it to be. He escaped censure at the time, but was forced to resign later in the month. The causes of his resignation were complex but, in part, came from a widespread perception that he had in fact been duplicitous. The lesson drawn by commentators was, however, that it was the press and not Parliament that had forced the resignation, by making Byers a liability for the government through constant, negative reportage which served to prevent transport policy from being anything other than a 'bad news' story whilst he was in charge of it.

In conclusion, it has been argued that insofar as the convention of accountability is for all practical purposes expressed by the formulation set out in *The Ministerial Code*, the charges made in the question are largely substantiated. There are still very broad and vaguely defined areas where information may be withheld; the Code does not appear to tackle the culture of giving only partial information, and it allows ministers to deny that they have misled Parliament by reference to their own subjective and possibly eccentric interpretations, instead of requiring adherence to a more objective standard. It is therefore submitted that while the present position does represent a small advance upon that which existed pre-Scott, the accountability regime requires both greater strength and greater clarity. Whether the Freedom of Information Act 2000 will significantly strengthen the ability of Parliament – and the press – to hold ministers to account will depend, crucially, on the readiness of the Information Commissioner to order the release of information relying on the public interest test in the Act, and on how often ministers are prepared to take the possibly damaging step of invoking the ministerial veto against an order to release information relating to their own departments.

NOTE

1 Students could note that this is an advance on the previous position, whereby the obligation as set out in *Questions of Procedure for Ministers* (the forerunner of *The Ministerial Code*) was produced simply as a unilateral act of government, thus allowing government to determine the extent of its own accountability. The new statement of the obligation was at least approved by Parliament. However, it should be noted that the wording of the obligation was suggested by the government for approval by Parliament, and that the government had rejected a more radically worded version produced by the Public Service Committee.

CHAPTER 7

JUDICIAL REVIEW

▌INTRODUCTION

This topic is very extensive and is often taught as a separate course on Administrative Law in the second or third year of degree courses. However, on constitutional law courses, it is of a manageable size and sometimes attracts two questions in exams – which can make it a good return for your revision (check your past papers!). In this area, extensive knowledge of case law is clearly necessary, but must be bound together and informed by a grasp of basic principle. Questions can appear as either essays or problems and quite often both appear in one paper. Essays will generally demand an evaluation of the effectiveness of judicial review in one form or other. If a problem question asks the student to advise clients, it is important to remember standing, amenability, procedure and remedies, bearing in mind the changes introduced by the Civil Procedure Rules (CPR). Some papers treat natural justice as a separate topic, and this has been reflected in the questions given below. In theory, a problem could combine traditional judicial review issues with questions arising under the Human Rights Act (HRA). However, the textbooks and most courses treat the HRA separately and examiners seem generally to be setting questions that test the student's knowledge of the English principles of judicial review, without confusing this with possible claims brought under the HRA – though again, you should check past papers on this. In addition, answering a problem question on the HRA would generally require knowledge of the European Convention on Human Rights' (ECHR's) case law, particularly in relation to Art 6, which first year students would not generally be expected to have. There is, in particular, a very complex legal issue as to how far judicial review of a decision taken by a body which does not itself satisfy the requirements of Art 6 of the ECHR can provide a level of protection such that overall, Art 6 is satisfied. Therefore, the answers given to the problem questions here do not include possible HRA points, except in one important area. The HRA has already had the effect of changing the ordinary English law on bias, with the courts accepting that Art 6 of the ECHR requires a modification of the previous *Gough* test. This is therefore included. Additionally, essay questions on judicial review may well ask for an analysis of how the HRA has changed the standard of substantive review in human rights cases. Such a question is included here.

Checklist

Students should be familiar with the following areas:

- the public/private law boundary: r 54 of the CPR, *locus standi*, time limits and amenability of bodies to review;

- procedural impropriety other than natural justice; mandatory/directory express requirements, for example, consultation;

- tests for the applicability of natural justice, including 'legitimate expectation';

- the *audi* rule – what it will demand in different situations: when are legal representation, witnesses, cross-examination or an oral hearing required?;

- the rule against bias: direct interests (*Pinochet*) and indirect interest – how the test for the latter has been changed by the HRA: *Porter v Magill (2002)*;

- illegality: fettering by policy, delegation, improper purpose, inferred purpose or plurality of purposes; irrelevant considerations and concept of error of law; the effect of rulings that all such errors are reviewable; substantive legitimate expectations;

- irrationality: is this the same concept as '*Wednesbury* unreasonableness'?; citiques of the notion;

- remedies: basic knowledge, discretion to refuse, instances when certain remedies are inappropriate or will not lie;

- the impact of the HRA; the possible development of proportionality as a ground of review.

Question 26

Prisoners at Burham prison occupy the roof in an attempt to air their grievances. After the disturbance has been brought under control, Abel and Bert, two of the prisoners, are charged with various offences against discipline as laid down in the Prison Rules 1964. Abel is charged with attempting to assault an officer by throwing a slate from the prison roof and is sentenced by the Board of Visitors to the forfeiture of 20 days' remission. Bert is charged with intentionally obstructing an officer in the execution of his duty. He is also dealt with by the Board, which imposes a punishment of 14 days' forfeiture of privileges and 28 days' stoppage of earnings.

Both Abel and Bert are allowed to appear in person at their respective hearings, but both are refused legal representation on the ground that the hearings must be dealt with swiftly. Abel is permitted to call one witness in his defence, but two others are refused on the ground that they have been dispersed to other prisons. Bert's request to call a witness is refused. Abel is allowed to remain present during his hearing while a prison officer gives evidence against him, but is refused permission to cross-examine him. The Board gives Bert a summary of the allegations made against him by a prison officer, but refuses to allow him to see the full statement. Bert is surprised by the content of the allegations, which appear to be more extensive than those appearing in the statement of charges given to him prior to the hearing. Despite this, the Board refuses to give him time to consider them.

Advise Abel and Bert as to any redress they might have. Disregard any possible impact of the Human Rights Act (HRA) 1998 in your answer.

Answer plan

This is a very straightforward question on the principles of natural justice. At the outset, it is very important to bear in mind that what is meant by a fair hearing will vary from hearing to hearing, and that the more serious the penalty, the higher the standards observed should be. Thus, it is probably a good idea to deal with the hearings separately. It must first be shown that the courts are prepared to review the decision in question on the ground of want of natural justice, and secondly in relation to each hearing separately, that a breach (or breaches) of natural justice has taken place. Although one serious breach might lead to the quashing of the decision, you should strengthen your argument by considering as many as possible.

Essentially, the following matters should be discussed:

- the preparedness of the courts to review prison disciplinary decisions on the ground of want of natural justice (*St Germain* (1979));
- the preparedness of the courts to review decisions of Boards in prison disciplinary hearings on the ground of want of natural justice (*Leech v Deputy Governor of Parkhurst Prison; Prevot v Deputy Governor of Parkhurst Prison* (1988));
- the discretion to allow the calling of witnesses;
- the discretion to allow cross-examination;
- the discretion to allow legal representation which was established in Boards of Visitors' hearings;
- the right of a prisoner to a full opportunity of hearing the allegations against him and to present his case.

Answer

Both Abel and Bert will wish to show that these decisions were made in breach of the principles of natural justice. In order to seek judicial review to challenge them, they must show that they have a sufficient interest in the matter to which the application relates (s 31(3) of the Supreme Court Act 1981). Clearly, both applicants satisfy this test, as they have both been directly and adversely affected by decisions which relate only to them. It must be determined whether decisions of Boards of Visitors are amenable to judicial review. The new test under r 54.1(2) of the CPR provides that judicial review 'lies to review the lawfulness of . . . a decision, action or failure to act in relation to the exercise of a public function'. Cases since the CPR were introduced indicate that this test is at least as broad as the old one; case law prior to the CPR indicates that decisions of Boards of Visitors are subject to judicial review (*Board of Visitors of Hull Prison ex p St Germain (No 1) (1979)*). It is clear also that judicial review is the appropriate mode of challenge to such decisions: the applicants have no private law right (*O'Reilly v Mackman (1983)*) which could be vindicated in an ordinary civil action; moreover, r 54.2 of the CPR has now clarified that judicial review 'must be used' where the applicant is seeking, *inter alia*, a quashing order, which will be the remedy sought by both Abel and Bert here. Permission to seek judicial review must be granted by the court (r 54.4); it must be applied for 'promptly, and in any event not later than three months after the grounds to make the claim first arose' (r 54), so Abel and Bert must be advised to make their application swiftly.

Having ascertained that there are no procedural barriers in the way of the applicants, it must next be determined whether the rules of natural justice apply to the process in question. As Abel and Bert are involved in two separate hearings, and the consequences for each differ in degree of seriousness, their cases will be considered separately. It was determined in *Board of Visitors of Hull Prison ex p St Germain (No 1) (1979)* that prison disciplinary hearings were subject to the principles of natural justice. Certain prisoners complained that the disciplinary proceedings which followed the Hull prison riots were not conducted in accordance with the principles of natural justice. The Court of Appeal, in the first such ruling since *Ridge v Baldwin (1964)*, held that prisoners only lose those liberties expressly denied them by Parliament – otherwise, they retain their rights under the law. 'The rights of the citizen, however, circumscribed by penal sentence or otherwise must always be the concern of the courts unless their jurisdiction is expressly excluded by statute' (*per* Shaw LJ). This has been followed in numerous cases since then.

The rules of natural justice will therefore apply in Abel's case; however, can it be said that they have been breached? One of the two main principles of natural justice is the right to a fair hearing: the *audi alteram partem* rule. The question, therefore, is whether a disciplinary hearing requires the calling of all or any of the witnesses requested by the prisoner, cross-examination of the witnesses or legal representation in order to be fair. These matters will be looked at in turn.

In *Board of Visitors of Hull Prison ex p St Germain (No 2) (1979)*, it was held that Boards of Visitors must be able to exercise a discretion to refuse a prisoner's request for witnesses if they feel that he is purposely trying to obstruct or subvert the proceedings by calling large numbers of witnesses, or if, where the request is made in good faith, they feel that the calling of large numbers of witnesses is unnecessary. However, mere administrative inconvenience would not support a decision to refuse such a request. The principles established in the above case were confirmed in *Deputy Governor of Long Lartin Prison ex p Prevot (1988)*, in which the refusal to allow a prisoner to call a material witness led to a decision of a prisoner governor being quashed by the House of Lords. In the instant case, it appears that the only reason for the refusal was the inconvenience involved in recalling the witnesses from other prisons. It seems, therefore, that the Board took into account a factor that it should have disregarded. It does not appear that Abel requested three witnesses with a view to subverting the proceedings. Furthermore, given the fact that Abel was allegedly merely one of a group of prisoners on the roof, it would seem essential that he should be able to challenge evidence that he was present, that he threw the slate and that in doing so, he was attempting to assault a prison officer. In other words, these are questions of disputed fact: it is precisely in such situations that first hand accounts by eye-witnesses are necessary. It seems unlikely that the case was so straightforward as to require only one witness for the defence. Therefore, if Abel can demonstrate that calling more than one witness was necessary due to the nature of his defence, it would follow that he should have been allowed to call them.[1] The refusal to allow him to do so would amount to a breach of the *audi* rule.

It was determined in *St Germain (No 2)* that cross-examination of hearsay evidence should be made possible if it appertains to the central question of guilt or innocence. In this instance, hearsay evidence is not being presented; nevertheless, many of the arguments used in *St Germain* as to the desirability of allowing cross-examination where hearsay evidence is presented are equally applicable where it is not. Further, in *Board of Visitors of Gartree Prison ex p Mealy (1981)*, it was held that the accused should have been allowed to ask questions of a defence witness. On this basis, it may be argued that Abel should have been allowed to cross-examine prison officers.[2]

Abel's final ground of complaint is that he received no legal representation. Does a fair hearing before a Board include the right to legal representation? In *Fraser v Mudge (1975)*, the Court of Appeal determined that a prisoner had no such right, while in *Maynard v Osmond (1977)*, it was held that it would not be normal to have such a right, although a friend or helper might be permitted to be present. However, in *Secretary of State for the Department ex p Tarrant (1985)*, although it was accepted, following Fraser v Mudge, that a prisoner could not claim a right to legal representation, it was ruled that a Board of Visitors must exercise a discretion as to its grant. The court then suggested certain factors which a Board could properly take into account. These included: the seriousness of the charge and of the penalty; the likelihood that points of law might arise; the ability of the prisoner to conduct his own case; and the need for speed in making the adjudication. The House of Lords in *Board of Visitors of HM Prison, the Maze ex p Hone (1988)* considered the issue afresh, but determined that no absolute right to legal representation in prison disciplinary hearings could be created; the position would remain as in Tarrant. In Hone, the House of Lords was eager to deny that a right to legal advice as opposed to a discretion to award it existed, on the basis that otherwise it would be hard to deny such a right in Boards' hearings. It therefore follows that a discretion to award legal advice does exist in Boards' hearings, although it is likely that it will rarely appear necessary to grant it.

On this basis, given that the request for legal advice in the instant case was refused due to the need for expedition, can it be argued that a Board which had properly exercised discretion would have granted it? The charge is fairly serious and it carries a serious penalty. Points of law might well arise; Abel might wish to argue that he did not possess the requisite *mens rea* for attempted assault. This is probably the strongest argument for the grant of legal representation, but possibly it is outweighed by the particular need for speedy adjudication due to the tense situation in the prison. It may be concluded that the Board did exercise its discretion properly.

Thus, proceedings in Abel's case seem to have breached the *audi* rule, in that he was not allowed witnesses and probably in that he was not allowed an opportunity for cross-examination.

The requirements of a fair hearing in Bert's case will differ from those in Abel's because the consequences for Bert are less serious than for Abel: he is losing privileges and earnings rather than being forfeited with remission. In *Aston University ex p Rothy (1969)*, it was held that natural justice would apply although there was no kind of legal right in the question; it was necessary to look at all the circumstances – the expectation of a fair hearing and the serious consequences which would follow from the decision. It appears to be only in 'bare application' cases, such as *McInnes v Onslow Fane (1982)* that there is no duty to afford some kind of right to be heard; here Bert is being deprived of something. Possibly, the loss of privileges might not alone be sufficiently serious to warrant the application of the principles of natural justice, but may be so coupled with the loss of earnings – deprivation of a legal right – and on this ground, natural justice may apply. Whether Bert would have been entitled to an oral hearing, had the prison not decided to hold one need not be determined (*R (West) v. Parole Board (No 2) (2006)* would suggest that he may well not have been): but once a hearing is held, it must be fair, or the purpose of having one at all will be defeated. On this argument, *Leech v Deputy Governor of Long Lartin Prison; Prevot v Deputy Governor of Long Lartin Prison (1988)* applies to Bert's hearing, which should therefore have been conducted in accordance with the principles of natural justice.

Was the *audi* rule breached in Bert's case? He has four grounds of complaint: he was not allowed to call witnesses; to have legal representation; or to see a full statement of the allegations against him; and it seemed that the allegations had been added to since he saw the statement of charges against him prior to the inquiry. Administrative inconvenience is likely to be allowed much more weight since loss of remission is not in question. The tests from *Tarrant* (above) may be applied in the instant case; it may then be argued that the triviality of the penalty involved coupled with the need for speed in making the adjudication outweigh other factors such as the need to deal with points of law, and therefore do not warrant the grant of legal representation.

However, it may be urged that the Board should have exercised its discretion in favour of allowing Bert to call a witness (and perhaps allowing cross-examination of the prison officer whose evidence is presented). The test from *St Germain (No 2)* seems to be satisfied: Bert appears to be making the request in good faith and there seems no sufficient reason for refusing it. The administrative inconvenience involved would be minor, since the witness is presumably present in the prison.

Furthermore, Bert is denied the opportunity to see a full statement of the allegations. The right of notice of the case against a person is normally treated as the most basic of all the requirements of natural justice, since without it, it is impossible for the subject of the allegations to make effective representations: *R v Governing Body of Dunraven School & Anor, ex parte B (by his Mother & Next Friend) (1999)*. It was determined in *Tarrant* that a prisoner should be given sufficient time to understand what is alleged against him and prepare a defence. Clearly, if somebody is unaware of the extent of the charges against him he will be unable to answer them; the inconvenience involved would have been very minor.

In *Board of Visitors of Gartree Prison ex p Mealy (1981)*, Mealy alleged unfairness, because when he came to answer the charges against him, he found that the order of the proceedings had been changed. This took him by surprise and, he believed, adversely affected his ability to defend himself. The Divisional Court found that chairmen of Boards of Visitors should guide prisoners through the proceedings and not surprise them by sudden changes of format. This could apply to the instant case, as Bert was upset by additional allegations which he had not expected.

Even where loss of liberty is not in question, a reasonable standard of fairness must be observed in prisoners' disciplinary hearings, which does not appear to be the case here. Therefore, Bert may be able to show that the *audi* rule has been breached with regard to all his complaints apart from denial of legal representation.

Thus, since both Abel and Bert are able to show breaches of the principles of natural justice, the decisions will be void. (In the *Anisminic* case (1969), the House of Lords held that a decision which breached the principles of natural justice would be void, not voidable.) Under r 54 of the CPR, a quashing order will be issued to quash the decision in each instance.

NOTES

1 A further case could be mentioned at this point: in *Board of Visitors for Nottingham Prison (1981)*, it was held that if it were established that a prisoner had asked for and been refused permission to call witnesses, this would *prima facie* be unfair.

2 Students could point out that cases in which the right to cross-examination has not been found to be required by the principles of fair procedure, such as *Bushell v Secretary of State for the Environment (1981)*, have occurred in contexts very different from prison disciplinary hearings. Such hearings are basically adversarial procedures where the purpose of the procedures in question is the determination of a person's guilt or innocence. In this respect, they are very similar to court proceedings. In cases involving more polycentric disputes, where an adjudicator is attempting to reach a conclusion on an administrative matter, after hearing evidence from numerous sources and weighing up the conflicting priorities bearing upon his decision, the courts are much more reluctant to impose formal, judicial-style practices, such as cross-examination.

Question 27

Blankshire County Council is empowered by s 3 of the (fictitious) Street Traders Act to grant licences to street traders and withdraw them for, *inter alia*, misconduct. It has been the custom of the Council to grant hearings to consider the case against proposed revocation of licences, provided that a written request is received within 14 days of the decision being announced. Under the Cautious Party, previously in control of the Council, such licences were granted sparingly. The Enterprise Party, now in power, has announced that in six months' time, 50 new licences are to be granted over a six-week period.

The following events occur:

Doreen, a current licence-holder, is disgruntled by the decision to grant new licences, fearing such a massive increase in competition; she requests a hearing from the Council. She receives a letter in reply stating that normally, only revocation of a licence gives rise to a hearing and that in any event, unprecedentedly low Council funds forbid a hearing.

Vic and William receive notification that their licences are to be revoked for misconduct, subject to their right to put their case against the revocation. William is given a fair chance to state his case at a meeting of the Licensing Board. However, he recognises one of the five members of the Board, Bert, as the former husband of

Alison; Alison recently left Bert for William in an episode which generated much publicity. The Board orders revocation. After the hearings are over, it emerges for the first time that Bert covertly encouraged Alison to have the affair with William so that he could divorce her and marry his secret, long standing mistress, with whom he is now blissfully happy.

Vic is unhappy because it was only at his hearing that he was told full details of the case against him: that there was evidence that specific products sold from his stall were unsafe. Previously he had only been told that his licence was being revoked 'on health and safety grounds'. The Board orders revocation. Vic is indignant because he claims he has detailed evidence of the safety of his products, which he could have raised in evidence in the hearing, had he known the true grounds of the Council's case.

Jane applies for a licence to run a stall but is refused. She is indignant, because the Council have provided no reasons for the refusal.

Discuss the issues of 'procedural impropriety' raised by the above.

Answer plan

This is a long and initially rather confusing question. On analysis, however, it can be seen to break down into a number of fairly distinct issues surrounding fair procedure. Students must take care to work out the application of all the given facts to all the applicants before starting to answer the question; for example, the fact that persons whose licences have been revoked have been customarily granted a hearing is primarily relevant not to Vic and William, but to Doreen. Note that discussion of remedies and procedure is *not* required, as the question calls for a discussion of the issues of procedural impropriety, not for advice to be given to possible applicants for judicial review.

Essentially, the following areas should be covered:

- do the rules of natural justice require a hearing for Doreen or at least an opportunity for her to make representations?; the argument for 'legitimate expectation' by analogy from existing custom with respect to revocation;
- is there an infringement of the *nemo judex* rule regarding William's hearing?; the test for bias is now *Porter v Magill (2002)*; the effect of facts pointing to bias at the time of the hearing, but not subsequently;
- Vic – failure to give a person full notice of the case against them;
- Jane – failure to give reasons for an administrative decision.

Answer

Blankshire Council may have been guilty of procedural impropriety during the revocation of licences, the refusal of Jane's licence, and in the taking of the decision to grant new licences.

The question of Doreen's possible entitlement to a hearing will be considered first. One of the two rules of natural justice is *audi alteram partem* which, at its most basic level, denotes that both sides should be heard in making certain decisions. In *Ridge v Baldwin (1963)*, Lord Reid, in the course of his judgment, stated (strictly *obiter*) that the crucial characteristic of a hearing or decision which would render it subject to the rules of natural justice is that a person's rights would be affected by the outcome; he disposed of the fallacy that the proceedings had to have the further characteristic of being quasi-judicial. In the instant case, Doreen could claim that her right to trade granted by her licence would be affected to her detriment by a massive increase in competition.

Further, it can be argued that Doreen has a 'legitimate expectation' of a hearing. This notion was first formulated by Lord Denning MR in *Schmidt v Home Secretary (1969)* and its principles were clarified in *Council of Civil Service Unions v Minister for the Civil Service (1984)*. Lord Fraser stated that a legitimate expectation 'may arise either from an express promise or from the existence of a regular practice which the claimant can reasonably expect to continue'. Doreen may be able to argue that she has a legitimate expectation based on the Council's 'custom' of consultation over revocation of licences. It is arguable that if it is legitimate to expect consultation over revocation of licences – an expectation particularly strong where economic loss may be caused by the revocation – then it would also be reasonable to expect consultation over a decision which would greatly devalue licences in existence and similarly cause economic loss. Lord Denning put forward this line of reasoning (*obiter*) in *Liverpool Corp ex p Liverpool Taxi Fleet, etc (1972)* (a decision approved in *Devon County Council ex p Baker; Durham County Council ex p Curtis (1995)*), in which it was held that taxi drivers were entitled to be consulted over a proposal to increase the number of taxicabs; however, in that case, an express promise had been given of full consultation with existing taxi drivers, so it is not directly applicable to the instant situation.

However, the Council would argue that, while Dorothy might be entitled to make representations as to the increase in licences, she is not entitled to a hearing, especially in light of its unprecedented shortage of funds: Doreen is not being deprived of a benefit but merely subject to increased competition. *R (West) v Parole Board (2006)* strongly suggests that an oral hearing would not be considered necessary in such a marginal case. The court would then, probably take the view that while Doreen is not entitled to a full hearing, she should have had an opportunity to make full representations to the Council: the court is likely to take this view if it believes that the opportunity to make representations in writing will give Doreen a proper opportunity to put her case: *Lloyds v McMahon (1987)*. The Council, then, will almost certainly not be obliged to give Doreen an oral hearing – the consequences for her in this case are far less grave than those in *Lloyds*, which involved a massive surcharge on negligent councillors. However, its failure to grant Doreen a right to make written representations is probably in breach of the *audi* rule.[1]

Vic appears to have a relatively clear case. The right to full notice of the case against a person is the lowest level of procedural protection; if you have no notice of the case against you then clearly you cannot make any effective representations on your own behalf. In *R v Governing Body of Dunraven School & Anor, ex p B (by his Mother & Next Friend) (1999)*, a 15-year-old boy was excluded from school. He successfully applied for judicial review on the basis that he had not been informed of the main evidence against him (provided by another boy). Therefore the right to notice is only likely to be denied either for particular reasons of public policy (e.g. national security) or where the applicant is very much in the position of merely applying for a benefit, for example, applying for a licencse. Neither is the case here and it is clear that holding a hearing, at which one side cannot, through the other's failure to inform them properly, present their side of the argument properly, is a breach of the duty to act fairly.

Finally, the fact that Bert sits on the Board which hears William's case fails to be considered. Clearly, the perception of his probable hostility towards William raises questions about the fairness of William's hearing. The second main rule of natural justice, *nemo judex in causa sua*, is commonly expressed to forbid bias on the part of the decision-maker. It must initially be established whether personal animosity towards the applicant by the decision-maker can amount to bias for the purposes of natural justice. The persuasive authority of *Re Elliott (1959)* suggests that it can, and in the recent decision of *Locabail (2000)*, Lord Woolf expressly mentioned 'personal animosity' as a circumstance that could found a legitimate claim of bias. However, in cases where the decision-maker has neither a pecuniary interest in the outcome, nor is actually involved with an organisation which is a party to a case (the further category added by the *Pinochet* decision: *Bow Street Stipendiary Magistrates ex p Pinochet Ugarte (No 2) (2000)*), it is not enough simply to establish the facts pointing to bias, without more. The new test for such cases, following the House of Lords' decision in *Porter v Magill (2002)*, is that the decision will be quashed where 'the fair-minded and informed observer, having considered the [relevant] facts would conclude that there was a real possibility that the tribunal was biased'. Thus, the court is concerned not to ascertain whether there was *in fact* 'a real danger of bias' (the old test under *Gough (1993)*). It is concerned with whether a fair-minded observer would so conclude, in recognition of the fact that the appearance of the matter is just as important as the reality (as Lord Nolan observed in *Pinochet*). Such an observer would not have to think that it was more probable than not that there was bias, merely that it was a real, and not a fanciful possibility. On the facts of the present case, a perception of bias might well have arisen at the time of the hearing, since observers would know only that Bert's wife had left him for William – presumably common knowledge in view of the widespread 'publicity' that the affair created – and would therefore be very likely to apprehend bias on the part of Bert. The ruling in *Bremer Handelsgesellschaft mbh v Ets Soules et Cie (1985)* suggested that 'the apparent fairness of the process must be judged in the light of the facts as they would have appeared to the reasonable man *at the time when they mattered, that is, when the procedure was in progress*' (emphasis added), presumably in reliance on the well known principle that justice must not only be done, but must be seen to be done. However, in *Steeles v Derbyshire CC (1985)*, the court stated that the reasonable man in making his judgment knows all relevant matters whether available to the public or not. Dicta in the recent decision in *Director General of Fair Trading v Proprietary Association of Great Britain and Proprietary Articles Trade Association (2001)*, however, support the approach in *Bremer*: the judges repeatedly spoke of what the perception would be 'at the material time', which must mean the time when the decision was made. Even if, therefore, it could be established in evidence that given that his wife's departure was not unwelcome to him, Bert bears no grudge against William, a court would probably find that a fair-minded observer would inevitably have suspected bias at the time. If this were the case, the decision relating to William would be quashed.

Jane's only ground of complaint is that she has not been given reasons for her decision. There is no general duty to give reasons for administrative decisions, but the courts are rapidly developing broad categories of cases in which reasons must be given. Unfortunately for Jane she does not appear to fall within any of them and *R v Lancashire CC ex p Huddleston (1986)* is authority for the proposition that reasons do not have to be given for the refusal of a discretionary benefit. Jane has not suffered an interference with her legal rights or other 'highly regarded interests' (*R v Secretary of State for the Home Department ex p Doody and ors (1994)*), and nor is there any particular feature of the decision, such as its being inexplicable *Sinclair (1992)* or against her legitimate expectations (*R v Criminal Injuries Compensation Board ex p Cunningham (1991)*) that might require reasons to be given.[2] Jane is a 'bare applicant' for a benefit, and as such is most unlikely to be held to be entitled to anything more than that the decision-maker is unbiased and the decision not perverse (*Mc Innes v Onslow Fane (1982)*).

NOTES

1 Though the point is strictly outside the ambit of the question, it could be noted that if the application for judicial review was not heard until after the issuing of the licences, a court might refuse to issue a quashing order on the basis that

substantial prejudice would result to the new licence-holders from the invalidation of their licences.

2 Further examples of instances in which reasons have to be given could be given; they include cases which are particularly 'judicial' in character (*Stefan v General Medical Council (1999)*) and instances in which there is a conflict of factual evidence, and it is unclear what view of the facts the decision-maker took: *R v Criminal Injuries Compensation Board ex p Cummins (1992)*. Neither of these are applicable to Jane.

Question 28

The Opticians' Regulatory Body, established by statute, is empowered to designate certain opticians' practices as being 'ORB approved', if it appears to the ORB that the practice concerned is 'a credit to the profession'. Upon such a designation being made, a central government grant will be made to the practice. ORB may also publicly designate opticians it considers to be 'negligently run' as 'not recommended'. The following events occur in Dansfield Town:

(a) Edward's practice is designated 'not approved'; at his hearing, the Dansfield Town branch of the ORB tells him that it considers his practice 'too small to provide an efficient service'. Edward is very unhappy with this decision, but puts off seeking legal advice for some time because of his fear of going to court.

(b) Thirty practices, making up the I Can See Clearly conglomerate, are given block approval by the Dansfield Town branch of the ORB. In response, Julia, the chair of the national Citizens Against Government Waste (CAGW) group, points out that many of the ORB members sit on the Dansfield local council, which is very concerned about unemployment among secretaries in the area; she admits, however, that all the practices concerned are meritorious.

(c) Three months after the announcement of the block approval, Fanny, who has been running a practice for two months which has been lauded as a model of efficiency in letters to the *Dansfield Herald*, requests a favourable designation from the Dansfield Town branch of the ORB. At her hearing, she is told that the body has a policy of refusing to approve practices which are less than one year old, and that in any case, an optician in her practice has been accused of failing to diagnose cataracts in a patient. The Panel tells her that the evidence of this came from gossip overheard by an ORB member in a pub. Fanny indignantly denies that any such misdiagnosis has ever taken place. Her practice is not approved.

You may assume that all the hearings given are in accordance with the principles of natural justice.

Advise Edward and Fanny, who wish to challenge the decisions about their practices, and Julia, who wishes to question the legality of the block approval of 30 practices.

Answer plan

This is a fairly typical problem question which includes decisions that may be open to attack under various heads of judicial review. Students should note that unlike in the last question, they are asked to advise possible claimants, rather than to 'discuss issues'. Consequently, matters of standing, procedure and remedies *must* be covered. Natural justice should obviously not be discussed here; it should be noted, however, that one issue of natural justice is sometimes thrown into a question which is otherwise mainly concerned with illegality and irrationality.

The following areas should be covered:

- a brief mention that the ORB as a public body will be subject to judicial review if grounds exist;
- the procedure for all three claimants; r 54 of the Civil Procedure Rules (CPR), time limits – applicability to Edward; *locus standi* – requires a full argument in Julia's case; standing not to be considered wholly separately from merits;
- Edward's challenge – illegality: error of law/jurisdictional fact; misinterpretation of grounds; remedy;
- Fanny's challenge – illegality: the fettering of discretion in relation to policy; basing a decision on no evidence; irrationality in deciding on the basis of gossip; remedy;
- Julia's challenge: irrelevant considerations; partially improper purpose and the correct purpose inferred from the Act; remedy.

Answer

The Opticians' Regulatory Body is a public body, established by statute; its decisions will therefore be subject to the supervisory review jurisdiction of the High Court on the basis that it clearly exercises a 'public function' as r 54.1(2) of the CPR requires. This would also be so under the case law prior to the new CPR. If the above applicants are to succeed in challenging any of the Body's decisions, they must use the correct procedure, demonstrate that they have the requisite standing and make out a case that the ORB's decisions impugn one or more of the various principles of judicial review.

It is clear that judicial review is the appropriate mode of challenge to such decisions: the applicants have no private law right (*O'Reilly v Mackman (1983)*) which could be vindicated in an ordinary civil action; moreover, r 54.2 of the CPR has now clarified that judicial review 'must be used' where the applicant is seeking either a quashing order or mandatory order, which will be the remedies sought by the applicants here. Under r 54.4 of the CPR, applicants must initially seek the courts' permission to apply for judicial review; this must be done 'promptly, and in any event not later than three months after the grounds to make the claim first arose' (r 54.5 of the CPR). It will be assumed that all three potential claimants are within this basic time limit. However, in *Independent Television Commission ex p TVNI (1991)*, the Court of Appeal emphasised that applications for judicial review would be refused if not made with the utmost promptness, even if within the three-month time limit. Since Edward has delayed his application for no good reason, he may be refused leave; however, the Court of Appeal indicated that leave is more likely to be refused if third party rights are involved, which is not the case here.

Applicants must show that they have a sufficient interest in the matter to which the application relates (s 31(3) of the Supreme Court Act 1981). Edward and Julia will be seeking a quashing order to annul the relevant ORB decisions, while Fanny will require a mandatory order to compel a reappraisal of the decision not to approve her. The standing required for both remedies was equated in *IRC ex p National Federation of Self-Employed, etc (1982)*. Clearly, Edward and Fanny have sufficient interest, as the decisions by the ORB have given them an individual grievance. Julia, however, may have more difficulty establishing standing. In *ex p National Federation*, the House of Lords held that the National Federation did not have a sufficient interest to challenge the legality of an IRC decision to grant an amnesty to casual labourers over previous tax avoidance. The fact that it had no personal interest in the IRC decision was decisive. However, although Julia also does not have any personal grievance, her case can be distinguished from *ex p National Federation*. Lord Wilberforce seems to have been much influenced in his judgment by the fact that the affairs of any individual taxpayer are strictly confidential; he considered that allowing judicial review of the way the IRC had dealt with such individuals would breach that principle of confidentiality. In the instant case, the result of ORB approval is a government grant; it can be argued that the outlay of government money *is* a matter for public concern and scrutiny, unlike the affairs of individual taxpayers. However, the decision in *Secretary of State for the Environment ex p Rose Theatre Trust Co (1990)*, which indicates that pressure groups whose only interest in a decision is concern about the issues involved will not in general have *locus standi* to challenge the decision, represents a further difficulty.

However, since the *Rose Theatre* decision, the courts have begun to take a much more flexible and accommodating approach to the question of standing when a sufficiently important issue is raised by the application, such that the case is now generally regarded as being out of line with the general thrust of judicial policy. Thus, in *Secretary of State for Foreign and Commonwealth Affairs ex p Rees-Mogg (1994)*, it was found that the applicant had standing 'because of his sincere concern for constitutional issues'. In *Secretary of State for Foreign Affairs ex p the World Development Movement (1995)*, the WDM was granted *locus standi* on the basis of a number of factors, including the importance of the issue raised (the possibly illegal use of the government's overseas aid budget), the absence of any other challenger and the prominence and expertise of the applicant pressure group in relation to the issues raised by the case. In other cases, the courts have stressed the importance of pressure groups representing people living in the area affected by the contested decision. Thus, in *Inspectorate of Pollution ex p Greenpeace (1994)*, the judge stressed the fact that 2,500 supporters of Greenpeace lived in the local area (Cumbria), the health of whom might be affected by emissions from a nuclear plant; the court therefore found that members of the group had a personal interest in a matter of substantial concern – public health. Similarly, in *Secretary of State for the Environment ex p Friends of the Earth (1994)*, in which Friends of the Earth and its director were granted leave to challenge a decision related to the quality of drinking water in certain specified areas, the fact that the director lived in one of those areas – London – and hence had a personal local interest in the matter was stressed as significant. The expertise of the respective pressure groups as a factor in their favour was also emphasised in both cases.

Thus, in cases involving decisions with a particular impact on one region or area of the country, the courts seem to stress the importance of pressure groups having a genuine interest in that area, via their membership (see Hilson and Cram (1996) 16(1) LS 3). The pure 'public interest' approach appears so far to have been saved for cases such as *World Development Movement* and *Rees-Mogg*, where the decisions were of general national importance, with no particular local interest.

Applying these criteria to Julia and the CAGW, her claim for standing appears rather weak. The challenge is mainly one of local interest, so the pure public interest approach is not really applicable; applying the *Greenpeace* and *Friends of the Earth* cases cited, the courts will probably inquire whether Julia or the group have any local connection, as the general public interest in the issue appears quite weak. On the other hand, the CAGW may have some expertise in the area of government waste, a point which would count in its favour. Probably, the issue of standing would ultimately therefore turn upon whether the courts considered that Julia's challenge raised serious issues of possible unlawful action, a matter which will be considered below.

The substantive merits of each of the applicant's challenges will now be considered, starting with the decision to designate Edward's practice as 'not approved'. Such a designation may be made only if the ORB considers a practice to be 'negligently run'. There is, it is submitted, a clear argument that the ORB has made an error of law by misinterpreting the word 'negligent'. The word would probably be treated as a legal term of art like the words 'successor in title' in *Anisminic Ltd v Foreign Compensation Commission (1969)* and, as such, its interpretation would be a matter for the court to decide upon if necessary, substituting its own judgment for that of the ORB (as confirmed in *O'Reilly v Mackman (1982)*). An error in interpreting such a word would mean, as *Anisminic* established, that the decision-making body would have 'asked itself the wrong questions . . . thereby stepping outside its jurisdiction'.

It is apparent from the reasons given to Edward that the ORB has taken the word 'negligently' to mean 'not sufficiently efficient'. It is therefore apparent that the question asked by the ORB in the course of deciding Edward's case was: 'Does Edward's practice conform to a certain standard of efficiency?' This may conceivably connote an ordinary usage of the word 'negligently', but it is not the legal understanding. Assuming that the courts would view the word as a term of legal art, it is submitted that the question which should have been asked was: 'Is Edward's practice run with a lack of reasonable care for those who might foreseeably be harmed by lack of such care on his part?' It is apparent that the answer to that question would be in the negative, as the only complaint against Edward is that the practice is small, not that it is run with lack of reasonable care. (There is no suggestion that the practice is so small that it creates a risk to the health of those using it.) If it is accepted that the ORB has asked itself the wrong question, the result would be, *per* Lord Diplock in *Re Racal Communications Ltd (1981)*, 'that the decision they reached would be a nullity', as it would have decided a matter which it was not empowered to decide and thus exceeded its *vires*. Therefore, a quashing order will lie to quash the decision.

The ORB might argue in its defence that the decision as to whether a practice is 'negligently run' is, rightly construed, one of fact and that errors of fact are not generally a ground of challenge on judicial review. However, an important exception relates to what are known as 'jurisdictional facts'. This exception refers to instances where the decision-maker is only entitled to enter upon his inquiry if a particular fact exists. Here, 'the exercise of power, or jurisdiction, depends on the precedent establishment of an objective fact. In such a case, it is for the court to decide whether that precedent requirement has been satisfied' (*Khawaja v Secretary of State for the Home Department (1983)*). Since the ORB may only take the decisive action of designating a business as 'not approved' should it be 'negligently run', it would seem possible to characterise the existence of such negligence as a precedent fact, and therefore a matter for the court. If 'negligence' is taken as a factual, rather than a legal term, the court is likely to attribute a rather more broad range of meanings to it, but the notion of 'inefficiency' *simpliciter* does not, on its face, seem congruent with the concept of negligence. The ORB might, however, argue that to make the court the assessor of whether a given business is 'negligently run' is to deprive it of the exercise of judgment in its area of expertise – a freedom which Parliament intended to give it under the statute. In other words, it could contend that the finding of negligence is not a precedent fact which entitles it to enter upon the real inquiry, but rather one of the principal roles it is given under the statute. Recent developments, however, indicate that the courts are becoming more willing to strike decisions down on the basis of error of fact, even if that fact is not jurisdictional. In *Criminal Injuries Compensation Commission ex p A (1999)*, four of their Lordships accepted that a decision on a 'crucial matter' which was tainted with a material error of fact could be quashed. *Adan v Newham BC (2002)* made it clear however that the courts will not attempt to investigate complex factual disagreements but only intervene in clear cases. Clearly, the finding that Edward's business is 'negligently run' is the crux of the matter. Provided that the error is clear and unarguable, rather than a contested matter of opinion on which the court would consider itself bound to defer to the expertise of the ORB, Edward should succeed on this ground.

The decision not to approve Fanny's practice now falls to be considered. The ORB's policy with respect to recently established practices will be considered first. There can be, as Lord Reid observed in *British Oxygen Co Ltd v Board of Trade (1971)*, 'no objection' to a body evolving even a fairly precise policy with respect to its area of remit. What it must not do is apply this policy rigidly in every case; it must still decide each case on its merits and consider whether an exception to the policy should be made. Thus, in the *British Oxygen* case, the Board had a policy of not giving grants for items costing less than £25, but their Lordships found that it was willing to hear reasons from any applicant as to why the policy should not be applied in his case. Similarly in *R v Secretary of State for the Home Department ex p Hindley (2000)*, the setting of a 'whole life' tariff for a murderer was lawful provided it was kept under review. By contrast, in *Secretary of State for the Environment ex p Brent LBC (1982)*, the minister refused to hear representations from the authority before applying his policy; consequently, his decision was unlawful. In the instant case, the ORB granted Fanny a hearing; if it could show that it knew the age of Fanny's practice before it held the hearing, there would be a strong inference that it was prepared to consider making an exception, since otherwise the hearing would have been a waste of time. This argument would be hard to refute; it could be claimed that the ORB only held the hearing to avoid falling foul of the rules of natural justice, and if Fanny could convince the court that the apparent preparedness to consider exceptions was only a sham, *North West Lancashire Health Authority ex p A and Others (2000)* is authority for the proposition that the policy would therefore be considered as truly rigid and thus unlawful. However, without actual evidence of this, it would be hard to destroy the inference that the ORB must have been holding the possibility open of making an exception to its policy, and therefore made a lawful decision.[1]

The ORB's other ground for making its decision about Fanny may now be considered. Clearly, if the allegation in the overheard gossip against Fanny's practice were to be true, the practice could not reasonably be considered a 'credit to the profession', and approval would have been properly withheld. The ORB may, however, have made a finding of fact on the basis of no evidence. There is much *dicta* of high authority to support the proposition that, as du Parcq LJ said in *Bean v Doncaster Amalgamated Collieries Ltd (1944)*, 'to come to a conclusion which there is no evidence to support is to make an error in law'. Thus, in *Coleen Properties v Minister of Housing and Local Government (1971)*, the minister had disagreed with an inspector's recommendation that it was not reasonably necessary to purchase a given property in order to redevelop an area, but had cited no evidence to justify his disagreement. The decision was quashed. However, it would appear that in cases where there is any evidence at all, however flimsy, 'its weight is entirely for the inferior court' (*per* Lord Sumner in *Nat Bell Liquors Ltd (1922)*). The exception appears to be where the evidence is so flimsy that reliance upon it may be considered perverse. In *Puhlhofer v Hillingdon LBC (1986)*, Lord Brightman remarked:

> Where the existence or non-existence of a fact is left to the judgment and discretion of a public body, and that fact involves a broad spectrum ranging from the obvious to the debatable to the just conceivable, it is the duty of the court to leave the decision of that fact to [that body], save where it is obvious that the public body, consciously or unconsciously, is acting perversely.

However, the recent decision in *ex p A* (above) may have tightened up this requirement. It could, in any event, plausibly be argued on behalf of Fanny that to make an important decision with a severe effect on someone's livelihood, on the basis of unsubstantiated gossip from what may be an anonymous source, is a wholly irresponsible and indeed perverse act, or alternatively that such gossip cannot reasonably be said to amount to 'evidence' at all.[2] Either argument would seem likely to succeed.

The decision not to approve Fanny's practice could also be attacked under the head of irrationality. It is arguable that in effect, to condemn a practice which has been widely praised because of overheard gossip which could well be malicious or mere rumour is a decision which is 'so outrageous in its defiance of logic or of accepted moral standards that no sensible person who had applied his mind to the question could have arrived at it' – the test laid down in the *GCHQ* case. Such an argument may well have more chance of success than the illegality argument, although because of the somewhat subjective nature of the irrationality head, it is difficult to predict how a court will receive it. It is therefore submitted that Fanny has some chance of success on this basis.[3] She will probably be seeking a mandatory order to compel the ORB to reassess her practice, as in *Padfield v Minister of Agriculture (1968)*.

Julia's grounds of complaint will now be considered. It is well established that where an authority is endowed with power to achieve one goal, and uses it to achieve another, that exercise of power is unlawful (*Hanson v Radcliffe (1922)*). In the instant case, no purpose is stated in the parent Act, but the courts have been prepared on a number of occasions to infer a purpose (as in *Padfield's* case) and then hold a decision *ultra vires* for not conforming with that purpose. It could be sensibly inferred here that the statute creating the ORB had the purpose of raising standards amongst opticians by providing performance incentives through grants to meritorious practices. If the block approval was made with the purpose of decreasing unemployment (the hope being that the practices receiving the grants would expand and employ more staff), or even if the ORB was influenced by that consideration, then the decision will be a nullity for illegality or possibly for unreasonableness.

The situation is, however, complicated by the fact that all the practices approved are, as Julia concedes, meritorious and therefore could properly be approved within the purposes of the Act. Where a decision has been taken with both a proper and an improper purpose in mind, the approach of the courts has been to ask whether it would have been taken in the absence of the improper consideration. If it would not (as in *ILEA ex p Westminster City Council (1986)*), then the decision is unlawful. If the same decision would have been taken without the improper motive, as in *Brighton Corp ex p Shoosmith (1907)*, then it will be allowed to stand. In the instant case, the motives behind the ORB's decision would be a matter for evidence, but *prima facie* it would seem unlikely that a block approval of 30 practices would have taken place without the additional motive of the Councillors. Moreover, the *ILEA* case also suggested that the test of whether the improper purpose 'materially' affected the decision could be used; a test which would clearly be easier to satisfy. Assuming that the ORB was materially influenced by the desire to address the problem of unemployment, Julia would have a reasonable chance of demonstrating the decision to be unlawful. If so, as discussed in relation to Edward, a quashing order would lie to quash it.

NOTES

1 Students could note that any policy developed must be consistent with the objects of the relevant Act. If it is not, then paying heed to it would amount to taking irrelevant factors into account when making a decision which can render a decision vitiated for unreasonableness as, for example, in *Padfield v Minister of Agriculture (1968)*. The statute creating the ORB can reasonably be presumed to have the purpose of raising standards amongst opticians by providing performance incentives through grants to meritorious practices. It may be considered reasonable to withhold approval from practices until they have established their efficiency over a reasonable period of time, in order to avoid grants being given on the basis of a very short term effort by a practice.

2 Students could put the further, alternative argument that the case can be distinguished from *Nat Bell*, because that case involved a criminal trial in which

the laws of evidence disallowed the kind of 'evidence' upon which Fanny's case has been decided, so that Lord Sumner was pronouncing upon evidence which did have some basic credibility as being legally admissible.

3   The further point could be made that for the case built on the ORB's consideration of the gossip against Fanny to be successful, Fanny would also have to satisfy the tests considered in the last paragraph of the text above relating to Julia.

Question 29

'It is often said that judicial review is intolerably uncertain and amounts to little more than a licence for judges to interfere arbitrarily with the machinery of government and administration' (Emery and Smythe).

Is this a fair criticism? If so, is this a failure on the part of the judiciary?

Answer plan

This is a fairly typical essay question on judicial review, in that it demands an evaluative approach. Essays in this area are often concerned with the efficacy of judicial review. In this case, the focus is narrowed to a discussion of the charge of uncertainty, but this still leaves a very large area which could be discussed. However, students would not be expected to assess every sub-head of judicial review for certainty. A sensible solution, therefore, would be to focus on the controversial, ambiguous areas, while indicating briefly what are the more settled grounds. The answer below selects certain of these areas; it would be perfectly legitimate, however, to use other examples, such as the uncertain scope of the duty to give reasons or the issue of when legitimate expectations may receive substantive protection.

Essentially, the following areas should be covered:

- natural justice: the duty to act fairly – the vagueness of the test for applicability and over what level of procedural protection is needed;
- illegality: notions of fettering by policy/delegation are reasonably settled; the notion of error of law: inconsistencies and the problem of determining error in applying law to facts; improper purpose – a problematic notion; uncertainty in determining what is a relevant or irrelevant consideration;
- irrationality: incoherence of the notion; its essentially subjective nature;
- conclusion: an uneven picture.

Answer

A comprehensive discussion of the above criticism of judicial review would clearly be impossible in this context if any depth of discussion is to be maintained. Accordingly, in what follows, discussion will focus on those heads which are the subject of particular debate and controversy. An effort will be made to ascertain how fixed the principles governing intervention are, and to reveal whether, in certain cases, apparent principles are merely a cloak to allow improper intervention.

Procedural impropriety is one of the three main grounds of review identified by Lord Diplock in *Council of Civil Service Unions v Minister for the Civil Service (1984)*. In the area of natural justice, the *audi* rule will be discussed as being the less settled of the two rules. There are perhaps two main questions to be considered. One is the issue as to when the rules will apply, the other the controversy concerning what will satisfy the rules in a given situation. In their treatment of the second of these areas, the courts have again taken the flexible approach – in this case, by allowing compliance with the *audi* rule to be fulfilled by widely differing conduct in different situations.[1]

The growth of the notion of the 'duty to act fairly' (perhaps originating from *Re HK (1967)*), an even more flexible concept than the *audi* rule, epitomises the apparent determination of the judiciary to avoid laying down rigid rules or to force administrative decision-makers into adopting a more judicial approach. For example, the House of Lords in a recent 2005 ruling was only able to give us general guidance that an oral hearing will sometimes be required depending on the facts of the case and whether it would assist in the just disposition of the matter: *R (West) v Parole Board (2006)*; although it is fairly well settled that cases involving interferences with legal rights or 'highly regarded interests' will give rise to a higher level of procedural protection than those in which the applicant is a mere applicant: *Doody (1994)*. Rawlings, among others, has commented that from the point of view of an administrator anxious to know what he must do to ensure his decision is correct, this notion is 'hopelessly imprecise', for 'all [the administrator] knows is that he must be "fair" – and what fairness requires in the particular circumstances he can only find out when the court . . . tells him that he has or has not been fair' ((1986) 64 *Public Administration* 140–141).

It is arguable that Rawlings is somewhat overstating the case: for example, an administrator *does* know that a person must be informed of the substance of the case against him (*Secretary of State, etc ex p Philippine Airlines Inc (1984)*), but his argument that flexibility has been taken too far is certainly attractive. It is, however, difficult to see how a degree of uncertainty could have been avoided, given the huge range of situations to which natural justice applies. A greater rigidity in the rules might create the risk that either low-level administrative decisions would be shackled with inappropriately stringent procedural requirements, with a consequent loss of efficiency and speed, or that disciplinary hearings would give insufficient procedural safeguards to those whose cases they were trying. Again, in allowing the situation to develop as it has, Parliament must shoulder some responsibility for not attempting greater clarification through legislation.[2]

In considering the head of 'illegality', one might reasonably expect that the tests determining when a body has stepped outside its jurisdiction would be more precisely defined; indeed, this expectation is to a certain extent borne out by practice. There are a number of reasonably clearly defined acts that will render a body's decision unlawful. These include doing an act which an authority is not in the simplest sense empowered to do (for example establishing a commercial laundry when empowered to provide municipal wash houses: *AG v Fulham Corp (1921)*), and effectively failing to exercise a statutory discretion by applying a policy rigidly in every case or by improperly delegating the decision to another body or person (*Secretary of State for the Environment ex p Brent LBC (1982)* and *Ellis v Dubowski (1921)* respectively). It is also clear law that public bodies may not use powers granted to fulfil one objective for quite another (*Porter v Magill (2002)*).

It could be noted, however, that ambiguity can arise in the case of decisions made for a plurality of purposes – some proper, some improper. This ambiguity is nicely illustrated by the fact that Glidewell LJ, embroiled in the complexities of such a case in *ILEA ex p Westminster City Council (1986)*, drew 'comfort' from the fact that the area was admitted by De Smith to be 'a legal porcupine which bristles with difficulties'. A further issue in the application of the 'purpose axiom' arises from those cases where the statute under which the body makes its decisions does not lay down its overall purpose or does so only in the most general terms. In dealing with this area, the courts have been accused of using their practice of inferring a purpose as a means whereby to interfere with policy. Often, the purpose inferred is uncontroversial or the courts only go so far as stating – in effect – that, whatever the purpose of the body's power may be, it is not to enable it to do the act complained of (as in the well known case of *Barnsley MBC ex p Hook (1976)*). In other cases, however, the judiciary has been accused of inferring an unwarrantably narrow purpose from an act which appears to grant broad discretion, and then holding a decision unlawful because it is not in conformity with this purpose. Arguably, this technique was adopted by the Lords in *Bromley London Borough Council v GLC (1983)* in order to quash a GLC policy to subsidise public transport from the rates.

Other difficulties arise in relation to the principle that taking into account irrelevant considerations can invalidate a decision, as can failure to have regard to mandatory relevant matters: *ex p Fewings (1993)*. The problem is simply that it may be extremely difficult for a decision-maker to predict what will be seen as a relevant or irrelevant matter by a court. Again, Parliament must share some of the responsibility here, as it very often paints discretion in the broadest of language, leaving it almost wholly unclear as to what may or may not be taken into account, as in *Fewings* itself. For example, the courts have had to face, in a number of recent cases, the question of whether local authorities, in making various decisions which involve resources (e.g. provision for old people and children with special educational needs), may take into account their own limited financial resources, and if so, at what stage of the decision-making process. In *Gloucester County Council ex p Barry (1997)*, the Council, if it considered that a disabled person had certain 'needs', was under a statutory duty to make arrangements to cater for them. Barry had been previously assessed as having certain needs, which were fully catered for in 1992 and 1993. In 1994, the Council told him that due to central government cuts in its funding, it was no longer able to provide for his full needs. The House of Lords held, by a 3:2 majority, that in assessing 'need', the Council had to consider what was an acceptable standard of living. In assessing that, the authority could have regard to its own resources, and so had not acted unlawfully. In contrast, in *Sefton Metropolitan Borough Council ex p Help the Aged (1997)*, the court drew a distinction between: (a) assessing a person's needs; and (b) deciding what to provide in order to meet those needs. In determining the first question, the court said that an authority could, following *Barry*, take into account resources, but once it had decided that a particular person was in need, it came under a binding duty to provide for those needs and lack of resources was not relevant. *Barry* was distinguished again in *East Sussex County Council ex p Tandy (1998)*. Here, a local authority had a duty to provide 'suitable education' for the children in its area. Tandy had been unable to attend school and had received five hours a week tuition, funded by the Council. In 1996, the authority reduced this to three hours because of financial constraints. On its face, the situation seemed very similar to *Barry* – an initial provision being reduced to save money. However, the court found that the concept of 'suitable education', unlike a person's 'needs' (as in *Barry*), was objective, and did not vary according to resources. In taking account of its own resources in deciding what was 'suitable', the authority had had regard to an irrelevant consideration. These cases scarcely leave local authorities with clear guidance on the issue. How was a council to know in advance that the concept of a 'suitable education' is to be assessed entirely independently of resource availability, whereas a person's 'needs' are resource-relative? It could in fact be argued that it is difficult to assess what is a suitable education without considering the resources available for that and other levels of education, whereas the concept of 'need' is more objective. There is a strong whiff of arbitrariness about these decisions; they certainly provide the most uncertain guidance to councils struggling to reconcile statutory duties with scarce resources.

In contrast, it has been clearly established, by *Anisminic Ltd v Foreign Compensation Commission (1969)* that any error of law made by a body, such as misinterpreting a statutory provision as in *Anisminic* itself, will (as Lord Diplock said in *Re Racal (1981)*) 'result in [it] having asked [itself] the wrong question with the result that the decision . . . would be a nullity', a finding clearly and emphatically restated by the House of Lords in the case of *Boddington v British Transport Police (1998)*. The rationale is that by asking the wrong question, the body had decided an issue it was not empowered to decide and thus exceeded its *vires*. The courts have certainly made a great stride towards greater clarity and simplicity in the law by abolishing the arcane and elusive distinction between jurisdictional and non-jurisdictional errors. The basic principle is now clear enough, but probing deeper, one may find areas of uncertainty. Just one will be highlighted here, namely, the defining of errors of law made in applying the law to the facts or drawing inferences. While it is now clear that any error of law can lead to the decision being quashed, the question is what is meant by 'error'. In many cases, the answer to what the law requires will be one on which reasonable people will disagree. Will the court invariably substitute its opinion of what the law is or what finding it should yield in the particular case for the opinion of the tribunal? The courts have drawn a distinction here between two things: (a) what is the correct interpretation of the law?; and (b) what is the 'right answer' when a decision-maker applies that legal test to the facts of the situation?

Broadly speaking, the courts have held that they can substitute their opinion on (a) for the original decision-maker, but that when it comes to (b), they will take a more restrained approach. A good illustration of the distinction and its application may be seen in the case of *Monopolies and Mergers Commission ex p South Yorkshire Transport Ltd (1993)*. Here, the Secretary of State could refer a proposed merger to the Commission if the merger would mean that the supply of over 25 per cent of the service in question 'in a substantial part of the United Kingdom' would be in the hands of only one person. The question at issue was whether the 'substantial part of the UK' test was satisfied. On the interpretation point, the House of Lords said that it was the courts' role to decide what 'substantial' meant in the context of that statute. But if, having been defined, the test for 'substantial' was so imprecise that different decision-makers, applying it to the facts in front of them, might reasonably come to different conclusions, the conclusion the decision-maker had reached would only be quashed if it was not within the range of reasonable responses open to a reasonable decision-maker.

One objection to this is that it imports the inherently uncertain *Wednesbury* unreasonableness test into what is supposed to be the more 'hard edged' area of illegality. However, it seems apparent that the practice of drawing a distinction between the question of what the word 'substantial' means when used in a particular statute, and whether any given geographical area in fact fits that definition is eminently sensible. For the test appears, broadly speaking, to assign questions of statutory interpretation to the specialists in that area (the judiciary) and what are ultimately questions of fact and common sense to those with the relevant knowledge of the area concerned. Moreover, it acknowledges openly that the question whether a given piece of land comes within an inherently broad and flexible test such as 'substantial' has no 'right' answers, so that the decision may as well be taken by the person with the best knowledge of local, relevant circumstances. There is clearly room for differences of judicial opinion as to what kind of decisions on factual matters are perverse, or outside the range of reasonable possible responses, and therefore a degree of uncertainty is associated with the test. However, it is submitted that it is based on reasonably workable distinctions and cannot therefore be fairly assessed as intolerably uncertain.

This accusation can, it is submitted, have more applicability to the head of irrationality. The head seems to be expressed in two different ways, both of which reveal muddled judicial thinking. Lord Diplock's definition of irrationality in the *GCHQ* case seems essentially redundant; it is hard to visualise circumstances in which a decision which is outrageously immoral or illogical would not in any event be seen by the judiciary as being outside the purposes of the governing statute and therefore *ultra vires*. The head of irrationality is alternatively expressed as referring to decisions which are so unreasonable that no reasonable person could come to them. Three comments can be made about this definition. First, such decisions would again surely be outside the purpose of the parent Act; second, as Jowell and Lester argue, the definition is tautologous (a decision is unreasonable if a reasonable man could not have made it). Third, the definition seems to be merely another way of saying that the decision has fallen foul of the test considered above: in other words, the decision-maker has come to a conclusion which is not *capable* of being considered correct. For these reasons, it is submitted that the doctrine of unreasonableness as currently understood adds nothing to the law of judicial review and should be abandoned as its subjective nature inevitably renders it uncertain. In that respect, Lord Cooke's recent comment in *Secretary of State for the Home Department ex p Daly (2001)*, 'I think that the day will come when it will be more widely recognised that [*Wednesbury*] was an unfortunately retrogressive decision in English administrative law', is a welcome harbinger of possible future change. However, in going on to say only that it 'may be that the law can never be satisfied' merely by finding that a decision was not absurd, Lord Cooke adds further uncertainty to the law.

It is clear that, overall, a mixed picture has emerged. In some cases, incoherent doctrines have left judges open to charges of unwarranted interference. However, many workable principles have been developed, and uncertainty can be due to the range of situations to which review applies, or to Parliament's failure to legislate clearly on the subject in hand. The charge of intolerable uncertainty can therefore, it is submitted, have only uneven application to the law of judicial review.

▌NOTES

1 Examples could be given of this wide variation. Thus, in the context of disciplinary hearings of prisoners before the Board of Visitors, the rules of natural justice (in tandem with limited statutory provision) demand that prisoners should be allowed to call witnesses, cross-examine those giving evidence against them (*Board of Visitors of Hull Prison ex p St Germain (No 2)*

(1979)) and, in some circumstances, be allowed legal advice (*Secretary of State for the Home Department ex p Tarrant (1985)*) while, at the other end of the scale, in the context of a decision by the minimum wage board, natural justice did not require an oral hearing (*Judge Amphlett (1915)*).

2 Students could note that in the area of determining when natural justice will apply, the judiciary can be criticised not only for leaving the law uncertain but for unwarranted intervention in decision-making. In *Home Secretary ex p Khan (1984)*, the court held that the Home Secretary could not depart from a previously expressed policy under which a foreign child would have been given clearance to enter the UK, without notifying the applicant (who wished to adopt the child) of the change. In its judgment, the Lords was arguably blurring the notion of the applicant's right to be heard in relation to the new policy with the notion that the applicant had a right *simpliciter* that the policy would remain the same as it had been. It can be contended that here, the judiciary was using a flexible principle as a cloak under which to reverse a change of policy which it considered unfair.

Question 30

'The law of judicial review before the Human Rights Act 1998 provided uncertain and unsatisfactory levels of protection for civil rights and freedoms.'

Consider how far you agree with this statement, and how far the Human Rights Act has changed this situation. Take into account decided cases under the Act.

Answer plan

This question is currently a very popular subject with examiners, given the current dynamic state of the law in this area. Essentially, the following matters should be discussed:

- the traditional approach of judicial review to civil rights;
- the 'common law constitutional rights' approach;
- how this approach found some acceptance in subsequent case law;
- conclusion on the state of protection prior to the HRA;
- the impact of the HRA: the rights and exceptions to them;
- the new duty of statutory construction: infringement of rights has become a new ground of review.

Answer

Historically, judicial review has not been greatly concerned with the protection of human rights *per se*. Since its traditional basis has been the *ultra vires* doctrine, and since liberties have been mainly residual rather than being granted positively by statutes, this is perhaps not surprising. Cases such as *GCHQ (1984)* showed some recognition of the importance of civil rights – in that case, freedom of association – but up until quite recently, they have generally played a marginal role in public law. This essay will examine how much impact the more rights-orientated approach of recent years has had, the limitations inherent in this approach, and the change brought about by the Human Rights Act (HRA) 1998.

Calls for a more rights-based approach to judicial review had multiplied in the years before the HRA. Jowell and Lester, in a well known article ([1987] PL 368) argued that the *Wednesbury* unreasonableness test had for some time been used as a cloak under which substantive principles of review – proportionality, respect for human rights and legal certainty – had been cautiously and sporadically deployed. The authors called for a more explicit acceptance and application of these values; they made the concrete proposal that the courts, when reviewing decisions taken under statute, could perfectly legitimately apply a presumption – displaceable only by clear statutory language – that Parliament did not intend to authorise actions incompatible with the UK's obligations under the European Convention on Human Rights (ECHR).

Such an approach was roundly rejected by the House of Lords in the *Brind* case (*Secretary of State for the Home Department ex p Brind (1991)*), on the basis that the imposition of such a presumption would amount to *de facto* incorporation of the Convention 'by the back door', since the effect would be to render all administrative decisions violating the Convention unlawful, even if the statute had granted a broad discretion which on its face encompassed rights-violating action. This, the Lords thought, would be a usurpation of judicial power, given Parliament's persistent refusal to introduce the Convention through legislation.

Partly in response to this decision, which rejected the proposal to develop judicial review principles by reference to the then un-incorporated Convention, Laws J put forward a thesis as to how judicial review could be developed ([1993] PL 59) which, he argued, avoided their Lordships' objection to the Jowell and Lester approach, but would afford far greater protection to fundamental rights than the traditional *Wednesbury* grounds. The main thrust of his argument is briefly as follows. Laws J proposed that review could develop such that in a case in which the exercise of discretion could have an adverse impact on fundamental rights, a two-stage test would be imposed by the courts. The first stage would be the imposition of an interpretative presumption, that no statute's purpose could include interference with fundamental rights embedded in the common law, and that such interference will only be allowed if it is demonstrated that reading the statute to permit such interference is the only interpretation possible. Laws argued that their Lordships had been invited in *Brind* to make a presumption that the statute they were considering was not intended to give power to infringe Art 10 of the ECHR. This approach was rightly rejected, he argued, on separation-of-powers principles, which forbade incorporation 'through the back door'. The correct approach, he argued, would be to view the norms implicit in the ECHR as already reflected in the common law – an approach which gained some support from the House of Lords' decision in *Derbyshire (Derbyshire CC v Times Newspapers (1993))* – and to argue that it is the importance that the common law consequently attaches to fundamental rights which makes a presumption that statutes do not intend to facilitate infringement of such rights a permissible, indeed, legitimate one.[1]

This approach was demonstrated in some notable cases. *Lord Chancellor ex p Witham (1997)*, a judgment of Laws J himself, concerned a challenge to a decision of the Lord Chancellor, who, acting under a general power to make regulations as to the level of court fees, removed the exemption from such fees for persons on income support. Given that the fee for issuing a High Court writ was simultaneously increased to £500, this effectively meant that unemployed people were not able to commence proceedings, and hence effectively were denied access to the courts. Following his own suggested approach, the judge first of all found that access to the courts was a fundamental right; second, that in the absence of very clear wording, it was presumed that Parliament had not given power to a minister to invade this right; and third, that the statute did not contain any such wording, being phrased in general terms. He thus adjudged the rule removing the exemption from court fees for those on income support to be *ultra vires* and struck it down.

This approach gained acceptance from the House of Lords in two important decisions. Lord Hoffmann remarked in *Secretary of State for the Home Department ex p Simms (2000)* that 'fundamental rights cannot be overridden by general or ambiguous words'. The House of Lords found that general words in a statute were not sufficient to warrant a rule laid down by the Home Secretary that prevented a prisoner from contacting journalists with a view to starting a campaign that his own conviction amounted to a miscarriage of justice. Freedom of expression was held to be a common law right, to be ousted only by express words or necessary implication. In *Secretary of State for the Home Department ex p Pierson (1998)*, Lord Browne-Wilkinson summarised the principle thus:

> A power conferred by Parliament in general terms is not to be taken to authorise the doing of acts by the donee of the power which adversely affect the legal rights of the citizen . . . unless the statute conferring the power makes it clear that such was the intention of Parliament.

These decisions show how far the basic doctrine of *ultra vires*, coupled with a readiness to impose strong presumptions as to legislative intent on Parliament, can go.[2] Indeed, in stating that express words would be required to remove the right of access to the courts, Laws J in *Witham* effectively gave notice that there were certain rights in defence of which the judiciary would be prepared to suspend the doctrine of implied repeal, an approach which, as we shall see, is actually more radical than that of the HRA itself. The essential problem with this situation was that with the exception of certain established categories, it was very difficult to know when a judge would decide that a given right was sufficiently firmly 'embedded' in the common law to justify the imposition of such strong legislative presumptions. Privacy, for example, was clearly not such a right, at least according to earlier decisions like *Malone (1979)*.

The second stage of Laws' suggested approach was perhaps more ambitious. He notes that it is well established that the courts insist that relevant considerations should be taken into account when making a decision, but hold that the *weight* to be given to those considerations is entirely for the decision-maker to determine. He then suggests that on principle, while this may be a reasonable approach when the matter under consideration involves such issues as economic policy, in cases where fundamental rights are at stake, this would mean that the decision-maker would be free 'to accord a high or low importance to the right in question, as he chooses' which 'cannot be right' if the right is to be taken seriously. The courts, he suggested, should therefore insist that the right could only be overridden if an 'objective, sufficient justification' existed so that the infringement was limited to what was strictly required by the situation.

In *Ministry of Defence ex p Smith (1996)*, this approach appeared to find partial acceptance: Sir Thomas Bingham MR accepted the following submission of David Pannick QC that ' . . . the more substantial the interference with human rights, the more the court will require by way of justification before it is satisfied that the decision is reasonable' (p 263). This sounds almost like an echo of Laws' prescription. However, the sting lies in the meaning of the word 'reasonable'; it denotes only a decision which is 'within the range of responses open to a reasonable decision-maker'. In other words, the prescription adopted seems to be this: the decision-maker is required to take account of human rights in appropriate cases; further, he must have a more convincing justification the more his decision will trespass on those rights. But that decision remains primarily one for the decision-maker. The courts will only intervene if the decider has come up with a justification which no reasonable person could consider trumps the human rights considerations – a position which seems to take us almost back to classic *GCHQ* irrationality. At present, therefore, the more rights-oriented approach may appear merely as a gloss only superficially overlaying traditional principles.

Where, therefore, the *ultra vires* approach used in *Simms* and *Witham* could not plausibly be used, and the approach had to be framed in terms of *Wednesbury*, the attempt to utilise judicial review to provide a strong defence of rights outside the context of freedom of expression and access to a court met with flat rejection from the higher judiciary. In *Cambridge Health Authority ex p B (1995)*, which concerned a challenge to the Health Authority's decision not to allocate funds to the treatment of a young girl suffering from leukaemia, Laws J applied his own second stage approach, reasoning that the girl's right to life, threatened by the Authority's decision, could only be overridden by a substantial public interest justification, the sufficiency of which would be determined by the judge. Finding that no such justification had been provided, he found the Authority's decision to have been unlawful. His judgment was swiftly overturned on appeal. Lord Bingham MR found that the appropriate test was straightforward, narrow *Wednesbury:* the court could only intervene to quash a manifestly perverse decision. The threshold of unreasonableness had not even been approached by the Authority and its decision should stand. This decision was indeed not surprising, given that Laws J's judgment had interfered in the discretionary allocation of resources – an area in which the judiciary have always tended to grant a great deal of leeway to the decision-maker.

Thus, the pre-HRA position revealed great potential in the law of judicial review for greater rights protection and some manifestation of that potential. But, it also revealed divisions within the judiciary, uncertainty as to which rights will merit strong protection and disagreement as to how strong that protection should be. In some cases, such as *ex p Smith*, the rhetoric of rights yielded barely any greater protection in practice than the old *Wednesbury* approach. Moreover, there are cases on the books in which may be found refusals even to recognise the existence of the claimed right (privacy in *Malone (1979)*) or, less extremely, denials of any duty to modify the traditional grounds of review to ensure rights protection (*Secretary of State for the Environment ex p Nalgo (1993)*). Consistency and coherence were conspicuously lacking.

How far then was this situation remedied by the introduction of the HRA? It is suggested that six key changes have been brought about. These are considered in turn, with discussion of relevant case law where necessary.

First of all, the Act, by incorporating the ECHR, has made it clear which rights are recognised as fundamental; this is no longer left to the views of individual judges. Second, the Convention spells out the permissible grounds for derogating from the rights. Although the exceptions to Arts 8–11 are expressed in very broad and general terms, Arts 3 and 6 have no express exceptions, whilst Arts 2, 4 and 5 permit only tightly defined and narrow exceptions. Moreover, even in relation to the rights with generalised exceptions (Arts 8–11), at least some of the detailed work in elucidating the appropriate balance between particular rights and particular exceptions has been done by the ECHR; such jurisprudence has to be taken into account by UK judges (s 2 of the HRA). Moreover, *dicta* in *Alconbury (2001)* instruct the courts that they should follow the 'clear and settled' case law of the ECHR, save in exceptional circumstances.

Third, and perhaps most importantly of all, s 6(1) of the HRA makes it clear beyond doubt that infringement of a Convention right will, *per se*, render an administrative decision or provision in delegated legislation unlawful, unless the enabling legislation clearly allows for or mandates the infringement (s 6(2)). Thus, there is now no uncertainty as to whether Convention rights are restraints upon broad discretions, mandatory considerations or even optional considerations, although as we shall see in a moment, that straightforward provision has given rise to a surprising amount of difficulty for the judiciary.

Fourth, the pre-HRA doubts as to whether legislation can be presumed not to give power to infringe rights has been dispelled: in accordance with s 3(1) of the HRA, past and future legislation has to be read and given effect in a way which is compatible with Convention rights, if this is possible, although (incompatible legislation remains valid and of full effect (s 3(2) and s 4). The decision in *A (2001)* has made it clear that this very powerful rule of construction is to be applied rigorously, and may allow for the implication of words into statutory provisions, as well as strained readings of statutory language. *Re W and B (Children) (Care Order) (2002)* has tempered the strongly activist stance taken in *A* by clarifying that the courts may not effectively read entirely new provisions into statutes.

It is fair to say that decisions on s 3(1) have not removed all uncertainty as to its scope. Lord Nicholl said in *Re W and B* that a reading of legislation under s 3(1) should not 'depart substantially from a fundamental feature of an Act of Parliament' and similar *dicta* may be found in *Poplar Housing (2001)*, *per* Woolf CJ and in *Lambert (2001)*, *per* Lord Hope, but arguably this is precisely what occurred in *A*. The provision in question was intended to *exclude* judicial discretion to admit evidence of a woman's sexual history with the defendant, unless the specified, very narrow conditions set out by Parliament in the provision in question were met. The effect of the majority decision was effectively to restore that discretion. Similarly, in *Ghaidan v Mendoza (2004)*, the House of Lords arguably overruled Parliament's clear intention in the relevant housing legislation to extend tenancy succession rights to heterosexual couples living together as husband and wife, but *not* to gay couples in the same situation. Conversely, *Bellinger v Bellinger (2003)* clearly indicated that the courts will sometimes refuse to engage even in relatively straightforward re-interpretation of legislation, in terms of linguistics, where it is felt that the change is complex and significant enough to require consideration by Parliament. In that case, the House of Lords refused to interpret the word 'female' in the Matrimonial Causes Act 1973 to reflect modern understandings of the protean nature of gender so that it included post-operative male to female transsexuals and would thus allow the applicant validly to marry a man. To change the meaning of a single word in this way was clearly a 'possible' interpretation even under the most modest views of what that elusive word means. However, the interpretation was rejected and a declaration of incompatibility made instead. How far s 3(1) allows the judiciary to go has not therefore been wholly settled. But the position is still far clearer than before the HRA.

The fifth effect of the Act is that it is no longer necessary to 'tag' human rights arguments onto existing grounds, such as *ultra vires* or *Wednesbury*, as in the cases discussed above. Section 7 of the HRA provides for proceedings against public authorities simply on the basis that they have infringed Convention rights.

The final effect of the HRA is not as clear cut. On the face of it, the wording of s 6(1), 'It is unlawful for a public authority to act in a way that is inconsistent with a Convention right,' meant that questions of whether rights have been violated become a matter of statutory construction of the Convention and its case law: thus, so it appeared, the question would be a hard-edged legal one, for determination by judges. There would be no more division between a primary decision by the decision-maker and a secondary review of it by the courts: the issue of infringement would be one in relation to which the courts must substitute their judgment of the matter for that of the decision-maker. So, at least, one would think from a straightforward reading of s 6(1) (see, for example, Leigh [2002] PL 265). However, the position, it turns out, is more muddy than that (see, for example, *Blessing Edore v Secretary of State for the Home Department (2003)*, in which Simon Brown LJ said that it would be 'unhelpful' to think of Convention proportionality as a question of law). In order to understand why, it is necessary to rehearse the three-stage proportionality test as developed by the European Court of Human Rights which is applied to determine whether a *prima facie* violation of a right is nevertheless justified (the court must also find a basis in law for the interference). First, it must be asked whether the purpose served by the proposed restriction on the right falls into one of the exceptions set out in the relevant Convention Article. In other words, was there a 'legitimate aim'? Second, if so, is it 'necessary in a democratic society' to protect the value threatened by the right? This has been interpreted as requiring a court to ask whether there is a 'pressing social need' so to act. Third, it must be asked whether the action taken to protect the value in question went no further than was necessary.

It is in conducting this proportionality inquiry that the courts have somewhat detracted from the clear change that s 6(1) appeared to bring about. Some early judgments seemed intent on watering down s 6(1) into merely a modified *Wednesbury* test, so that the court would merely *review* the minister's own decision as to whether infringement of a Convention right was justifiable, interfering only if he had struck a manifestly unfair balance between the primary right and the competing social interests (see, for example, *Mahmood (2001)*). The courts in such cases emphasised that the HRA did not mean that they now stood in the minister's shoes, deciding for themselves whether the actions taken breached the Convention. Laws LJ spoke of a 'principled distance' between the courts' review and the minister's original decision. Standing in the minister's shoes seemed, however, to be precisely what s 6(1), in making the matter one of *law*, required of the courts and it was not long before the House of Lords reminded the lower courts of this, in *Daly (2001)*. Lord Bingham said clearly that 'domestic courts must *themselves* form a judgment whether a Convention right has been breached', while Lord Steyn stressed that under the Convention proportionality test, the courts were required to assess the balance struck by the decision-maker between the primary right and the competing interests, looking at the previously forbidden territory of the *weight* assigned by the decision-maker to the various factors in the balance. *Daly* therefore seemed to have scotched any attempt to equate the protection given under the ECHR with the heightened *Wednesbury* test used in *Smith* (above), though as Leigh notes, the decision in *Samaroo (2001)*, with its emphasis on assessing whether the decision-maker had struck a 'fair balance' between the right and societal interests, was an attempt to shift the ground back to the *Mahmood* approach.

However, even if further cases stamp out these backslidings, one principle that judges have developed, related to the approaches taken in *Samaroo* and *Mahmood*, will continue to inject uncertainty into the rigour of the courts' review of Convention compliance in ministerial and other decisions. This is the notion of the 'area of discretionary judgment'. Essentially, when the court is deciding whether a given decision, which impacted on a Convention right, was proportionate to the aim pursued, it will extend an area of latitude to the body it is reviewing, thus abjuring a rigorous inquiry into proportionality, in deference to the 'area of judgment' or 'discretion' of another body. *DPP ex p Kebilene (1999)* provided an early endorsement of this doctrine, and it has been deployed in many cases since: *Brown v Stott (2001))* was an early important example; it was seen in perhaps its most marked form in *ProLife Alliance (2003)*. Effectively, the court affords great weight to the view of the decision-making body itself on the question of proportionality; this can lead it to intervene only where that body has manifestly got the question wrong. This can lead straight back to the approach in *Mahmood* and a dilution of the Convention protection. On the other hand, in some cases, it would seem undesirable for the court to rush to substitute its judgment where the matter was primarily one of real expertise, or of a considered social policy choice made by the legislature. Conversely, in cases concerning grave invasions of the core of rights held dear by the judiciary, a rigorous approach towards assessing proportionality has been taken. The outstanding example is *A v Secretary of State (2004)*, in which, in the context of the detention without charge of suspected terrorists, the House of Lords firmly rejected the submission of the A–G that because national security was in play, the courts should largely defer to the view of the executive as to what was required to protect it, on democratic grounds. Lord Bingham said, trenchantly: 'the function of independent judges charged to interpret and apply the law is universally recognised as a cardinal feature of the modern democratic state, a cornerstone of the rule of law itself'. The trouble at present is that some uncertainty has been imported into the application of the HRA, in that the courts have made only limited progress in indicating when it is appropriate to apply a wide area of discretion, and when a narrow, or no area; as Lord Steyn observed in *Daly*, 'In law, context is everything'.

In conclusion, the HRA has forcibly plunged the judiciary into the task of interpreting a series of broadly worded guarantees, around which a formidable and complex jurisprudence has already been generated. While this will create a period of uncertainty as to the detailed accommodation to be made between the rights and their inbuilt exceptions, particularly when further latitude – of as yet uncertain scope – has to be given to the views of the original decision-maker, the advent of the HRA has firmly dispelled the quite fundamental uncertainties as to the place fundamental rights hold in public law which pertained before its coming into force.

▌NOTES

1 Students could note the problem with this approach, namely, that it is uncontroversial to assume that power is only granted on the understanding that it will be exercised rationally – indeed this could be said to be a basic requirement of the rule of law. By contrast, to assume that power is never granted to infringe basic liberties is to make a *substantive* claim about Parliament's values and priorities – a far more controversial claim.

2 It could be pointed out that both of these cases were examples of a rights-based approach sheltering behind an apparent deference to Parliament's intent. The real concern of the courts was not to enforce Parliament's intent, but to prevent the government from invading individual rights. The notion that Parliament could not have intended such outrages was largely a fiction.

NOTES

CHAPTER 8

OMBUDSMEN

▌INTRODUCTION

Questions about the Ombudsman system tend to concentrate on the Parliamentary Commissioner for Administration (PCA), but the Ombudsman system has been extended into a number of areas, including in Scotland and Wales, and, as explained below, does not operate in the same way in each. Therefore, it is necessary to be aware of other Ombudsmen. A knowledge of parliamentary procedures and of the scope of judicial review is valuable in tackling this area, because a typical question might concern the extent to which the Ombudsman system provides remedies for the aggrieved citizen not available by those means. The question most commonly asked concerns the efficacy of the Ombudsman despite the limitations of the system.

Checklist

Students should be familiar with the following areas:

- the provisions of the Parliamentary Commissioner Act 1967 and the setting up of the Ombudsman system, in particular: the nature of 'maladministration' under s 10(3);

- matters excluded from the scrutiny of the Ombudsman under Scheds 2 and 3 to the Act;

- the extension of the system: Local Commissioners, Health Service Commissioners, the Parliamentary Commissioner for Northern Ireland; the Scottish and Welsh Ombudsmen;

- the characteristics of the system (which do not apply equally to all Ombudsmen): lack of direct access, informal procedures, lack of formal remedies, the ability to persuade bodies to make widespread changes in administrative practices;

- the efficacy of the Ombudsman: governmental compliance with recommendations;

- the reforms suggested by the Cabinet Office Review (2000) and the limited Government response in Cabinet Office, *Reform of the Public Sector Ombudsmen in England (2005)*;
- the use of parliamentary procedures as a means of providing redress for maladministration.

Question 31

'The constraints on the Parliamentary Commissioner which appear to limit his power are actually a source of strength; if they were lifted, his role would, paradoxically, be less valuable.'

Discuss.

Answer plan

A question concerning the extent to which the Parliamentary Commissioner, or Ombudsman, is effective despite several factors impairing his efficiency is commonly set and is quite straightforward. This question introduces a variation on that theme, as it suggests that the Ombudsman is effective because of the restrictions rather than despite them. However, the issues to be discussed are the same in either case: what are the restrictions and what effect do they have? The further issue that this particular question raises concerns the extent to which the restrictions are beneficial and probably inherent in his role. A distinction could be drawn between such restrictions (if any) and those which are arguably not a necessary concomitant of his role.

The following matters should be considered:

- the aim in setting up the Ombudsman system;
- the nature of 'maladministration';
- the matters excluded from scrutiny;
- the detriment caused by the lack of direct access to the Parliamentary Commissioner for Administration (PCA);
- the informal procedure adopted by the PCA;
- the lack of coercive remedies available to the PCA and the beneficial and detrimental impacts of this;
- the impact of reforms suggested by the Cabinet Office Review (2000) – the limited Governmental response.

Answer

In addressing this question, a distinction will be drawn between two types of constraint on the PCA: first, those that appear to be a necessary concomitant of his role as presently conceived and which, if removed, would arguably create not only a completely different body but also a less effective one; second, those which, it will be argued, are *not* a necessary concomitant of his office and that impair his efficacy. The thrust of the argument will be that on the whole, contrary to the statement to be discussed, constraints on the PCA weaken his efficacy, although it will be agreed that some are indeed a source of strength.

It will first be necessary to consider the role the PCA was set up to fulfil. The system was set up under the Parliamentary Commissioner Act 1967 (hereafter 'the Act') as a result of the perception which arose after the Crichel Down affair in 1954 that pre-existing judicial and parliamentary remedies did not provide adequate redress for members of the public who had suffered as a result of maladministration in central government. The PCA was given the ability to investigate a wider range of complaints than could be investigated in a court and given greater investigative powers than those available to MPs. He is empowered to consider 'maladministration' (under s 10(3) of the Act) as opposed to illegality. There will be some overlap between the range of administrative actions he can consider and those which can consider where there is a statutory right of appeal or in judicial review proceedings, but it will not be great. A court can intervene in judicial review proceedings only where a decision is *ultra vires*, where it is considered *Wednesbury* unreasonable, where there has been a breach of natural justice or a breach of rights protected under the European Convention on Human Rights (ECHR), as incorporated into UK law via the Human Rights Act (HRA) 1998 (s 6(1)). In contrast, 'maladministration' has been described as 'bias, neglect, inattention, delay, incompetence, ineptitude, perversity, turpitude, arbitrariness and so on' (Richard Crossman in the debate on the Parliamentary Commissioner Bill 1967). The PCA in 1994 fleshed out the definition a little, making clear that it also included matters such as rudeness, discrimination, refusal to answer reasonable questions, neglecting to inform a person of a right of appeal against decisions and 'failure to mitigate the effects of rigid adherence to the letter of the law where that produces manifestly inequitable treatment' (HC 345, 1993–94, para 10). Although these words are wide, they suggest a limitation of his role in that the PCA is, on the whole, concerned with procedural defects rather than with the merits of a decision. This distinction is contained in s 12(3) of the Act, which provides that the PCA may not investigate the merits of a decision taken without maladministration.

However, the distinction between substance and procedure is not always easy to draw (as appears from the contrast between the judgment of Nolan J at first instance and that of Lord Donaldson in the Court of Appeal in *Local Commissioner ex p Eastleigh BC (1988)*) and the PCA has complied with the demand from the Parliamentary Select Committee on the PCA to interpret his role widely. Therefore, this apparent limitation on the PCA's remit is less significant than may at first appear.

It must not be forgotten that once maladministration is found, it must be shown that it caused 'injustice' (s 10(3) of the Act). It was recently clarified in the case of *Parliamentary Commissioner for Administration ex p Balchin (No 2) (2000)* that 'injustice' is specifically *not* limited to identifiable loss or damage, but includes 'a sense of outrage caused by unfair or incompetent administration'.

However, there are a number of limitations on the powers of the PCA which, it will be argued, are *not* inherent in the nature of his office and *do* impair his efficacy. He is unable to investigate at all in certain areas. The bodies affected by the Act, which are set out in Sched 2, do not include public corporations, tribunals, the Criminal Injuries Compensation Board or, crucially, the police (although the Independent Police Complaints Commission now provides a robust mechanism for police complaints). The system has been expanded to cover the National Health Service and local authorities – Local Commissioners were established in 1974. Prior to 1987, the PCA's jurisdiction was limited to central government departments and agencies, but the Parliamentary and Health Service Commissioners Act 1987 amended the 1967 Act in order to add about 50 non-departmental public bodies (NDPBs) such as the Arts Council and the EOC to its remit. In 2006 the PCA acquired a new area of work, in hearing complaints from victims of crime in relation to the criminal justice system under the new Victims Code (2006).

The Scotland Act 1998 requires the Scottish Parliament to legislate for the creation of an Ombudsman to investigate actions of the Scottish Executive (s 91), and the Scottish Public Services Ombudsman Act 2002 created an Ombudsman with a much broader remit than the PCA, encompassing the devolved institutions, local government and the Scottish NHS. In relation to Northern Ireland, an Assembly Ombudsman was established under the Northern Ireland Act 1998 (see SI 1996/1298 (NI 8)). The Public Services Ombudsman for Wales, introduced by the Public Services Ombudsman (Wales) Act 2005 will be able to investigate matters relating to local government, social housing, health, the Welsh Assembly, certain Welsh public authorities and (so far as their conduct impacts upon Wales) certain other public authorities. In relation to the UK PCA, certain matters, set out in Sched 3 to the Act, are excluded from investigation. These include extradition and fugitive offenders, the investigation of crime by or on behalf of the Home Office, security of the State, action in matters relating to contractual or commercial activities, court proceedings and personnel matters of the armed forces, teachers, the Civil Service or police. The government has always resisted the extension of the Ombudsman system into these areas.

Of these restrictions, those attracting the most criticism have been the exclusion of contractual and commercial matters and of public service personnel matters. The *Fourth Report from the Select Committee on the PCA*, 1979, considered that both exclusions were unjustified. It considered that government was under a duty to use its purchasing power fairly and that this was particularly important where there was a risk that such power might be used as a political weapon. Therefore, where commercial decisions were taken with maladministration, the PCA should be able to question them. Drewry comments that, 'Looking at other Ombudsman systems, such exclusions are rare – and the Northern Ireland PCA (whose office is modelled closely on that of the mainland PCA) does exercise jurisdiction in this area, without this causing any apparent difficulties' ('The Ombudsman: parochial stopgap or global panacea?', in Leyland and Woods (eds), *Administrative Law Facing the Future*, 1997, p 99). However, as Seneviratne notes (*Ombudsmen in the Public Sector*, 1994), in practice, this exception 'has accounted for few rejections [of complaints to the PCA], perhaps because its scope has been limited by successive PCAs who have decided that a service does not become commercial [merely] because a charge is made for it' (p 23). As regards public service personnel, the Select Committee accepted that matters relating to discipline, promotion and rates of pay should be outside the PCA's remit, but considered that no evidence had been shown of harm likely to accrue if other purely administrative acts of the government in its capacity as an employer were brought within it. Whatever justification might be put forward for this limitation, it is hard to show that the PCA derives positive benefit from being excluded from these areas and the PCA himself has said that such exclusion from his scrutiny may not reflect Parliament's intentions (PCA Annual Report for 1988). The Cabinet Office Review was generally cautious as to jurisdiction, merely recommending that there should be no overall reduction in the jurisdiction of the new Commission. By contrast, the Public Administration Committee, in its Report on the Review (HC 612, 1999–2000), took a more radical line: in answering the question, 'Should the legislation specify the bodies which are not within the Ombudsmen's jurisdiction, rather than those which are?', it answered, firmly, 'This change has been consistently recommended by our predecessor Committees and it should be seen as a basic principle of any new system'. One of their witnesses put it thus: 'The onus of jurisdiction needs to be shifted in favour of the complainant. All State agencies and their activities should be in jurisdiction unless otherwise specifically excluded.'

A further important limitation, the system of making the complaint through a Member of Parliament, has been much criticised: it is thought that this 'screening' of complaints does not serve the best interests of complainants.[1] The screening of complaints by MPs either before or after the PCA receives them could arguably undermine the importance of the PCA as a means of making up for the inefficacy of some parliamentary procedures. Select Committees and Questions in the House operate within the doctrine of ministerial responsibility; in other words, the expectation is that the minister in question will remedy matters. The PCA, on the other hand, looks behind that expectation and considers the workings of the administrative body itself. The involvement of MPs in the process may mean that complaints which should lead to investigation in the department in question are dealt with through inadequate parliamentary procedures. The present system, as Justice pointed out in 1979, weakens the PCA, because he is unable to publicise himself as available to receive complaints when he is not so available.[2]

Some amelioration of this system has occurred: since 1978, where the PCA receives a complaint directly from a member of the public, the complainant's MP will be contacted and, if he is in agreement, the PCA will investigate. This system does not, however, encourage citizens to complain directly to the PCA and, due to his low profile, many will in any event be unaware that a complaint is possible. The primary concern of MPs about removing their screening function is the fear that allowing direct access would undermine their constitutional role as defenders of the citizen against the Executive (the main recent discussion may be found in the Select Committee Report, HC 33–II, 1993–94). Apart from any symbolic undermining, the concrete threat, according to the Select Committee, appears to boil down to the fear that 'direct access will result in the denial to members of expertise in the problems facing their constituents . . . This is to impoverish parliamentary, and thus, political life' (para 76). This argument seems flawed in its own terms: it fails to recognise that direct access by the public to the PCA need not necessarily cause any decrease at all in either the involvement of MPs in the matters raised or in the flow of information to them, the second of which is certainly vital to their role as scrutinisers of the Executive. The Committee argued that 'the publication of anonymised reports can never be a genuine substitute for direct involvement in the case which the member has referred' (HC 33–11, 1993–94). But this is not the only alternative to the present system. If direct access were introduced, the continued involvement and knowledgability of MPs could be ensured very simply: the PCA would (with the complaint's permission) simply copy the appropriate MP in with any complaint received, and with news of the investigation of the complaint (if he decided to take it up) as it proceeded. It does not seem clear that MPs' constitutional role necessarily demands that they should have to make the decision as to whether a complaint should be investigated, particularly as it may reasonably be feared that their political allegiance could distort their judgment in sensitive cases. It may be added that MPs would, of course, continue to receive numerous complaints on a variety of matters, many of which would be outside the PCA's jurisdiction. There thus seems to be no sufficient argument for requiring complaints to come only via MPs. In New South Wales, where complaints can come directly from the public or from MPs, the vast majority of complaints come directly from the public.

At one point, it appeared that the above arguments had won the day and that the days of the MP filter were numbered. The Cabinet Review (2000), the PCA himself and the Public Administration Committee (Third Report, HC 612, 1999–2000) agreed that the MP filter had outlived its usefulness and should be removed. Recently, the PCA commented: 'in the 21st Century it really is not defensible for citizens not to have direct access to a public sector ombudsman', (Public Administration Committee, Minutes of Evidence (2003–04 HC41-i). It is particularly significant that the Public Administration Committee, whose predecessor Committees, as seen above, had consistently argued for the *retention* of the filter, has now changed its view and expressed it in such firm terms: 'We believe that the idea of an MP filter . . . is now inconsistent with the world of public service charters and ought to be replaced by direct public access to the public sector Ombudsmen' (para 12). It is noteworthy that there is no equivalent filter in the Scottish Public Services Ombudsman Act 2002, nor in the equivalent legislation for Wales (above). The government has in principle accepted that the filter should be removed from the PCA (see HC Debs, 20 July 2001, WA Col 464w). However, now six years on from the Cabinet Office Review, and five years after this statement by the Government, no time has yet been found for primary legislation to remove the filter. The latest report from the Cabinet Office, Cabinet Office, *Reform of the Public Sector Ombudsmen in England (2005)* (hereafter "the 2005 Review) advocates making certain changes to streamline the English Ombudsmen system by way of regulatory reform through secondary legislation, but this route does not allow for removal of the filter – a major disappointment (see M. Elliot, (2006) PL 84, for comment and criticism).

The current lack of direct access to the PCA may account for the very small number of complaints received in comparison with the number of administrative decisions taken. The Select Committee on the PCA, in its 1994 Report (HC 64, 1993–94), noted the far greater volume of complaints received in a sample year, 1991, by Ombudsmen in countries with far smaller populations than the UK: the Danish Ombudsmen, catering for a population of five million, received 2,000 complaints; the Swedish Ombudsmen, 4,000 complaints (population eight million); while the UK Ombudsmen, from a population of 55 million, received at that time only 766 complaints. These figures are striking. Moreover, the majority of complaints are rejected as being outside the jurisdiction of the PCA, or for some other reason. The case load of the PCA has only been one-sixth of what was anticipated, though it continues to rise quite sharply, climbing to 1,933 in 1996 and levelling out at 1,721 in 2001 and 1,853 in 2005 (parliamentary cases only).

A further limitation on the role of the PCA arises due to the lack of power to award a remedy. The PCA can neither order compensation nor apply to a court to enforce his findings; compliance is therefore voluntary. The remedies recommended vary: *ex gratia* payments to individuals adversely affected by maladministration appear to be made in roughly half the cases in which the PCA makes a finding against the department concerned (in 92 out of 177 cases in 1992, and in 108 cases out of 236 in 1995). However, although this inability to award compulsory remedies might appear to weaken the PCA severely, it is arguable that the need for such a limitation is inherent in his role. If the PCA could award remedies, it would be hard to avoid making the investigative proceedings more formalised so as to give the body complained of a full opportunity to answer the allegations made. Probably, some of the procedures would have to be conducted in public. The fact that the PCA operates informally and privately has been thought to enhance his powers of persuasion. Where a particular complaint seems to be merely symptomatic of a deep-seated problem in a department, the PCA can sometimes persuade it to change its general procedure. This occurred in the *Ostler case (1977)*: the Department of the Environment was persuaded to introduce new procedures in order to prevent a repetition of the situation which led to Ostler's complaint. In his Annual Report for 1993, the PCA noted that as a very significant byproduct of his investigation into the mishandling of claims to disability living allowance, the Department of Social Security was persuaded to revise its general departmental compensation scheme. Similarly in her report for 2006, the PCA noted that the Department of Health intended to integrate the handling of health and social care complaints, something which was recommended in the PCA's 2005 report on the NHS complaints system. Thus, this apparent weakness in the PCA's powers may underlie one of his main strengths.

Furthermore, research indicates that the influence of the PCA is far greater in practice than his limited formal powers might suggest. Writing in 1994, Rodney Austin noted that 'Whitehall's record of compliance with the nonbinding recommendations of the Ombudsman is actually outstanding: on only two occasions have government departments refused to accept the PCA's findings and, in both cases, the PCA's recommendations were [nevertheless] complied with' ('Freedom of information: the constitutional impact', in Jowell and Oliver (eds), *The Changing Constitution*, 1994, p 443). Since this was written, the government rejected the adverse findings of the PCA's report on the blight caused by the Channel Tunnel Rail Link (HC 193, 1994–95); although faced with unanimous Select Committee backing for the PCA's findings (HC 270, 1994–95), the relevant department did eventually agree to award some *ex gratia* compensation to some of those affected, though without admitting any fault. However, since then there, disturbingly, been two rejections by the Government of PCA findings in only 12 months. The first related to a report entitled *A Debt of Honour* (July, 2005), dealing with *ex-gratia* payments to former British civilian internees in the Far East. However, while initially rejecting the PCA's findings, the Government eventually relented, and by the time the PCA produced her annual report for 2006, she was able to report that the MOD had agreed to expand the eligibility criteria for compensation. The second instance related to more widespread problem. '125,000 people lost significant parts of defined benefit occupational pensions when such schemes wound up between April 1997 and March 2004 without sufficient funds to pay the benefits promised', due, the PCA found, to Government maladministration (Select Committee on Public Administration

(SCPA, 6th Report (2005–06). Information provided by the Government had been, she said, 'incomplete, unclear and inconsistent' (Annual Report, 2006 HC 1363). She recommended that the Government consider restoring benefits to those affected, a recommendation brusquely rejected by the Government. The PCA commented:

> There appears to be an emerging attitude amongst Government departments that they can properly, and with impunity, reject my independent assessment of their actions, and my findings of maladministration

Given that the entire system depends upon the government of the day accepting an obligation to implement PCA recommendations, and that this sense of obligation rests partly upon the practice of successive governments to do so, such instances threaten gradually to undermine the whole basis of the PCA system.

It is sometimes further argued that if the PCA appears too demanding and, *a fortiori*, if he were afforded coercive powers, she might exacerbate the very problems she is expected to solve. Administrators might be reluctant to take bold decisions for fear of the consequences; 'defensive administration' might be undertaken: time-wasting procedures designed not to further administrative efficiency but to deflect criticism. However, against this, it could be argued that administrators take the benefit of a courageous decision which turns out well in the form of promotion and will, therefore, accept the risk that it will turn out badly. It could be argued that the PCA has gone too far in the direction of placating government departments to the detriment of citizens who have been maltreated.

It may be said that accepting the need to appear reasonably emollient is endemic in the PCA system and even desirable, as being more likely to allow its persuasive powers to take effect. However, this assumption could be attacked on the basis that if other restrictions were lifted, the PCA might not have to tread such a careful path. Probably, the need to do so is inherent in the role of the PCA as currently conceived, but it is arguable that it is not a necessary part of it. If, for example, members of the public could contact the PCA directly, and if her role were publicised, she might feel more able to incur the displeasure of government departments because she would be supported by public opinion.

Thus, although the PCA at present has arguably evolved a limited role for herself as a gentle instrument of change which may represent a departure from the role it was hoped she would fulfil, it is submitted that this was not inevitable but occurred due to some of the constraints that were externally imposed. In this respect, a distinction should be drawn between allotting the PCA formal powers to award coercive remedies which, as argued above, might well detract from her efficacy, and removing certain of the limitations on her particularly as regards direct public access. The removal of such limitations would, it is submitted, lead to a bolder approach and would benefit the people she is expected to serve.

NOTES

1 It could be mentioned here that there is wide variation among MPs as to the number of complaints they submit each year to the PCA. For example, in 1986, 40 per cent of MPs submitted no complaints at all. Therefore, the availability of the PCA service may depend on where a complainant happens to live.

2 It could further be noted that limitation of access also prevents the PCA reporting directly to the complainant. Further, Ombudsmen cannot transfer complaints to one another. The Cabinet Office Review proposes unifying all the various Ombudsmen, including the PCA, into one Public Sector Ombudsman, so that the public would have a one-stop shop with any complaint about public sector matters. Complaints would be channelled internally.

Question 32

'In a number of respects, the Ombudsman system has proved more effective as a means of providing redress for the citizen mistreated by government authorities than have judicial and parliamentary remedies.'

Discuss.

Answer plan

A more straightforward question than the last. It again raises the question of whether the Ombudsman system is effective, but it is of wider scope as it: (a) includes a comparison with two other means of redress; and (b) concerns the whole of the Ombudsman system, not just the Parliamentary Commissioner for Administration (PCA). It must be remembered that in some respects, certain Ombudsmen may be more effective than others in comparison with other available remedies.

The following matters should be considered:
• the aim in setting up the Ombudsman system;
• the extension of the system;
• the nature of 'maladministration' as opposed to illegality;
• the informal procedure adopted by the PCA: comparison with the courts;

- the lack of coercive remedies available to the PCA: the impact of such a lack with particular reference to the Local Commissioners; comparison with the Welsh Ombudsman;
- the use of parliamentary procedures as a means of providing redress for maladministration;
- the detriment caused by the lack of direct access to the PCA;
- the matters excluded from scrutiny;
- the reforms suggested by the Cabinet Office Review (2000), as relevant.

Answer

In addressing this question, it should be borne in mind that the Ombudsman system was not set up as a replacement for other remedies, but in order to remedy their deficiencies and to fill gaps they created. It will be argued that although the system does have advantages over pre-existing judicial and parliamentary remedies, its limitations mean that it is hampered in fulfilling its aims. As the statement applies to the whole of the Ombudsman system, it will be argued that in some respects, certain Ombudsmen may be more effective than others in comparison with other available remedies.

The PCA was set up under the Parliamentary Commissioner Act 1967 (hereafter 'the Act') as a result of the perception which arose after the Crichel Down affair in 1954 that pre-existing judicial and parliamentary remedies did not provide adequate redress for members of the public who had suffered as a result of maladministration in central government. Thus, defective administrative action was going unremedied either because it fell outside the jurisdiction of the courts or because MPs did not have sufficient powers to investigate it satisfactorily. In providing a further means of investigating complaints, the intention was that the PCA would not only uncover maladministration, but would also enable civil servants wrongly accused of maladministration to clear their names. The Ombudsman system has been extended to the NHS, to Northern Ireland under the Commissioner for Complaints Act (Northern Ireland) 1969, and to local government under the Local Government Act 1974. Prior to 1987, the PCA's jurisdiction was limited to central government departments and agencies, but the Parliamentary and Health Service Commissioners Act 1987 amended the 1967 Act in order to add about 50 non-departmental public bodies (NDPBs) such as the Arts Council and the EOC to its remit. In 2006 the PCA acquired a new area of work, in hearing complaints from victims of crime in relation to the criminal justice system under the new Victims Code (2006). The Scotland Act 1998 requires the Scottish Parliament to legislate for the creation of an Ombudsman to investigate actions of the Scottish Executive (s 91), and the Scottish Public Services Ombudsman Act 2002 created an Ombudsman with a much broader remit, encompassing the devolved institutions, local government and the Scottish NHS. In relation to Northern Ireland, an Assembly Ombudsman was established under the Northern Ireland Act 1998 (see SI 1996/1298 (NI 8)). The Public Services Ombudsman for Wales, introduced by the Public Services Ombudsman (Wales) Act 2005 will be able to investigate matters relating to local government, social housing, health, the Welsh Assembly, certain Welsh public authorities and (so far as their conduct impacts upon Wales) certain other public authorities.

In being required to consider 'maladministration' (under s 10(3) of the Act) as opposed to illegality, Ombudsmen are empowered to investigate a wider range of complaints than could be investigated by a court. A court can intervene in judicial review proceedings only where a decision is *ultra vires*, or where it is considered *Wednesbury* unreasonable, or where there has been a breach of natural justice or a breach of rights protected under the European Convention on Human Rights (ECHR), as incorporated into UK law via the Human Rights Act (HRA) 1998 (s 6(1)). Alternatively, in some instances, there may be a statutory right of appeal to a tribunal. 'Maladministration' may cover some instances which would give rise to redress in a court or tribunal, but it goes further than that. It has been described as 'bias, neglect, inattention, delay, incompetence, ineptitude, perversity, turpitude, arbitrariness and so on' (Richard Crossman in the debate on the Parliamentary Commissioner Bill 1967). Where a court or tribunal could consider such defective administration, the PCA will not investigate the matter unless it would not be reasonable to expect the complainant to seek redress in litigation.

Although maladministration is a wide concept, it does mean that the PCA is broadly concerned with procedural defects rather than with the merits of a decision. This distinction is contained in s 12(3) of the Act, which provides that the PCA may not investigate the merits of a decision taken without maladministration. However, the distinction between substance and procedure is not always easy to draw (as appears from the contrast between the judgment of Nolan J at first instance and that of Lord Donaldson in the Court of Appeal in *Local Commissioner ex p Eastleigh BC (1988)*), and the PCA has complied with the demand from the Parliamentary Select Committee on the PCA to interpret his role widely. Therefore, this apparent limitation on the PCA's remit is less significant than may at first appear.

Procedurally, the Ombudsman system may have advantages over a court hearing: its informality in investigation may be more effective at times in discovering the truth than the adversarial system in the courts. It is also, of course, free to use. Moreover, in court, the Crown may plead public interest immunity to avoid disclosing documents; in contrast, the PCA can look at all departmental files.[1] Such flexibility is also reflected in the fact that the Ombudsman procedure is not circumscribed by rules as regards time limits, and therefore may provide a remedy in instances which cannot be considered by a court. The *Ostler case (1977)* illustrates the advantage of such flexibility in comparison with judicial review proceedings. The challenge concerned a complaint that there had been a secret agreement between the department concerned and a third party. The Court of Appeal held that the complainant's challenge to the proposals in question was barred because the statutory time limit for challenges had expired. Ostler then complained to the PCA, with the result that the department made him an *ex gratia* award to cover his court costs and also introduced changes in its procedures in order to deal with the problems exposed by his complaint.

On the other hand, unlike a court, the PCA lacks the power to award a remedy, although *ex gratia* payments to individuals may at times be made. In some situations, this lack might be said to amount to a weakness in the PCA system. In *Congreve v Home Office (1976)*, the applicant succeeded in showing that the Home Office had acted unlawfully as regards television licence fees and a refund was awarded. The situation had already been investigated by the PCA, which had found inefficiency on the part of the Home Office but had not recommended a remedy for licence-holders. However, although the lack of formal power to award a remedy might appear to weaken the PCA severely, it is arguable that the need for such a limitation is inherent in his role. If the PCA could award remedies, it would be hard to avoid making the investigative proceedings more formalised, so as to give the body complained of a full opportunity to answer the allegations made. Probably, some of the procedure would have to be conducted in public. The fact that the PCA operates informally and privately has been thought to enhance his powers of persuasion. Where a particular complaint seems to be merely symptomatic of a deep-seated problem in a department, the PCA can sometimes persuade it to change its general procedure. As already mentioned, this occurred in the *Ostler* case. Thus, the apparent weakness of the PCA's powers may underlie one of his main strengths.

This is not, however, true of all Ombudsmen. The Local Commissioners have sometimes reported difficulty in securing compliance with their recommendations.[2] Seneviratne notes that by 1992, the total number of cases in which 'the local authority has not provided a satisfactory remedy after a finding of maladministration and injustice' amounted to 186, 'about 6 per cent of all cases of maladministration and injustice'. She concludes that 'Noncompliance is, therefore, a serious problem . . . [as] recognised by Justice which felt that it was bringing the LGO [Local Government Ombudsmen] into disrepute' (Seneviratne, *Ombudsmen in the Public Sector*, 1994, pp 98–99). Sections 26 and 28 of the Local Government and Housing Act 1989, which amended the Local Government Act 1974, were supposed to address this difficulty but have been criticised for their very modest nature (see, for example, Jones [1994] PL 608). The provisions require a statement to be made by the local authority within three months from the date of an

Ombudsman's adverse report as to the action to be taken in response, and for publication of a statement giving reasons for the decision not to comply with it where that is the case. In contrast, when the Commissioner for Complaints in Northern Ireland finds that an individual has sustained injustice as a result of maladministration, the individual concerned can apply to the county court under s 7(2) of the Commissioner for Complaints Act (Northern Ireland) 1969, which may award damages at its discretion. The new Welsh Ombudsman (above) may, if s/he is satisfied that a public authority has disregarded a report served on it without lawful excuse, issue a certificate to that effect to the High Court (s 20). It has been suggested by Birkinshaw and Lewis (*When Citizens Complain, 1993*) that giving the LGO powers to enforce their findings would imperil their relationship with local authorities which, they fear, would become defensive and 'minimalist' in their responses to LGO recommendations; the current practice of negotiating the response of the authorities in a consensual and informal way would be placed in jeopardy (p 39). In response to this, it may be argued that even if the LGO were given enforcement powers, consensual methods would still be used; that they would still be, and would be presented as being very much the norm; that court action would be kept largely out of mind, seen as an exceptional and rarely resorted-to last resort. It must be borne in mind that arguments as to the harm which might be caused by the introduction of enforcement powers are in the end speculative hypotheses which must be weighed against a concrete harm – the 6 per cent of LGO findings which are currently going unenforced. Overall, however, the Cabinet Office Review (2000) drew favourable conclusions as to the work of the LGO: 'Stage II of the Financial Management and Policy Review of the CLA in 1996, which drew on polls by MORI in 1995, concluded that the work of the LGO was generally well respected by complainants, their advisers and local authorities; although there was widespread concern about delays. A survey by MORI of complainants to the LGO in 1999 reported "a broadly encouraging improvement from the 1995 survey"' (para 1.5).

It may be concluded that where a body is susceptible to informal persuasion, this method has advantages over litigation as a means of improving administrative procedures. Otherwise, it is arguably desirable to make the Ombudsman's recommendations enforceable in the courts, on the basis that it would be worth the risk of damaging the relationship between him and the body in question in order to bring about such enhancement of his power. Where there is a need for such enforcement which has not yet been met, it may be argued that litigation, where it is available, may represent a surer means of bringing about change. It is worth noting in this respect that the Cabinet Office review recommended that the Ombudsman should continue to work by persuasion, rather than having the power to award compulsory remedies. Aside from the reasons canvassed above, it was feared that if the Commissioner had such a power, it could become subject to Art 6 of the ECHR, thus imposing a more formal, court-like procedure.

Thus, the statement that the Ombudsman system offers advantages which litigation does not, has some substance but needs qualification. On the other hand, there are clear advantages for the aggrieved citizen in using the Ombudsman service rather than relying on an MP to resolve the problem. Although MPs are of course able to hear a wide range of complaints, their powers of investigation are limited. The PCA in contrast has wide powers of investigation. Under s 7 of the Act, he may examine all documents relevant to the investigation, and the duty to assist him overrides the duty to maintain secrecy under the Official Secrets Acts. Furthermore, MPs may be hampered or may appear to be hampered by their political allegiance, in contrast to the Ombudsman, who is independent. Although MPs may not know the political allegiance of a constituent who makes a complaint regarding the activities of central government and might, in any event, be uninfluenced by it, the constituent might assume that the complaint would be more forcibly pursued by an Opposition MP.

Parliamentary procedures such as Questions and Select Committees are plainly less efficacious than the Ombudsman. Such procedures operate within the doctrine of ministerial responsibility; in other words, the expectation is that the minister in question will remedy matters. The PCA, on the other hand, looks behind that expectation and considers the workings of the administrative body itself. The PCA's procedure can be more flexible than that of a Select Committee due to its informal, private nature and may get closer to the root of a problem.

However, although the Ombudsman system may offer an effective means of redress to citizens who manage to invoke it, many citizens who need to do so cannot get access to it either because they do not know of its existence or because, having contacted an MP with a complaint, the MP decides not to refer the complaint on to the PCA. The PCA cannot be contacted directly by a citizen, because it is thought that to allow such contact would be to undermine the constitutional principle that an MP should defend the citizen against the Executive. However, Local Commissioners can now be contacted directly and, since 1978, where the PCA receives a complaint directly from a member of the public, the complainant's MP will be contacted and if he is in agreement, the PCA will investigate it. Inroads have therefore been made into the principle of disallowing direct access, but it still remains as an obstacle which may account for the very small number of complaints received in comparison with the number of administrative decisions taken. Clearly, the PCA cannot address the difficulties created by his low profile while he cannot advertise himself as available to receive complaints.

Even if a complaint is referred to the PCA, it may be rejected as being outside his jurisdiction. The PCA cannot investigate bodies which are not ultimately under ministerial control. Various bodies, as already mentioned, have their own Ombudsmen, but this division of jurisdiction between Ombudsmen creates difficulties of access, as one Ombudsman cannot refer a complaint directly to another. Second, certain matters, set out in Sched 3 to the Act, are excluded from investigation. These include extradition and fugitive offenders, the investigation of crime by or on behalf of the Office, security of the State, action in matters relating to contractual or commercial activities, court proceedings and personnel matters of the armed forces, teachers, the Civil Service or police (although the Independent Police Complaints Commission now provides a robust mechanism for police complaints). The government has always resisted the extension of the Ombudsman system into these areas. The fact that contractual and commercial matters and public service personnel matters are excluded has, in particular, led to the rejection of many complaints.

Therefore, as a system, the Ombudsman has many limitations; its informal procedures can be effective in securing change, but at the same time, in comparison with litigation, may lead to problems of enforcement. Lack of direct access to the Ombudsman or want of jurisdiction can mean that for many citizens the system is merely irrelevant; the screening of complaints by MPs, either before or after the PCA receives them, may undermine the importance of the PCA as a means of making up for the inefficacy of some parliamentary procedures. Moreover, the recent review by the Cabinet Office (2000) found a further, major problem with the current Ombudsman system. In order to combat these problems, the Review recommended a radical solution – the restructuring of the PCA, Local Commissioners and Health Service Commissioners into one collegiate structure of Public Sector Ombudsmen, able to take complaints about any matter within jurisdiction regardless of whether it concerned a local authority, the NHS or a government department. Its recommendations still await implementation.

▌NOTES

1 It could be noted here that the PCA does not, however, have access to Cabinet papers; the courts, on the other hand, claim the power to order such access.

2 However, the Report of the Local Commissioners 1992 showed an improvement in this respect; few local authorities had failed to comply with the reports of the Commissioners.

CHAPTER 9

PROTECTION FOR HUMAN RIGHTS

▍INTRODUCTION

The Human Rights Act 1998 (HRA) has now been in force for nearly seven years (it came into force in 2000), so it is possible to make an interim assessment as to its efficacy in protecting human rights and freedoms in the UK. It affords further effect to a number of the rights protected under the European Convention on Human Rights. It remains a controversial piece of legislation; for example, in 2006, in a distorted and misleading fashion, parts of the media blamed it for weakening the UK in its 'war' against terrorism, and for the early release of criminals. The Conservative party has stated that its policy is to repeal the Act if a Conservative government is elected at the next general election, and to replace it with a 'British Bill of Rights'. Assuming that a Conservative government is elected and carries out this pledge, such a Bill of Rights could be in place by 2010; it would presumably protect the Convention rights that are currently protected under the HRA, so the respect in which it would sharply differ from the HRA is unclear. In this forensic climate it is important to examine the background to the Act and to look carefully at what it can and cannot do. Its effects in fields ranging well beyond the criminal justice or terrorism ones must also be considered.

The very first edition of this book dealt in considerable detail with the Bill of Rights debate pre-1998, the advantages and disadvantages of a written human rights guarantee and the deficiencies of the European Convention on Human Rights (hereafter 'the Convention'). It also considered the various human rights enforcement mechanisms. The reception of the Convention into UK law via the Human Rights Act 1998 has rendered that debate largely defunct, but knowledge of the history of the Convention in the UK remains essential to an understanding of the background to the HRA, and the legal context that it should be placed in. Political and public support for some form of Bill of Rights grew overwhelming by the mid-1990s, but the resulting statute, the HRA, bears the marks of several compromises.

By 2007 the debate was centred upon the status of the Convention in UK law, its effectiveness as a human rights guarantee and the improvements in domestic human rights protection which had already resulted from it and would be likely to result from the introduction of the HRA. Essay questions are likely to ask you to consider the way that the courts have dealt with the interpretation over the first years of its life of the key sections of the Act – ss 3 and 6; they are also likely to focus on gaps and inadequacies in both the Convention and the 1998 Act. Now that the HRA has been fully in force for nearly seven years, some commentary on the significant early case law will be expected. The role of the judges has now come under fresh scrutiny, since they hold an important and enhanced role as human rights watchdogs, yet under the HRA lack the ultimate power of overriding legislation which breaches the Convention. Many different styles of essay question are possible on this large and wide ranging topic; the following questions cover most of the debate at the time of writing. Certain relevant issues are also touched on in Chapter 2.

Checklist

Students must be familiar with the following areas and their interrelationships:

- the legal protection for civil liberties before the introduction of the HRA and the former difficulties of relying on the European Convention on Human Rights in UK courts;
- the drive towards incorporation of the Convention;
- the doctrine of parliamentary sovereignty;
- the key provisions of the HRA and the Convention, especially ss 2,3,6,4,10,12, Arts 3,5,6,8,10,11;
- key case law on the Convention;
- key HRA cases, especially on ss 3 and 6;
- key statutes in the area of civil liberties, including the Police and Criminal Evidence Act 1984, as amended, and the Public Order Act 1986, as amended, the Terrorism Act 2000.

Question 33

Critically examine the implications of introducing the Human Rights Act1998 as the UK's human rights guarantee, giving consideration to the interpretations of ss 3 and 6 in recent cases.

Answer plan

This is a reasonably straightforward essay question which is commonly set. However, it is important that the answer should not degenerate into a list of advantages and disadvantages of the Human Rights Act 1998 and the European Convention on Human Rights (ECHR). The implications include: a comparison with the previous situation; the changed role of judges; the impact on public authorities; and the new dimension to all domestic legal cases which raise human rights issues. A number of the early decisions on ss 3 and 6 must be examined, indicating how far the HRA's protection for the ECHR rights has been enhanced or diminished by them. One further implication, which should be touched on briefly, is the choice of the HRA mechanism as opposed to the introduction of a Bill of Rights on the US model. This has pertinence, given David Cameron's (Leader of the Conservative Party) expressed predilection for a 'British Bill of Rights', possibly to be introduced around 2010, although of course it would be unlikely that it would be modeled on the US Constitution.

The following matters should be discussed:

- the comparison with the pre-HRA position with examples of statutory provisions;
- the impact of the Act on post-HRA legislation – s 19;
- the interpretative obligation under s 3: recent case law, giving examples of its use in practice;
- the change in the judicial role;
- the impact on public authorities of s 6; relevant HRA case law
- the choice of the HRA mechanism, as opposed to entrenching the Convention;
- an interim evaluation of the implications of relying on the HRA as the UK's human rights' guarantee.

Answer

Until 1998, the precarious and disorderly state of civil liberties and human rights in the UK was a strong argument in favour of the adoption of some form of Bill of Rights. In certain areas of civil liberties, the existing statutory and common law safeguards against abuse of power were less comprehensive and, arguably, less effective than in many other democratic countries. Citizens of the UK did enjoy a reasonable level of tolerance of individual behaviour, but there were serious gaps and the tolerance itself, because it was not bolstered by a formal guarantee of rights, was fragile, especially in times of crisis. The law sought to protect certain values, such as the need to maintain public order but, in doing so, curtailed the exercise of certain freedoms because nothing prevented it from disregarding them. Thus, human rights (recognized as 'liberties' in the UK) had a precarious status, in that they only existed, by deduction, in the interstices of the law.

For example, the Public Order Act 1986 contains extensive provisions in ss 12 and 14 which allow stringent conditions to be imposed on marches and assemblies. They are not balanced by any provision in the 1986 Act which takes account of the need to protect freedom of assembly. Equally, the Official Secrets Act 1989 arguably provides a more efficient means of preventing the disclosure of official information than did its predecessor, but it was not intended to allow the release of any information at all to the public (although later statutes – in particular the Freedom of Information Act 2000 – have done just that).

Not all statutes suggest the same reluctance to protect the freedom which their provisions may infringe; the Contempt of Court Act 1981, while primarily concerned with protecting the administration of justice, contains provisions in s 5 for allowing 'discussions in good faith of public affairs . . . if the risk of prejudice to the particular legal proceedings is merely incidental to the discussion'. However, the Contempt of Court Act 1981 was, in fact, passed in response to the ruling by the European Court of Human Rights (ECtHR) in the *Sunday Times case (1979)* that UK contempt law had infringed Art 10 of the Convention. The Contempt of Court Act may be contrasted with the Broadcasting Act passed in the same year, which allowed the Secretary to prohibit the broadcasting of 'any matter or class of matter'. This Act, like the Public Order Act, is typical of a number of provisions in domestic law which had the potential to undermine human rights very significantly and would have done so, had not discretion been exercised in their interpretation and invocation. This essay will argue that the Convention, as afforded further effect in domestic law by the Human Rights Act (HRA) 1998, would appear to provide a better safeguard than the previous reliance placed upon such forbearance. In particular, it should largely obviate the need to enforce rights at Strasbourg, as occurred in the *Sunday Times* case.

In contrast to the previous situation, the HRA now represents a minimum guarantee of freedom. Certain fundamental values have been placed, theoretically and temporarily at least, out of the reach of any political majority, unless the government decides to seek to persuade Parliament to pass legislation which deliberately infringes the Convention rights, or covertly undermines them, or decides that it will bring forward legislation to seek to repeal or modify the HRA itself. Nothing in the HRA prevents such repeal or modification. The HRA allows Parliament to pass legislation incompatible with the Convention rights (see s 19(1)(b), s 6(2) and s 3(2)), but it is notable that only one Bill has been presented to Parliament unaccompanied by a statement of its compatibility with the rights – the Bill that became the Communications Act 2003. Even the Anti-Terrorism,

Crime and Security Act 2001 was accompanied by a statement of compatibility, although the government had to derogate from Art 5(1) in order to make the statement.

Formally speaking, citizens of the UK no longer have to rely upon the ruling party to ensure that its own legislation does not infringe freedoms. They can at least be sure that the government has made some effort to ensure that a Bill is Convention-compliant before it becomes an Act of Parliament. If, despite the statement of compatibility, statutory provisions are passed which conflict with some fundamental Convention guarantee, courts will now have to interpret such provisions in order to bring them into compliance with the Convention if at all possible under s 3 of the HRA (see *R v A (No 2) (2001)*). They must also do so in respect of pre-HRA statutes. They have to consider, taking account of the Convention jurisprudence under s 2, to what extent, if at all, the freedoms may legitimately be curtailed. If, having striven to achieve compatibility, it is found to be impossible, a court of sufficient seniority can issue a declaration of incompatibility (s 4), although it will merely have to go on to apply the law in question (see *H v Mental Health Tribunal, North and East London Region and Another (2001)*). The position under s 3 is in strong contrast to the prior situation, where the courts had no choice but to apply a provision of an Act of Parliament, no matter how much it might breach the Convention if it unambiguously expressed Parliament's intention to allow such a breach (where there was ambiguity, a Convention-compliant interpretation was usually adopted in the years immediately preceding the inception of the HRA). Section 3 goes well beyond resolving ambiguity in legislation in favour of the Convention-compliant interpretation and has received a fairly generous interpretation in the courts (see *Ghaidan v Mendoza (2004)*). Under s 3 HRA words can even be read into a statute in order to achieve Convention-compliance (*Ghaidan and R v A*), so long as the changes do not oppose a pervasive feature of the statute (*R (on the application of Anderson) v Secretary of State for the Home Dept (2002)*). This stance was taken in *Re S and Re W (2002)*; as Kavanagh argues, the courts demonstrated that although they are prepared to read words into statutes, as in *R v A*, they will not do so, 'as a way of radically reforming a whole statute'. If a court does issue a declaration of incompatibility, it is expected that the government will act promptly to take remedial action – although it does not have to do so (s 10).

The HRA 1998 has therefore created a far more active judicial role in protecting basic rights and freedoms. The interpretation of the US constitution illustrates what could happen in this country, although probably to a lesser extent; vast edifices of civil rights have been constructed out of innocuous and ambiguous phrases. The generality of the terms of the Convention means that its interpretation is likely to evolve in accordance with the UK's changing needs and social values; this is, in any case, one of the basic principles of Strasbourg-based Convention jurisprudence, since the Convention is intended to be a living document which is not bound by time or venue, but can develop to suit both in any jurisdiction. Thus, it is possible that eventually there will be two versions of the Convention relevant to the UK: the domestic version as incorporated by the HRA and interpreted domestically (see *Campbell v MGN (2004)*); and the Convention as interpreted at Strasbourg, providing a still-existing opportunity to take a persistent grievance to the ECtHR. The UK version could be more generous than the Strasbourg one; this is however at present still a matter of controversy.

Incorporation of the Convention under the HRA has already had a number of advantages. Citizens may obtain redress for human rights breaches without needing, except as a last resort, to apply to the ECtHR in Strasbourg. This saves a great deal of time and money for the citizen and thus greatly improves access to human rights protection. The range of remedies available under the HRA is the same as in any ordinary UK court case (apart from criminal sanctions), and so includes injunctions and specific performance where appropriate, rather than simply damages. British judges are already making a contribution to the development of a domestic Convention rights jurisprudence (see, for example, *Lambert (2001), Offen (2001)* and *A (2001)*).

But a major disadvantage, or at least a source of anxiety, is the doubt as to whether UK judges can be trusted to give a vigorous interpretation to the Convention. The British judiciary is, in general, highly regarded, but it is an elite group, drawn mainly from a certain stratum of society, dominated by males at the higher levels and, arguably, to varying degrees, out of touch with the working class and with minority groups. The judiciary has been trained in techniques of legal analysis which include deciding cases without the responsibility of considering their human rights repercussions, although it is fair to say that its attitude to such repercussions was changing in the years immediately prior to the inception of the HRA (see *ex p Simms (1999)*). It is doubtful whether a brief period of human rights awareness training will have overturned years of adoption of its traditional stance.

The interpretations given by judges to the Convention have the ability to dilute its impact greatly. The watering down of Art 6 which occurred in *Brown v Stott (2001)* and, arguably, of Art 5 in *Gillan (2006)* exemplified this problem. Further, the new role of the judiciary, which is more important and, therefore, more overtly political might eventually mean moves towards more political involvement in its appointments – a development which has taken place in the US. Conversely, it may be argued that pre-HRA UK judges have at times shown themselves capable of bearing in mind the public interest in, for example, freedom of speech. Apart from *ex p Simms*, a clear example comes from Scott J's ruling in *AG v Guardian (No 2) (1988)* (the *Spycatcher* case), which boldly rejected the argument that the need to maintain confidentiality outweighed the public interest in freedom of expression. Post-HRA the judges have shown themselves capable of human rights activism in the area of privacy in *Douglas v Hello! (2001)* and the *Campbell case (2004)*. Although *A v B and C (2002)* may be viewed as sounding a clear cautionary note, that decision has now been superceded. Thus the HRA appears to have aided in the creation of a more comprehensive right to respect for private and family life than the patchy and piecemeal one previously protected under various other names in domestic law. The judges have also shown themselves willing to take an activist stance in protecting the right to liberty: key provisions of the Anti-Terrorism, Crime and Security Act 2001 Part 4 were declared incompatible with Arts 5 and 14 of the ECHR (protecting the rights to liberty and to freedom from discrimination) by the House of Lords in *A and Others v Secretary of State for the Home Dept (2005)*, in a constitutionally significant, and human rights-oriented decision.

Apart from its implications for legislation, public authorities have been greatly affected by the inception of the HRA due to the requirements of s 6. Under s 6, it is unlawful for a public authority to act in a way which is incompatible with a Convention right. This is the main provision giving effect to the Convention rights; rather than 'incorporation' of the Convention, it is made binding against public authorities. Under s 6(6), 'an act' includes an omission, but does not include a failure to introduce in or lay before Parliament a proposal for legislation or a failure to make any primary legislation or remedial order. Section 6(6) was included in order to preserve parliamentary sovereignty and prerogative power: in this case, the power of the Executive to introduce legislation. Thus, apart from its impact on legislation, the HRA also creates obligations under s 6 which bear upon 'public authorities'. Such obligations have a number of implications. Independently of litigation, public authorities must put procedures in place in order to ensure that they do not breach their duty under s 6. A number of public authorities and bodies that have a public function have already undergone HRA training and have had to modify their practices in response to the HRA. Thus, the HRA has had immense implications for all bodies in the UK that are public authorities or have a public function. In stark contrast to the previous situation, such bodies act illegally if they fail to abide by the Convention rights. Previously, unless forced impliedly to adhere to a particular right legislatively (for example, under s 58 of the Police and Criminal Evidence Act 1984, imposing on the police, in effect, a duty to abide by one of the implied rights within Art 6(1)), they could disregard the rights in their day to day operations with impunity.

Under s 6 public authorities are either 'core' or 'functional'; if the latter, they are only bound by the Convention in relation to their public, not their private, functions. The division between functional public authorities and purely private bodies remains one of the most controversial and difficult matters under the HRA. Obviously its resolution has very strong human rights implications since a person affected by a rights-infringing action of a private body has no cause of action under the HRA, s 7. One of the early leading decisions on this matter was *Poplar Housing & Regeneration Community Association Ltd v Donoghue (2001)*. A local authority, Tower Hamlets, was under a statutory duty under s 188 of the Housing Act 1996 to provide or secure the provision of housing to certain homeless people. Poplar was set up by Tower Hamlets as a registered social landlord specifically for the purpose of receiving its housing stock. Five members of Tower Hamlets were on the board of Poplar and it was subject to the guidance of the Council as to the manner in which it acted towards its tenants. Poplar sought vacant possession of accommodation let to the claimant tenant, Donoghue. Donoghue claimed that this would violate her right to a home under Art 8 ECHR and that Poplar Housing was bound under s 6 HRA to respect her Art 8 right because it was a public authority under the Act. Poplar claimed, inter alia, that it was neither a standard public authority (which the Court of Appeal accepted) nor a body performing a function of a public nature. As to this latter point, Lord Woolf said that an act can be 'public' for HRA purposes where a combination of features is present. Statutory authority for what is done can help to mark the act as being public; so can the extent of control over the function exercised by another body which is a public authority. 'The more closely the acts that could be of a private nature are enmeshed in the activities of a public body, the more likely they are to be public.' But he said that the supervision of the acts by a public regulatory body would not necessarily indicate that they were of a public nature, in a manner analogous to the position in judicial review. The Court found that Poplar *was* exercising a public function in relation to the management of the social housing it had taken over from Tower Hamlets because it was so closely associated with Tower Hamlets, a core public authority.

One of the key points in the judgment was the holding to the effect that where a function (such as managing social housing) had been transferred to a private body, the simple fact that it had previously been carried out by a public authority did not make it a public function in the hands of the private body. Where no public function has been transferred, the question appears to be whether the function in question should be viewed as inherently private or public, not whether the body in question is a private or public institution (*Parochial Council of the Parish of Aston* (2003)). Focussing on the function rather than the institution, is a more generous means of delimiting the concept of a public authority, and therefore allows for a wider protection for the Convention rights.

So far, this essay has indicated that the HRA has immense implications for the interpretation of legislation and for the operations of a large number of bodies in the UK. But there are limitations on its impact. The choice of the HRA as the enforcement mechanism for the Convention itself has implications since at present, the use of a different, more effective, mechanism is precluded. Currently, the Convention is incorporated into domestic law, but not entrenched on the US model; thus, its direct effects on UK law via ss 3 and 6 could be removed by the simple method of repeal of the HRA. The UK would remain bound by the Convention at the international level. It is submitted that this is a constitutionally appropriate situation at present, both in terms of the maintenance of parliamentary sovereignty and to avoid handing over too much power to the unelected judiciary. Moreover, the judiciary cannot strike down incompatible legislation. However, it does mean, as indicated earlier, that Parliament can deliberately legislate in breach of the Convention. It also means that if prior or subsequent legislation is found to breach the Convention in the courts, and cannot be rescued from doing so by a creative interpretation under s 3, it must simply be applied. If no statute is applicable, and the rights-infringing body is not a public one under s 6, a citizen will not be able to obtain legal protection for his or her Convention right, unless there is an existing common law cause of action that can be utilised (*Campbell (2004)*), and even then there would be no certainty of vindication of the right even if a breach was found. Thus, citizens cannot always be certain of being able to rely on their Convention rights domestically.

In conclusion, the HRA is allowing for the incremental improvement of the UK's recognition and enforcement of domestic human rights. Certain weaknesses are identifiable[1] within the HRA 1998 and the Convention, but the method chosen is a reasonable compromise between protection for human rights and parliamentary sovereignty. It represents a first step towards creating a rights-based culture in UK law and society.

▌NOTE

1 Obvious deficiencies of the HRA include: the missing Art 13 (guarantee of a legal remedy for infringement of a Convention right); the exceptions made in the definition of 'public authority'; the narrow definition of a 'victim'; the fact that most of the Convention rights which it incorporates are heavily qualified, or weak (Art 14); and (arguably) the lack of a direct power by which courts could strike down offending legislation. Each of these could be discussed in greater detail.

Question 34

Critically evaluate the provisions of the Human Rights Act 1998 which are intended to ensure that legislation is compatible with the European Convention on Human Rights, and comment on their impact in practice.

Answer plan

This is a question which requires a sound knowledge of ss 3, 4, 10, Sched 2 and 19 of the Human Rights Act (HRA) 1998, of some of the academic criticism generated by those provisions and of the key cases. Close analysis of those provisions of the Act, which are in some respects quite technical, is required. This is a question which is highly likely to be set at the present time. Note that the question does not require you to consider the efficacy of the Convention itself or the implications of receiving it into UK law. Also, it deliberately focuses on s 3 and the related provisions; it does not ask you to discuss the definition of a public authority under s 6.

The following matters should be discussed:

- the interpretative obligation under s 3: its use in practice so far in key cases;
- the declarations of incompatibility under s 4: their use in practice in key cases;
- the 'fast track' procedure under s 10 and Sched 2;
- the impact of the Act on post-HRA legislation – s 19;
- evaluation of the efficacy of this aspect of the HRA scheme.

Answer

The Human Rights Act (HRA) 1998 is of immense constitutional significance. The Act provides further protection for the European Convention on Human Rights in UK law. Once it came fully into force in 2000, UK citizens had, for the first time, human rights (in the sense of rights which may be claimed against public authorities) instead of liberties: instead of having residual freedoms they had from 2000 onwards guarantees of rights. However, the likely impact of the reception of the Convention into domestic law is still unclear, since the Act contains a number of complex, intriguing and unusual features which are determining and will determine its impact in practice.

The intention was not simply to incorporate the Convention into domestic law so that it became, in effect, a statute. The most significant provision, which largely determines the status of the Convention in domestic law, is s 3. Under s 3(1), primary and subordinate legislation must be given effect in a manner which makes it compatible with the Convention rights; the judiciary is under an obligation to ensure such compatibility 'so far as it is possible to do so'. This goes well beyond resolving ambiguity in statutory provisions by adopting the Convention-based interpretation which, of course, was already occurring in the pre-HRA era. Section 3 appears to place the judiciary under an obligation to render legislation compatible with the Convention if there is any loophole at all allowing it to do so.

It is now apparent that s 3(1) of the HRA may allow judges to read words into statutes (*R v A (2001), Ghaidan v Mendoza (2004)*) or to adopt a broad or doubtful interpretation; in *Cachia v Faluyi (2001)*, the Court of Appeal held that 'action' in s 2(3) of the Fatal Accidents Act 1976 should be construed as 'served process'. In *Secretary of State for the Home Department ex p Aleksejs Zenovics (2002)*, the Court of Appeal added the words 'in respect of that claim' in the Immigration and Asylum Act 1999 to the end of the provision in question. Section 3(1) does not, however, allow for wholesale revision of the statute: *Re S and W (Care Orders) (2002)*; *Donaghue v Poplar Housing (2001)*. In other words, the changes must not oppose a pervasive feature of the statute (*Anderson (2003)*). This stance was taken in *Re S and Re W (2002)*; as Kavanagh argues, the courts have demonstrated that although they are prepared to read words into statutes, as in *R v A*, or in *Ghaidan* (2004), they will not do so, 'as a way of radically reforming a whole statute'.

The judges may also be reluctant to read in words where the provisions themselves offer no reasonably ready 'avenue' to so doing. Even where such an avenue is available, the judges may be reluctant to use it. In *Bellinger v Bellinger (2003)*, as Phillipson argues, it would have been more than possible, as a matter of linguistics, to interpret the single word 'female' as including a 'female' who had arrived at that gender as a result of human intervention (i.e. post-operative transsexuals). Nevertheless, the House of Lords refused to reinterpret the word in the way suggested, taking into account a range of what were essentially policy matters – the far-reaching practical effects of the change. Also Parliament had indicated that it would legislate on the subject. Thus, it is clear that the judges are prepared – where they view it as appropriate, taking account of the factors indicated – to use the powerful interpretative tool of s 3(1) to its fullest extent, even if this means twisting or ignoring the natural meaning of the statutory words or, most dramatically, reading words into statutory provisions. Thus, the judges have in some instances adopted a role which is close to a legislative one. Possibly, in so doing, they have pushed the interpretative obligation under s 3 too far, as in *R v A*, and in that instance should instead have issued a declaration of incompatibility under s 4.[1]

Section 3(2) provides that this interpretative obligation does not affect the validity, continuing operation or enforcement of any incompatible primary legislation. Thus, the Convention cannot be used to strike down any part of an existing statute as unconstitutional. This is clearly an important limitation. It means that parliamentary sovereignty is at least theoretically preserved, since prior and subsequent legislation which cannot be rendered compatible with the Convention cannot be struck down due to its incompatibility by the judiciary.

If a court cannot render a statutory provision compatible with the Convention, despite its best efforts, the claimant wishing to rely on the right will have to suffer a breach of his/her Convention rights for a period of time. This is clearly unsatisfactory; the solution chosen by the Labour government was to include ss 4, 10 and Sched 2 in the Act. Section 4 allows certain higher courts to make a declaration of incompatibility, while s 10 and sched 2 allows for a 'fast track' procedure, whereby a Minister may by order, approved by both Houses of

Parliament, amend the offending primary or subordinate legislation if there are compelling reasons to do so. A number of comments may be made on this procedure. In general, executive amendment of legislation is objectionable. However, Parliamentary scrutiny of the order is provided for under sched 2; Parliament will normally have 60 days to consider the order before voting on it, although in urgent cases the order can come into effect immediately, subject to later approval by both Houses. Further, the usual objections to such a procedure are arguably inapplicable since the order is intended to bring UK law into harmony with the Convention, thereby raising the standard of human rights often at the expense, in effect of the executive.

Other objections to this procedure are less easily overcome. The Minister is under no obligation to make the amendment(s) and may only do so if there are 'compelling' reasons. In other words, the fact that a declaration of incompatibility has been made is not, in itself, a compelling reason. Thus, there may be periods of uncertainty during which citizens cannot rely on aspects of their Convention rights. Further, in some instances, a declaration of incompatibility may not be obtained for some time. For example, a lower court (a court outside the meaning of 'court' within s 4(5)) might find in criminal proceedings that the police have bugged a person's home in accordance with the Regulation of Investigatory Powers Act 2000 (RIPA), but, it appears, contrary to Art 8 (providing a right to respect for private life) of Sched 1 to the HRA 1998. The court could not make a declaration of the incompatibility, and the defendant would have no interest in appealing to a higher court in order to obtain such a declaration, since it would provide him with no personal benefit. No damages could be awarded due to the provisions of s 6(2). Thus, changes to particular parts of the law in order to ensure compatibility with the Convention rights may be slow in coming.

The courts may seek to address the inadequacy of the declaration of incompatibility procedure – the awarding to the claimant of a 'booby prize' – in two ways. First, the lower courts may come to be very reluctant to find that a statutory provision is incompatible with the Convention. Given the broad and open-ended wording of the Convention, it will often be easy to find that compatibility exists. In the example given above, the lower court could seek to manipulate or modify the wording of RIPA to ensure compliance with Art 8. The danger in this approach is that instead of 'levelling up', that is, bringing UK law up to the level of the Convention standards, UK courts may level down – adopt the interpretation of the Convention which gives the lowest possible level of protection. It is suggested that this occurred in *Brown v Stott (2001)*, in which Art 6(1) was watered down in order to avoid having to declare s 172 of the Road Traffic Act 1988 incompatible with it. Second, the defendant – often a public authority – may tend to appeal to a higher court on the issue of compatibility, arguing that once the relevant UK law was properly interpreted, it could be found to be in compliance with the Convention. The defendant would hope that a higher court would be prepared to adopt a more creative interpretation than the lower one and that the interpretation obtained would be favourable to him. This occurred in the *Alconbury case (2001)*; the declaration was over-turned in the House of Lords. These tendencies, while avoiding making declarations of incompatibility, are tending to place aspects of Convention rights in a doubtful and precarious position. This is especially a matter of concern where criminal proceedings are in question, due to the implications for the defendant while the matter of compatibility is being resolved.

Declarations of incompatibility in civil proceedings might appear to be less likely to occur than in criminal proceedings, or proceedings relating to state detention decisions. The Convention, as a civil rights measure, consists of a series of rights guaranteed to the citizen against the power of the State. That power is usually, although by no means always, encapsulated in the criminal law. A glance through the pages of texts on the Convention as an international instrument will show that proceedings brought against Member States often began as criminal proceedings in the Member State. Thus, many cases in which Convention rights are invoked in UK courts are criminal ones, or relate to matters of detention, and the question raised tends to concern an aspect of criminal procedure (see *A (2001)* and *Offen (2001)*) or the substantive issue of the right to liberty. Thus Articles 5 and 6 are frequently invoked since they protect, *inter alia*, a fair criminal trial and the right to liberty of the person. The key provisions of the Anti-Terrorism, Crime and Security Act 2001 Pt 4 were declared incompatible with Arts 5 and 14 of the ECHR (protecting the rights to liberty and to freedom from discrimination) by the House of Lords in *A and Others v Secretary of State for the Home Dept (2005)*, in a constitutionally significant, and human rights-oriented decision. In *H v North and East Region Mental Health Tribunal (2001)* a declaration was made in relation to ss 72 and 73 Mental Health Act 1983, on the basis that they infringed Art 5(1) and (4) of the Convention since they placed the burden of proof on the patient to prove that he/she was not suffering from mental illness and so should no longer be detained. In response, the government used its power under s 10 to make a remedial order, amending the 1983 Act.

It might appear that declarations of incompatibility in civil proceedings, especially those between private parties, would be less likely to occur, although if a statute affects the legal relations between private individuals (for example, employment statutes which cover private companies and their employees), ss 3 and 4 apply. But Convention issues giving rise to the possibility of a declaration of incompatibility are arising in civil proceedings, either substantively under, for example, Art 8 (*Re S and W (Care Orders) (2002)*) or procedurally under Art 6(1) as in *Alconbury* and in *Wilson (2003)*. *Wilson* concerned two private parties, one a large Company.

One problem is that if a statute governing part of the civil law was found in a lower court to be incompatible with the Convention, the claimant or defendant would be denied a remedy, even if their Convention rights had been breached. The claimant or defendant could in theory appeal to a higher court, arguing that no incompatibility arose. However, since public funding is likely to be unavailable, only those persons who can fund the action themselves will have any certainty that they will be able to do so. Others may be able to do so on a contingency fee basis, but Convention-based cases tend to be especially unpredictable, and therefore lawyers may tend to consider that the chances of success are insufficiently high.

The key weakness of this scheme is clearly that the government may not be willing to bring forward a remedial order under s 10. In *R(M) v Secretary of State for Health (2003)* the government sought to persuade the court that a declaration of incompatibility in relation to ss 26 and 29 Mental Health Act 1983 was not needed as legislation to remedy the incompatibility was in contemplation, The court was unpersuaded by the argument and made the declaration. In the event, in 2006 the Mental Health Bill, which apparently would have remedied the incompatibility, was dropped. If s 10 is not relied upon to introduce remedial legislation, then, unless the claimant takes the case to Strasbourg, he or she will merely have to continue to suffer a breach of their Convention rights. In contrast, if the Convention guarantees affect an area of the common law, including areas that apply between private individuals, such as breach of confidence, the common law can be interpreted or reformed to harmonise with the Convention (see *Douglas v Hello! (2001), Campbell (2004)*) under s 6 HRA.

Thus some previous legislation has already been found to be incompatible with the Convention, and further incompatible legislation is likely to persist for some time, even though the HRA is fully in force, since it is largely a matter of chance whether a suitable case comes to court. The Mental Health Act 1983 provides an example of a previous statute which cannot be rendered Convention-compatible by the use of s 3. Subsequent legislation is arguably in a somewhat different position due to the provisions of s 19. Under this section, when a Minister introduces a Bill into either House of Parliament, he must make and publish a written statement to the effect either that, in his view, the provisions of the Bill are compatible with the Convention rights, or that although he is unable to make such a statement, the government wishes nevertheless to proceed with the Bill. If the latter statement is made, it is possible that the judiciary will allow the provisions of the legislation to override the Convention, just as it would if a clause was included in it stating 'this statute is to be given effect notwithstanding the provisions of Art X of the Human Rights Act 1998'. But clearly the better argument is that s 3 still applies and the judges should therefore strive to achieve compatibility through interpretation, even if ultimately it is impossible to do so. So far, all legislation passed post-HRA, apart from the Communications Act 2003, has been accompanied by a statement of its compatibility with the rights.

If the relevant Minister makes a statement to the effect that the legislation is compatible with the Convention, but subsequently it appears that it is not compatible, it would seem that in such circumstances, the judiciary may be prepared to do its utmost to ensure compatibility, even going so far as to disregard the absolutely plain meaning of statutory language, on the basis that Parliament must have intended this to occur. Its duty to do so will arise both from the general need to construe legislation in order to ensure compatibility with the Convention if at all possible (s 3), and from the particular need flowing from s 19 to do so where subsequent legislation was thought to be compatible with the Convention when introduced into Parliament. But in the alternative, the court can issue a declaration, meaning that Parliament has to – in effect – try harder to achieve compatibility – if the government accepts that remedial legislation is necessary or that the offending provision must merely be repealed. The Anti-Terrorism, Crime and Security Act 2001 Pt 4 was accompanied by a declaration of compatibility, although a derogation from Article 5 was needed to make the declaration. In the event the provisions of Pt 4 were declared incompatible with Arts 5 and 14 of the ECHR (protecting the rights to liberty and to freedom from discrimination) by the House of Lords in *A and Others v Secretary of State for the Home Dept* (2005). In other words, the Lords did not consider that s 3 could be used to create compatibility. The government decided to repeal Pt 4 and to introduce instead control orders under the Prevention of Terrorism Act 2005.

In conclusion, it may be said that for the reasons discussed, the impact of the HRA is being realised slowly in practice. Nevertheless, it represents a radical change in the traditional means of protecting civil liberties. It has become much less likely that legislation will be introduced which will have the clear effect of limiting a liberty, since such legislation might eventually be declared incompatible with the guarantees of rights under the Act (s 4). Further, when the legislation was introduced, the relevant minister would have to declare that a statement of compatibility could not be made under s 19 – something that ministers are clearly reluctant to do due to the political embarrassment which would be created. Even future non-liberal governments would probably be deterred thereby from an obvious infringement of the Convention guarantees. Similarly, existing legislative protection for a Convention right is unlikely to be repealed, since a citizen might then challenge breaches of the right under s 7(1)(a), so long as the right was one exercisable against a public authority. Thus, the Act, despite its complexities and limitations, represents a break with previous legislative tradition; due to the operation of s 3, it is creating a much greater awareness in the judiciary of fundamental human rights issues. But while the operation of s 3 has had this laudable effect, it may also be pointed out that the judiciary should bear in mind the mechanisms of the HRA which were supposed to preserve parliamentary sovereignty – ss 3(2) and 4 – and show a greater preparedness to use them.

NOTE

1 An example could be given which would illustrate the complexity of the process of reform. Section 10 of the Contempt of Court Act as currently interpreted is

arguably incompatible with Art 10 of the Convention due to the ruling to that effect of the European Court of Human Rights in *Goodwin v UK (1996)*. Thus, s 10 was a possible candidate for reform under s 3 of the HRA. But it is clear that no declaration of incompatibility is necessary. Courts could simply re-interpret s 10 using s3 HRA in the light of the ruling of the European Court, overturning the ruling of the House of Lords in *X v Morgan Grampian Publishers (1991)*, which led to the ruling in *Goodwin v UK*. This would be a bold move, but it is arguable that it is required. At present, the House of Lords has, however, avoided a finding that *Morgan Grampian* has been over-turned on the basis that there was sufficient flexibility in the *Goodwin* case to allow the two to be reconciled: see *Ashworth v MGN (2002)*.

Question 35

In terms of enhanced human rights protection, would it have been better to have introduced a tailor-made Bill of Rights for the UK rather than enacting the Human Rights Act 1998?

Answer plan

This is a fairly demanding question which requires quite detailed knowledge of the European Convention on Human Rights (the Convention), the Human Rights Act (HRA) 1998, early decisions on it and key Convention decisions. It is also necessary to say something about the differences between an entrenched Bill of Rights and the HRA in terms of enhanced human rights protection, although it should be pointed out that a Bill of Rights need not be entrenched. It is quite a pertinent question at the present time, given David Cameron's (Leader of the Conservative Party) expressed predilection for a 'British Bill of Rights', possibly to be introduced around 2010 – if a Conservative government comes to power. This essay asks a straight question, and therefore you must come down on one side or the other, albeit while acknowledging the force of the arguments on the other side. The essay below answers the question posed in the affirmative.

Issues to be discussed include:

- the possibilities available in terms of constructing a tailor-made Bill of Rights;
- the exceptions to the primary rights of the Convention;

- the effect of the margin of appreciation in certain European Court of Human Rights (ECtHR) decisions;
- the general restrictions on Convention rights;
- the weaknesses of some substantive Convention rights, for example, Art 14;
- the (arguable) deficiencies of the HRA 1998 in comparison with an entrenched Bill of Rights – early HRA cases illustrating the problems.

Answer

The HRA 1998 has given the European Convention on Human Rights and Fundamental Freedoms further effect in UK law, as will be discussed, using the mechanism of an ordinary Act of Parliament. It has not sought to entrench its own provisions or the Convention, and it has not introduced any new rights other than from those of the Convention. (It may be noted that not all the Convention rights were included in Sched 1 HRA – Art 1, Art 13 and the Protocols, apart from the First and Sixth ones, were excluded.) The possibility of introducing a tailor-made Bill of Rights had been considered but rejected. Apart from the cumbersome nature of the process of deciding on the rights to be protected, a Bill of Rights might have taken too much account of the interests of the government in power at the time when it was passed. But although producing a tailor-made Bill of Rights would certainly have been difficult, it can be argued that the UK should nevertheless have attempted it, rather than incorporating the ready-made Convention, which is arguably defective in content. This essay will argue that the attempt should have been made to introduce a Bill of Rights which would have been unique to the UK. It will also consider the possibility of entrenchment, which is associated with Bills of Rights – as in the US. The HRA is arguably a weak mechanism for the protection of human rights when compared to an entrenched Bill of Rights.

The Convention is a cautious document: it is not as open-textured as the American Bill of Rights and it contains long lists of exceptions to most of the primary rights – exceptions which suggest a strong respect for the institutions of the State. These exceptions have at times received a broad interpretation in the ECtHR and it is likely that such interpretations will have a great influence on domestic courts as they apply the rights directly in the domestic arena under the HRA. For example, Art 10, which protects freedom of expression, contains an exception in respect of the protection of morals. This was invoked in the *Handyside case (1976)* in respect of a booklet aimed at schoolchildren which was circulating freely in the rest of Europe. It was held that the UK government was best placed to

263

determine what was needed in its own country in order to protect morals, and so no breach of Art 10 had occurred. The decision in *Otto-Preminger Institut v Austria (1994)* was on very similar lines: it was found that the 'rights of others' exception could be invoked to allow for the suppression of a film which might cause offence to religious people since, in allowing such suppression, the State had not overstepped its margin of appreciation. A somewhat similar course was adopted in *The Observer and The Guardian v UK (1991)* (the *Spycatcher* case), which will be considered in some detail as an example of the readiness of the ECtHR to afford a wide meaning to the exception provisions of the Convention.

The newspapers claimed that temporary injunctions granted to restrain publication of material from *Spycatcher* by Peter Wright violated the Art 10 guarantee of freedom of expression. The Strasbourg Court found that, although the injunctions clearly constituted an interference with the newspapers' freedom of expression, those in force during the period before publication of the book in the US in July 1987 were justified under the exception provided for by para 2 of Art 10 in respect of protecting national security. The injunctions had the aim of preventing publication of material which, according to evidence presented by the Attorney General, might have created a risk of detriment to MI5. The nature of the risk was uncertain, as the exact contents of *Spycatcher* were not known at that time, since the book was still only in manuscript form. Further, the Court accepted the argument that there was a need to ensure the preservation of the Attorney General's right to grant a permanent injunction; if *Spycatcher* material had been published before that claim could be heard, the subject matter of the action could have been damaged or destroyed. In the court's view, these factors established the existence of a pressing social need, which the injunctions answered.

The court then considered whether the actual restraints imposed were proportionate to the legitimate aims represented by the exceptions. It found that the injunctions did not prevent the papers from pursuing a campaign for an inquiry into the operation of the security services, and although preventing publication for a long time – over a year – the material in question could not be classified as urgent news. Thus, it was held that the interference complained of was proportionate to the ends in view. It is suggested that in this ruling, the court accepted very readily the view that the authority of the judiciary could best be preserved by allowing a claim of confidentiality, set up in the face of a strong competing public interest, to found an infringement of freedom of speech for over a year.[1] The Court did find a violation of Art 10 in that the injunctions were continued after the publication of the book in the US.

In other areas, there has been an equal willingness to allow the exceptions a wide scope in curtailing the primary rights. In *CCSU v UK (1988)*, the European Commission on Human Rights, in declaring the unions' application inadmissible, found that national security interests should prevail over freedom of association, even though the national security interest was weak, while the infringement of the primary right was very clear: an absolute ban on joining a trade union had been imposed. It is worth noting that the ILO Committee on Freedom of Association had earlier found that the ban breached the 1947 ILO Freedom of Association Convention.

However, these were all instances in which the doctrine of the 'margin of appreciation' had an influence on the decision in question. In other words, the view was taken that in certain particularly sensitive areas, such as the protection of morals or of national security, the domestic authorities had to be allowed a certain discretion in determining what was called for. In less sensitive areas, the ECtHR has been bolder. In the *Sunday Times case (1979)*, it determined that the exception to Art 10, allowing restraint of freedom of speech in order to protect the authority of the judiciary, was inapplicable in an instance where the litigation in question which could have been affected was dormant. The Court has also been relatively bold in the area of prisoners' rights, holding in *Golder (1975)* and *Silver (1983)* that a prisoner's right to privacy of correspondence must be respected, and rejecting the UK government's arguments that an express or implied exception to Art 8 could be invoked.

It is not possible at the moment to come to general conclusions about the response of UK judges under the HRA to interpretations of the Convention rights at Strasbourg, but some observations can be made. The judges are failing to take the view that they should not apply a particular decision because it has been affected by the margin of appreciation doctrine. In other words, they could be said to be importing the doctrine 'through the back door', even though it is an international law doctrine that has no application in the domestic sphere. To an extent, this was the approach adopted in the leading pre-HRA case of *DPP ex p Kebilene (1999)*; although the doctrine itself was rejected, the outcomes of applications at Strasbourg were taken into account without adverting to the influence the doctrine had had on them. Arguably, a similar stance was taken in the post-HRA case of *Alconbury (2001)*. Thus, the watering down effect at Strasbourg of this doctrine may also be occurring under the HRA. The judges are also giving full weight to the express exceptions under Arts 8–11 of the Convention, even where possibly Strasbourg might have decided on a different outcome. This may be said of *Interbrew SA v Financial Times Ltd (2002)*, where the Court of Appeal found that on the facts of the case no protection for a media source need be given. In *R(on the application of Gillan) v Commissioner of Metropolitan Police (2006)* the House of Lords found that, assuming that Arts 8 and 10 were applicable, the exceptions under them were satisfied, without engaging in any proportionality analysis.

Apart from the express exceptions to Arts 8–11, there are also general restrictions to the operation of the rights. All the Articles except Arts 3, 4(1), 6(2) and 7 are subject to certain restrictions, either because certain limitations are inherent in the formulation of the right itself, or because it is expressly stated that certain cases are not covered by the right in question. Even the right to life under

Art 2 is far from absolute: 'unintentional' deprivations of life are not covered, and the use of necessary force is justified even where it results in death. Derogations from certain rights are also possible under Art 15. Now that the Convention has been incorporated and the interpretative jurisprudence of the ECtHR is being used in domestic cases as a guide (s 2 of the HRA), such exceptions and restrictions tend to offer judges a means of avoiding a controversial conflict with the government and possibly make it unlikely that a radical impact on UK law will exist in the long term. Lord Bingham has made it clear that Convention rights should be argued only where they truly apply and that any sudden explosion of human rights arguments, where unnecessary under Strasbourg jurisprudence, will not be supported (*Ullah (2004)*). Indeed, the domestic courts have succeeded in finding exceptions even to rights that appear to be largely unqualified, such as Art 6(1): this was evident in *Brown v Stott (2001)* and in *Alconbury (2001)*. They have done so by relying on a case at Strasbourg, *Sporrong and Lonnroth v Sweden (1982)*, in which it was said that the search for a balance between individual rights and societal concerns is fundamental to the whole Convention. Thus, it may be argued that the domestic judiciary has explored methods of watering down the rights which might not have been so readily available had a tailor-made Bill of Rights been introduced.

However, the judges do have an important function in giving the language of rights primacy, even if, eventually, an exception to a particular right is allowed to prevail. The Strasbourg jurisprudence and the rights themselves make it clear that the exceptions are to be narrowly construed and that the starting point is always the primary right. This is in contrast to the previous position, in which the judges merely applied the statute in question without affording much or any recognition to the freedoms it affected. This could bring about important changes in relation to such statutes, including the Public Order Act 1986 and the Official Secrets Act 1989. In considering the effect of such statutes, their human rights dimension should at least be recognised even if, as in the *Shayler case (2002)*, it has not yet prevailed. A tailor-made Bill of Rights could hardly have afforded greater primacy to the primary rights, even though, in theory, it could have included exceptions that were more narrowly drawn and perhaps a greater number of absolute rights, on the lines of the First Amendment in the US.

However, it can also be argued that a tailor-made Bill of Rights could have contained a more extensive list of rights including social and economic rights. In particular it could have included a free-standing anti-discrimination guarantee. In contrast, Art 14 of the Convention prohibits discrimination on 'any ground such as sex, race, colour, language, religion', but only in relation to any other Convention right or freedom. It has been determined in a string of Strasbourg cases since *X v Federal Republic of Germany (1970)* that Art 14 has no separate existence, but that, nevertheless, a measure which is, in itself, in conformity with the requirement of the Convention right governing its field of law may, however, infringe that Article when it is read in conjunction with Art 14, for the reason that it is discriminatory in nature. In *Abdulaziz, Cabales and Balkandali v UK (1985)*, it was held that although the application of Art 14 does not presuppose a breach of the substantive provisions of the Convention and is therefore, to that extent, autonomous, it cannot be applied unless the facts in question fall within the ambit of one or more of the rights and freedoms. Thus, in one sense, Art 14 is largely ineffective in strengthening the existing provisions of sex discrimination and race relations legislation which tends to be invoked in the context of employment, because general employment claims fall outside the ambit of the other rights and freedoms.

Yet, conversely, Art 14 is has had an impact on the forms of discrimination which are unlawful in situations where another Convention right or freedom does apply (*Ghaidan v Mendoza (2004)*), since Art 14 prohibits discrimination on any ground, without the restrictions in the UK's current anti-discrimination scheme (for example, discrimination on grounds of sexual orientation can occur in the contexts of goods and services, education, housing, without giving rise to a cause of action under current legislation. Strasbourg case law exists on discrimination on the basis of sexuality and transsexuality, religion, lifestyle, political opinion, or residence, which has the potential to broaden the UK's relatively narrow anti-discrimination laws considerably, at least as far as the activities of public authorities are concerned. Further, it should be remembered that Strasbourg cases clearly state that discrimination on grounds of sex or race will be very difficult to justify (see, for example, *Schmidt v Germany (1994)*) within the ambit of a Convention right.

The HRA itself has limitations in terms of enhanced human rights protection. The choice of the HRA as the enforcement mechanism for the Convention means that the Convention is incorporated into domestic law, but not entrenched on the US model; thus, it could be removed by the simple method of repeal of the HRA, as argued for in 2006 by the Conservative party. Moreover, the judiciary cannot strike down incompatible legislation. Entrenchment was rejected in order to maintain parliamentary sovereignty and to avoid handing over too much power to the unelected judiciary. This means that Parliament can deliberately legislate in breach of the Convention (ss 19 and 3(2)), and the incompatible legislation will be effective. It also means that if prior or subsequent legislation is found to breach the Convention in the courts and cannot be rescued from doing so by a creative interpretation under s 3, it must simply be applied (see *H v Mental Health Tribunal, North and East London Region and Another (2001)*), although a declaration of the incompatibility can be made under s4, as it was in that instance. In *R(M) v Secretary of State for Health (2003)* a declaration of incompatibility was made in relation to ss 26 and 29 Mental Health Act 1983 but by 2007 the government had failed to introduce remedial legislation. On the other hand the key provisions of the Anti-Terrorism, Crime and Security Act 2001 Part 4 were declared incompatible with Arts 5 and 14 of the ECHR (protecting the rights to liberty and to freedom from discrimination) by the House of Lords in *A and Others v Secretary of State for the Home Dept (2005)*; the government bowed to the pressure and repealed Pt 4. But it is clear that citizens cannot always be certain of being able to rely on their Convention rights domestically. An entrenched Bill of Rights on the US model would have provided them with that certainty and, at the sacrifice of parliamentary sovereignty as traditionally understood in the UK, would have therefore delivered an enhanced degree of rights protection.[2]

The use of ss 3 and 6 HRA as the means of affording the Convention further effect in domestic law means that there are inherent limitations to the rights protection the HRA offers. If no statute is applicable in a particular instance, and the rights-infringing body is not a public one under s 6, a citizen will not be able to obtain legal protection for his or her Convention right, unless there is an existing common law cause of action that can be utilised (*Campbell (2004)*), and even then there would be no certainty of vindication of the right even if a breach was found. This would be the case even if the citizen could probably obtain redress at Strasbourg in the particular circumstances (see *Von Hannover v Germany (2005)*).

In reaching a conclusion on the question posed, it should be borne in mind that the Convention was never intended to be used as a domestic Bill of Rights. It has been argued that the creation of such a new guarantee from scratch would have been an incredibly difficult and complex task, and so it is understandable why the incorporation of the Convention was chosen as a (comparatively) quick and easy 'fix'. But it may further be argued that due to the deficiencies of the Convention as a human rights guarantee for the UK, there should be a commitment towards creating a new Bill of Rights in the future, once it can be judged to what extent the HRA 1998 has been a success. Once the impact of the HRA can be more fully evaluated, there will be room to consider whether further entrenched rights legislation is necessary and the form it should take. If such a course were taken in the UK, then it would be brought into line with the experience of most of the other European signatories. These States already possess codes of rights enshrined in their constitutions, but the majority also adhere to a general practice of incorporation of State Treaties into domestic law, either automatically, as in Switzerland, or upon ratification, as in Luxembourg. The dual system of the Convention rights and a domestic code of rights seems to operate well in these countries. Thus, the HRA could become an interim measure to secure the further protection of the rights provided by the Convention, in the hope that a domestic Bill of Rights would later cure the gaps, defects and inadequacies of the Convention. If a domestic Bill of Rights is ever created (in spite of the current government's lack of will to do so, as evidenced in the Green Paper, *Bringing Rights Home (1997)*), then the two documents could exist side by side in UK law and each could be invoked when its protection of rights on a point was stronger than the other.[3] However, while the deficiencies identified here leave room for argument that at some stage, a supplementary and complementary Bill of Rights should be enacted in order to create a more tailor-made and comprehensive human rights guarantee for the UK, the likelihood that this will occur does not appear to be very great, under the current Labour government. The very reasons for settling on the compromise of the HRA would continue to preclude it.

NOTES

1 Further features of this decision could be considered: the court seems to have been readily persuaded by the Attorney General's argument that a widely framed injunction was needed in July 1987, but it is arguable that it was wider than it needed to be to prevent a risk to national security. It could have required the newspapers to refrain from publishing Wright's material which had not been previously published by others until (if) the action to prevent publication of the book was lost. Such wording would have taken care of any national security interest; therefore, wording going beyond that was disproportionate to that aim.

2 It could be pointed out that there are advantages in incorporating the Convention as opposed to introducing a domestic instrument. In particular, if a right is violated here, since primary legislation mandates the violation, the possibility of recourse to Strasbourg is afforded encouragement.

3 An example could be inserted here. Cyprus adopted a course similar to this when it became independent in 1960. It used the Convention as a drafting prototype for certain fundamental rights and freedoms which then became part of its new constitution. The Convention itself was incorporated into the law of Cyprus and was then invoked before the Cypriot courts as a supplementary aid to interpreting corresponding Articles of the constitution. This apparently circular method is not without success and may be likely to highlight weaknesses in the constitutional protection for human rights.

Question 36

Critically evaluate the extent to which the Human Rights Act 1998 is bringing about change in substantive law in the 'civil liberties' field and the extent to which it is likely to have a further impact.

Answer plan

This is becoming a common type of examination question, although it may appear in many forms. The question is confined to the 'civil liberties' field and within that field you will have to be selective – and make your selection clear at the outset. In order to answer the question, it is essential that you should be able to explain and evaluate cases on selected rights of the European Convention on Human Rights (the Convention), at Strasbourg and domestically, and further, to predict whether and how UK law may have to change further in the coming years to reflect those Convention rights and the relevant jurisprudence. Changes that have already occurred should be identified. When a question is phrased as generally as this one, students should avoid the temptation to refer to a long list of instances where domestic law will be likely to be challenged; it is more important to consider instances where domestic law has been challenged, and crucial to include some depth of argument and analysis of the case law. Examiners may also ask students to refer to one or more specific areas of domestic law, such as criminal law and evidence, or to refer to one or more Convention rights, such as privacy, expression, discrimination or torture. It is therefore essential that students have detailed knowledge of current issues concerning Convention rights and their status in domestic law. If the question is phrased generally, it will be necessary to be selective about the rights referred to in the answer and to make this clear in the introduction.

The following matters must be considered:

- the ways in which the Human Rights Act (HRA) 1998 is able to have an impact on domestic law;
- the leading European Court of Human Rights (ECtHR) cases which raise issues about the UK's enforcement of human rights in key areas, for example, privacy, police powers of covert surveillance and freedom of protest;
- key aspects of relevant statutes, including the Anti-Terrorism, Crime and Security Act 2001, the Regulation of Investigatory Powers Act 2000, the Terrorism Act 2000 and the Prevention of Terrorism Act 2005;
- examination of the current and probable impact of the HRA in the areas chosen; key post-HRA cases;
- evaluation – the role of domestic courts and Parliament in interpreting and giving effect to the Convention rights.

Answer

Under s 3 of the HRA, many statutes have been opened to rights-based scrutiny; some, such as the Mental Health Act 1983 have shown themselves to be vulnerable to declarations of incompatibility issued by a higher court under s 4. A tide of legislation in the civil liberties field apparently designed to be Convention compliant has also been introduced, including, for example, the Regulation of Investigatory Powers Act 2000, the Terrorism Act 2000, the Anti-Terrorism, Crime and Security Act 2001 (although Pt 4 required a derogation from Art 5) and the Prevention of Terrorism Act 2005. Since October 2000, public authorities within the UK have been under a duty to act in compliance with the Convention (s 6 HRA). Since the term 'public authorities' includes the courts, significant changes in UK law have occurred, since the courts must seek to ensure that current common law doctrines are in compliance with the Convention rights, as discussed below. Courts are being deluged with arguments based on the Convention, and so the existing case law of the ECtHR has become a vital tool for interpretation purposes, although it is not binding (s 2 of the HRA). However, it continues to be the case that the interpretation of Convention rights taken by the government (as evidenced in new Bills put forward to Parliament) and by the judiciary provide in some instances a watered down version of the rights compared to the interpretation of the rights at Strasbourg. Obviously, that has led to a diminution of the impact of the Convention in certain areas of law.

It should be remembered that neither the HRA 1998 nor the Convention, takes the stance that human rights are absolute; each instrument has its own exceptions and limitations. The key HRA provisions, especially ss 3(1), 3(2), 6(1) and 6(2), show that it is intended to create a delicate political balance; the rights which it contains only bind public authorities, not private bodies, and public authorities need not abide by the Convention if incompatible primary legislation means that they must act in contravention of the right (s 6(2)). Existing legislation which contravenes the rights cannot be rendered automatically invalid by the courts, but can remain in force under s 3(2) although a declaration of its incompatibility is made under s 4. Art 13 of the Convention, the right to an effective remedy before a domestic court, has 'disappeared' from the text of the Act. It would have been possible, although unlikely, for very little change to result from the whole exercise if the government frequently sought to persuade Parliament to decide to take advantage of its power to legislate contrary to the rights. In fact that has only occurred once – overtly – in relation to the Communications Act 2003.

The Convention was itself a compromise document which attempted to identify core values applicable in a range of very different signatory countries: it contains no overtly economic and social rights; a number of the rights it does contain have exceptions for such matters as national security and the prevention of crime (Arts 8–11). Art 14 can only operate within the ambit of another Convention right. The doctrine of the 'margin of appreciation' has traditionally allowed a significant leeway to States as regards the means and methods of upholding rights (*Otto-Preminger*, *Handyside*). In spite of these and other limitations, it is, however, possible to predict many fields of law which will require at least re-evaluation in the light of Convention rights. Since the potential areas of change in the 'civil liberties' field are so many and varied, the current and future impact on three will be examined here: privacy, police powers of surveillance and freedom of public protest.

In the field of public protest it is now clear, due to the HRA, that the Convention, Arts 10 and 11, must be taken into account. Where protest is in question, there seems to be a preparedness evident from the decision in *DPP v Percy (2001)* to look to Art 10. In other words, protest is not merely treated under the HRA as a form of disorder, as it often was in the past, but as an exercise of freedom of expression; the freedom of expression dimension is recognised – even afforded weight. When new public order statutory provisions, such as ss 132–8 of the Serious and Organised Crime Act 2005, are passed, their impact on freedom of assembly and public protest has to be considered so that it can be declared compatible with the Convention rights under s 19. Clearly, it is possible that a minimal interpretation of the Convention requirements are being relied upon, but at least the human rights dimension of such statutes is being recognised. They are no longer considered in Parliament only in terms of their ability to curb the activities of football hooligans or late night revellers, as in the past. Thus, for example, s 41 of the Criminal Justice and Police Act 2001 was considered to be compatible with Arts 10 and 11. Clearly, the courts may take a different view when cases arise under it; if so they can use s 3 of the HRA to seek to bring s 41 into conformity with the rights if that has not already been achieved. However the fact that the freedom of expression or assembly dimension of a protest is recognized, does not mean that Arts 10 and 11 are necessarily being afforded full weight. In *R(on the application of Gillan) v Commissioner of Metropolitan Police (2006)* the House of Lords found that, assuming that Art 10 was applicable in relation to an application of s 44 Terrorism Act, one of the exceptions under it was satisfied, without engaging in any proportionality analysis.

There is no substantive right to privacy in either domestic law or, strictly speaking, under the Convention. However, domestic law has long recognised a collection of disparate privacy-related rights, which fall within the scope of land law, tort, criminal law and a handful of statutes, including the Data Protection Act 1998. Article 8 of the Convention requires respect for family and private life, and it is this requirement which has aided in bringing about change in domestic law now that the HRA 1998 is in force. Whilst the relevant ECtHR cases are qualified and the European Court has arguably tended towards caution in its interpretation of Art 8, it is clear that both respect for private life and for family life require greater protection than they had pre-HRA in domestic law. The case of *X and Y v The Netherlands (1986)* held that the State is under a positive obligation to ensure respect for an individual's private and family life, even where the interference comes from a non-State source, such as another private individual. *Von-Hannover (2004)* made it clear that this was the case. Domestically, under the HRA, such an individual is not bound by the Convention rights, but since the Court itself is a public authority under s 6 of the HRA, it has a duty to develop existing common law doctrines (in particular, in this instance, breach of confidence) compatibly with Art 8.

In the case of *Douglas v Hello! (2001)*, it appeared that due to the influence of Art 8, s 12 and to an extent s 6, a right to respect for privacy might be emerging from the doctrine of confidence. The findings in *A v B and C (2002)* confirmed that those who wish to assert 'privacy rights' will have to rely on confidence, but they can seek to rely on the Court's duty under s 6 in relation to the development of that area of law. *Campbell (2004)* gave support to this stance and also confirmed that the doctrine of confidence had developed – partly under the influence of Art 8 – in such a way that it had transmuted itself into a an action for the protection of personal information, whether or not a pre-existing relationship of trust, imposing confidentiality obligations could be identified, as had been required in the past. Section 12 of the HRA was not found to mean that freedom of expression takes priority over right to protection of personal information where there is a conflict.

The legal basis for powers of covert surveillance and of interception has undergone a change, partly as a result of the inception of the HRA. In this instance, the change has been statute-based, rather than relying on judicial interpretation. There is a right to peaceful enjoyment of the home (*Sporrong and Lonnroth v Sweden (1982), Powell and Rayner v UK (1990)*). Invasions of the home or office, even when carried out under warrant by State officials, are open to special scrutiny (*Niemietz v Germany (1993)*). The interception of communications and covert surveillance must be carried out only in accordance with stringent safeguards and with an easily accessible method of appeal for an aggrieved party (*Khan v UK (2000); Klass v Germany (1979)*). The Regulation of Investigatory Powers Act 2000 was introduced in order to provide a broader statutory basis for surveillance and interception, to ensure that the 'in accordance with the law' requirement of Art 8(2) was met. The Act probably meets that objective. However, it arguably fails to meet the standards laid down at Strasbourg in terms of proportionality and necessity under Art 8(2), since it provides such wide powers for the interception of communications and for surveillance accompanied by a low level of protection for the privacy of citizens.

The key provisions of the Anti-Terrorism, Crime and Security Act 2001 Pt 4 were declared incompatible with Arts 5 and 14 of the ECHR (protecting the rights to liberty and to freedom from discrimination) by the House of Lords in *A and Others v Secretary of State for the Home Dept (2005)*, in a constitutionally significant, and human rights-oriented decision. This led to the introduction of the Prevention of Terrorism Act 2005, which itself allows for detention without trial, if a derogation is introduced, and for the use of control orders in a manner that has been found in *Secretary of State for the Home Dept v JJ, KK etc (2006)* to be incompatible with Art 5.

It has been argued that the HRA has so far had a patchy impact on certain existing areas of law. As indicated above, legislation has been introduced post-HRA which has been said by the government to be in compliance with the Convention and which is apparently intended to ensure that the exercise of powers by certain State bodies is human rights compliant. Such legislation includes the Regulation of Investigatory Powers Act 2000, which has already been discussed, and the Terrorism Act 2000. However, it is arguable that the Terrorism Act, with its extremely broad definition of terrorism in s 1 and the Regulation of Investigatory Powers Act, which places 'directed surveillance' on a statutory basis but provides very meagre human rights safeguards, are based on minimal readings of the Convention.[1] Thus, it is concluded that while an awareness of the human rights dimension of legislation and of the common law is becoming apparent, the pace of change is likely to be very slow. This is largely due, it is suggested, to the readiness with which minimal interpretations of the Convention rights can be adopted both by the judiciary and by the government.

NOTE

1 The example of Part III of the Anti-Terrorism, Crime and Security Act 2001 could also be given. A broad statutory basis for the sharing of personal and other information by public authorities has been created, which affords minimal respect for Art 8 rights.

CHAPTER 10

FREEDOM OF EXPRESSION AND FREEDOM OF INFORMATION

❚ INTRODUCTION

Freedom of expression is a key area in the protection of human rights element of constitutional law courses. Examiners tend to set general essays in this area; the emphasis is usually on the degree to which a balance is struck between freedom of expression and a variety of other interests. It is now essential in your answers to take the European Convention on Human Rights (the Convention) into account, especially Art 10, which provides a guarantee of freedom of expression. The Convention was received into UK law when the Human Rights Act (HRA) 1998 came fully into force in October 2000. Until that time, Art 10 and other Convention Articles relevant in this area were not directly applicable in UK courts, but the judiciary referred to the Convention more and more in resolving ambiguity in statutes in the run-up to the inception of the HRA. The HRA has now been in force for over seven years and there are certain early significant decisions in the field of freedom of expression (such as *Prolife Alliance (2003), Ashworth (2002), Interbrew SA v Financial Times Ltd (2002), Punch (2003)* and *Shayler (2002)*). Whether any particualr case is relevant will depend of course on the essay title.

Section 3 HRA requires that: 'So far as it is possible to do so, primary and subordinate legislation must be read and given effect in a way which is compatible with the Convention rights.' Section 3(2)(b) reads: ' . . . this section does not affect the validity, continuing operation or enforcement of any incompatible primary legislation.' This goes beyond the *current* obligation to resolve ambiguity in statutes. All statutes affecting freedom of expression and media freedom therefore have to be interpreted so as to be in harmony with the Convention if that is at all possible. Under s 6 of the HRA, Convention guarantees are binding only against public authorities. These are core or functional public authorities (defined as bodies which have a public function (see Chapter 9)). The definition is therefore quite wide, but means that private bodies, including most of the media (apart from the 'public' bodies, such as Ofcom, the BBC (probably), and the Press Complaints

Commission) can violate Convention rights unless a part of the common law, which also should be interpreted in conformity with the Convention, bears on the matter.

Thus, exam questions currently reflect the demands of the HRA in this extremely significant area and will expect an awareness of the Art 10 jurisprudence and of the impact of the HRA on freedom of expression.

This chapter considers other values that often oppose freedom of expression such as the administration of justice or official secrecy. One of the main concerns of certain of the questions in this chapter is with the methods employed by governments to ensure that official information cannot fall into the hands of those who might place it in the public domain, and with methods of preventing or deterring persons from publication when such information has been obtained. The balance between what may be termed State interests, such as defence or national security, and the individual entitlement to freedom of expression and information is largely struck by the Official Secrets Act 1989 and various common law provisions. However, the interpretation of the 1989 Act and the application of those provisions may be affected by the Convention rights as applied under the Human Rights Act 1998.

Freedom of information, in contrast to freedom of expression, concerns the ability of the citizen to gain access to state information even from an unwilling speaker. The most important value associated with freedom of information is the need for the citizen to understand as fully as possible the working of government, in order to render it accountable. This chapter therefore places a strong emphasis on the choices that were made as to the release of information relating to public authorities – not only to central government – in the Freedom of Information Act 2000 (in force 2005).

Examiners tend to set general essays rather than problem questions in this area; the emphasis is usually on the degree to which a balance is struck between the interest of the individual in acquiring government information and the interests of public authorities, in withholding it. Where information held by central government or by other public authorities is not covered by the 1989 Act, the citizen may be able to obtain access to it under the Freedom of Information Act 2000. The 2000 Act is a significant development which is highly likely to feature on exam papers.

Checklist

Students should be familiar with the following areas:

- the Official Secrets Act 1989;
- DA Notices;

- the basic scheme of the Public Records Act 1958 and key aspects of the Data Protection Act 1998;
- basic aspects of freedom of information measures in other countries, particularly Canada and the US;
- the doctrine of breach of confidence as used by the government;
- central aspects of the previous voluntary government Code on Access to Information, relied on prior to the Freedom of Information Act;
- the key aspects of the Freedom of Information Act 2000; aspects of the early work of the Information Commissioner;
- Art 10 of the Convention, other relevant rights such as Art 6, Art 10 jurisprudence;
- the Human Rights Act 1998, especially ss 3,4,6,12;
- early decisions taking account of the HRA and Art 10, such as *Prolife Alliance (2003), Ashworth (2002) Interbrew SA v Financial Times Ltd (2002), Campbell (2004)* and *Shayler (2002)*;
- key aspects of the Contempt of Court Act 1981 and common law contempt.

Question 37

'The Freedom of Information Act 2000 is a grave disappointment to those who are genuinely committed to the principle of freedom of information.' Do you agree?

Answer plan

This is a very specific essay question which requires a detailed and critical evaluation of the 2000 Act. It should not be attempted unless the student has quite detailed knowledge (with references to sections) of this complex Act. In a form similar to that taken here, this question is highly likely to appear on exam papers at the present time.

Essentially, the following matters should be discussed:

- the general right of access to information under the Act;
- the exemptions under the Act; implications of the tests for exemptions;
- the use of and nature of the harm tests;

- the role of the Information Commissioner; aspects of her early work;
- the enforcement mechanisms in general;
- concluding evaluation of the Act.

Answer

'Unnecessary secrecy in government leads to arrogance in governance and defective decision-making . . . people expect much greater openness and accountability from government than they used to' (White Paper: *Your Right to Know*, Cm 3818). These words expressed the intentions of the Labour government in introducing the freedom of information legislation.

The Freedom of Information Act 2000 provides a general right of access to the information held by a range of bodies. The Act covers 'public authorities' and s 3 sets out the various ways in which a body can be a public authority. In Sched 1, the Act covers all government departments, the House of Commons, the House of Lords, quangos, the NHS, administrative functions of courts and tribunals, police authorities and chief officers of police, the armed forces, local authorities, local public bodies, schools and other public educational institutions and public service broadcasters. Under s 5, private organisations may be designated as public authorities insofar as they carry out statutory functions, as may the privatised utilities and private bodies working on contracted-out functions.

Section 1(1) provides that any person making a request for information under the 2000 Act to a public authority is entitled to be informed of whether it holds information of the description specified in the request and if it holds the information it must communicate it. Thus, the right of access to the information is accompanied by a right to know whether or not the information is held by the body in question – this is referred to in the Act as 'the duty to confirm or deny'. From 2005 onwards, when the Act came into force, individuals were able to gain access to information relating to them personally, such as tax and medical records. They also now have the right to obtain information on other, general matters from the departments and bodies covered. For example, journalists and consumer groups might wish to obtain information concerning food safety, medical safety or pollution.

As indicated, the Act begins with an apparently broad and generous statement of the rights it confers; it is also generous in its coverage.[1] However, the rights are subject to a wide range of exceptions and exemptions. In this crucial respect, it will be argued, the Act is indeed a disappointment to those who are committed to the freedom of information ideal. In particular, the Act came as a disappointment after the White Paper, which did not propose a wide range of exemptions. Under the

White Paper, seven specified interests were indicated. The test for disclosure was, with one exception, will this disclosure cause substantial harm to one of these interests? The first of these interests covered national security, defence and international relations. A further six interests were: law enforcement, personal privacy, commercial confidentiality, the safety of the individual, the public and the environment, and information supplied in confidence.

Thus, the exemptions under the White Paper were relatively narrow and were subject to quite a strict harm test. They may be sharply contrasted with those that emerged under the Act. The harm-based exemptions under the Act are similar to those indicated in the White Paper: they require the public authority to show that the release of the information requested would (or would be likely to) cause prejudice to the interest specified in the exemption. However, this test for harm is of course less restrictive than that proposed under the White Paper. Further, a number of exemptions are class-based, meaning that in order to refuse the request, the authority only has to show that the information falls into the class of information covered by the exemption, not that its release would cause or be likely to cause harm or prejudice.

However, the Act provides a public interest test in relation to some but not all of the class exemptions, and almost all of the 'harm exemptions'. The authority, having decided that the information is *prima facie* exempt (either because the information falls into the requisite class exemption or because the relevant harm test is satisfied, as the case may be), must still then go on to consider whether it should be released under the public interest test set out in s 2. This requires the authority to release the information unless 'in all the circumstances of the case, the public interest in maintaining the exemption outweighs the public interest in disclosing the information'. It has been argued that the application of the public interest test to class exemptions in effect transformed them into 'harm-based' exemptions. However, where information falls into a class exemption and an authority objects to disclosure even under the public interest test, it can not only argue that the specific disclosure would have harmful effects, but also that the public interest would be harmed by any disclosure from within the relevant class of documents, regardless of the consequences of releasing the actual information in question. By contrast, under a prejudice test, the authority must be able first to identify that harm would be caused by releasing the *specific information* requested, and then go on to show that that specific harm outweighs the public interest in disclosure. It should be noted that the Information Commissioner takes the view that there is a presumption running through the Act that openness is, in itself, to be regarded as something which is in the public interest.

The discussion in this essay cannot cover all of the freedom of information class exemptions, but will consider some of the more controversial ones. Section 23(1) covers information supplied by or which relates to the intelligence and security services. The bodies mentioned in this exemption are not themselves covered by the

Act at all. This exemption therefore applies to information which is held by *another public authority*, but which has been supplied by one of these bodies. Because it is a class exemption, it applies to information which has no conceivable security implications, such as evidence of a massive overspend on MI5 or MI6's headquarters. Bearing in mind the complete exclusion of the security and intelligence services from the Act, the use of this class exemption, unaccompanied by a harm test and not subject to the public interest test, means that sensitive matters of great political significance will remain undisclosed, even if their disclosure would ultimately benefit those services or national security. Section 32 covers information *which is only held* by virtue of being contained in a document or record served on a public authority in proceedings, or made by a court or tribunal or party in any proceedings, or contained in a document lodged with or created by a person conducting an inquiry or arbitration, for the purposes of the inquiry or arbitration. The public interest test does not apply.

Information the disclosure of which would be an actionable breach of confidence (s 41) is exempt and the duty to confirm or deny does not apply if compliance with it would itself amount to a breach of confidence. The problem is that governments could seek to protect all information supplied by third parties simply by agreeing with the third party at the time of the communication of the information that it would be treated in confidence. The information would then become confidential, provided that it was not already in the public domain, and subject to the public interest test and, possibly, to the need to show detriment. This potential problem – of 'contracting out' of the obligations under the Act – has however been recognised. The Access Code issued by the Lord Chancellor takes the clear stance that when entering into contracts public authorities should refuse to include contractual terms which purport to restrict the disclosure of information held by the authority and relating to the contract beyond the restrictions permitted by the Act. Public authorities cannot 'contract out' of their obligations under the Act.

Certain class exemptions are subject to the public interest test. In relation to these exemptions, in practice, while the Information Commissioner always has the last word on whether the information falls into the class in question, she will not always be able to enforce a finding that it should nevertheless be released on public interest grounds if the information is held by certain governmental bodies, since the ministerial veto may be used (see below). Section 30(1) provides a sweeping exemption, covering all information, whenever obtained, which relates to investigations that may lead to criminal proceedings. It represents a specific rejection of the recommendation of the Macpherson Report that there should be no class exemption for information relating to police investigations. It overlaps with the law enforcement exemption of s 31, which does include a harm test. There are certain aspects of information relating to investigations which would appear to require disclosure in order to be in accord with the principle of openness enshrined in the Act. For example, a citizen might suspect that his telephone had been tapped without authorisation or that he had been unlawfully placed under surveillance by other means. Under the Act, no satisfactory method of discovering information relating to such a possibility will exist. It is therefore unfortunate that telephone tapping and electronic surveillance were not subjected to a substantial harm or even a simple harm test.

The s 30(1) exemption extends beyond protecting the police and the Crown Prosecution Service (CPS). Other bodies are also protected: it covers all information obtained by safety agencies investigating accidents. It covers routine inspections as well as specific investigations, since both can lead to criminal prosecution. Thus, anything from an inspection of a section of railway track by the Railway Inspectorate to a check upon hygiene in a restaurant by the Health and Safety Executive may be covered. It is particularly hard to understand the need for such a sweeping class exemption when s 31 specifically exempts information which could prejudice the prevention or detection of crime, or legal proceedings brought by a public authority arising from various forms of investigation. That exemption ensures that no information is released which could damage law enforcement and crime detection.

The other major class exemption in this category, under s 35, has been equally criticised. It amounts to a very broad exemption covering virtually all information relating to the formation of government policy. This exemption is presumably intended to prevent government from having to decide policy in the public gaze – to protect the freeness and frankness of Civil Service advice and of internal debate within government – but once again it appears to go far beyond what would sensibly be required to achieve this aim. Section 36 contains a harm-based exemption which covers almost exactly the same ground. Since it covers all information whose release might cause damage to the working of government – and is framed in very broad terms – it appears to be unnecessary to have a sweeping class exemption covering the same ground. Moreover, this exemption is not restricted to Civil Service advice; it covers also the background information used in preparing policy, including the underlying facts and their analysis.

The Act is much more restrictive in this respect than the previous voluntary Code of Practice on Access to Government Information. The latter required both facts and the analysis of facts underlying policy decisions, including scientific analysis and expert appraisal, to be made available once decisions were announced. Material relating to policy formation could only be withheld under a harm test – if disclosure would 'harm the frankness and candour of internal discussion'. The White Paper preceding the 2000 Bill proposed that there should be no class exemption for material in this area, but rather that, as under the Code, a harm test would have to be satisfied to prevent disclosure. While information in this category under the Act is subject to a public interest test, it is important to note that because by definition it is generally information held by a government department, if the Commissioner orders disclosure on public interest grounds, the ministerial veto is available to override her.[2] However, the Commissioner has issued important guidance on this provision which all but changes it into a 'harm-based' test. In one of the strongest pronouncements made on the interpretation of the Act, the guidance states that the Information Commissioner's view is that there must be some clear, specific and credible evidence that the formulation or development of policy would be materially altered for the worse by the threat of disclosure under the Act.

The Information Commissioner has issued a series of guidance notes on the interpretation and operation of the Act, one of which deals with the 'prejudice' test. As to the meaning of prejudice, the Commissioner indicates that the term is to be interpreted, in general terms as meaning that the prejudice need not be substantial, but the Commissioner expects that it be more than trivial. This indicates that, at the least, the Commissioner is not minded to countenance trivial claims of prejudice. As noted above, the prejudice based exemptions can be pleaded on the basis that prejudice would be 'likely' to be caused by the release of information; it is not necessary to show that it would definitely occur. The phrase 'likely to prejudice' has been considered by the courts in the case of *R (on the application of Alan Lord) and The Secretary of State for the Home Department (2003)*. Although this case concerns the Data Protection Act, the Commissioner regards this interpretation as persuasive. Following this judgment the probability of prejudice occurring need not be 'more likely than not', but there should certainly be substantially more than a remote possibility. Once again, this approach will help to rule out flimsy or implausible claims of prejudice.

The Commissioner's decision in a recent decision notice has also given guidance as to the legal professional privilege qualified exemption (under s 42 of the Act). A freedom of information request was submitted to the Department for Trade and Industry for information regarding an investigation into smuggling allegations made against British American Tobacco. In response to the request, the DTI withheld some information comprising legal advice and sections of submissions to ministers on the basis that the legal professional privilege qualified exemption applied. The applicant appealed to the Information Commissioner. On applying the public interest test, the Information Commissioner held that there were strong public interest arguments for maintaining legal professional privilege but she noted that this privilege could and should only be outweighed in exceptional cases where there were compelling contrary arguments.

The enforcement review mechanism under the Act is clearly crucial, but it is also open to criticism in certain key respects. The rights granted under the Act[1] are enforceable by the Data Protection Commissioner, now known as the Information Commissioner. Importantly, the Commissioner has security of tenure, being dismissible only by the Crown following an address by both Houses of Parliament. An appeal lies from decisions of the Commissioner to the Information Tribunal which is made up of experienced lawyers and 'persons to represent the interests' of those seeking information and of public authorities (Sched 2, Pt II).

Section 50 provides that any person can apply to the Commissioner for a decision as to whether a request for information made by the complainant to a public authority has been dealt with in accordance with the Act. In response, the Commissioner has the power to serve a 'Decision Notice' on the authority, stating what it must do to satisfy the Act. She may also serve 'Information Notices' upon authorities, requiring the authority concerned to provide her with information about a particular application or its compliance with the Act generally. The Commissioner may ultimately force a recalcitrant authority to act by serving upon it an 'Enforcement Notice' (s 52(1)) requiring it to take the steps specified in the Notice. If a public authority fails to comply with a Decision, Enforcement or Information Notice, the Commissioner can notify the High Court, which (s 52(2)) can deal with the authority as if it had committed a contempt of court. At present it appears that the Commissioner is finding difficulty in dealing with the number of complaints she is receiving. The Campaign for Freedom of Information reported that, as at November 2005, only 11 months after the Act came into force, there was a backlog of over 1,300 cases, and that some complaints had been with the Commissioner's office for more than 6 months without even being allocated to an investigating officer.

The Commissioner's decisions are themselves subject to appeal to the Information Tribunal, and this power of appeal is exercisable upon the broadest possible grounds. The Act provides that either party may appeal to the Tribunal against a Decision Notice and a public authority against an Enforcement or Information Notice (s 57(2) and (3)) either on the basis that the notice is 'not in accordance with the law', or 'to the extent that the Notice involved an exercise of discretion by the Commissioner, that he ought to have exercised his discretion differently' (s 58(1)). The Tribunal is also empowered to review any finding of fact on which the Notice was based. There is a further appeal from the Tribunal to the High Court, but on a 'point of law' only (s 59). In practice, this will probably be interpreted so as to allow review of the Tribunal's decisions, not just for error of law, but also on the other accepted heads of judicial review. The Convention rights under the Human Rights Act 1998 could be invoked at this point.

Enforcement can be affected by the ministerial veto, which is another highly controversial aspect of the Act. The veto can be exercised if two conditions are satisfied under s 53(1): first, the Notice which the veto will operate to quash must have been served on a government department, the Welsh Assembly or 'any public authority designated for the purposes of this section by an order made by the Secretary of State'; second, the Notice must order the release of information which is *prima facie* exempt but which the Commissioner has decided should nevertheless be released under the public interest test in s 2. The White Paper made no provision for such a power of veto, on the basis that to do so would undermine confidence in the regime. Such a veto clearly dilutes the basic freedom of information principle that a body independent from government should enforce the rights to information.

In late 2006 it became apparent that the Government was proposing a number of changes to the Freedom of Information Act 2000. There are apparently plans to make it harder to make 'the most difficult requests', including imposing a flat rate fee for requests to deter 'serial requesters', as well as a fee structure that allows the time taken by public authorities when considering difficult requests to be taken into account. The leaked memo reportedly estimates that these proposals would deter around 17 per cent of individuals who are considering making a request from doing so. Lord Falconer has since confirmed that he wishes to introduce changes to the Act to stop requests for large numbers of files that constitute 'fishing exercises' and that, while a review of the freedom of information fee structure is underway, a flat fee is unlikely as it would not be cost-effective.

In conclusion, it is suggested that the Act is indeed disappointing. It creates so many restrictions on the basic right of access that depending upon its interpretation, much information of any conceivable interest can still be withheld. How far this turns out to be the case in practice depends primarily upon the robustness of the stance taken by the Commissioner, particularly in applying the public interest test to the class exemptions under the Act, where it provides the only means of obtaining disclosure. However, certain restrictions, in particular that represented by the ministerial veto, are difficult, if not impossible, to overcome, however robust a stance is taken. Nevertheless, the Act does represent a turning point in British democracy since, for the first time in its history, the decision to release many classes of information has been removed from government and from other public authorities and placed in the hands of an independent agency, the Information Commissioner. Most importantly, for the first time, a statutory 'right' to information, enforceable if necessary through the courts, has been established.

NOTES

1 The use of statutory publication schemes under the Act could be considered briefly here as part of the discussion of the more favourable aspects of the Act.

2 The issue of exemptions could be considered further and it could be pointed out that the Act, through amendments to the Public Records Act, provides that some of the exemptions will cease to apply after a certain number of years, though these limitations are hardly generous. Examples of exemptions that will cease to apply at all after 30 years (s 63(1)) can be given, for example, s 28 (inter-UK relations), s 30(1) (information obtained during an investigation), s 32 (documents generated in litigation) and s 36 (information which could prejudice effective conduct of public affairs). Still less generously, information relating to the bestowing of honours and dignities (s 37(1)(b)) only ceases to be exempt after

60 years, while it will be necessary to wait 100 years before the expiry of the exemption for information falling within s 31. One of the absolute exemptions – information provided by the security, intelligence, etc, services (s 23(1)) – will cease to be absolute after 30 years, that is, the public interest in disclosure must be considered once 30 years has expired.

3 It could also be noted that there is a duty to provide advice and assistance so far as reasonable to the individual seeking information, provided for in s 16 of the Act. The Code of Practice published by the Department for Constitutional Affairs deals with the s 16 duty, stating that Authorities should, as far as reasonably practicable, provide assistance to the applicant to enable him or her to describe more clearly the information requested.

Question 38

Critically evaluate the means currently available to the government to prevent disclosure of information. Taking account of relevant developments, including the introduction of the Freedom of Information Act 2000, would it be fair to say that the tradition of government secrecy is finally breaking down?

Answer plan

This is clearly quite a general and wide ranging essay which requires knowledge of a number of different areas. It is concerned with restrictions on access to state information, methods of ensuring that information cannot fall into the hands of those who might place it in the public domain, and with methods of preventing or deterring persons from publication when a leak has occurred. The latter two issues are both aspects of freedom of expression, but the first is given greater prominence here. The question asks you, in essence, to present a critical analysis of the current scheme preventing disclosure of certain state information, and to consider whether the right of access to information introduced in the 2000 Act is dramatically improving the public's access to information. Since the essay is so wide ranging, you are not expected to engage in a detailed analysis of the 2000 Act.

Essentially, the following areas should be considered:

- the impact of the Official Secrets Act 1989: 'harm tests' and the Public Interest Disclosure Act 1998;
- the relationship between the Official Secrets Act, the Security Services Act 1989, the Intelligence Services Act 1994, the Interception of

Communications Act 1985 and the Regulation of Investigatory Powers Act 2000 in terms of creating secrecy (detailed knowledge of these statutes is not needed, except of the 1989 Act);

- the use of the common law docrine of breach of confidence as a means of preventing disclosure of state information;

- mention of a comparison with the DA Notice system – criticism of the system as currently operated;

- freedom of information measures in other countries;

- mention the operation of the Public Records Acts 1958 and 1967, as amended, and the Data Protection Act 1998, as amended;

- the effect of the Freedom of Information Act 2000; briefly mention the efficacy of the previous voluntary Code.

Answer

It has often been said that the UK is more obsessed with keeping government information secret than any other Western democracy. It is clearly advantageous for the party in power to control the flow of information in order to ensure that citizens are unable to scrutinise some official decisions. The justification for this climate of secrecy is that freedom of information would adversely affect 'ministerial accountability'. In other words, ministers are responsible for the actions of civil servants in their departments, and must therefore be able to control the flow of information emanating from the department in question. However, this doctrine is not easy to defend in a democracy; it might be thought that ministers would be made more accountable, not less, if the workings of officials were made fully open to public scrutiny. However, s 2 of the Official Secrets Act 1911 created a climate of secrecy in the Civil Service which greatly hampered the efforts of those who wished to obtain and publish information about the workings of government.

The Official Secrets Act 1989, which decriminalised disclosure of some official information, was therefore heralded as amounting to a move away from obsessive secrecy. However, since it was in no sense a freedom of information measure, it did not allow the release of any official documents into the public domain, although it does mean that if certain information is disclosed outside the categories it covers, the official concerned will not face criminal sanctions. (He might, of course, face an action for breach of confidence as well as disciplinary proceedings.)

The narrowing down of the official information covered by the Act was supposed to be achieved by introducing 'harm tests', which took into account the substance of the information. Clearly, such tests are to be preferred to the width of s 2 of the Official Secrets Act 1911, which covered all official information, no matter how trivial. However, there is no test for harm at all in the category of information covered by s 1(1) of the 1989 Act, which prevents members or former members of the security services from disclosing anything at all about the operation of those services. All such members come under a lifelong duty to keep silent, even though their information might reveal serious abuses of power in the security services or some operational weakness (see *Shayler (2003)*). Equally, there is no test for harm under s 4(3) of the Act, which covers information obtained by or relating to the issue of a warrant under the Interception of Communications Act 1985 or the Security Services Act 1989.

The harm tests under the Act are further diluted in various ways. Under s 3(1)(b), which covers confidential information obtained abroad, the mere fact that the information is confidential 'may' be sufficient to establish the likelihood that its disclosure would cause harm. In other words, a fiction is created that harm may automatically flow from such disclosure. The Act contains no explicit public interest defence and it follows from the nature of the harm test that one cannot be implied into it; any good flowing from the disclosure of the information cannot be considered, merely any harm that might be caused. Moreover, no express defence of prior publication is provided; the only means of putting forward such an argument would arise in one of the categories in which it was necessary to prove the likelihood that harm would flow from the disclosure; the prosecution might find it hard to establish such a likelihood where there had already been a great deal of prior publication. Thus, the Act was unlikely to have a liberalising impact on the publication of information allowing the public to scrutinise the workings of government.

The Public Interest Disclosure Act 1998 is also far from being a likely source of greater freedom of information; although, in principle, it affords a defence of 'public interest' disclosure to those facing Official Secrets Act disciplinary proceedings, full protection only exists where the disclosure is made in good faith to an employer or regulatory body. Thus, disclosure to the media is still a risky method and will be justified only where the malpractice is exceptionally serious or the whistleblower acts to avoid victimisation or a cover-up, or an inept official investigation has occurred.

The Official Secrets Act 1989 works in tandem with other measures designed to ensure secrecy. Sections 1 and 4(3) work in conjunction with the provisions of the Security Services Act 1989 to prevent almost all scrutiny of the operation of the security service. Even where a member of the public has a grievance concerning the operation of the service, it will not be possible to use a court action as a means of bringing such operations to the notice of the public – under s 5 of the Security Services Act, complaints can only be made to a tribunal and, under s 5(4), the decisions of the tribunal are not questionable in any court of law. Furthermore, the

Act provides for no real form of parliamentary oversight of the security service, but this has to some extent been remedied by s 10 of the Intelligence Services Act 1994, which set up for the first time a Parliamentary Committee to oversee the operation of MI5, MI6 and Government Communications Headquarters (GCHQ). However, since the Committee is not a Select Committee, its powers are limited. In a similar manner, s 4(3) of the Official Secrets Act, which prevents disclosure of information about telephone tapping, works in tandem with the Regulation of Investigatory Powers Act 2000. Under the 2000 Act, complaints can be made only to a tribunal (set up under the Act), with no possibility of scrutiny by a court.

Developments in the use of the common law doctrine of confidence as a means of preventing disclosure of information provide a further method of ensuring secrecy where information falls outside the categories covered by the Official Secrets Act, or where it falls within one of them, but a prosecution is not undertaken. *AG v Guardian Newspapers (1987)*, which concerned the publication of material from *Spycatcher* by Peter Wright, demonstrated that temporary injunctions could be obtained to prevent disclosure of official information, even where prior publication has ensured that there is little confidentiality left to be protected. The House of Lords decided (relying on *American Cyanamid Co v Ethicon Ltd (1975)*) that temporary injunctions could be continued where there was still an arguable case for permanent injunctions. However, the House of Lords eventually rejected the claim for permanent injunctions on the basis that the interest in maintaining confidentiality was outweighed by the public interest in knowing of the allegations in *Spycatcher*. Moreover, it was impossible to sustain a restriction based on confidentiality when the worldwide publication of the book meant that the information it contained was clearly in the 'public domain'.

There are other methods of seeking to deter persons from publishing information relating to the security and intelligence services. In *AG v Blake (2000)*, a former security services operative published his memoirs. The Attorney General did not seek an injunction on grounds of breach of confidence, because the information concerned was at least 30 years old, and did not in itself prejudice national security. The House of Lords, however, held that the Attorney General was entitled to an account of any profits from the publication of the memoirs, because such publication involved a breach of a contractual duty on the part of the operative, dating from his employment by the security services, not to disclose any information about his work.

A restraint over obtaining an injunction or damages for breach of confidence is now to be found in s 12 of the HRA 1998. This requires any court considering such relief not to grant any interim injunctions unless it is satisfied that the claimant is likely to be successful at trial. Moreover, it must have particular regard to the importance of freedom of expression, and in relation to journalistic, literary or artistic material, consider both the public interest and the extent to which the relevant information is or is about to be in the public domain. It therefore appears that in future, courts will apply existing statutory and common law rules with a far greater focus upon the public right to know. In this respect, the case of *AG v Times (2001)* is significant. A former MI6 officer wrote a book, *The Big Breach*, about his experiences in MI6 which *The Sunday Times* intended to serialise. There had been a small amount of publication of the material in Russia. The Attorney General sought an injunction to restrain publication. It was found that he had failed to demonstrate why there was a public interest in restricting publication; therefore, no injunction was granted. The requirement to seek clearance should not, it was found, be imposed: the editor had to form his own judgment as to whether the material could be said to be already in the public domain. That position was, the court found, most consonant with the requirements of Art 10 and s 12. This decision suggests that bearing in mind the requirements of the HRA, an injunction is unlikely to be granted where even a very small amount of prior publication has already taken place.

The position was affected by the decision of the House of Lords in *Cream Holdings Limited and others v Banerjee (2004)*. This decision gives the definitive interpretation of the meaning of section 12(3) HRA, which provides, *inter alia*, that no relief affecting the Convention right to freedom of expression ' . . . is to be granted so as to restrain publication before trial unless the court is satisfied that the applicant is likely to establish that publication should not be allowed.' The effect of the decision of the House of Lords is that, in nearly all cases – absent the claim of immediate and serious danger to life, limb, or presumably national security – the party seeking the injunction, that is the government in these kinds of cases, must show not only an arguable case, as previously, but that it is "more likely than not" that they will succeed at final trial. This approach, assuming it is applied consistently to *Spycatcher*-type cases, should make it significantly harder for future governments to obtain gagging injunctions against the media.

Apart from the action for breach of confidence, the government can seek to prevent the publication of some forms of information by means of a curious institution known as the DA Notice system. This system, which effectively means that the media censor themselves in respect of publication of official information, may preclude the need to seek injunctions to prevent publication. The DA Notice Committee was set up with the object of letting the press know which information could be printed: it was intended that if sensitive political information was covered by a DA Notice, an editor would decide against printing it.[1]

It is clear from the discussion so far that the government has a range of measures available to it to prevent publication of forms of State information, but that the measures have recently become more liberal. The 1989 Act is a narrower measure than its predecessor and the action for breach of confidence has a narrower application due to the impact of the HRA. However, the narrowing down of the measures available to the State to prevent disclosure of information does not in itself mean that access to official information is available. The mere fact that a

Crown servant will not be prosecuted for disclosing information and is unlikely to face civil liability does not in itself mean that the citizen can obtain access to the information.

Information of historical interest may be obtainable via the UK Public Records Act 1958, as amended by the Public Records Act 1967 and the Freedom of Information Act 2000. However, under the 1958 Act, public records in the Public Records Office are not available for inspection until the expiration of 30 years, and longer periods can be prescribed for sensitive information. Some information can be withheld for 100 years or forever and there is no means of challenging such decisions. For example, at the end of 1987, a great deal of information about the Windscale fire in 1957 was disclosed, although some items are still held back. Thus, the 1958 Act, even after amendment, can hardly be viewed as being equivalent to a statutory right of access to current information.

However, for the past decade, there has been a slow but progressive movement towards freedom of information legislation for the UK, culminating in the Freedom of Information Act 2000. The then Conservative government published a White Paper in July 1993 setting out its intentions in relation to freedom of information, which included the means of allowing citizens access to some government information. A voluntary Code allowing the citizen access to official information in certain specified areas was introduced in 1994. Voluntary open government asks the citizen to trust the government to act against its own interests. Clearly, government departments may be prepared voluntarily to release some information which is innocuous, but they are less likely to do so where the information will cause political embarrassment and may enable the Opposition to make a more informed and therefore more damaging attack on government.

When the Labour government came to power in 1997, it promised to introduce a Freedom of Information Act in the White Paper: *Your Right to Know*, Cm 3818. This promise took shape in the form of the Freedom of Information Act 2000, which came into force in 2005. The Act has a number of important consequences. Primarily, it places a general right of access to information on a statutory basis for the first time, in s 1. The right allows the public access to information held by a very wide range of public authorities, including local government, the NHS, schools and colleges, and the police. An Information Commissioner has been appointed who supervises the scheme and the public can contact her directly. Public authorities must, on request, indicate whether they hold information required by an individual and, if so, communicate that information to him within 20 working days.

It may be noted that the 2000 Act is not the only freedom of information measure available, and different bodies may be affected by other measures even though they are not public authorities for the purposes of the 2000 Act. For example, the Information Commissioner has issued a decision notice which provides that Network Rail is caught by the definition of 'public authority' under the

Environmental Information Regulations 2004. This decision indicates that a 'public authority' under the Regulations encapsulates a different group of organisations to those caught by the Freedom of Information Act 2000 and, unlike the Act, includes some private companies such as Network Rail, who had argued previously that as a 'private company' they were not bound by the Regulations.

Under the 2000 Act a number of forms of information are exempt, including that relating to security matters or which might affect national security, defence or the economy. The exemptions proposed under the White Paper were relatively narrow and were subject to quite a strict harm test. They may be sharply contrasted with those that emerged under the Act. The harm-based exemptions under the Act are similar to those indicated in the White Paper: they require the public authority to show that the release of the information requested would or would be likely to cause prejudice to the interest specified in the exemption. However, this test for harm is less restrictive than that proposed under the White Paper. Further, a number of exemptions are class-based, meaning that in order to refuse the request, the authority only has to show that the information falls into the class of information covered by the exemption, not that its release would cause or be likely to cause harm or prejudice.

However, the Act provides a public interest test in relation to some, but not all, of the class exemptions and almost all the 'harm exemptions'. The authority, having decided that the information is *prima facie* exempt (either because the information falls into the requisite class exemption, or because the relevant harm test is satisfied, as the case may be), must still go on to consider whether it should be released under the public interest test set out in s 2. This requires the authority to release the information unless 'in all the circumstances of the case, the public interest in maintaining the exemption outweighs the public interest in disclosing the information'.

Section 32 provides a particularly controversial class exemption: it covers information *which is only held* by virtue of being contained in a document or record served on a public authority in proceedings, or made by a court or tribunal or party in any proceedings, or contained in a document lodged with or created by a person conducting an inquiry or arbitration, for the purposes of the inquiry or arbitration. The public interest test does not apply. It overlaps with the law enforcement exemption of s 31, which does include a harm test. The other major class exemption, under s 35, has been equally criticised. It amounts to a very broad exemption covering virtually all information relating to the formation of government policy. Section 36 contains a harm-based exemption which covers almost exactly the same ground.

The imprecise terms used to indicate the exempted information and the introduction of class exemptions may be allowing the government to exempt from the disclosure provisions much information which is merely embarrassing or damaging to its reputation. Some such information may also be subject to the ministerial veto, where it relates to central government, which means that it cannot be disclosed even if it is not exempt.[2] However, where the veto is not used, a right to appeal to the information tribunal is granted by the Act to complainants and much will depend upon future interpretations of the statute by the Commissioner and the courts. To an extent, it remains to be seen whether the Act will be a substantial step towards greater openness in central government. In relation to other public authorities operating in non-exempt areas, the Act clearly represents a significant further step in the direction of freedom of information. It is concluded that the developments described here do suggest that a movement away from the tradition of government secrecy has been occurring over the last two decades, culminating in the Act of 2000. Nevertheless, the existence of class exemptions in the Act and of the ministerial veto suggest that some aspects of that tradition are reflected, ironically, in that Act.

NOTES

1 It could be pointed out that the system is entirely voluntary, and in theory, the fact that a DA Notice has not been issued does not mean that a prosecution under the Official Secrets Act 1989 is precluded, although, in practice, it is very unlikely. Press representatives sit on the Committee as well as civil servants and officers of the armed forces.

2 The veto can be exercised if two conditions are satisfied under s 53(1): first, the Notice which the veto will operate to quash must have been served on a government department, the Welsh Assembly or 'any public authority designated for the purposes of this section by an order made by the Secretary of State'; second, the Notice must order the release of information which is *prima facie* exempt but which the Commissioner has decided should nevertheless be released under the public interest test in s 2. The White Paper made no provision for such a power of veto, on the basis that to do so would undermine confidence in the regime. Such a veto clearly dilutes the basic freedom of information principle that a body independent from government should enforce the rights to information.

Question 39

'A comparison between the previous Code of Practice on access to government information introduced by the Conservative government and the Freedom of Information Act 2000 demonstrates that the Act is inadequate, since it provides very little more than the Code. It therefore appears that although with the introduction of the Act, the UK has gone some way down the path towards freedom of information, there is still a long way to go.'

Discuss.

Answer plan

This is clearly quite a specific topic which calls for an answer confined to access to information, rather than a general and wide ranging answer looking at the whole area of government secrecy. In order to answer it, it is necessary to have detailed knowledge of both the Code and the key provisions of the Act of 2000.

Essentially, the following areas should be considered:

- the previous Code of Practice on access to government information – exceptions and enforcement;
- the general right of access to information under the Act;
- the exemptions under the Act; implications of the tests for exemptions;
- the use of and nature of the harm tests;
- the role of the Information Commissioner;
- the enforcement mechanisms in general;
- a comparison between the Code and the statutory right of access to government and public authority information under the 2000 Act;
- conclusions as to the stage reached in freedom of information terms.

Answer

The then Conservative government published a White Paper in July 1993 which set out its intentions in relation to freedom of information. Instead of freedom of information legislation, the Major government favoured the introduction of an unenforceable Code of Practice on access to government information. It came into effect in 1994 and the second edition was published in 1997. In contrast to the voluntary Code, the Labour government promised a statutory right of access to official information and this was established with the introduction of the Freedom of Information Act in 2000 which came into force in 2005. In the following discussion, certain key features of the Code will be identified and these will be contrasted with the provisions of the Act. When the Code is compared with the Freedom of Information Act, it is found that both exhibit features which are found in freedom of information Codes or Acts abroad, but in almost every instance where various possibilities are available, the Code chooses the course which disadvantages the seeker of information and undermines the principle of 'openness'. The picture that emerges under the Act is more mixed. Four particular key features of the Code will be considered in order to emphasise the contrasts between the Act and the Code. The argument will be that the Act creates a superior freedom of information scheme, but that it displays a number of weaknesses.

The Code provided that non-exempted government departments would publish a range of information and also provide information on receipt of specific requests. The presumption was in favour of disclosure; after the 1997 revision, the Code provided that information should be disclosed, unless the harm likely to arise from disclosure would outweigh the public interest in making the information available: Pt II. The 2000 Act is based on similar principles, but in strong contrast to the unenforceable Code, it gave UK citizens, for the first time, a statutory right to non-exempt official information enforceable by an independent Information Commissioner, who as a last resort can enforce her orders through invoking the courts' power to punish for contempt of court.

One of the weaknesses of the Code was that it only provided for release of information as opposed to documents (para 4 of Pt I). As the Campaign for Freedom of Information has pointed out, this was 'a potentially overwhelming defect: the opportunities for selective editing were obvious'. In contrast, the right conferred under s 1(1)(b) of the Freedom of Information Act covers original documents as well as 'information'. Section 84 defines information broadly to cover information 'recorded in any form', and in relation to matters covered by s 51(8), this includes unrecorded information. In this respect, the Act is clearly an improvement on the Code.

The implied and express exemptions from the Code were extremely wide. Certain matters set out in Sched 3 to the Parliamentary Commissioner Act (PCA) 1967 were excluded from the investigation by the Parliamentary Commissioner for Administration (PCA). These included the investigation of crime by or on behalf of the Home Office, security of the State, and personnel matters of the armed forces, teachers, the Civil Service or police. A large number of matters were excluded from the Code, although the majority of these – after the 1997 revision – were subject to a harm test. They included defence, security and international relations; internal discussion and advice; law enforcement and legal proceedings; immigration and nationality; effective management of the economy and of the public service; research, statistics and analysis; privacy of an individual; and information given in confidence. Of these restrictions, those attracting the most criticism were the exclusion of contractual and commercial matters and of public service personnel matters.

In relation to major policy decisions (para 3(i) of Pt I), the Code related only to information considered relevant by the government. In countries which have freedom of information legislation, the usefulness or relevance of documents containing information is determined by the person who seeks it rather than by government ministers or civil servants. Usefulness is not an objective quality, but depends on the purposes of the seeker which only he can appreciate.

The introduction of harm tests, which mirror some of those under the Official Secrets Act 1989, was welcome since it limited the width of the exemption in question, but the tests were so wide and imprecise that they did not have much impact in narrowing the exemptions. The harm tests were varied and some were more complex than others, but none of them provided a precise explanation of the meaning of 'harm'. Thus, in relation to defence, security and international relations, part of the harm test was concerned with 'information whose disclosure would harm national security or defence'. Exemption 2 covered 'information which would harm the frankness and candour of internal discussion'.

The exceptions under the Act of 2000 are, on the whole, less wide ranging than those under the Code, taking into account the limitations of the PCA's remit – the PCA does not cover many of the bodies which are covered by the Act and therefore the question of exemptions does not arise. In certain respects, however, the Code was on its face more generous. In particular, the total exemption under s 21 did not appear in the Code in as broad a form (para 8 of the Code referred to information obtainable under existing statutory rights) and the exemption under s 35 is broader than the equivalent exemption under the Code (in para 2). The exemptions under the Act rely on the key distinction between 'class' and 'harm-based' exemptions. The harm-based exemptions under the Act are similar to those indicated in the White Paper: they require the public authority to show that the release of the information requested would or would be likely to cause prejudice to the interest specified in the exemption. However, a number are class-based, meaning that in order to refuse the request, the authority only has to show that the information falls into the class of information covered by the exemption, not that its release would cause or would be likely to cause harm or prejudice.

The Act provides a public interest test in relation to some but not all of the class exemptions and almost all the 'harm-based exemptions'. However, where information falls into a class exemption and an authority objects to disclosure even under the public interest test, it is able not only to argue that the specific disclosure would have harmful effects, but also that the public interest would be harmed by any disclosure from within the relevant class of documents, regardless of the consequences of releasing the actual information in question.

This discussion cannot cover all of the Freedom of Information Act class exemptions, but will consider some of the more controversial ones. Section 23(1) covers information supplied by or which relates to the intelligence and security services. The bodies mentioned in this exemption are not themselves covered by the Act at all. This exemption therefore applies to information which is held by *another public authority*, but which has been supplied by one of these bodies. Because it is a class exemption, it could apply to information which had no conceivable security implications, such as evidence of a massive overspend on MI5 or MI6's headquarters. The use of this class exemption unaccompanied by a harm test and not subject to the public interest test is likely to mean that sensitive matters of great political significance remain undisclosed, even if their disclosure would ultimately benefit those services or national security. Section 32 is another broad and controversial class exemption; it includes information *which is only held* by virtue of being contained in a document served on a public authority in proceedings or made in any proceedings. The public interest test does not apply.

Section 30(1) provides a sweeping class exemption, covering all information whenever obtained which relates to investigations that may lead to criminal proceedings. It represents a specific rejection of the recommendation of the Macpherson Report that there should be no class exemption for information relating to police investigations. This s 30 exemption extends beyond protecting the police and the Crown Prosecution Service. Other bodies are also protected: it covers all information obtained by safety agencies investigating accidents. It is particularly hard to understand the need for such a sweeping class exemption when s 31 specifically exempts information which could prejudice the prevention or detection of crime, or legal proceedings brought by a public authority arising from various forms of investigation.[1]

A further major class exemption under s 35 has been equally criticised. It amounts to a very broad exemption covering virtually all information relating to the formation of government policy. This exemption is not restricted to Civil Service advice; it covers also the background information used in preparing policy, including the underlying facts and their analysis. Section 36 contains a harm-based exemption which covers almost exactly the same ground.[2] In contrast to the position under most other freedom of information regimes, s 35 allows the *analysis* of facts to be withheld. The 2000 Act is much more restrictive in this respect than the voluntary Code of Practice. The latter required both facts and the analysis of facts underlying policy decisions, including scientific analysis and expert appraisal, to be made available once decisions were announced. Material relating to policy formation could only be withheld under a harm test. While information in the s 35 category is subject to a public interest test, it is important to note that because by definition it is generally information held by a government department, if the Commissioner orders disclosure on public interest grounds, the ministerial veto is available to override her (see below).

The third feature of the Code to be considered relates to the role of the Parliamentary Commissioner for Administration (Ombudsman) in policing it. If a citizen failed to obtain information or full information in a non-exempt area, he could complain to an MP, who would probably pass the complaint to the Ombudsman. If the Ombudsman recommended that a department should reveal information and the department did not accept the recommendation, the department might be called upon to justify itself before the Select Committee on the PCA. However, the Committee could not compel a department to release information. Thus, the Ombudsman had no means of enforcing his recommendations unless he took the means of redress into his own hands by disclosing the disputed information. No provision of the Code envisaged that he might do this. He would have been reluctant to take this course since it would have damaged relations between himself and the department in question, which would almost certainly have had repercussions in relation to other aspects of his role. Thus, the Code was most open to criticism due to its lack of 'teeth'.

The enforcement review mechanism under the Act is far stronger than the mechanism that was established under the Code. The internal review of a decision to withhold information, established under the Code, was formalised under the Act and the role of the Ombudsman was taken over by that of the Information Commissioner. The Commissioner's powers are much more extensive than those of the Ombudsman: she has the power to order disclosure of the information by means of an enforcement notice (s 52(1)) and can report a failure to disclose information to the High Court (s 52), which can treat it in the same way as contempt of court.[3] However, the ministerial veto weakens the enforcement of the access where government departments are involved. It is therefore another highly controversial aspect of the Act. The White Paper made no provision for such a power of veto, on the basis that to do so would undermine confidence in the regime. Such a veto clearly dilutes the basic freedom of information principle that a body independent from government should enforce the rights to information, and since in cases where the release of information could embarrass ministers, it constitutes them as judge in their own cause, it is objectionable in principle.[4] Thus, the enforcement mechanism under the Act, while stronger than that available under the Code, exhibits clear failures of commitment to the freedom of information ideal.

The final and most fundamental criticism of the Code was that in principle, the case for a voluntary Code as opposed to a general statutory right of access to information is not a strong one, mainly because voluntary open government asks the citizen to trust government to act against its own interests. Clearly, government departments may be readily prepared to release voluntarily some information which is out of date or innocuous for some other reason, but this is less likely where the information will cause political embarrassment and may enable the Opposition to make a more informed and, therefore, more damaging attack on the governing party. The grace and favour nature of this scheme, it is argued, was entirely inappropriate in relation to freedom of information, although the recommendatory nature of the PCA is appropriate in relation to his main function. The fact that the PCA operates informally and privately has been thought to enhance his powers of persuasion. However, in relation to complaints under the Code, the lack of a power to award a remedy was in some situations a weakness in the PCA system. The fact that adherence to the Code was voluntary may have meant that it was not taken seriously unless the PCA took up a complaint.[5]

It is argued that the introduction of a statutory right of access to official information was clearly preferable to relying on a voluntary Code. However, it must be acknowledged that the Commissioner's power to force government to disclose information is weakened by the existence of the ministerial veto. This is one of the major concerns about the Act. The other is the great number and width of the exemptions it contains and the fact that many of these amount to class exemptions. It is concluded that the Code of Practice on access to government information, and the developments preceding it, represented a clear movement towards freedom of information, but an inadequate one. Despite the concerns expressed above, it is suggested that a far more significant step in that direction was taken by the Act of 2000.

▌NOTES

1 It could be pointed out that where it has been decided that the information falls into the protected class, the authority must then go on to consider whether it should be released under the public interest test. Since most of the information above will not be held by a government department (discussed later in the essay), the Commissioner can order disclosure if she thinks that the information should be released under this provision, with no possibility of a ministerial veto.

2 The sole, and very limited exception to this exemption appears in sub-s (2) of s 35; it applies only 'once a decision as to government policy has been taken' and covers 'any statistical information used to provide an informed background to the taking of the decision'.

3 Further discussion of the enforcement mechanism could be included. The Commissioner's powers are buttressed by powers of entry, search and seizure to gain evidence of a failure by the authority to carry out its obligations under the Act or comply with a Notice issued by the Commissioner (detailed in Sched 3). However, the Commissioner's decisions are themselves subject to appeal to the Tribunal, and this power of appeal is exercisable upon the broadest possible grounds (s 57(2) and (3); s 58(1)). The Tribunal is empowered to review any finding of fact on which the Commissioner's notice was based and, as well as being empowered to quash decisions of the Commissioner, may substitute any other notice that he could have served. It may also be noted that no civil liability is incurred if a public authority does not comply with any duty imposed by the Act (s 56).

4 For the veto to be exercisable, two conditions must be satisfied under s 53(1): first, the Notice which the veto will operate to quash must have been served on a government department, the Welsh Assembly or 'any public authority

designated for the purposes of this section by an order made by the Secretary of State'; second, the Notice must order the release of information which is *prima facie* exempt but which the Commissioner has decided should nevertheless be released under the public interest test in s 2.

5 A survey published in March 1997 (see the journalists' magazine, *UKPG*, 7 March 1997, para 9) showed that public bodies were not meeting the standards of openness laid down in the previous government Code. Fifty government departments were asked for information to which the public is entitled under the Code. Eleven gave wrong or inadequate information and three refused to reply at all. Among those showing poor practice were the Legal Aid Board and the Commission for Racial Equality. The Department for Education and Employment and the Office for National Statistics were among those which refused to reply.

Question 40

In the light of statutory developments in the fields of official secrecy, the administration of justice and protection for journalistic sources in the 1980s and the 1990s, how far, if at all, does UK law require reform in order to ensure compatibility with Art 10 of the European Convention on Human Rights, Sched 1, Human Rights Act 1998?

Answer plan

This is clearly a fairly narrowly focused essay. Note that only *statutory* developments in the two areas in question need be considered, although of course that means that case law on the statutes in question must also be considered. Also, unless the answer is not to become unmanageably long, it would be wise to interpret the question as unconcerned with other aspects of freedom of expression such as public protest (see Chapter 12) or freedom of information – which is linked to media freedom of expression. Usually, if a question expects those aspects to be discussed, it will make that clear.

The following matters should be considered:

• Article 10 European Convention on Human Rights and the HRA – ways in which the HRA influences the law, especially ss 3, 6;

• key aspects of the Strasbourg freedom of expression jurisprudence;

- the Official Secrets Act 1989; *Shayler (2002)*;
- ss 2 and 5 of the Contempt of Court Act 1981;
- s 10 Contempt of Court Act 1981 – *Goodwin v UK (1996)*;
- *Interbrew SA v Financial Times Ltd (2002); Ashworth Hospital Authority v MGN Ltd (2002)*;
- conclusions.

Answer

Freedom of expression tends to come into conflict with other interests to a greater extent than any other liberty, and this is equally true of protection of journalistic sources as an aspect of freedom of expression. In considering how far the 'balance' between freedom of expression and other interests, in particular official secrecy and the administration of justice, was affected by statutory developments in the field of freedom of expression in the 1980s and the 1990s, it should be remembered that freedom of expression is not affected only by changes in domestic law. Art 10 of the European Convention on Human Rights (the Convention) guarantees freedom of expression to citizens of Member States and, although the Convention was not at the time directly applicable in UK courts, it had some influence on domestic law in this area, since the judiciary increasingly referred to the Convention in resolving ambiguity in statutes.

The Human Rights Act 1998 received the Convention, including the guarantee of freedom of expression under Art 10, into domestic law. Thus public authorities and the courts became bound under s 6 HRA by Article 10. Legislation must be read by the courts in a manner which gives effect, so far as is possible, to the Convention rights (s 3 of the HRA); if this is not possible, a declaration of incompatibility may be issued (s 4), and remedial action may be taken as a result (s 10). Further, the HRA gives special regard to the importance of freedom of expression and forbids restraint of publication before a full trial of an injunction, unless the court is satisfied that the applicant is more likely than not to win at trial (s 12).

The Strasbourg freedom of expression jurisprudence demonstrates that Art 10 is one of the most significant Articles of the Convention. The Court has repeatedly asserted that freedom of expression 'constitutes one of the essential foundations of a democratic society' (*The Observer and The Guardian v UK (1991)*) and that it is applicable not only to 'information' or 'ideas' that are regarded as inoffensive, but also to those that 'offend, shock or disturb' (*Thorgeirson v Iceland (1992)*). Particular stress has been laid upon 'the preeminent role of the press' which, 'in its vital role of 'public watchdog', has a duty 'to impart information and ideas on matters of public interest' which the public 'has a right to receive' (*Castells v Spain (1992)*). However, it is a marked feature of the Strasbourg jurisprudence that clearly political speech receives a much more robust degree of protection than other types of expression. Thus, the 'political' speech cases of *Sunday Times (1979), Jersild v Denmark (1994), Lingens v Austria (1986)* and *Thorgeirson v Iceland (1992)* all resulted in findings that Art 10 had been violated and all were marked by an intensive review of the restriction in question in which the margin of appreciation was narrowed almost to vanishing point. By contrast, in cases involving artistic speech, an exactly opposite pattern emerges: applicants have tended to be unsuccessful and a deferential approach to the judgments of the national authorities as to its obscene or blasphemous nature has been adopted (*Müller v Switzerland (1991)*; *Handyside v UK (1976)*; *Otto-Preminger Institut v Austria (1994)*; *Gay News v UK (1982)*).

It may be noted that in the years immediately preceding the inception of the HRA, UK free speech judgments gave a similar weight to freedom of speech – or, as the judges might put it, discovered that they were in any event a significant aspect of the common law. As Lord Steyn has put it: 'freedom of speech is the lifeblood of democracy' (*Secretary of State for the Home Department ex p Simms (1999)*).

Thus, it is submitted that the statutory developments to be considered in this essay are undergoing, and will undergo, fresh scrutiny under the HRA, creating further possible changes in the balance they create between protecting freedom of expression and protecting other interests, such as the need for official secrecy and the administration of justice. This is especially the case where the statutes in question restrict political speech, broadly defined. Art 10, unlike domestic law, provides a clear means of attempting to consider the extent to which the 'balance' in question is maintained, since its starting point is the primacy of freedom of expression, and Art 10(2) provides a number of tests that must be satisfied before a restriction of expression can be justified.

The Official Secrets Act 1989 represents a highly significant development which is arguably likely to prove more effective in preventing disclosure and publication of information than its predecessor. The Act was supposed to bring about an increase in the information which could be disclosed to the public without incurring criminal liability, by introducing a test which took into account the substance of the information. However, it is apparent that there is no test for harm at all in certain of the categories of information covered, including s 1, which prevents members of the security services disclosing anything, however trivial, about the operation of those services. In the categories covered by s 3(1)(b), although there appears to be a test for harm, it may in fact be satisfied merely by establishing the nature of the information. In other words, once it is shown that the information is of a certain nature, it is accepted that harm may automatically flow from its disclosure. The Act contains no explicit public interest defence and it follows from the nature of the harm test that one cannot be implied into it; any good flowing from the disclosure of the information cannot be considered, merely any harm that might be caused. Thus, the Act was always unlikely to have a liberalising impact on the publication of information, allowing the public to scrutinise the workings of government. It might therefore have been expected that the HRA could have a liberalising effect on it, that s 3 could be used to impose an Art 10-friendly interpretation on the statutory provisions, especially as they affect political expression. The provisions prevent civil servants divulging relevant information to journalists, and journalists themselves are also threatened with sanctions if they publish material covered by the 1989 Act (s5).

However, the *Shayler* case (*2002*) put paid to the expectations that the HRA would have a liberalising effect on ss 1 and 4 of the 1989 Act. In 2002 David Shayler was tried under the 1989 Act on the basis that he had infringed ss 1 and 4 by divulging MI6 secrets. He alleged that MI6 had been involved in a plot to assassinate Colonel Gaddafi; further allegations exposed, Shayler claimed, serious illegality on the part of MI6, and were necessary to avert threats to life and limb and to personal property. Since the HRA was in force, Shayler could seek to rely on s 3 which provides: 'So far as it is possible to do so, primary and subordinate legislation must be read and given effect in a way which is compatible with the Convention rights.' Since s 1 of the 1989 Act provides no means of balancing any harm to the security and intelligence services against the interests of freedom of expression, it might have been expected that it would be found to be incompatible with Art 10. A preliminary hearing was held regarding the effect of the HRA on s 1(1). It was argued that since ss 1(1) and 4(1) are of an absolute nature, they are incompatible with Art 10 of the Convention under the HRA, owing to the requirement that interference with expression should be proportionate to the legitimate aim pursued. In other words, using s 3 of the HRA in a creative fashion to seek to resolve the incompatibility would be unfruitful, since compatibility could not be achieved.

This argument was rejected by the House of Lords (*Shayler (2002)*) on the basis that avenues of complaint were available to Shayler. There were various persons to whom the disclosure could be made, including those identified in s 12. Further, significantly, under s 7(3) of the 1989 Act, a disclosure can be made to others if authorised; those empowered to afford authorisation are identified in s 12. Shayler could have sought authorisation to make his disclosures from those identified under s 12 or from those prescribed as persons who can give authorisations. Thus while a truly blanket ban on disclosure of the information in question could not have been viewed as proportionate to the aim sought to be achieved, under Art 10(2), the ban was not absolute, and therefore proportionality was achieved. Assuming that this ruling is not over-turned in a subsequent House of Lords' decision, and applications on this matter are not made to Strasbourg, Art 10 will have no impact on ss 1(1) and 4(1) since, according to this ruling, there is no incompatibility between Art 10 and the two provisions.

The problem with the argument accepted by the House of Lords is that the means viewed as available to members or former members of the security services to expose iniquity are very unlikely to be used. It seems, to say the least, highly improbable that such a member would risk the employment detriment that might be likely to arise, especially if he then proceeded to seek judicial review of the decision. It appears that it would place him in an impossible position vis à vis colleagues and superiors. Thus, both current and former members may be deterred from using this route. Moreover, they would probably view it as inefficacious. It would probably be impossible to prove to a court that security service work was creating dangers to persons without adducing evidence which itself would be covered by s 1(1). One of the most important principles recognised at Strasbourg is that rights must be real, not tokenistic or illusory. It is argued that the right to freedom of expression – one of the central rights of the Convention – is rendered illusory by ss 1(1) and 4(1) of the Official Secrets Act in relation to reporting on or communications about allegedly unlawful activities of the security services – a matter of great significance in a democracy.

If ss 1 and 4 of the Official Secrets Act make little effort to balance national security and the protection for use of covert surveillance against freedom of expression, the Contempt of Court Act 1981 in contrast does make an effort to create a balance between protecting the administration of justice and media freedom of expression. The 1981 Act was designed to modify the common law in response to the findings of the European Court of Human Rights in the *Sunday Times* case *(1979)* without bringing about radical change. It introduced various liberalising factors, but it was intended to maintain the stance of the ultimate supremacy of the administration of justice over freedom of speech, while moving the balance further towards freedom of speech. In particular, it introduced stricter time limits (s 2(3)), a more precise test for the *actus reus* (s 2(2)) and allowed some articles on matters of public interest to escape liability even though prejudice to proceedings was created (s 5).

Section 5 reflects the guarantee under Art 10. It affords a high value to political speech, broadly defined, and therefore reflects the value placed upon such speech at Strasbourg. If it appears that s 2(2) is fulfilled, it must next be established that s 5 does not apply. *AG v English (1983)* is the leading case on s 5 and is generally considered to provide a good example of the kind of case for which s 5 was framed. Lord Diplock's test under s 5 may be summed up as follows: looking at the actual words written (as opposed to considering what could have been omitted), was the article written in good faith and concerned with a question of general legitimate public interest which created an incidental risk of prejudice to a particular case? It seems that the discussion can be triggered off by the case itself; it need not have arisen prior to it. This ruling gave an emphasis to freedom of speech which tended to bring the strict liability rule into harmony with Art 10 as interpreted by the European Court's ruling in the *Sunday Times* case. Due to the interpretation afforded to s 5, it is probable that the 1981 Act is already in harmony with the demands of Art 10 and therefore the inception of the HRA may not require a change in the balance it strikes between the two interests in question.

However, in other respects, it might have been expected that the 1981 Act would require reform or at least re-interpretation due to the inception of the HRA. Section 10 of the 1981 Act provides some protection for media sources, unless a court finds that disclosure is necessary in the interests of justice or national security or for the prevention of disorder or crime. Thus, s 10 creates a presumption in favour of journalists who wish to protect their sources which is, however, subject to four wide exceptions, of which the widest arises where the interests of justice require that disclosure should be made. The House of Lords clarified the nature of the balancing exercise to be carried out under s 10 in *X v Morgan Grampian Publishers and Others (1990)*, and moved that balance away from protection for media freedom, in its finding that the applicant's right to take legal action against the source outweighs the journalist's interest in maintaining the promise of confidentiality made to him. In *Goodwin v UK (1996)*, the European Court found that Art 10 had been infringed in the *X v Morgan Grampian Publishers* decision, since insufficient weight had been given to the need of journalists to protect their sources. It might have appeared, therefore, that s 10 would require re-interpretation under s 3 once the HRA was in force, in order to take the *Goodwin* decision into account.

However, in *Interbrew SA v Financial Times Ltd (2002)* and *Ashworth Hospital Authority v MGN Ltd (2002)*, the Court of Appeal and House of Lords respectively considered that the journalists in question had to reveal the source of the information in the interests of justice, interpreting that phrase very widely. The two decisions therefore clearly do not offer reassurance to sources who are uncertain whether to come forward, although it could be argued that the source in the *Interbrew* case came forward for his own (arguably improper) motives, and was hardly in the position of the nervous source who wishes to reveal wrongdoing but is afraid of the repercussions. On the other hand, potential sources are unlikely to understand the nuances of the cases, but may merely receive the message that the protection for their anonymity is in jeopardy. Although this comment is arguably inapplicable or not fully applicable to these two cases themselves, it might appear in general that the courts are protecting the right of institutions or companies to bring actions against employees and others in order to ensure that they can maintain effective cover-ups. In *Ashworth*, it is suggested, the Lords did not examine the question of proportionality in detail, but appeared to assume impliedly that since there was such a pressing need to protect medical records in the instant case, the measure in question was proportionate to the aim pursued. Thus they did not engage in a full application of the *Goodwin* proportionality tests under a strict level of scrutiny. The House of Lords in *Ashworth* purported to do what the European Court did in *Goodwin*, but, it is argued, mis-weighed both the harm done to the privacy interest and the value of the speech. In the context the privacy interest in secrecy was less pressing since some of the patients at Ashworth appeared to want to bring malpractice to the attention of the authorities and so appeared to be content with disclosure of the medical records. Both these decisions took account of the effect of the HRA and the courts considered that the outcomes were consistent with the demands of Art 10 of the Convention.

In the post-HRA instances considered so far, the interests of the State or its agents in keeping sensitive information secret, or the interests of justice have tended to prevail over free speech interests despite the effects of Art 10. However, it is not suggested that the judiciary is unconcerned with the need to protect freedom of speech, whether as a result of the HRA or of following common law principle. It is suggested, rather, that they wish to provide such protection, but are most confident in doing so when faced with a competing public interest lying outside the areas under discussion, in which they have traditionally been receptive to claims that freedom of expression must be suppressed.

In conclusion, it appears that while the HRA may not ensure that protection of freedom of speech is enhanced where it comes into conflict with the interests of the State, especially the interest of national security, the judiciary does show an awareness of the need to afford such protection. The HRA 1998 requires judges to take an activist stance in this area and it is possible that eventually Art 10 will be used to create clearer, fairer boundaries to restrictions on freedom of expression, outside matters relating to the security and intelligence services. However, judicial determination to create a proper balance between freedom of speech and other interests may find expression only where it is not countered by judicial reluctance to allow the needs (or apparent needs) of national security to be abrogated. It would appear that the UK statutory provisions in question do not require reform in order to ensure compatibility with Art 10 of the Convention under the HRA, but that this does not necessarily mean that freedom of expression clearly receives the degree of protection it would receive at Strasbourg.

CHAPTER 11

THE INDIVIDUAL AND THE STATE: POLICE POWERS AND COUNTER-TERRORIST MEASURES

▎INTRODUCTION

This chapter concerns the balance struck by the law between 'ordinary' powers conferred on the police, counter-terrorist measures, and the maintenance of individual freedom and of due process.

Examiners often set problem questions in the area of 'ordinary' police powers, since the detailed rules of the Police and Criminal Evidence Act 1984 (hereafter PACE), as amended, and the Codes of Practice (current versions 2006) made under it lend themselves to such a format. (Note also the power to stop and search arising under the Misuse of Drugs Act 1971 s 23(2).) The questions usually concern a number of stages from first contact between police and suspect in the street up to the charge. This allows consideration of the rules governing stop and search, arrest, searching of premises, seizure of articles, detention, treatment in the police station and interviewing. (It must be borne in mind that interviews do not invariably take place in the police station; an important area in the question may concern an interview of the suspect which takes place in the street or in the police car.) You need to be aware of changes made to the PACE Codes in 2006. In particular, a new arrest Code, Code G, and a special new Code, Code H (covering police detention of terrorist suspects) were introduced in 2006. The Codes, especially Code C, are very long and detailed; you only need, however, to be aware of the key provisions – the ones mentioned in the questions below. You also need to be aware of ss 34–37 of the Criminal Justice and Public Order Act 1994, as amended, which curtail the right to silence and therefore affect police interviewing. (In freedom of assembly questions involving police powers, covered in Chapter 12, you also need to be aware of the extension of police powers in the public order context, contained in Part V of the 1994 Act.) The common law power to arrest to prevent a breach of the peace is still extensively used and may need to be considered.

The rules governing obstruction and assault on a police officer in the execution of his duty under s 89 of the Police Act 1996 may be relevant as necessitating analysis of the legality of police conduct, in order to determine whether or not a police officer was in the execution of his duty. Finally, the question may call for an analysis of the forms of redress available to the suspect in respect of any misuse of police power. If essay questions are set, they often tend to place an emphasis on the balance struck by PACE between the suspect's rights and police powers.

Police powers to deal with 'ordinary' suspects differ from those available to deal with terrorist suspects; in general the level of due process available in relation to terrorist suspects is lower. Also, post-9/11 special measures were introduced to deal with terrorist suspects outside the normal criminal justice process – these were and are proactive measures, including detention without trial, designed to deal with terrorist activity before it occurs. So this chapter deals with a range of police powers applicable to 'ordinary' suspects and also aspects of the current counter-terrorist scheme. The Codes of Practice made under the Police and Criminal Evidence Act 1984 (revised and added to in 2006) reflect the differences between terrorist suspects and non-terrorist suspects since terrorist suspects are no longer covered by Code C (the Code covering interviews and police detention) but by Code H. Police powers in relation to terrorist suspects, special terrorism offences and sanctions operating outside the criminal justice system are contained in the Terrorism Act 2000, as amended, especially by the Terrorism Act 2006, and the Prevention of Terrorism Act 2005. Part 4 Anti-Terrorism, Crime and Security Act 2001 – the key UK counter-terrorist response to 9/11 – has been repealed. However, this chapter takes account of it in order to place the 2005 Act in its proper context. The provisions of the Prevention of Terrorism Act 2005 and those of the 2000 and 2006 Acts may be consolidated in a new comprehensive Terrorism Act to be introduced in 2007 or 2008. Thus the powers discussed below will still be of relevance under the new Act. Counter-terrorism powers are most likely to be discussed in essay question format. It should be noted that some Public Law courses may not cover counter-terrorism powers, or may cover only the 'police powers' aspects.

Articles 5 and 6 of the European Convention on Human Rights (hereafter the Convention), which provide guarantees of liberty and security of the person and of a fair trial respectively, were received into UK law once the Human Rights Act (HRA) 1998 came fully into force in 2000. It should be noted that Art 6 protects a fair hearing in the civil and criminal contexts, but our concern is with the criminal context, and in particular with pre-trial procedures which may affect the fairness of the trial and which, therefore, may need to be considered under Art 6 *(Teixeira v Portugal* (1998), *Khan v UK* (2001)). Under the HRA, Arts 5 and 6 and other Convention Articles relevant in this area, such as Art 8 (which provides a right to respect for private life and for the home), are directly applicable in UK courts since the courts are bound by them (s 6HRA). The police and other public authorities involved in the criminal justice process are also so bound. The rights should also be taken into account in relation to interpreting and applying common law and statutory provisions affecting the powers of State agents, including the police, and counter-terrorist powers. Section 3 of the HRA requires that: 'So far as it is possible to do so, primary and subordinate legislation must be read and given effect in a way which is compatible with the Convention rights.' Section 3(2)(b) reads, 'this section does not affect the validity, continuing operation or enforcement of any incompatible primary legislation.' This goes well beyond the previous obligation to resolve ambiguity in statutes by reference to the Convention. All statutes affecting this area, in particular, PACE, the Terrorism Act 2000 and the Prevention of Terrorism Act 2005 therefore have to be interpreted so as to be in harmony with the Convention, if that is at all possible.

So the application of the powers under all these statutes, in specific instances, should be in harmony with all the Convention rights, since those applying the powers, including the courts, are bound by those rights, under s 6HRA. As Chap 9 explained, under s 6, Convention guarantees are binding only against public authorities. In this context, if the police or other state agents use powers deriving from any legal source in order to interfere with the liberty or privacy of the citizen, this means not only that the rights should be adhered to, but that the citizen may be able to bring an action against them under Arts 5, 6 or 8 (and/or any other relevant Article). Within the criminal process, citizens can rely on Art 6 in order to ensure the fairness of the procedure, under s 7(1)(b) of the HRA. Also, in a hearing relating to interference with the liberty of terrorist suspects *outside* the normal criminal process Art 6 will be applicable. Exam questions therefore demand awareness of the Arts 5, 6 and 8 jurisprudence and of the impact of the HRA in this area. It is not good practice merely to refer to the HRA in answers; you should refer to specific sections of the HRA, usually ss 3 or 6 and to the relevant Convention right; reference should also be made to the Convention jurisprudence and to the domestic use of the Convention in relevant post-HRA cases.

Checklist

Students must be familiar with the following areas:

- the key provisions under PACE, as amended, in particular by s110 Serious and Organised Crime Act 2005, the PACE Codes of Practice (2006) affecting the areas mentioned above, especially Codes A and C, and ss 1, 2, 17, 18, 32, 24, 28, 58, 76, 78 PACE;
- s 23(2) Misuse of Drugs Act 1971;
- key cases on PACE and related provisions, especially *R v Samuel* (1988), *R v Loosely* (2001), *R v Khan* (1996), *Osman* (1999), *DPP v Hawkins* (1988), *R v Beckles* (2004), *R v Condron* (1997), *R v Delaney* (1988), *R v Parris* (1993), *Gillan* (2006);
- the provisions under the Criminal Justice and Public Order Act 1994, as amended, relevant to police powers, especially ss 34, 36, 37 and 60;

- s 58 of the Youth Justice and Criminal Evidence Act 1999 – inserts 34(2A) into the Criminal Justice and Public Order Act 1994;
- the offences of obstruction and assault on a police officer in the execution of his duty under s 89 of the Police Act 1996;
- the issues raised by the revisions of the Codes of Practice made under PACE; latest revisions 2006; new arrest Code, Code G, introduced in 2006;
- the PACE rules governing exclusion of evidence, particularly s 78;
- the relevant tortious remedies;
- the police complaints mechanism under Police Reform Act 2002 Part 2 and Sched 3;
- police powers contained in the Terrorism Act 2000, as amended, especially by the Terrorism Act 2006; PACE Code H (2006);
- counter-terrorist offences under the Terrorism Act 2000;
- counter-terrorist measures under the Prevention of Terrorism Act 2005;
- Part 4 Anti-Terrorism, Crime and Security Act 2001;
- Arts 3,5, 6 and 8 of the Convention; relevant ECHR case law, especially *Khan v UK* (2001), *Condron v UK* (2001), *Beckles v UK* (2003);
- the HRA, especially ss 2, 3, 6.

Question 41

Albert and Bill, two policemen in uniform and driving a police car, see Colin outside a factory gate at 11.30 pm on a Saturday. Albert and Bill know that Colin has a conviction for burglary. Colin looks nervous and is looking repeatedly at his watch. Bearing in mind a spate of burglaries in the area, Albert and Bill ask Colin what he is doing. Colin replies that he is waiting for a friend. Dissatisfied with this response, Bill tells Colin to turn out his pockets, which he does. Bill seizes a bunch of keys which Colin produces and, still suspicious, tells Colin to accompany them to the police station. Colin then becomes abusive; Bill takes hold of him to restrain him, and Colin tries to push Bill away. Albert and Bill then bundle Colin into the police car, telling him that he is under arrest. Colin does not resist them. They then proceed to Colin's flat and search it, despite his protests. They discover nothing relating to a burglary, but do discover a small amount of cannabis, which they seize.

Albert and Bill then take Colin to the police station, arriving at 12.20 am. He is cautioned under s 10.5 Code C, informed of his rights under Code C by the custody officer, and told that he is suspected of dealing in cannabis. Colin asks if he can see a solicitor, but his request is refused 'for the time being'. Colin is then questioned and eventually admits to supplying cannabis. The interview is tape recorded. He is then charged with supplying cannabis and with assaulting a police officer in the execution of his duty.

Advise Colin.

Answer plan

This is a reasonably straightforward question, but it does cover a very wide range of issues. The most significant and difficult issue is that of the arguably unlawful arrest(s) – so that should form a large part of the answer. The most straightforward approach is to consider the legality of the police conduct at every point. Once this has been done, the applicability of the possible forms of redress can be considered. It should be noted that the examinee is merely asked to 'advise Colin'; therefore, all relevant possibilities should be discussed – albeit briefly due to the time constraint. European Court of Human Rights (ECtHR) cases should be considered in relation to the relevant Articles of the Convention, contained in Sched 1 to the HRA, and the effects of ss 3 and 6 of the HRA should be mentioned where relevant.

Essentially, the following issues should be considered, using case law to support your points and mentioning the HRA, with relevant cases, where applicable at various points:

- the legality of the search under ss 1 and 2 of the Police and Criminal Evidence Act (PACE) 1984 and Code of Practice A (2006); Art 5 of the Convention;
- assaulting a police officer in the execution of his duty under s 89(1) of the Police Act 1996;
- the legality of the arrest under s 24 of PACE, as amended 2005; mention Code G (2006);
- the legality of the search of premises and the seizure of the cannabis under ss 18 and 19 of PACE; Art 8 of the Convention;
- access to legal advice under s 58 of PACE – legality of the refusal of advice; Art 6 of the Convention under HRA;
- exclusion of evidence under ss 76 and 78 of PACE; relevance of Art 6 of the Convention under HRA;
- possible free-standing action under s 7(1) (a) of the HRA relying on Art 8;
- relevant tortious remedies;
- the police complaints procedure under the Police Reform Act 2002.

Answer

The legality of the police conduct in this instance will be considered first; any possible forms of redress open to Colin will then be examined. The impact of the Human Rights Act 1998 (HRA) which affords the European Convention on Human Rights (ECHR) further effect in domestic law will be taken into account at a number of significant points.

The first contact between the police officers and Colin appears to be of a voluntary nature: the officers are of course entitled to ask questions, which Colin may answer if he wishes to (*Rice v Connolly* (1966)). It is not therefore necessary to ask whether Albert and Bill are invoking powers of stop and search under s 1 of PACE at this stage. Further, a failure to co-operate in answering questions as part of a voluntary contact with police cannot of itself give rise to reasonable suspicion, allowing for a stop and search (*Samuel v Commissioner of Police for Metropolis* (1999)). When Colin is asked to turn out his pockets, this appears to be part of a voluntary search. However such searches are now forbidden under Code A s 1.5 (2006). Thus under s 1.5 the search and seizure of the keys should be part of a lawful stop and search. Thus, it must be shown that the police officers complied with the provisions of ss 1 and 2 of PACE and of Code A. Under s 1(2), a police officer may search for stolen or prohibited articles if he has reasonable grounds (s 1(3)) for believing that he will find such articles.

The necessary reasonable suspicion is defined in s 2 of Code A, especially s 2.2. There must be some objective basis for it which will relate to the nature of the article suspected of being carried. Various factors could be taken into account in arriving at the necessary reasonable suspicion on an objective basis. These include the time and place, the behaviour or demeanor of the person concerned (see *Slade* (1996)) and the carrying of certain articles in an area which has recently experienced a number of burglaries (see *Black v DPP* (1995) where, however, although the place where the suspect was was taken into account, it was not found to be sufficient to give rise to reasonable suspicion). In the instant situation, the lateness of the hour and the fact that Colin is outside a factory in an area which has recently experienced burglaries, coupled with his nervous behaviour, might give rise to a generalised suspicion, but it could be argued that the suspicion does not relate specifically enough to a particular article, since there is very little to suggest that Colin is carrying any particular article (this was found in *Black v DPP* (1995) and in *Francis* (1992)). Colin's conviction cannot be taken into account (s 2.2 Code A). The case law makes it very difficult to come to a conclusion on this point since, following *Slade* the level of suspicion is probably high enough, but following *Black* (in which the suspicion was viewed as too general as it merely related to the area that the suspect was in) it is arguable that it is not. Following this argument, it is doubtful whether a power to stop and search arises. But in any event, even if it could be established that reasonable suspicion is present, the search is unlawful, since the procedural requirements of s 2 of PACE are breached[1] (*Osman* (1999)); the seizure of the keys is therefore also unlawful. It does not appear necessary to comply with the demands of Art 5 which the police must abide by under s 6 of the HRA since short detentions for stop and search purposes appear not to engage Art 5 (*Gillan* (2006)).

The demand made to come to the police station may assume that Colin will come on a voluntary basis but it is not phrased as a request so it is necessary at this point to consider whether a power to arrest arises. Also under s 3.2 Code C he must be informed that if he is not under arrest, he is free to leave, and under s 3.4 Code C he should be cautioned. Under Code G s 1.3 less intrusive means than arrest should be considered by the officers. After Colin becomes abusive, Bill takes hold of him to restrain him. If this restraining is not part of a lawful arrest and therefore lawful under s 117 of PACE, it could be characterised as an assault on Colin. Have Albert and Bill a power to arrest at the point when they state that he must accompany them to the station? Any such power would have to concern an arrest on suspicion of participation in burglary and therefore would arise under s 24 PACE, as fleshed out in Code G, the Arrest Code (2006). In order to invoke the power under s 24, Albert and Bill would have to show reasonable suspicion that Colin is involved in burglary (that he is about to commit burglary in relation to s 24(1)(a)(c)) and, as already considered in relation to s 1, it is doubtful whether such suspicion arises on the facts. The finding of the keys adds to the suspicion already present (this conclusion would appear to accord with the findings in the leading case on reasonable suspicion, *Castorina v Chief Constable of Surrey* (1988)), since there is a need for an objective basis for suspicion, even if it is not of a very high level. *O'Hara* (1997) does not appear to be relevant since, although the police have received intelligence regarding burglaries, they have not received intelligence stating that they should arrest Colin. Probably reasonable suspicion is present. The police also need to show that the arrest is needed to allow the prompt and effective investigation of the suspected offence in question or to prevent prosecution of the offence from being hindered by Colin's disappearance (s 24(5)(e) and(f)). It is probable that one of these conditions will be found to be satisfied in relation to most arrests, although it should be pointed out in the instant case that there is no proof that an offence has actually been committed.

In any event, even if s 24 PACE is satisfied, s 28 is not, since no reason is given for the arrest and the fact of the arrest is not stated, although it is later. At this point, before Colin becomes abusive, it would be practicable to state the fact of and reason for the arrest as required by s 28 since Colin has been co-operative so far; therefore the arrest becomes unlawful at that point (*DPP v Hawkins* (1988)). Therefore, since no power to arrest arises the restraint of Colin is unlawful. In any event, it seems that the restraint may not have been an integral part of an arrest; if so, following *Kenlin v Gardner* (1967), it was clearly unlawful. Either argument obviously produces the same result. Under s 2.2 Code A officers need to inform the suspect of the fact of the arrest even if it is obvious; they also need to inform of the reason for the arrest. A strict approach to s 28 PACE also accords with the demands of Art 5(2), under the HRA.

Albert and Bill then arrest Colin. This may be for simple assault or for assault on a police officer in the execution of his duty, an offence arising under s 89(1) of the Police Act 1996, but this reason is not given. Is the arrest lawful, meaning that there would only be a short period of time during which an unlawful arrest had occurred (*DPP v Hawkins* (1988))? There is no power to arrest under s 89 of the Police Act 1996. Therefore, the arrest power must arise, if it arises at all, under s 24 or at common law, on the basis that the assault amounted to a breach of the peace. If it is to arise under s 24, two tests must be satisfied. First, it must be shown that one of the general arrest conditions under s 24 arises; the police need to show that the arrest is needed to allow the prompt and effective investigation of the suspected offence in question or to prevent prosecution of the offence from being hindered by Colin's disappearance (s 24(5)(e) and (f)). As already indicated, it is probable that one of these conditions will be found to be satisfied in relation to most arrests, and an offence has already occurred. It may be argued that the arrest was necessary to prevent Colin causing further physical harm to Bill; in that case, the condition under s 24(5) (c) would be satisfied.

Second, Albert and Bill must be able to show that Colin is guilty of an offence – that the assault has been perpetrated or that they have reasonable suspicion that is guilty of the offence (s 24(2)(3)). It can be argued that Bill was not at that point in the execution of his duty, as he had laid hands on Colin unlawfully; therefore, can Albert and Bill be said to have reasonable suspicion as to that aspect of the offence? It may be argued, following *Marsden* (1868) and *Fennell* (1970), that since Bill had exceeded his authority in restraining Colin, Colin was entitled to resist by way of reasonable force; any such resistance would be lawful and therefore could not amount to an assault on an officer in the execution of his duty, so on this argument the offence under s 89 Police Act is not made out. Simple assault would not be made out either since he was entitled to resist. Assuming that Colin's action amounted to no more than reasonable force, he has not committed an assault. However it could be argued that even if at trial assault could not be established, reasonable suspicion of it could arise at this point. Albert and Bill may not be expected to appreciate the niceties of the law on assault in the heat of the moment. A further possibility is that Albert and Bill would again have to show reasonable suspicion that Colin is involved in burglary (that he was about to commit burglary) as already discussed. Even assuming that reasonable suspicion is present of assault or burglary, no reason is given for the arrest.

Any reason given for the arrest, following *Christie v Leachinsky* (1947) and receiving some support from *Abassy v Metropolitan Police Commissioner* (1990), must ensure that the arrested person knows which act he has been arrested for. This is enshrined in s 28 PACE. In *Mullady v DPP* (1997), where the arrest reasons were given as 'obstruction' (which is also not arrestable), it was held that where the reasons given to a suspect for his arrest are invalid or are the wrong reasons, then the arrest itself is unlawful. The reason should be correct (*Wilson v Chief Constable of Lancashire Constab* (2000)). The reason should be given if it is practicable to do so (*Edwards v DPP* (1993) and *Hawkins* (1988)). No clear reason was given in the instant case even though it might appear to be apparent that the arrest was for pushing Bill. The reason must be clearly stated and information as to the reasons why both elements of s 24 are satisfied must be given (s 2.2 Code G). However, it might be argued that since Colin had become violent it was not practicable to give the reason at that point (*Hawkins* (1988)).

Thus, it is arguable that the arrest was therefore unlawful for a period of time, before Colin pushed Bill. It arguably became lawful for a period of time, but then again became unlawful when the point came and passed at which Colin could have been given the reason (under s 28 and s 2.2 Code G) – in the police car. On this argument, when Colin is bundled into the car, Albert and Bill are entitled to use reasonable force under s 117, as they are in the exercise of an arrest power. But they are not entitled to use force before Colin pushes Bill. The subsequent detention – after the point when they could have informed Colin of the reason for the arrest – is also unlawful. These findings as to the arrest would appear to accord with the demands of Art 5(1) and (2) under the HRA.

The search of Colin's flat also appears to be unlawful. Under s 18, a power to enter and search premises after arrest arises, in instances covered by s 24. Since the arrest appears to be unlawful at this point this condition is not satisfied. It follows from this that the power of seizure under s 19(2) does not arise, as it may only be exercised under s 19(1) by a constable lawfully on the premises. The seizure of the cannabis is therefore unlawful. The search of the home also appears to breach Art 8 under the HRA and gives rise to an action in trespass. The search should also comply with Code B, but Colin is not given a notice of powers and rights as the Code requires. S 30(1) PACE requires that Colin should be taken to the police station as soon as practicable after arrest; since there is no basis for the search, it appears that s 30(1) has not been complied with.

At the police station, Colin is denied access to legal advice. Delay in affording such access will only be lawful if one of the contingencies envisaged under s 58(8) of PACE will arise if a solicitor is contacted. Following *Samuel* (1988), the police must have a clear basis for this belief. In this instance, the police made no effort to invoke one of the exceptions and have therefore breached s 58 and para 6 of Code C (1996), which provides that once a suspect has requested advice, he must not be interviewed until he has received it.

Having identified a series of illegal acts on the part of the police, it will now be necessary to consider the redress, if any, available to Colin in respect of them. The first such act was the unlawful seizure of the keys. The appropriate tortious cause of action in this instance will be trespass to goods; damages will, however, be minimal.

In taking hold of Colin outside the context of a lawful arrest, Bill commits assault and battery and breaches Art 5 of the Convention. The facts of the instant case closely resemble those of *Collins v Willcock* (1984) or *Kenlin v Gardner* (1967), which established this principle. Further, the unlawful arrest and the subsequent unlawful detention in the car and police station will support a claim of false imprisonment. The search of the home, based on an unlawful arrest, will give rise to an action in trespass to land. The seizure of the cannabis was part of an unlawful search; Colin could therefore sue the police authority for trespass to land and to goods. Alternatively, Colin could sue under s 7(1)(a) of the HRA, in relation to the breach of Art 5, seeking to receive compensation either under Art 5(4) or s 8 HRA, or under ss 7(1)(a) and s 8 HRA for an arguable breach of Art 8 in respect of the entry of his home. But, since the tort actions are available, there would be no need to rely on the HRA.

Colin may hope that the keys and cannabis will be excluded from evidence under s 78 of PACE, as found during the course of unlawful searches. However, according to *Thomas* (1990) and *Effick* (1992), and confirmed in *Khan* (1997) and *Loosely* (2001), physical evidence is admissible subject to a very narrow discretion to exclude it. That discretion might be exercised if it was obtained with deliberate illegality. The first instance decision in *Edward Fennelly* (1989), in which a failure to give the reason for a stop and search led to exclusion of the search, is entirely out of line with the other authorities. It may be that Albert and Bill merely misconstrued their powers in thinking that a power to search and of entry to premises arose in the circumstances, rather than deliberately perpetrating illegal searches. In any event, it may be very hard to show that they acted in bad faith. If so, it appears that no strong argument for exclusion of the cannabis or keys from evidence arises, and this outcome appears to be in accordance with the demands of Art 6 under s 3 of the HRA. Section 78 must be interpreted in accordance with Art 6, under s 3 HRA, but no change in the current interpretation appears to be required due to the findings in *Khan v UK* (2001).

Can a reasonable argument be advanced that Colin's admissions in the police station interview should be excluded from evidence under s 76? Following *Alladice* (1988) and *Hughes* (1988), unless it can be shown that the custody officer acted in bad faith in failing to allow Colin access to a solicitor, it seems that s 76(2)(a) will not apply. Following *Delaney* (1989), it is necessary to show under s 76(2)(b) that the defendant was in some particularly difficult or vulnerable position, making the breach of PACE of special significance. Since this does not appear to be the case here, it seems that s 76(2)(b) cannot be invoked.

On the other hand, Colin's admissions may be excluded from evidence under s 78 on the basis that the police breached s 58. Following *Samuel* (1988), it must be shown that the breach of s 58 was causally related to the admissions made in the second interview. It may be that Colin was aware that he could keep silent (although from the s 10.5 Code C caution he thought that this might disadvantage him at trial), but decided to make admissions and would have done so had he had advice. This argument succeeded in *Dunford* (1990) and *Alladice* (1988), on the basis that the appellants in those cases were experienced criminals, aware of their rights. (It should be noted that the wrong caution was given; the caution should have been that of Annex C para 2 Code C since the restriction on drawing adverse inferences from silence applied as he had been denied access to legal advice.) It appears that Colin did remain silent for some time; possibly, therefore, he would have made the admissions in any event. It might be argued that access to legal advice would have added little to his ability to weigh up the situation. However, since he was not afforded an opportunity to have legal advice (s 34(2A) CJPOA), the advisor could have warned him that there was probably no risk involved in staying silent under s 34 CJPOA.[2] On this analysis, it is possible that the requisite causal relationship exists and the admissions might, therefore, be excluded from evidence under s 78.

The ECtHR has placed considerable importance on the right of access to legal advice in cases such as *Murray (John) v UK* (1996) and *Averill v UK* (2000). It has held that delay in access where the defendant faces the possibility that adverse inferences may be drawn from silence can amount to a breach of Art 6 of the Convention. These cases were decided in relation to defendants who did remain silent but may neverthless encourage courts to be more willing to exclude admissions obtained when access to legal advice was refused. It is concluded that taking Art 6 into account, the admissions are likely to be excluded from evidence under s 78, especially as Colin was mislead by the caution (as it was the wrong one).

There is also the possibility of Colin being able to bring an action against the police under s 7(1)(a) of the HRA 1998, claiming infringement of his Art 6 rights but it is unlikely that a court would view Art 6 as giving rise to a cause of action, on the basis that its demands should be satisfied in the trial. A further possibility is that the actions of the police in breaching the PACE Codes and PACE itself could be the subject of a complaint, as could the other unlawful actions mentioned, under the Police Reform Act 2002.

Finally, Colin may want to know whether the charge of assaulting a police officer in the execution of his duty will succeed. Clearly, it will fail on the argument that Colin's actions did not amount to an assault, as he was entitled to resist Bill. Moreover, it has been determined that Bill was outside the execution of his duty since he was in the course of perpetrating an unlawful arrest.

Thus, in conclusion, a number of tort actions are available to Colin, as well as the possibility of an HRA 1998 action, under s 7(1)(a), in respect of the breaches mentioned of the Convention rights, or of making a complaint in respect of Albert and Bill's behaviour. It further seems that the charge of assaulting a police officer will be unsuccessful. It is probable that Colin's admissions will not be admissible in evidence against him and therefore there may not be enough evidence to support the burglary charge. The cannabis found will probably be admissible in evidence against him.

NOTES

1 Had it been found that the stop and search was lawful, the seizure of the keys would be lawful on the basis that the keys fall into the category of articles which may be seized if discovered under s 1(6) PACE.

2 This argument could be explored in more detail. It could be argued that despite his conviction, Colin may not be well equipped to withstand questioning. Possibly, had his solicitor been present, he might have been able to help Colin to keep silent (if that appeared to be in his best interests) even after the prolonged questioning. The provision of s 36 of the Criminal Justice and Public Order Act 1994 (that – in this instance – a failure to account for having the keys in his possession might lead to the drawing of adverse inferences at trial) would not appear to apply since the restriction on drawing adverse inferences from silence in Code C applied.

Question 42

At 12 midnight on Saturday, Carl and Bert, two policemen in uniform and driving a police car, see Ali, an Asian youth, hurrying through the street. Bearing in mind a knife attack perpetrated at 11.50 pm by Asian youths in the area, they approach Ali and ask him where he has just been. He refuses to answer their questions and they ask him to get into the police car. Bert then says, 'We're going to search you. OK?'. Ali does not reply but makes no resistance to the search. Carl and Bert then search him and discover a knife. Carl cautions Ali, and then questions him as to the whereabouts of the others involved in the attack; Ali admits that he was with some other youths in the street where the attack took place at 11.50 pm. No notes are taken during the questioning. Bert then informs Ali that he is under arrest for wounding.

They arrive at the police station at 12.35 am. Ali is re-cautioned and informed of his rights under Code C by the custody officer, Doris. He makes a request to contact his solicitor but Eileen, the investigating officer, is unable to contact the solicitor. Eileen then asks Ali whether he is prepared to go ahead with the interview without a solicitor and he reluctantly agrees to do so. A period of two hours elapses. He is then questioned and after half an hour, he admits that he participated in the knife attack, although he says that he acted in self-defence. (The interview is tape recorded.) He is asked to sign the notes (compiled later in the station) of the questions and answers in the police car and does so.

At 8 am on Sunday morning, he is charged with wounding and is remanded in custody.

Ali (who has no previous convictions but was cautioned for theft two years previously when he was 16) now alleges that his confession was untrue, that he knew nothing of the attack until informed of it by the police and was merely carrying the knife as a precaution. He says: '1 only confessed because 1 was desperate to get home. I wasn't even there; I only said I was because I was scared of them.'

Advise Ali as to whether the interviews and the finding of the knife will be admissible in evidence against him. Do *not* consider any other possible advice that could be given regarding other aspects of the problem.

Answer plan

This is a fairly tricky problem question since, in contrast to the last one, it involves police behaviour that is close to rule bending as opposed to rule breaking. It is fairly narrowly focused: it is concerned *only* with the question of exclusion of evidence. It must first be established that any breaches of the Police and Criminal Evidence Act (PACE) 1984, as amended, or of the PACE Codes (2006), have occurred. Then it should be asked whether or not they are likely to lead to exclusion of admissions made during any interview affected and/or of any physical evidence obtained during the whole course of the investigation – in this case the knife found during the search of Ali. You should take into account the cautioning provisions under Code C. Note that the question *expressly* does not call for consideration of forms of redress available to Ali other than exclusion of evidence. Also, it does not ask you to consider whether adverse inferences will be drawn from his silence, assuming that it is not excluded from evidence.

Essentially, the following matters should be considered:

- the lawfulness of Ali's arrest under s 24 of PACE, as amended in 2005; Code of Practice G (2006); Art 5 of the Convention binding on officers under s 6 HRA;
- the legality of the stop and search; Art 5 of the Convention not engaged – *Gillan* (2006);
- the applicability of the prohibition on interviews outside the police station under s 11.1 Code C, bearing in mind the exception under s 11.1(b);
- the possible breach of s 11.7 Code C in respect of the first interview (in the police car): impracticability of contemporaneous recording?;

- the exclusion of the first interview from evidence under ss 76 and 78 of PACE; relevance Art 6 of the Convention;
- the possible breach of s 6.6 of Code C affecting the second interview in the station; the admissibility of the second interview; Art 6;
- the likelihood that the second interview will be excluded from evidence; ss 76 and 78 of PACE; relevance of Art 6 of the Convention under the Human Rights Act (HRA) 1998;
- the likelihood that the knife will be excluded from evidence under s 78; relevance of Art 6 of the Convention; *Khan v UK* (2001); *R v Loosely* (2001).

Answer

Confessions may be excluded from evidence under s 78 or s 76 of PACE. Non-confession evidence, in this instance, the knife, may be excluded from evidence under s 78 of PACE. A first step in the direction of exclusion from evidence of the admissions made by Ali in the car and the station, and the knife is to demonstrate that substantial and significant breaches of PACE or the Codes have occurred (*R v Walsh* (1990), *R v Samuel* (1988)). The impact of the Human Rights Act 1998 (HRA), which affords the Convention further effect in domestic law will be taken into account at a number of significant points.

The knife is discovered during the course of a stop and search of doubtful legality. Any illegality of the stop and search is significant. It may be argued that the stop and search was unlawful; it was based on s 1 of PACE, which requires reasonable suspicion that prohibited objects or offensive weapons are being carried. The nature of the suspicion required is described in s 2.2 of Code A. The fact that Ali was Asian and was hurrying through the street near the scene of the attack only 10 min after it had taken place might be enough to give rise to the reasonable suspicion that a weapon was being carried as is required by s 2.2 of Code A (see *Slade* (1996)) since in terms of place, time and identifying features he fits the profile of the suspects.[1] However, Carl and Bert do not provide Ali with the information specified under s 2 of PACE, thereby rendering the search unlawful (*Osman* (1999)). The possible consequence of the unlawful search in evidential terms will be discussed below.

The facts of the instant case may support an argument that Ali was unlawfully arrested. If the arrest was unlawful, the subsequent detention would also be unlawful, as his detention is dependent on the power to detain for questioning under s 37(2) of PACE, which is in turn dependent on an 'arrest', not an unlawful arrest. If his detention was found to be unlawful, this would support an argument for excluding evidence obtained during it. Ali is arrested for wounding, an offence arising under s 18 or s 20 of the Offences Against the Person Act 1861. He could be arrested under s 24 of PACE, as amended in 2005. In order to arrest under the section, it is necessary to show that Carl and Bert had reasonable grounds for suspecting that Ali had committed the wounding (s 24(2),(3). Ali fits the broad description of the suspects; also his proximity in time and place to the offence, coupled with his possession of the knife is, it is submitted, sufficient to give rise to the necessary suspicion, which is not of a very high level (*Castorina* (1988)). Nevertheless, nothing in PACE provides that evidence obtained from an unlawful search may not be used to fuel reasonable suspicion under s 24, allowing for an arrest. Further, if the above argument as to the reasonable suspicion is correct, there may be sufficient suspicion for s 24 purposes, even without the finding of the knife. Thus, on this argument also, s 24 would be satisfied. This outcome would appear to be consistent with the demands of Art 5 which the police must abide with under s 6 of the HRA, since it appears that the exception under Art 5(1)(c) applies. The police also need to show that the arrest is needed to allow the prompt and effective investigation of the suspected offence in question or to prevent prosecution of the offence from being hindered by Ali's disappearance (s 24(5)(e) and (f)). It is probable that one of these conditions will be found to be satisfied in relation to most arrests, and it appears that both would be here.

The officers satisfy s 28 PACE by giving him the grounds of arrest. Code G (2006) s 1.3 demands that the arrest be proportionate to the objectives of the investigation; this requirement is probably satisfied in that this is a serious offence which requires immediate investigation, although on the other hand it could be argued that the officers make no attempt to ask Ali if he will cooperate in the investigation without being arrested. Section 1.3 of Code G should be interpreted compatibly with Art 5 of the Convention under s 3 of the HRA, meaning that a strict view should be taken of its provisions, giving the emphasis to the primary right (*Murray v UK* (1994)). Nevertheless, it does not appear that there is a strong argument that the arrest is unlawful; therefore, support is not afforded to the argument for exclusioin of evidence obtained in the station, as discussed below.

The next question to consider is whether by questioning Ali in the police car, Carl and Bert breached the prohibition on interviews outside the police station under s 11.1 of Code C. If s 11.1 is to apply, two conditions must be satisfied: the questioning must constitute an interview under s 11.1 A of Code C; and the decision to arrest must have been made at the point when the questioning took place. It is apparent that the first of these conditions has been met, as questions were put to Ali which concerned his suspected involvement in the wounding. The second is less clearly satisfied: the police might argue that until Ali admitted that he was in the street where the wounding took place, the level of suspicion was not high enough to justify an arrest. However, the stronger argument is that the other factors present (the finding of the knife, his proximity to the offence already observed by the officers; he fits the description of the suspects) gave rise to a level of suspicion sufficient to justify an arrest, even before the admission in question was made. Therefore, the questioning falls within s 11.1 and should not have taken place at all until the police station was reached, unless the exception under s 11.1(b) can apply. The exception may be invoked if a delay in interviewing would be likely to 'lead to the alerting of other persons suspected of having committed an offence but not yet arrested for it'. The questions were directed to determining the whereabouts of the other youths involved in the attack who might be alerted by the news of Ali's arrest. It is only necessary to show a likelihood that such a contingency might arise, not a reasonable suspicion; therefore, it appears that this exception may be invoked. No breach of s 11.1 has therefore occurred.

If an interview takes place outside the police station but falls outside the s 11.1 prohibition, the verifying and recording provisions under ss 11.7–11.11 Code C will apply, with the proviso that contemporaneous recording may be impracticable. Section 11.7(c) Code C provides that recording should be contemporaneous unless impracticable. The mere fact that an interview is conducted in the street or in a police car, as here, may not be enough to support an assertion that it could not be contemporaneously recorded. This seems to follow from the decision in *Fogah* (1989). What is impracticable does not connote something that is extremely difficult, but must involve more than mere inconvenience (*Parchment* (1989)). In *Parchment* note-taking while the suspect was dressing and showing the officers round his flat was held to be impracticable. However, Carl and Bert are in the police car at the time and Ali has shown no sign of violence or non-co-operation. While it might have been slightly inconvenient to record the interview in the police car, it would not have been difficult. It appears, then, that s 11.7 has been breached. It should be noted that Carl and Bert assumed wrongly that the minimum level of protection provided by s 11.7 or by s 13 Code C for comments made outside the context of an interview applied: a written record was made at the police station of the interview and the notes were offered to Ali to sign.

It will be argued that insufficient effort was made to comply with Ali's request for legal advice. Under para 6.6(d) of Code C, a suspect who has requested advice can change his mind and consent to the commencement of the interview even though he has not obtained it. However, it can be argued that the suspect should not be misled into giving such consent. Once she had failed in her effort to contact Ali's solicitor, Eileen failed to inform him that he could obtain the services of the duty solicitor; it could therefore be argued that his consent was vitiated as based on the misapprehension that unless he obtained advice from his own solicitor, he could not obtain it at all. However, in the case of *Hughes* (1988), the Court of Appeal considered that a consent to go ahead with an interview after a suspect had been led to believe that the duty solicitor was unavailable could be treated as a genuine consent. The police had given this information in good faith although the duty solicitor was, in fact, available. In principle, there is little difference between leading a suspect to believe that the duty solicitor is unavailable and failing to inform the suspect of the duty solicitor scheme. Thus, following *Hughes*, Ali's consent to go ahead with the interview could be treated as genuine; on this analysis, s 6.6 has not been breached.[3]

On the other hand, even if Eileen acted in good faith, it could be argued that a requirement to inform of the duty solicitor scheme is implied in s 6 Code C (rather than arising only from Note 6B, which is not a Code provision according to s 1.6 of Code C) and that therefore the instant situation is not analogous to that in *Hughes*. Further, s 6.6(d)(iii) was breached since an officer of the rank of Inspector or above should have asked Ali the reasons for his change of mind and given authority for the interview to proceed. It appears then that s 6.6 is breached. It is submitted that this is the better view, since it accords with the prominence given to legal advice in the PACE scheme. It is also in accordance with the need to interpret the Code provisions compatibly with Art 6 under s 3 of the HRA. The European Court of Human Rights has placed considerable importance on the right of access to legal advice in cases such as *Murray (John) v UK* (1996) and *Averill v UK* (2000). It has held that delay in access where the defendant faces the possibility that adverse inferences may be drawn from silence can amount to a breach of Art 6 of the Convention. Adoption of this interpretation is supported by the provision of s 6.4 Code C that no attempt must be made to persuade the suspect to forgo advice; a failure to provide the requisite information could be characterised as part of such an attempt in the sense that it might have the effect of persuading the detainee to forgo advice. It is also supported by the first instance decision of *Vernon* (1988) which concerned a situation almost exactly in point with that of the instant case, and by the strict approach to the legal advice provisions taken in *Beycan* (1990) by the Court of Appeal. On this argument, a breach of s 6.6 Code C has occurred.

Could it be argued that the interview in the car should be excluded under s 76 as it was not contemporaneously recorded in breach of s 11.7 and occurred after an unlawful arrest? Under s 76(2)(a), the prosecution must prove beyond reasonable doubt that Ali's confession was not obtained by oppression. According to the Court of Appeal in *Fulling* (1987), 'oppression' should be given its dictionary definition: ' . . . the exercise of authority or power in a burdensome, harsh or wrongful manner.' The breach of s 11.5 Code C could fall within this definition on the basis that the police acted in a wrongful manner. However, the Court of Appeal in *Hughes* (1988) ruled that oppression could not arise in the absence of 'misconduct' on the part of the police; in the context of the case, 'misconduct' clearly meant bad faith. On that basis, and assuming that Carl and Bert merely misinterpreted the level of suspicion connoted by the wording of s 11.1 Code C, the holding of the interview in the police car could not be termed oppressive.

Under s 76(2)(b), it is necessary to show that something was said or done in the first interview in circumstances conducive to unreliability. Following the rulings of the Court of Appeal in *Delaney* (1989) and *Barry* (1991), it is essential under this head to identify some special factor in the situation (such as the mental state of the defendant or an offer made to him) which makes it crucial that the interview should be properly recorded. In other words, a single breach of PACE cannot amount to both 'circumstances' and 'something said or done' under s 76(2)(b).

However, even if the first interview is admissible under s 76, the trial judge will still have a discretion to exclude it from evidence under s 78 if, due to the circumstances in which it was obtained, its admission would have a significantly adverse effect on the fairness of the trial (*Samuel* (1998), *Canale* (1990), *Scott* (1991)). Can it be argued under s 78 that the first interview should be excluded from evidence as unreliable due to the lack of contemporaneous recording? Ali is not alleging that he did not make the admissions in question, but that they are untrue. Presumably, he signed the interview record as a means of indicating his acceptance that he had made the admissions, although he intended to allege later that he had lied out of fear. Thus, admission of the first interview which was not recorded contemporaneously may not have the necessary adverse effect on the fairness of the trial: its recording non-contemporaneously may be sufficient and therefore may not lead to its exclusion under s 78.2 But a judge might exclude it from evidence on the basis that unreliable admissions should not go before a jury since they could be viewed as more prejudicial than probative.

It will now be considered whether the second interview would be excluded from evidence under s 76, due to the breach of s 6.6 Code C on the basis that Ali's consent to be interviewed without legal advice must be treated as vitiated due to the failure to advise him of the duty solicitor scheme (this argument was considered above). Unless it can be shown that Eileen acted in bad faith in failing to inform Ali of the duty solicitor scheme (which as argued above does not appear to be the case), s 76(2)(a) will not apply (*Alladice* (1988)). As noted above, if an argument under s 76(2)(b) is to succeed, it would have to be shown that Ali was in a vulnerable position in the interview. No specific factor can be identified which might support such an argument. The courts appear to take the view (see *Canale* (1990)) that when a defendant of ordinary ability to withstand questioning is interviewed in breach of one of the PACE provisions, s 78 should be considered rather than s 76(2)(b). Therefore, although it could be argued that the failure to afford him legal advice could amount to 'something said or done' conducive to unreliability, some special circumstance as identified in *Delaney* is missing.

It will now be considered whether a reasonable argument for the exclusion from evidence of the second interview under s 78 can be advanced. Again, it will be necessary to identify some impropriety occurring in the police station. A breach of s 6.6 Code C has been established. However, this breach may not be causally related to the admissions made in the interview (see *Samuel* (1988)). It may be that Ali would have made the admissions had he had advice. This is suggested since the solicitor would be aware that under s 34 of the Criminal Justice and Public Order

Act 1994, recognised in the s 10.5 caution, it is disadvantageous to a defendant to hold back a defence. On the other hand, his confession in the interview may suggest that he gave in eventually to pressure to confess and that the 'defence' he puts forward is just part of a false confession. A solicitor who believed him would probably still have advised him to remain silent. On this analysis, it is possible that the requisite causal relationship exists, and the interview may therefore be excluded from evidence under s 78, following *Samuel*. Such an interpretation would appear to accord with the demands of Art 6(1), on the basis of the argument that where a detainee has not had access to legal advice and makes admissions, that fact may suggest that he is more vulnerable than a detainee who manages to remain silent. Also the solicitor might have realized that the wrong caution had been used – on the assumption that Ali's consent to the interview without legal advice had been vitiated. The caution arguably should have been the Annex C, para 2 one. Had Ali remained silent, a breach of Art 6(1) would probably have been established if the interview was admitted into evidence and adverse inferences drawn from the silence (*Murray v UK*). It could also be argued – regardless of the precise interpretation of Code C – that Ali did not obtain a full opportunity to have legal advice as required by Art 6, following *Murray* where adverse inferences could potentially be drawn from silence; the fact that he did not remain silent should not detract from seeking to uphold his Art 6 right. The court is bound to ensure that Art 6 is not infringed, taking the procedure pre and at trial into account (*Teixiera v Portugal* (1998)).

Will the knife be excluded from evidence under s 78? According to the analysis above, the stop and search could be characterised as unlawful. On that basis, it would be possible to argue, bearing the breach of s 2 of PACE in mind, that following *Edward Fennelly* (1989), the products of the search should be excluded from evidence. According to *Thomas* (1990), however, physical evidence will be excluded only if obtained with deliberate illegality.

Following the decision of the House of Lords in *Khan* (1997), evidence, other than involuntary confessions, obtained improperly is nevertheless admissible, subject to a narrow discretion to exclude it. The House of Lords took Art 6 of the Convention into account in reaching this conclusion. They found that Art 6 does not require that evidence should be automatically excluded where there has been impropriety in obtaining it, basing this finding on *Schenk v Switzerland* (1988). In *Khan* itself, it was found that the trial judge had properly exercised his discretion to include the improperly obtained evidence under s 78. In general, the courts have been prepared to exercise the discretion under s 78 to exclude confessions (for example, *Scott* (1991)) or identification evidence (for example, *Payne and Quinn* (1995)) where a substantial and significant breach of PACE has occurred. They have been much less ready to exclude physical evidence, and this position has been unaffected by the reception of Art 6 into domestic law under the HRA (*AG's Reference (No 3 of 1999)* (2001); *R v Loosely* (2001)) on the basis that the admission or exclusion of evidence is largely a matter for the national courts. The courts have therefore taken the view that the position that has developed under s 78 regarding non-confession evidence need not be modified by reference to s 3 of the HRA or to the duty of a court under s 6. Therefore, it is probable that a judge would exercise his discretion to include the knife in evidence under s 78, despite the breach of s 2. In conclusion, the stronger argument seems to be that the second interview will be excluded from evidence under s 78. The first interview may be found inadmissible under s 78. The knife will, however, probably be admissible in evidence. It remains uncertain whether Ali would be convicted of an offence relating to the knife attack, on that evidence. Ali could be convicted of the offence under s 139 Criminal Justice Act 1998 of having a knife in a public place; the burden of proof would be on Ali to show that he had it for an innocent reason (see *L v DPP* (2002)).

NOTES

1 The question of the meaning of reasonable suspicion could be considered in more detail at this point, bearing in mind the provision of s 2.2 of Code A, which states that reasonable suspicion cannot be supported on the basis of personal factors (including colour) alone. However, where colour is a genuinely identifying factor, as it appears to be in this instance, it would appear that it should be taken into account, although the extent to which it is identifying will depend on the racial mix of the persons in the area at the time in question.

2 However, if, at trial, the particular unfairness likely to arise from the improper recording is not specified but the breaches of the recording provisions affecting this interview are pointed out, it may appear that it cannot be relied on; it will then be excluded from evidence under s 78. A similar situation arose in *Keenan* (1989); the Court of Appeal held that the admissions in question should have been excluded under s 78. In *Canale* (1990), the importance of contemporaneous recording was stressed. However, in those instances, the defendant had not signed the interview record. Thus, although these points might be raised, the conclusion will remain the same.

3 There is a further argument which could be used to escape from this conclusion. It might be possible to show that Eileen deliberately failed to mention the duty solicitor scheme in order to obtain a confession from Ali more readily. In *Hughes*, the consent in question would have been treated as vitiated had the police acted in bad faith. However, it may be that the failure to advise Ali of the duty solicitor scheme arose because Eileen mistakenly believed that he did not need to be specifically advised of it again after the notification of rights by Doris and the reminder before the third interview that advice was available. Eileen is not specifically required to remind a suspect unable to obtain advice from his own solicitor of the duty solicitor scheme before he gives consent to be interviewed, although this can perhaps be implied from the wording of Note 6B.

Question 43

Toby, who has a history of mental disorder and has two convictions for possessing cannabis, is standing on a street corner at 2 am on Sunday when he is seen by two police officers in uniform, Andy and Beryl. Andy says: 'What are you up to now, Toby? Let's have a look in your pockets.' Toby does not reply, but turns out his pockets and produces a small quantity of Ecstasy. Andy and Beryl then ask Toby to come to the police station; he agrees to do so.

They arrive at the police station at 2.20 am. Toby is cautioned, informed of his rights under Code C by the custody officer and told that he is suspected of dealing in Ecstasy. He asks if he can see a solicitor, but his request is refused by superintendent Smith, on the ground that this will lead to the alerting of others whom the police suspect are involved. Toby is then questioned for two hours, but makes no reply to the questions. He then has a short break; when the interview recommences, he is re-cautioned and reminded of his right to legal advice although he is again told that he cannot yet exercise the right. After another hour, he admits to supplying Ecstasy. The interviews are tape recorded. He is then charged with supplying Ecstasy.

Toby now says that he only confessed because he thought he had to in order to get home.

Advise Toby as to any means of redress available to him.

Answer plan

This question is fairly demanding and quite tricky, since it covers the problem of apparently voluntary compliance with police requests and the particular difficulties created when the police are dealing with a mentally disordered person. The most straightforward approach is probably to consider the legality of the police conduct at every point. Once this has been done, the applicability of the possible forms of redress in respect of each possible breach can be considered. As special problems arise in respect of each, they should be looked at separately. It should be noted that the examinee is merely asked to 'advise Toby as to any means of redress'; therefore, all relevant possibilities should be discussed. It is important to remember to consider whether adverse inferences are likely to be drawn at trial from Toby's silence under ss 34 and 36 of the Criminal Justice and Public Order Act 1994, as amended.

Essentially, the following issues should be considered:

- the legality of the search under s 23(2) of the Misuse of Drugs Act 1971 and Code A of the Police and Criminal Evidence Act (PACE) 1984 (2006);

- is this a voluntary detention or an arrest under s 24 of PACE? – legality of the arrest?;

- access to legal advice under s 58 of PACE – exceptions under s 58(8) – the legality of the refusal of advice;

- the failure to ensure that an appropriate adult was present during the interview as required under s 11.15 Code C and Annex E;

- exclusion of evidence under ss 76 and 78 of PACE – relevance of ss 34 and 36 of the Criminal Justice and Public Order Act 1994; Art 6 of the Convention under the HRA; *Khan v UK* (2000);

- inferences to be drawn at trial from Toby's silence under s 34 of the Criminal Justice and Public Order Act 1994; relevance of ss 34(2A) and 36; Art 6 of the Convention under HRA; *Murray v UK* (1996);

- relevant tortious remedies;

- police complaints and disciplinary action.

Answer

The legality of the police conduct in this instance will be considered first; any possible forms of redress open to Toby will then be examined. In both instances, the impact of the Human Rights Act (HRA) 1998 will be taken into account.

The first contact between the police officers and Toby appears to be of a voluntary nature: the officers are entitled to ask questions; equally, Toby can refuse to answer them (*Rice v Connolly* (1966)). No adverse inference can be drawn from his silence at this point since he is not under caution – s 34(1)(A) of the Criminal Justice and Public Order Act (he has also not had therefore had any warning that he should seek an opportunity of having legal advice (s 34(2A)).

When Toby is asked to turn out his pockets, this appears to be a request. He cannot be subject to a voluntary search under s 1.5 Code A (2006). Thus, the search should not have taken place unless the police officers can show reasonable suspicion as the basis for the exercise of the power. In order to do so, it must be shown that the police officers complied with the provisions of s 23(2) of the Misuse of Drugs Act 1971 and of Code A. Under s 23(2), a police officer may search for controlled drugs if he has reasonable grounds for believing that he will find such articles. The necessary reasonable suspicion is defined in s 2.2 and 2.3 of Code A (2006). There must be some objective basis for it, which might include various objective factors, including the time and place and the behaviour of the person concerned. In the instant situation, the lateness of the hour might give rise to some suspicion, but it is apparent that the suspicion does not relate specifically enough to the possibility that Toby is in possession of drugs (*Black v DPP* (1995)). In *Slade* (1996) the suspect's demeanour gave rise to suspicion; here Toby has done nothing that might arouse suspicion since he is merely standing on a corner. His convictions cannot be viewed as relevant under s 2.2 Code A. Following this argument, no power to stop and search arises; the search itself and the seizure of the Ecstasy are therefore unlawful. It should further be noted that the procedural requirements of s 2 PACE are breached since the officers do not identify themselves or give the other required information (see *Osman v DPP* (1999), in which it was found that s 2 is mandatory). There are therefore two bases on which to find that the search is unlawful.

The request made to come to the police station appears to assume that Toby will come on a voluntary basis; however, it might be argued that if Toby is deemed incapable of giving consent to a stop and search, he cannot be viewed as capable of consenting to a voluntary detention. He has a history of being mentally disordered and, as the police know him, they may be aware of this fact (see s 1.4 Code C, below). Even if they are not aware that he has a specific mental disorder, they may recognise him as a person incapable of giving an informed consent to come to the station. When he is cautioned he must also be told that he is free to leave if he is not under arrest (s 3.21 Code C). It is not clear that this is done. Arguably, since the police must abide by Art 5 of the Convention under s 6 of the HRA, the better view is that he has not given a true consent to the detention, on the ground that where there is a doubt as to consent to a deprivation of liberty, a strict view should be taken giving the emphasis to the primary right (*Murray v UK* (1994)).

Again, the demands of Art 5(1) would favour this view. If this assumption is correct, it is necessary to consider whether a power to arrest arises. Toby is presumably arrested for possessing Ecstasy, an offence arising under s 5(3) of the Misuse of Drugs Act 1971. In order to arrest under s 24 PACE, it is necessary to show that Andy and Beryl had reasonable grounds for suspecting that Toby was in possession of the Ecstasy. Clearly, this is the case. The Ecstasy is discovered during the course of an illegal stop and search. It may appear strange that an illegal stop and search could provide the reasonable suspicion necessary to found a lawful arrest. However, nothing in PACE provides that it cannot do so. Nevertheless, even assuming that reasonable suspicion is present, the 'arrest' (if it may be characterised as such) is clearly unlawful due to the failure to state the fact of the arrest and the reason for it as required under s 28 of PACE and Art 5(2) of the Convention (see *Wilson v Chief Constable of Lancashire Constab (2000)*).

At the police station, Toby is not afforded access to legal advice. Delay in affording such access will be lawful only if it is the case that one of the contingencies envisaged under s 58(8) will arise if a solicitor is contacted. In this instance, the police will wish to rely on the exception under s 58(8)(b), allowing delay where contacting the solicitor will lead to the alerting of others suspected of the offence. Leaving aside the lack of any substantial evidence that others are involved at all, it will be necessary for the police to show, following *Samuel* (1988), that some quality about the particular solicitor in question could found a reasonable belief that he/she would bring about one of the contingencies envisaged if contacted. There is nothing to suggest that the police officers have any basis for this belief, especially as Toby has not specified the solicitor he wishes to contact. He may well wish to contact the duty solicitor. A further condition for the operation of s 58(8) is that Toby is being detained in respect of a serious arrestable offence. He is in detention at this point in respect of possession of Ecstasy. The concept of an arrestable offence under s 24 was abolished in 2005 when PACE was amended, so s 58(8) now covers indictable offences. So as supplying cannabis is an indictable offence, this condition is fulfilled. However, the lack of any basis for the necessary reasonable belief under s 58(8) means that there has been a breach of s 58. This strict approach to s 58 is supported by *Samuel* (1988) and by the approach of the European Court of Human Rights to the right of access to legal advice under Art 6. It has placed considerable importance on the right in cases such as *Murray (John) v UK* (1996) and *Averill v UK* (2000). It has held that delay in access where the defendant faces the possibility that adverse inferences may be drawn from silence is likely to amount to a breach of Art 6 of the Convention. That strict approach should be followed under the HRA.

Since Toby is mentally disordered, he should not have been interviewed except in the presence of an 'appropriate adult' as required under para 11.15 of Code C. Under s 1.4 Code C if an officer has any suspicion that a person may be mentally disordered or mentally vulnerable then he should be treated as such for the purposes of the Code (see also Annex E). Therefore, a further breach of PACE has occurred, unless it could be argued that the officers were not aware of his disorder; if so, following *Raymond Maurice Clarke* (1989), no breach of the Code provision occurred. The behaviour of Andy suggests, however, that the officers were aware of Toby's condition.[1]

Having identified a series of breaches of PACE and the Codes on the part of the police, it will now be necessary to consider any redress available to Toby in respect of them.[2] The first such act was the unlawful seizure of the Ecstasy. The appropriate cause of action in this instance will be trespass to goods; damages will, however, be minimal.

Will the Ecstasy be excluded from evidence under s 78? According to the analysis above, the stop and search was unlawful. It would be possible to argue, following *Edward Fennelly* (1989), that the products of the search should be excluded from evidence on the basis that there was no power to search in the circumstances. According to *Thomas* (1990) and *Effick* (1992), however, physical evidence will be excluded only if obtained with deliberate illegality; the pre-PACE ruling of the House of Lords in *Fox* (1986) would also lend support to this contention. Following the decision of the House of Lords in *Khan* (1997), evidence other than involuntary confessions obtained improperly is nevertheless admissible, subject to a narrow discretion to exclude it. The House of Lords took Art 6 of the Convention into account in reaching this conclusion. They found that Art 6 does not require that evidence should be automatically excluded where there has been impropriety in obtaining it, basing this finding on *Schenk v Switzerland* (1988). In *Khan* itself, it was found that the trial judge had properly exercised his discretion to include the improperly obtained evidence under s 78. This position has been unaffected by the reception of Art 6 into domestic law under the HRA (*AG's Reference (No 3 of 1999)* (2001) and *Loosely* (2001)) on the basis that the admission or exclusion of evidence is largely a matter for the national courts. The courts have therefore taken the view that the position that has developed under s 78 regarding exclusion of non-confession evidence need not be modified. It may be concluded that the Ecstasy would not be excluded from evidence.

Toby could make a complaint under the provisions of the Police Reform Act 2002 in respect of the illegal seizure of the Ecstasy since it can be characterised as resulting from an unlawful search in breach of s 23(2) of the Misuse of Drugs Act 1971 and of s 2 PACE and Code A.

Assuming that the arrest was unlawful (which cannot be determined with certainty), Toby could bring an action for false imprisonment for the whole period of his detention. There is also the alternative possibility of taking action under s 7(1)(a) of the HRA 1998 based on the infringement of his rights under Art 5 of the Convention, but since the tort action is available this is unnecessary. A further option might be to make a complaint in respect of the failure to observe the provisions of s 28 of PACE.

Can a reasonable argument be advanced that the admissions made by Toby will be excluded from evidence under s 76? Following *Alladice and Hughes* (1988), unless it can be shown that the custody officer acted in bad faith in failing to allow Toby access to a solicitor, it seems that s 76(2)(a) will not apply. However, following *Delaney* (1989), which was concerned with the operation of s 76(2)(b), if the defendant was in some particularly difficult or vulnerable position, the breach of PACE may be of special significance. Toby may be said to be in such a position due to the fact that he is mentally disordered. On this basis, it seems that s 76(2)(b) may be invoked to exclude the admissions from evidence.

The admissions may also be excluded from evidence under s 78, on the basis that the police breached s 58. If so, following *Samuel* (1988) and *Alladice* (1988), it must be shown that the breach of s 58 was causally related to the admissions made in the second interview. It may be that Toby would have made admissions had he had advice. The adviser might have considered that he should make admissions, since a failure to account for the Ecstasy would be commented on adversely in court under s 36 of the Criminal Justice and Public Order Act 1994. On the other hand, the adviser might have considered that this risk should be taken, especially as it could probably be established that the wrong caution had been used; the correct caution is in Annex C para 2 and the adviser might have been aware of this. This seems the stronger argument, bearing in mind Toby's mental disorder. It appears that Toby may have needed such advice. This argument failed in *Dunford* (1990) and *Alladice* (1988) on the basis that the appellants in those cases were experienced criminals, aware of their rights. It appears that Toby did remain silent for some time; possibly, therefore, he would have made the admissions in any event. As he has convictions, he will be aware of police procedures and know that he can keep silent. It might be argued that access to legal advice would have added nothing to his understanding of the situation. On the other hand, given his mental condition, it is unlikely that he would fully understand the implications of silence; he was obviously more vulnerable than the appellant in *Dunford*. On this analysis, the requisite causal relationship exists and the admissions may also be excluded from evidence under s 78. This approach is given additional weight by the importance attached to access to legal advice by the European Court in cases such as *Murray (John) v UK* (1996) and *Averill v UK* (2000). Under ss 6 and 2 of the HRA 1998, those decisions need to be taken into account in considering whether the evidence should be excluded; they would be likely to tip the balance in favour of exclusion.

It has further been argued that a breach of s 11.15 of Code C occurred, in that Toby was interviewed, although no appropriate adult was present.[3] Following DPP v *Blake* (1989), the judge would therefore be likely to use his discretion to exclude the interview under s 78 on the basis that it may be unreliable or because Toby would not have made the admissions at all had the adult been present.[4]

The breach of s 58 could also be the subject of a complaint, as could the breach of s 11.15 of Code C.

It follows from the above analysis that the first interview, which may be said to be causally related to the breach of s 6.6 Code C and s 58, may be excluded from evidence under s 78, since had Toby had legal advice, he might *not* have decided to remain silent. The solicitor, weighing up the situation, might well have decided that he should offer his explanation of the facts rather than risk an adverse inference being drawn at trial from a failure to do so. This would be in accordance with s 34 of the Criminal Justice and Public Order Act 1994, which provides that where a person fails to mention a fact which he subsequently relies on in his defence, adverse inferences can be drawn from such a failure. He has also failed to account for the presence of the Ecstasy. The solicitor might also have advised him to account for its presence since, under s 36 of the 1994 Act, an adverse inference can be drawn from a failure to so account. Exclusion of the first interview under s 78 would appear to accord with the duty of the court under s 6 of the HRA since the European Court of Human Rights has, as indicated above, held that delay in access where the defendant faces the possibility that adverse inferences may be drawn from silence is likely to amount to a breach of Art 6 of the Convention. Such a breach could be avoided by excluding the interview. On the other hand the courts, as indicated, are very reluctant to use the discretion under s 78 to exclude non-confession evidence (*Khan*).

Since there is a strong possibility that the interview will not be excluded cannot be ruled out, it must be considered whether adverse inferences would be likely to be drawn from Toby's silence during it. Section 34(2A) of the Criminal Justice and Public Order Act 1994, introduced in order to satisfy Art 6 of the Convention under the HRA, applies (see *Murray v UK*). Under s 34(2A), inferences cannot be drawn if the defendant has not had the opportunity of having legal advice. This appears to apply to Toby, especially as he has been unlawfully denied the opportunity, as argued above. Thus, no adverse inferences can be drawn.

▌NOTES

1   This point is strengthened by the provisions of Note 11B of Code C, in respect of the likelihood that mentally disordered persons might make an unreliable confession.

2   It could be noted that under s 67(10) of PACE, no civil liability can arise from a breach of the Codes.

3   The breach of para 11.14 could also be considered under s 76 but, if so, the argument would not differ from that in respect of the breach of s 58. Note that since Toby is mentally disordered, as opposed to mentally handicapped, the special provisions of s 77 in respect of the mentally handicapped do not apply. Nevertheless, as in *Delaney*, courts will be particularly vigilant when determining whether to exclude confessions of the mentally disordered under either s 76 or s 78. The ruling in *MacKenzie* (1993) supports this point.

4   It could be pointed out that if the police deliberately failed to afford Toby access to an appropriate adult, s 76(2)(a) might be invoked to exclude the admissions; alternatively (following *Alladice* (1988)), s 78 would be invoked without needing to discuss the question of reliability or of the requisite causal relationship between the breach and the confession.

Question 44

It is now over 20 years since the Police and Criminal Evidence Act 1984 (PACE) was enacted. PACE and the Codes of Practice made under it were supposed to strike a fair balance between increased police powers and greater safeguards for the suspect. Taking the effect of the Human Rights Act 1998, amendations to PACE and, in 2006, to the Codes, ss 34–37 Criminal Justice and Public Order Act 1994, and relevant aspects of the Police Reform Act 2002, into account, how far would it be fair to say that such a balance is still evident?

Answer plan

This is a reasonably straightforward essay question which is commonly set on PACE. It is clearly much more wide ranging than the one that follows it and therefore needs care in planning in order to cover provisions relating to the key stages in the investigation. Note that it does not ask you to comment on the treatment of terrorist suspects in the pre-trial investigation governed by the Terrorism Act 2000. It is clearly necessary to be selective in your answer. Essentially, the following points should be considered, mentioning relevant case law, including post-HRA cases at the various points:

- the arrest provision under s 24 of PACE , as amended in 2005; Art 5 of the Convention; Code G (2006);
- the stop and search provision under s 1 PACE and Code of Practice A (2006) and the efficacy of the procedural safeguards; s 60 of the Criminal Justice and Public Order Act 1994;
- the detention provisions under Pt IV PACE; Art 5 of the Convention;
- the safeguards for interviews under Pt V and Codes C and E (2006) – relevance of ss 34–37 under the Criminal Justice and Public Order Act 1994, as amended; Art 6 of the Convention under the HRA;
- a brief overview of the redress available for breaches of these provisions – tortious remedies, the police complaints mechanism (Police Reform Act 2002), exclusion of evidence; the impact of the Human Rights Act (HRA) 1998, especially Art 6 of the Convention.

Answer

It will be argued that although the Police and Criminal Evidence Act (PACE) 1984 and the Codes of Practice contain provisions capable of achieving a reasonable balance between increasing the power of the police to detain and question and providing safeguards for the suspect, that balance is not maintained in practice. Moreover it has changed significantly since PACE came into force. PACE has been amended, most significantly by s 110 of the Serious and Organised Crime Act 2005; the Codes have gone through a number of revisions, most recently in 2006;

new Codes have been introduced, including new Code G, the Arrest Code. Other provisions, including in particular s 34 Criminal Justice and Public Order Act 1994, and the Police Reform Act 2002, have been introduced. The safeguards in the Codes have been increased, but those in PACE itself have diminished while the powers have increased. The curtailing of the right to silence had a significant impact on the balance that was originally created under PACE. It is argued that the balance originally struck is no longer being maintained. This failure arguably arises partly due to the changes that have occurred since 1984, partly because many of the safeguards can be evaded quite readily, and partly because there is no effective sanction available for their breach. It will further be contended that while the relevant Articles of the Convention, afforded further effect in domestic law under the Human Rights Act (HRA), are likely to have some impact in encouraging adherence to the rules intended to secure suspects' rights, they will not have a radical effect, especially in terms of encouraging the exclusion of evidence where the rules have not been adhered to. Certain key provisions will be selected in order to illustrate this argument.

Before the inception of PACE, the police had no general and clear powers of arrest, stop and search or entry to premises. They wanted such powers put on a clear statutory basis, so that they could exercise them where they felt it was their duty to do so, without laying themselves open to the possibility of a civil action. In s 1, a general power to stop and search persons is conferred on the police if reasonable suspicion arises that stolen goods or prohibited articles may be found. This general power is balanced in two ways. First, the concept of reasonable suspicion, which is defined in s 2 of Code A (2006), appears to allow it to be exercised only when quite a high level of suspicion exists. However, the level of reasonable suspicion needed is not very high in practice (see *Slade* (1996)). Second, the police must give the person to be searched certain information, including the object of the search and the name of the police station to which the officer in question is attached. However, until recently these safeguards could be evaded if the search is made on an apparently voluntary basis, although the restriction on voluntary searches under Code A s 1.5, introduced in 2003 and continued in the 2006 revision, goes much of the way towards addressing this problem.[1]

It now appears unlikely that the HRA will tend to encourage a stricter adherence to the rules providing safeguards for suspects who are stopped and searched. The police are bound under s 6 of the HRA to adhere to the Convention requirements and, under s 3 of the HRA, PACE and other relevant provisions must be interpreted compatibly with those requirements if it is possible to do so. Art 5, contained in Sched 1 to the HRA, provides a guarantee of liberty and security of person. It appeared until recently that the short period of detention represented by a stop and search might be sufficient to constitute a deprivation of liberty (*X v Austria* (1979)). Deprivation of liberty can occur only on a basis of law and in certain specified circumstances, including, under Art 5(1)(b), the detention of a person in order to secure the fulfillment of any obligation prescribed by law and, under Art 5(1)(c), the 'lawful detention of a person effected for the purpose of bringing him before the competent legal authority on reasonable suspicion of having committed an offence'. The House of Lords recently decided in *Gillan* (2006) that Art 5(1) does not cover temporary detention for the purposes of a search; even if it did it would be likely in most situations that Art 5(1)(b) would apply. Art 5(1)(b) provides exceptions to a guarantee of a fundamental right, and therefore should not be interpreted broadly; Art 5 could have aided in requiring a restrictive approach to the use of the stop and search provisions. However *Gillan* appears to have closed off this possibility for the time being.[2]

Originally the police also acquired a general power of arrest under s 25. This power did not merely allow an officer to arrest for any offence so long as reasonable suspicion can be shown. Such a power would probably have been viewed as too draconian in 1984. It was balanced by what were known as the general arrest conditions which also had to be fulfilled. One of those conditions (s 25(3)(c)) consisted of a failure to furnish a satisfactory name or address, so that the service of a summons later on would be impracticable. The others concerned the immediate need to remove the suspect from the street. The inclusion of those provisions implied that the infringement of civil liberties represented by an arrest should be resorted to only where no alternative exists. However, s 25 was repealed in 2005 by s 110 Serious and Organised Crime Act 2005 and s 24 of PACE was amended, making the arrest powers available much broader. Under s 24 a person can be arrested on reasonable suspicion of having committed or being about to commit an offence – any offence. The arrest conditions originally under s 25 also have to be satisfied under s 24 but, crucially, two new ones have been added. The police also need to show that the arrest is needed to allow the prompt and effective investigation of the suspected offence in question or to prevent prosecution of the offence from being hindered by the suspect's disappearance (s 24(5)(e) and (f)). It is highly probable that one of these conditions will be found to be satisfied in relation to most arrests. Thus the police now have the broad power of arrest that would have been viewed as too draconian had it been introduced in 1984. Some attempt at balancing this power with increased safeguards for arrestees was made by the introduction of Code G, the arrest Code, in 2006. For example, s 1.3 Code G demands that the arrest be proportionate to the objectives of the investigation. Section 1 also reminds police that arrest should not be resorted to readily; it should only be used if other means of achieving the objectives of the investigation are not feasible. However, breach of Code G does not give rise to liability and it is possible that its safeguards will have little impact on street policing.

The concept of reasonable suspicion, which should ensure that the arrest takes place at quite a late stage in the investigation, limits the use of the s 24 power, although the concept tends to be flexibly interpreted. Art 5, as received into domestic law under the HRA, may eventually have some impact on the interpretation of the concept. This can be found if the leading post-PACE case on the meaning of the concept, *Castorina v Chief Constable of Surrey* (1988), is compared with the findings of the Strasbourg Court in *Fox, Campbell and Hartley v UK* (1990).

In *Castorina*, the grounds for suspicion regarding a burglary of a firm were that the suspect was a former employee who appeared to have a grudge and the burglary appeared to be an 'inside job'. However, the suspect was not considered by the victim to be likely to commit burglary and she had no criminal record. Nevertheless, the court found that reasonable suspicion had been established. In *Fox, Campbell and Hartley v UK* (1990), the applicants had been arrested in accordance with s 11 of the Northern Ireland (Emergency Provisions) Act 1978, which required only suspicion, not reasonable suspicion. The only evidence put forward by the government for the presence of reasonable suspicion was that the applicants had convictions for terrorist offences and that when arrested, they were asked about particular terrorist acts. The government said that further evidence could not be disclosed for fear of endangering life. The Court found that although allowance could be made for the difficulties of gathering evidence in an emergency situation, reasonable suspicion which arises from facts or information which would satisfy an objective observer that the person concerned may have committed the offence had not been established. The arrests in question could not, therefore, be justified. It is debatable whether the UK courts are in general applying a test of reasonable suspicion under PACE or other provisions for arrest which reaches the standards which the European Court had in mind, especially where terrorism is not in question. The departure which the HRA brings about is to encourage stricter judicial scrutiny of decisions to arrest.

Prior to PACE, the police had no clear power to hold a person for questioning. Such a power was put on a clear statutory basis under s 41, and it was made clear under s 37(2) that the purpose of the detention is to obtain a confession. The detention can be for up to 24 hours. In the case of a person in police custody for a serious arrestable offence (defined in s 116), it can extend to 36 hours with the permission of a police officer of the rank of superintendent or above, and may extend to 96 hours under s 44 after an application to a magistrates' court. These are very significant new powers. However, they are supposed to be balanced by all the safeguards created by Pt V of PACE and by Codes C and E. The most important safeguards available inside the police station include contemporaneous recording under s 11.7 of Code C, tape recording under s 3 of Code E, the ability to read over, verify and sign the notes of the interview as a correct record under s 11.9 and 11 Code C, notification of the right to legal advice under s 58 and s 3.1 of Code C, the option of having the adviser present under s 6.6 of Code C and, where appropriate, the presence of an appropriate adult under s 11.15 of Code C.[3]

However, there are methods of avoiding these safeguards without actually breaking the rules. For example, in *Hughes* (1988), the detainee, disappointed of obtaining advice from his own solicitor, inquired about the duty solicitor scheme, but was erroneously informed (but apparently in good faith) that no solicitor was available. Under this misapprehension, he gave consent to be interviewed and the Court of Appeal took the view that his consent was not thereby vitiated.

Further, access to legal advice and tape recording can be evaded and rendered worthless if the suspect is interviewed outside the police station. There has been an attempt to address the problem of such evasion: under s 11.1 Code C as revised, such interviewing can no longer occur unless the decision to arrest the person being interviewed has not been taken or the exchanges do not amount to 'the questioning of a person regarding his involvement or suspected involvement in a criminal offence or offences' (s 11.1 A Code C), or unless urgent interviewing is necessary to prevent various contingencies arising. This provision may have encouraged the police to take suspects to the police station to be questioned, where an arrest was likely to occur in any event, but it is unclear that the number of suspects questioned in the street has dropped significantly and in any event, the number and width of the express or implied exceptions to the prohibition are likely to have lessened its impact.

The right of access to legal advice was intended to bolster the right to silence. However, that right, originally included in the PACE scheme under since it was reflected in the Code C caution, was severely curtailed by ss 34–37 of the CJPOA 1994, thereby disturbing the 'balance' which was originally created. However, s 34(2A) was inserted into the CJPOA 1994 by s 58 of the Youth Justice and Criminal Evidence Act 1999. The amendments provide that if the defendant was at an authorised place of detention and had not had an opportunity of consulting a solicitor at the time of the failure to mention the fact in question, inferences cannot be drawn. This is a very significant change to the interviewing scheme, which was introduced as a direct response to the findings of the European Court of Human Rights in *Murray v UK* (1996). Had this change not been made, ss 34–37 might have been found to be incompatible with Art 6 under s 4 of the HRA.

However, it need not be assumed, conversely, that Art 6 will be satisfied where a defendant has access to legal advice before being questioned under caution. Cases such as *Condron* (1997) or *Bowden* (1999), where the defendants had had legal advice and had acted on it in remaining silent, should be considered on their particular facts, in relation to the Art 6 requirements. Such cases differ from *Murray* on the issue of the relationship between silence and legal advice. In *Condron*, the defendants acted on legal advice in refusing to answer questions; in *Murray*, a breach of Art 6(1) was found on the basis of inference-drawing in the absence of legal advice (not on the basis of inference-drawing *per se*). In *Condron*, the fact of having legal advice was not to the defendants' advantage, possibly the reverse, since in a sense they may have been misled into remaining silent. It is arguable that allowing adverse inferences to be drawn in that context – where the innocent explanation for silence was that it was on legal advice – could in certain circumstances be viewed as a breach of Art 6(1). For example, this might be argued where the adviser had failed to point out that adverse inferences might be drawn despite the advice and/or where the defendant could not be expected – due to his low intelligence, youth or other vulnerability – to decide to speak despite the advice. To hold otherwise might be viewed as undermining the value attached in *Murray* to granting access to legal advice where adverse inferences would be drawn from silence. The Court of Human Rights has found in *Beckles v UK* (2003) that a jury should not be advised to draw adverse inferences if they take the view that the defendant remained silent due to the legal advice. The Court of Appeal however, in *R v Beckles* (2004), has found that that a jury should be so advised if they take the view that the defendant *reasonably* remained silent due to the legal advice. Thus the domestic court appears to be taking a view of Art 6 that renders it less protective domestically than it is internationally.

It may appear that throughout PACE, a reasonable balance was originally struck between safeguards and increased police powers. However, as has been pointed out, the safeguards may be evaded, even though the powers may of course be used to the full. The HRA provides opportunities, as indicated, of seeking to restore the balance originally created by encouraging adherence to the rules in a Convention-compliant way. However, where evasion or breach of the safeguards has occurred, thereby destroying the balance, there will not always be an effective remedy available which could go some way towards restoring it. This may continue to be the case despite the inception of the HRA.

Damages will be available at common law in respect of some breaches of PACE. For example, if a police officer arrests a citizen where no reasonable suspicion arises under s 24 of PACE, an action for false imprisonment arises. Equally, such a remedy would be available if the provisions governing time limits on detention were breached.[4]

However, tortious remedies are inapplicable to the provisions of the Codes under s 67(10) and seem to be inapplicable to the most significant statutory interviewing provision, the entitlement to legal advice. There is no tort of denial of access to legal advice: the only possible tortious action is for breach of statutory duty. Whether this tort lies is a question of policy in relation to any particular statutory provision, and so the application of this remedy was purely conjectural.[5] Under s 7(1)(a) of the HRA 1998, it is possible to bring an action against the police for breach of the Convention rights. However, it is probable that this remedy is not available in relation to breaches of Art 6 (which would cover the legal advice scheme), on the basis that Art 6 is concerned with the trial as a whole and therefore potential breaches of it should be addressed within the trial itself.

The police complaints mechanism covers any breaches of PACE, including breaches of the Codes under s 67(8), but it is generally agreed that it is defective as a means of redress. It does not allow for compensation to the victim or for the victim to attend any disciplinary proceedings. In any event, most complaints do not result in disciplinary proceedings and it appears that none have been brought in respect of breaches of the Codes. The suspect concerned might, in many instances, be unaware that a breach of the Codes had occurred, and while theoretically another officer could make a complaint leading to disciplinary proceedings for such a breach, in practice, this appears to be highly unlikely. Furthermore, despite the involvement (albeit limited) of the Independent Police Complaints Commission, introduced by the Police Reform Act 2002, with a view to creating a stronger independent element in the system, the complaints procedure is still largely administered by the police themselves. The police disciplinary system has been found to provide an insufficient remedy for Convention breaches, under Art 13, in *Khan v UK* (2000), which criticised both its lack of independence and its lack of real remedies. The HRA 1998 ss 7 and 8 has gone some way towards redressing this problem by allowing Convention-related issues, including complaints of breaches of Arts 5 and 8 by the police, to be raised in ordinary courts and to receive the normal range of remedies.

The context in which many breaches of PACE have been considered is that of exclusion of evidence. Confessions may be excluded under s 76 if obtained by oppression or in circumstances conducive to unreliability. Any evidence may be excluded under s 78 if its admission would be likely to render the trial unfair. It must be borne in mind that the PACE mechanism for exclusion of evidence provides a means of redress for such breaches only in one circumstance – that the case is pursued to trial and the defendant pleads not guilty. In this one instance, they can be of great value, in that the defendant may be placed in the position he would have been in had the breach not occurred, and the police may seem to be 'punished' for their non-compliance with the rules by being prevented from profiting from their own breach. In this sense, exclusion of evidence does provide an effective means of redress. For example, in *Canale* (1990), the police failed to record an interview contemporaneously in breach of para 11.3 of Code C; it was excluded as possibly unreliable under s 78. In *Samuel* (1988), the police unlawfully denied the appellant access to legal advice; the court took the view that if a breach of s 58 had taken place which was causally linked to the confession, s 78 should be invoked. It could be said that in *Samuel*, the court succeeded in restoring the balance between the police power to detain and question, which had been used fully in the case, and the safeguards that the detainee should have had, in the sense that the outcome was what it would have been had the proper safeguards been in place. However, the provisions of ss 34–37 of the CJPOA 1994, reflected in the caution introduced under the 1995 revision of Code C, and continued in the 2006 version (unless the detainee has had no 'opportunity' to have legal advice in which case the 'old' caution should be used) make it less likely that advisers will advise silence, since adverse inferences may be drawn at trial from silence. Thus, it may be more difficult to establish the causal relationship in question relying on the method used in *Samuel*. Section 78 may become less effective as a means of maintaining the balance between police powers and suspects' rights.

Theoretically, the *Samuel* argument as to the causal relationship between an impropriety and a confession could be applied to non-confession evidence, but in practice, it appears that it will not be. According to *Thomas* (1990) and *Effick* (1992), physical evidence will be excluded only if obtained with deliberate illegality. Following the decision of the House of Lords in *Khan* (1997), evidence other than involuntary confessions obtained improperly is nevertheless admissible, subject to a narrow discretion to exclude it. The House of Lords took Art 6 of the Convention into account in reaching this conclusion. They found that Art 6 does not require that evidence should be automatically excluded where there has been impropriety in obtaining it, basing this finding on *Schenk v Switzerland* (1988). In *Khan* itself, it was found that the trial judge had properly exercised his discretion to include the improperly obtained evidence under s 78. This position has been unaffected by the reception of Art 6 into domestic law under the HRA (*AG's Reference (No 3 of 1999)* (2001), *Loosely* (2001)) on the basis that the assessment of evidence is largely a matter for the national courts. The courts have therefore taken the view that the position that has developed under s 78 regarding exclusion of non-confession evidence need not be modified under the HRA.[6]

Thus, although exclusion of evidence can provide a means of redress when police have not complied with one of the PACE safeguards, it is likely to be unavailable where the evidence obtained due to the breach is non-confession evidence. It may be unavailable in any event: first, even where a clear breach of PACE has occurred, the evidence may nevertheless be admissible; second, exclusion of evidence is irrelevant to the majority of defendants who plead guilty. Thus, the police had an incentive to break the rules by, for example, refusing a request for legal advice in the hope of obtaining admissions and a guilty plea. If, in such circumstances, a defendant did plead guilty, he had suffered denial of a fundamental right with no hope of redress apart from that offered by a complaint. Now, however, the HRA 1998 enables any person who considers that his arrest or trial have been unfair due to the behaviour of the police to argue breaches of, *inter alia*, Art 5 or 6, and *Khan* (2000) makes it clear that an effect on the fairness of proceedings, viewed as a whole, can create a breach of Art 6. Thus, courts are able to monitor and sanction police powers to a somewhat greater extent, and the remedies for most PACE breaches have been expanded. However, the relevant decisions so far under the HRA do not indicate that the HRA is having or is likely to have a significant impact in this context. This is particularly the case in relation to the decisions in *Gillan* (2006) and *Beckles* (2004), although the earlier decisions in *Osman* (1999) (in relation to adopting a strict view of the identification requirement of s 2 PACE) and *R v Chief Constable of Kent* (2000) (demanding that to accord with Article 5 reviews of detention should be in person, not by video link; the decision was reversed by s 73 Criminal Justice and Police Act 2001) suggested otherwise.

In conclusion, it appears that the balance between safeguards and police powers originally struck is not being maintained, due to the post-PACE changes, including in particular the 2005 change to the arrest power, and the ease with which certain of the domestic safeguards may be evaded or ignored. Clearly, if safeguards are not observed, the justification for increasing police powers to stop, arrest, search premises, detain and question is lost. It is possible that courts will use the HRA and the Convention to create stronger protection in these areas for individual rights, thus restoring the balance that has been lost, but so far no pattern of so doing is apparent in post-HRA decisions, such as *Gillan*.

▌NOTES

1 The problem of voluntary searches and provision for them could be considered in more detail. Prior to 2003 Note for Guidance 1E provided that certain persons – juveniles, the mentally handicapped or mentally disordered and any person who appears incapable of giving an informed consent – should not be subject to a voluntary search at all. However, this attempt to deal with the problem was recognised as inadequate and led to the prohibition on voluntary searches in 2003, now contained in s 1.5 Code A. There is however the problem that the Codes are of doubtful legal status since breach of a Code provision cannot give rise to civil liability. The courts should however treat a stop and search not based on reasonable suspicion as effecting a breach of s 1 PACE, rather than of s 1.5 Code A. It should also be pointed out that s 1 of PACE may be undermined in any event by s 60 of the Criminal Justice and Public Order Act 1994, which in certain circumstances allows stop and search without reasonable suspicion if authorisation has been given by a superintendent.

2 The exercise of the powers under s 60 of the Criminal Justice and Public Order Act (CJPOA) 1994 do not appear to need to fall within Art 5(1)(b) since, following *Gillan*, it appears that they do not engage Art 5. However, in appropriate cases, bearing in mind the recent evidence of a police tendency to show racial bias in decisions to stop and search, violation of Art 5(1)(b) or (c) might be found when read with the Art 14 guarantee of freedom from discrimination in the enjoyment of the Convention rights on the basis of an extended ambit for Art 5 where Art 14 is involved (see *Ghaidan v Mendoza* (2004)). This possibility may be of less significance given the amendments made to the Race Relations Act 1976 in 2000, allowing claimants to bring actions against the police in respect of direct or indirect discrimination in policing decisions, including decisions to stop and search. However, a defendant would also have the option of raising an Art 5 and 14 argument during the criminal process. The use of force in order to carry out a stop and search is permitted under s 117 of PACE, but under Art 3, the use of force must be strictly in proportion to the conduct of the detainee. Under it, the use of extreme force is permissible if necessitated by the conduct of the detainee, but if the use of such force causes death, it would appear to breach Art 2, which permits the use of lethal force to 'effect an arrest', not to effect a detention short of arrest.

3 It could be mentioned that a similar caution was shown in the introduction of video identification as an alternative to a parade or a group identification; it

was accompanied by various safeguards: under s 2.15 of Code D, the suspect must be reminded that free legal advice is available before taking part in the identification procedure and, under the new para 2.16, the identification procedure and the consequences if consent to taking part is not forthcoming must be explained in a written notice which the suspect must be given reasonable time to read.

4 Theoretically, use of a false imprisonment claim might be available; an argument could be advanced at this point that where gross breaches of the questioning provisions had taken place, such as interviewing a person unlawfully held incommunicado, a detention in itself lawful might thereby be rendered unlawful. However, although the ruling in *Middleweek v Chief Constable of Merseyside* (1985) gave some encouragement to such argument, it now seems to be ruled out, due to the decision in *Weldon v Home Office* (1991) in the context of lawful detention in a prison. It seems likely, therefore, that access to legal advice will continue to be unaffected by the availability of tortious remedies.

5 The question of whether damages are available in respect of property unlawfully seized was considered in *Chief Constable of Lancashire ex p Parker and McGrath* (1993). It was argued on behalf of the police that s 22(2)(a) of PACE, which allows the retention of 'anything seized for the purposes of a criminal investigation', would be superfluous, unless denoting a general power to retain unlawfully seized material. It was held, however, that the sub-section could not bear the weight sought to be placed upon it: it was merely intended to give examples of matters falling within the general provision of s 22(1). Therefore, the police were not entitled to retain the material seized. This decision re-affirmed the need to retain the balance between safeguards for the subject of the search and the police power to search, which might have been disturbed had the various issues been resolved differently.

6 This important issue could be considered further. The first instance decision in *Edward Fennelly* (1989) could be mentioned, in which a failure to give the reason for a stop and search led to exclusion of the search, is not consistent with *Khan*. Furthermore, even if the principles developed under s 78 with respect to confession evidence could properly be applied to other evidence, *Edward Fennelly* would still be a doubtful decision, as no causal relationship could exist between the impropriety in question and the evidence obtained.

Question 45

'The Police and Criminal Evidence Act 1984 as amended, and its Codes, provide important safeguards for the suspect during interviews in the police station, but no adequate means of redress is available if the police do not comply with them.'

Discuss, taking the impact of the Human Rights Act 1998 into account.

Answer plan

This is a reasonably straightforward essay question which is quite often set on the Police and Criminal Evidence Act (PACE) 1984. It is important to take ss 34–37, as amended of the Criminal Justice and Public Order Act (CJPOA) 1994 into account and to bear in mind the changes consequent to Code C, as well as its revision in 2006. It should be noted that it is *only* concerned with the interviewing scheme and its applicability inside the police station. It is not concerned therefore with safeguards for stop and search, for example, or for informal interviews outside the police station. It is obviously important to take the Human Rights Act (HRA) 1998 fully into account in your answer, since it provides new possibilities of creating redress in relation to safeguards for police interviews.

Essentially, the following matters should be considered:

- the nature of the safeguards available under Pts IV and V of PACE and Codes of Practice C, E and F (2006); Article 6 under HRA;
- the curtailed right to silence under ss 34–37 of the CJPOA 1994, as amended;
- the relevant tortious remedies;
- the efficacy of the police complaints mechanism;
- the nature of the PACE scheme for exclusion of evidence; the relevance of ss 34–37 of the CJPOA 1994, as amended, to arguments that adverse inferences should not be draw from silence; Art 6 under HRA;
- the value of exclusion of evidence as a form of redress;
- the possibilities of invoking the HRA 1998 to improve the protection for suspects.

Answer

It is generally accepted that the safeguards for interviews introduced by PACE, particularly access to legal advice, video and tape recording, can reduce the likelihood that an interview will be unreliable. However, it will be argued that the forms of redress available in respect of breaches of these provisions are inadequate, either as a means of encouraging the police to comply with them or as a means of compensating the detainee if they do not. The Human Rights Act 1998 (HRA) allows for European Convention on Human Rights (the Convention) arguments to be raised in any proceedings under s 7(1)(b), and provides for a free-standing cause of action where a public authority has breached a Convention right, under s 7(1)(a); remedies are available under s 8. Obviously, the extent to which the HRA can affect adherence to the interviewing rules depends on the relationship between the rules and the Convention Articles. This issue will be considered below. In general, it will be contended that while the relevant Articles of the Convention, afforded further effect in domestic law under the HRA, are having some impact in encouraging adherence to the interviewing rules, they have not had a radical effect, especially in terms of encouraging the exclusion of evidence where the rules have not been adhered to.

The most important safeguards available inside the police station include contemporaneous recording under s 11.7 of Code C or tape recording under s 3 of Code E, the possibility of video recording under Code F, the ability to read over, verify and sign the notes of the interview as a correct record under ss 11.9 and 11.11 of Code C, notification of the right to access to legal advice (s 3.1 Code C) under s 58, the option of having the adviser present in the interview under s 6.6 and, where relevant, the presence of an appropriate adult under s 11.15. The right to silence, encapsulated in the old Code C caution, had been viewed as a valuable safeguard, but it has now been greatly curtailed by ss 34–37 of the CJPOA 1994, which provide that in certain circumstances, adverse inferences can be drawn from silence. These provisions were reflected in the current and much more complex caution introduced in the 1995 revision of Code C. No adverse inference can be drawn from silence unless the suspect is under caution (s 34(1)(A) of the CJPOA 1994) and he has had the opportunity of having legal advice (s 34(2A)). Section 34(2A), inserted by s 58 of the Youth Justice and Criminal Evidence Act 1999, is therefore a significant provision since it may tend to encourage adherence to the legal advice scheme. It was introduced to satisfy the demands of Art 6 of the Convention. The 2006 version of Code C reflects ss 34–37, but s 34(2A) is also reflected in that the caution introduced in 1995 still applies, but a restriction on drawing adverse inferences from silence is apparent and reflected in the caution in Annex C, para 2.

The interpretation given to these provisions by the courts has meant that the circumstances in which non-compliance with a provision will be lawful have been narrowed down. In particular, in *Samuel* (1988), the Court of Appeal had to consider s 58(8), which provides that access to legal advice may be delayed where, *inter alia*, allowing such access might alert others involved in the offence. It was determined that s 58(8) could not be fulfilled by an unsubstantiated assertion that this contingency would materialise if a solicitor was contacted. After this ruling, in order to fulfil s 58(8), the police must be able to demonstrate a reasonable belief in some particular quality of naïvety or corruption possessed by the solicitor in question.

Equally, the courts have not been willing to accept that compliance with PACE was impracticable even in informal situations. In *Absolam* (1988), the custody officer questioned the detainee in the heat of the moment, without first advising him of his right to legal advice. At first instance, it was determined that the detainee was only entitled to his right to consult a solicitor as soon as it was practicable under s 3.1 of Code C and, further, that the questions and answers did not constitute an interview; therefore, s 3.1 did not apply. The Court of Appeal, however, held that the questions and answers did not constitute a formal interview, but were nevertheless an interview within the purview of (then) para 6.3. Since the appellant's situation was precisely the type of situation in which the Code's provisions were most significant, there could be no question of waiving them. Paragraph 3.1 of Code C (as it was then) had been breached.

However, although the courts may be quick to find that a breach of PACE has occurred, this does not mean that redress will automatically be available to the detainee who has thereby been disadvantaged. What form of redress might such a detainee seek?

Tort damages will be available in respect of some breaches of PACE. For example, if a police officer arrests a citizen where no reasonable suspicion arises under s 24 of PACE, an action for false imprisonment will be available. Equally, such a remedy would be available if the Pt IV provisions governing time limits on detention were breached. However, tortious remedies are inapplicable to the provisions of the Codes under s 67(10) and may not be available in respect of the most significant statutory interviewing provision, the entitlement to legal advice. There is no tort of denial of access to legal advice: the only possible tortious action would be for breach of statutory duty. Whether such an action would lie is a question of policy in relation to any particular statutory provision.[1] At present, the application of this remedy must be purely conjectural. Theoretically, an action for false imprisonment might lie; an argument could be advanced that where gross breaches of the questioning provisions had taken place, such as interviewing a person unlawfully held incommunicado, a detention in itself lawful might thereby be rendered unlawful. However, although the ruling in *Middleweek v Chief Constable of Merseyside* (1985) gave some encouragement to such an argument, it now seems to be ruled out due to the decision in *Weldon v Office* (1991) in the context of lawful detention in a prison. It seems likely, therefore, that access to legal advice, like the rest of the safeguards for interviewing, will continue to be unaffected by the availability of the established tortious remedies. However, the HRA provides various possibilities of redress which may affect adherence to the safeguards.

Access to custodial legal advice can be viewed as an implied right under Art 6(1), where the detainee is aware that adverse inferences may be drawn from silence (*Murray v UK* (1996); *Averill v UK* (2000)). However, at present, it is very improbable that Art 6 can be viewed as providing free-standing rights. Breaches of Art 6 are addressed within the criminal process itself. The Strasbourg jurisprudence does not cover instances in which the pre-trial procedure is flawed in a manner which might be viewed, potentially, as infringing the Art 6(1) guarantee of a fair trial, but where no court action in fact occurs. However, given that certain of the rights, and in particular the implied right of access to custodial legal advice under Art 6(3)(c), clearly have value outside the trial context, an action based on s 7(1)(a) or on a breach of the statutory duty under s 58 of PACE, but raising Art 6 (3)(c) arguments under s 7(1)(b), might resolve this issue in favour of the complainant, domestically. Other Convention Articles may have some impact on police interviewing practices and techniques, and where those Articles are breached during detention and interviewing, a free-standing action will arise.

Where provisions of Arts 3, 8, 5 or 14 are coterminous with Code safeguards, liability to pay damages under s 8 HRA for breach of the Convention guarantees might provide the Code provisions with a form of indirect protection, as the more detailed embodiment of the Convention requirements. Certain aspects of the Convention guarantees, including aspects of the Art 3 requirements, have no domestic statutory basis but are recognised only in certain Code provisions. In the *Greek* case (1969), the conditions of detention were found to amount to inhuman treatment owing to inadequate food, sleeping arrangements, heating and sanitary facilities combined with overcrowding and inadequate provision for external contacts. It was also found that conduct which grossly humiliates may amount to degrading treatment contrary to Art 3. The cases of *Tomasi v France* (1993), *Tekin v Turkey* (1998), *Selmouni v France* (1999) and *McGlinchey v UK* (2003) make it clear that standards change over time; so what might be viewed as degrading treatment in the past might now be viewed as torture. Ill treatment that might not have been viewed as 'degrading' twenty years ago might now fall within Art 3. The Scottish case of *Napier v Scottish Ministers* (2004) accepted that a broader concept of Art 3 treatment should now be adopted, but *Wainwright v HO* (2003) suggested that the English judiciary has not accepted the expanded definition of Art 3 treatment evident at Strasbourg and in the *Napier* case.

Article 3 treatment may include racially discriminatory and, probably, sexually discriminatory questioning and treatment in detention (*East African Asians* cases (1973)). In *Lustig-Prean and Beckett v UK* (1999) and *Smith and Grady v UK* (2000), it was found that grossly humiliating, intrusive interrogation could, if of an extreme and prolonged nature, amount to a breach of Art 3. Possibly, it could also fall within Art 8. Where discrimination is a factor, Art 14 would also be engaged. The creation of new tortious liability indirectly protective of the Code provisions but also creating new safeguards for interviewing under the HRA would be a very significant matter, since it might lead to a regulation of police interviewing practices and techniques which has been largely absent from UK law.

The police complaints mechanism covers any breaches of PACE, including breaches of the Codes under s 67(8), but it is generally agreed that it is defective as a means of redress, even after the reforms introduced under the Police Reform Act

2002 which introduced the Independent Police Complaints Commission. It does not allow for compensation to the victim or for the victim to attend any disciplinary proceedings. In any event, most complaints do not result in disciplinary proceedings and it appears that none have been brought in respect of breaches of the Codes. The suspect concerned might, in many instances, be unaware that a breach of the Codes had occurred, and while theoretically another officer could make a complaint leading to disciplinary proceedings for such a breach, in practice, this appears to be highly unlikely. Furthermore, despite the involvement (albeit limited) of the Independent Police Complaints Commission, the complaints procedure tends to be perceived as being administered largely by the police themselves, although a greater independent element was introduced in 2002 in the form of civilian investigators in certain cases. In *Khan v UK* (2000), the European Court of Human Rights (ECtHR) found a violation of Art 13 of the European Convention, on the basis that the Police Complaints Authority did not provide a sufficient means of redress for Convention breaches. It was found to be insufficiently independent as the provider of a remedial procedure since complaints could be handled internally, the chief constable of the area was able to appoint from his own force to carry out an investigation and since the Secretary of State was involved in appointments to the Police Complaints Authority. It is unclear that the 2002 reforms fully address these issues. Thus, further reform is arguably necessary.

The context in which breaches of Code C and of the entitlement to legal advice have been considered is that of exclusion of evidence. It must be borne in mind that the PACE mechanism for exclusion of evidence provides a means of redress for breach of the interviewing provisions only in one circumstance – that the case is pursued to trial and the defendant pleads not guilty. In this one instance, it can be of great value in that the defendant may be placed in the position he would have been in had the breach not occurred (the approach taken in *Absolam* (1988)), and the police may seem to be 'punished' for their non-compliance with the rules by being prevented from profiting from their own breach.

The Act contains three separate tests which may be considered after a breach of the interviewing rules has been shown and, in theory, all three could be considered in a particular instance. Under the 'oppression' test (s 76(2)(a)), once the defence has advanced a reasonable argument (*Liverpool Juvenile Court ex p R* (1987)) that the confession was obtained by oppression, it will not be admitted in evidence unless the prosecution can prove that it was not so obtained.[2] In *Fulling* (1987), the Court of Appeal proffered its own definition of oppression: 'The exercise of authority or power in a burdensome, harsh or wrongful manner.' The terms 'wrongful' and 'burdensome' used in this test could cover any unlawful action on the part of the police, and would therefore mean that any breach of the Act or Codes could constitute oppression. This wide possibility has been pursued at first instance (in *Davison* (1988)), but the Court of Appeal in *Hughes* (1988) held that a denial of legal advice due not to bad faith on the part of the police, but to a misunderstanding, could not amount to oppression. In *Alladice* (1988), the Court of Appeal also took this view in suggesting, *obiter*, that an improper denial of legal advice, if accompanied by bad faith on the part of the police, would certainly amount to 'unfairness' under s 78 and probably also to 'oppression'.

The test for oppression then does not depend entirely on the nature of the impropriety, but rather on whether it was perpetrated deliberately. Thus, bad faith seems to be a necessary, but not sufficient condition for the operation of s 76(2)(a), whereas it seems that it will automatically render a confession inadmissible under s 78.

The test under s 76(2)(b), the 'reliability' test, is concerned with objective reliability: the judge must consider the situation at the time the confession was made and ask whether the confession would be likely to be unreliable, not whether it is unreliable. It is not necessary under this test to show that there has been any misconduct on the part of the police.[3] In *Delaney* (1989), the defendant was 17, had an IQ of 80 and, according to an educational psychologist, was subject to emotional arousal which would lead him to wish to bring a police interview to an end as quickly as possible. These were circumstances in which it was important to ensure that the interrogation was conducted with all propriety. In fact, the officers offered some inducement to the defendant to confess by playing down the gravity of the offence and by suggesting that if he confessed, he would get the psychiatric help he needed. They also failed to make an accurate, contemporaneous record of the interview in breach of para 11.5 of Code C (now s 11.7). Failing to make the proper record was of indirect relevance to the question of reliability, since it meant that the court could not assess the full extent of the suggestions held out to the defendant. Thus, in the circumstances existing at the time (the mental state of the defendant), the police impropriety did have the necessary special significance.

Thus, it appears that the 'circumstances existing at the time' may be circumstances created by the police in breaching the interviewing rules; equally, following *Mathias* (1989), such a breach may amount to something said or done. However, a single breach of the interviewing rules, such as a denial of legal advice in ordinary circumstances, would not, it seems, fulfil both limbs of the test.

Due to the need to find some special factor in the situation in order to invoke either head of s 76, breaches of the interviewing rules unaccompanied by any such factor are usually considered under s 78. The idea behind the section was that the function of exclusion of evidence after police misconduct must not be disciplinary, but must be to safeguard the fairness of the trial. The first question to be asked under s 78 is whether a breach of the rules has occurred at all and then whether it is significant and substantial (*Keenan* (1989)). Once such a breach is found, the next question to be asked will be whether admission of the confession gained during the improperly conducted interview will render the trial unfair. This might occur if, for example, as in *Canale* (1990), there has been a failure to make contemporaneous notes of the interview in breach of s 11.7 of Code C. The defence may then challenge the interview record on the basis that the police have fabricated all or part of it, or may allege that something adverse to the detainee happened during the interview which has not been recorded. The court then has no means of knowing which version is true, precisely the situation which Code C was designed to prevent. In such a situation, a judge may well exclude the confession on the basis that it would be unfair to allow evidence of doubtful reliability to go before the jury.[4]

Breaches of the recording provisions will normally be considered under s 78 as opposed to s 76(2). Allegedly fabricated confessions cannot fall within s 76(2), due to its requirement that something has happened to the defendant which causes him to confess; its terms are not therefore fulfilled if the defence alleges that no confession made by the defendant exists. Second, s 76(2)(b) requires that something is said or done in special circumstances; a breach of the recording provisions could amount to something said or done in the *Delaney* sense (see above), but unless special circumstances such as the particular vulnerability of the defendant exist, the other test under the section is unsatisfied. In *Canale* (1990), the police breached the recording provisions and allegedly played a trick on the appellant in order to obtain the confession. Ruling that the confession should have been excluded under s 78, the Court of Appeal took into account the fact that the appellant could not be said to be weak-minded; it was therefore thought inappropriate to invoke s 76(2)(b). Equally, such instances would not normally fall within s 76(2)(a), because it may not be apparent that the police deliberately breached the recording provisions. On the other hand, if the defence alleges that the police made threats or *deliberately* tricked the detainee into confessing, the prosecution might not be able to prove beyond reasonable doubt that the police had in fact behaved properly, due to the breach of the recording provisions. This line of argument could have been considered in *Canale*.

Moreover, a significant and substantial breach of the interviewing rules, although unaccompanied by bad faith, may have caused the defendant to confess and on that basis, admission of the confession could be said to render the trial unfair, even though it appears that the confession is reliable. The difficulty here lies in determining whether the defendant confessed for other reasons. In *Samuel* (1988), the Court of Appeal determined that the police impropriety – a failure to allow the appellant access to legal advice – was causally linked to the confession: the appellant was not a sophisticated, hardened criminal able to handle the interview without advice. Conversely, in *Dunford* (1990), the Court of Appeal determined that the criminally experienced appellant had made his own assessment of the situation in deciding to make certain admissions and legal advice would not have affected his decision; the failure to allow legal advice was not therefore causally linked to the confession. Curtailment of the right to silence under ss 34–37 of the CJPOA 1994, as amended, means that legal advisers are less likely to advise silence and, therefore, the causal relationship in question will be more difficult to establish. Section 78 may therefore become less effective as a means of providing a form of redress where there is a failure to comply with the PACE provisions.[5] On the other hand, the importance attached to access to legal advice by the European Court in cases such as *Murray (John) v UK* (1996) and *Averill v UK* (2000) may encourage greater use of s 78, since the courts' duty under s 6 of the HRA 1998 means that these decisions should be taken into account in considering whether interviews should be excluded from evidence where breaches of the legal advice provisions have occurred.

Section 34(2A) of the CJPOA may be likely to encourage the police to afford access to legal advice. Whether it does so in practice will depend on the interpretation of the terms given to the provision. It provides essentially that adverse inferences shall not be drawn from a suspect's silence under caution before or after charge at an authorised place of detention if he has not been allowed an 'opportunity' to consult a solicitor before that point. Clearly, the term 'opportunity' may be taken to mean that formally, an opportunity had been offered, but the suspect had not availed himself of it. This interpretation would not curb the use of ploys by the police discouraging the suspect from having legal advice. Such an interpretation would not appear to accord with Art 6(1) jurisprudence, and therefore a broad interpretation of the term 'opportunity' could be adopted under s 3 of the HRA.

In conclusion, it is apparent that the courts are concerned to uphold the safeguards created by the PACE interviewing rules, but it must be questioned whether exclusion of evidence is an adequate or appropriate method of doing so. The majority of defendants plead guilty. Thus, the police have an incentive to break the rules by, for example, refusing a request for legal advice in the hope of obtaining admissions and a guilty plea. If, in such circumstances, a defendant does plead guilty, he has suffered denial of a fundamental right with little hope of redress, apart from that offered by a complaint. However, whilst not a direct remedy for breaches of PACE and its Codes, the incorporation of the Convention by the HRA 1998 has provided a separate method of redress for many situations which involve a PACE breach; if the pre-trial proceedings are unfair, viewing the trial process as a whole, then there will be a breach of Art 6, for which any domestic court may provide any available remedy (s 8 of the HRA), including excluding evidence or quashing any conviction obtained. Thus, the HRA may have some impact in making up for the deficiencies in the PACE remedial scheme.

▌NOTES

1 The tone of the only relevant case (a 1985 unreported application to prevent a breach of s 58) was unpropitious: ' . . . were I to make the order sought it would be unreasonable, a hindrance to police inquiries may be caused.'

2 The meaning of oppression could be considered in more detail. The only evidence given in the Act as to its meaning is the non-exhaustive definition contained in s 76(8): 'In this section, "oppression" includes torture, inhuman or

degrading treatment, and the use or threat of violence (whether or not amounting to torture).' The word 'includes' ought to be given its literal meaning according to the Court of Appeal in *Fulling* (1987). Therefore, the concept of oppression may be fairly wide: the question is whether it could encompass breaches of the interviewing scheme unaccompanied by any other impropriety.

3 There are two limbs to the test, as *Harvey* (1988) illustrates: the defendant, a mentally ill woman of low intelligence, may have been induced to confess to murder by hearing her lover's confession; the 'something said or done' (the first limb) was the confession of the lover, while the 'circumstances' (the second limb) were the defendant's emotional state, low intelligence and mental illness.

4 The question of any other available evidence as to what occurred could be pursued further at this point. In *Dunn* (1990), the defence had an independent witness to what occurred – a legal representative – and the judge admitted the confession as the defence had therefore a proper basis from which to challenge the police evidence.

5 For completeness, s 82(3), which preserves the whole of the common law discretion to exclude evidence, could be mentioned at this point, although it should be noted that in practice, its role in relation to breaches of the interviewing rules is largely insignificant, due to the width of s 78.

Question 46

The Terrorism Act 2000, as amended, introduced after the inception of the Human Rights Act 1998, was supposed to achieve Convention-compliance in increasing police powers, and creating a wider application of the special terrorism offences. How far would it be fair to say that this aim has been achieved?

Answer plan

This is a fairly tricky essay question which relates to a strong current theme regarding counter-terrorist measures and the Convention rights. It therefore needs care in planning in order to cover a reasonable range of the statutory provisions and their ECHR implications – not all the provisions could possibly be covered. Note that the Terrorism Act may be consolidated in a new Terrorism Act 2007 or 2008, so the provisions discussed below will still be of relevance from 2007 onwards. The question does not ask you to deal with the provisions of the Terrorism Act 2006, except in so far as they amend the Terrorism Act 2000. Essentially, the following points should be considered:

Check list

- the definition of terrorism under s 1 Terrorism Act 2000 (TA);
- amendments to the TA made under the Anti-Terrorism Crime and Security Act 2001 and the Terrorism Act 2006;
- proscription;
- special terrorism offences;
- aspects of the provisions applicable to terrorist suspects in pre-trial investigations;
- references to Arts 5, 6, 8, 10 and 11 of the Convention; relevant case law;
- the HRA, especially ss 2, 3 and 6.

Answer

This essay will focus on a number of the offences under the Terrorism Act 2000, as amended in 2001 and 2006, and on the special criminal justice regime for terrorist suspects pre-trial. In the Human Rights Act era, ironically, this scheme comes strongly into conflict with human rights in various respects. It is over-inclusive, covering on its face persons or groups who would not be termed 'terrorists' in many countries, or who do not appear to represent a threat to Britain itself. The key provisions of the scheme are in general extremely broad and imprecise; in particular, as discussed below, the definition of terrorism in the Terrorism Act itself is so broad as to be almost unworkable and it fails to distinguish between protest groups threatening direct action and terrorist groups.

The very broad definition adopted under s 1 of the Terrorism Act 2000 (TA) has three main elements. 'Terrorism' means, first, the use or threat of action involving serious violence against any person or serious damage to property, endangers the life of any person, or 'creates a serious risk to the health or safety of the public or a section of the public, or is designed seriously to interfere with or seriously to disrupt an electronic system.' Second, the use or threat must be for the purpose of advancing a 'political, religious or ideological' cause. Third, the use or threat must be 'designed to influence the government or to intimidate the public or a section of the public'. It may be noted that the third element is not needed if firearms or explosives are used. The Act applies wherever terrorist action takes place, under s 1(4).

This definition allowed many activities, previously criminal, to be re-designated as terrorist. The definition expressly covers threats of serious disruption or damage to, for example, computer installations or public utilities. The definition is therefore able to catch a number of forms of public protest. Danger to property, violence or a serious risk to safety that can be described as 'ideologically, politically, or religiously motivated' may arise in the context of many demonstrations and other forms of public protest, including some industrial disputes.

Under the TA the power of proscription, and all the previous proscription-related offences, were retained, and their impact was greatly extended. Section 3(1) TA provides: 'For the purposes of this Act an organisation is proscribed if it is listed in Schedule 2 . . . .' The power to add to or delete groups from the Schedule is exercised under s 3(3) by the Secretary of State, by order. Under s 3(4) the power may be exercised 'only if he believes that [the organisation] is concerned in terrorism'; this includes, under the Terrorism Act 2006, if it glorifies terrorism. In other words, groups which do not themselves fall within the s 1 definition but which are in any way 'concerned' in terrorism can be proscribed.

Under s 11(1) TA a person commits an offence if s/he belongs or professes to belong to a proscribed organisation; a maximum penalty of ten years' imprisonment is imposed. It is notable that there is no *mens rea* requirement.[1] Under s 12(1) TA it is an offence to solicit support, other than money or other property, for a proscribed organisation and it is also an offence under s 12(2) for a person to arrange, manage or assist in arranging or managing a meeting which he knows is to support (or be addressed by a member of) a proscribed organisation, These are broadly drawn offences, although they do include a *mens rea* ingredient. Their impact on speech, association and assembly is clearly far-reaching, bearing in mind the wide range of meetings, including very small, informal ones, covered. Restrictions on the use of badges or uniforms as signals of support for certain organisations are intended to have the dual effect of preventing communication – by those means – of the political message associated with the organisation and of tending to minimise the impression that the organisation is supported, thereby denying reassurance to its members, lowering their morale and preventing them from arousing public support. S 13 TA makes it an offence to wear an item of clothing, or wear, carry or display an article in a way that arouses reasonable suspicion that the person is a member or supporter of a proscribed organisation. Again it is notable that no element of *mens rea* is included.

The TA applies all the special 'terrorism' offences which were developed in the context of the previous terrorism legislation in relation to the IRA to an extremely wide range of organisations. Unless and until the Home Secretary proscribes a range of domestic animal rights' and environmental groups, the proscription-related offences will not apply to them. But all the special terrorist offences, which have no equivalents in ordinary criminal law, could be applied to a range of groups. The use of the stop and search power under s 44 TA, discussed below, in relation to reporters and protesters, is indicative of this possibility.

Section 56 TA makes it an offence to direct 'at any level' a terrorist organisation. Thus, the leaders, and all with some authority within the vast range of groups within the UK which may fall within the s 1 definition, are liable to a sentence of life imprisonment simply by virtue of their position. The police and prosecuting authorities have so far shown discretion in seeking to use this offence, and have not applied it to the leaders of, for example, protest groups advocating direct action, but it is unsatisfactory that the leaders of such groups should be placed in a precarious position in relation to the criminal law, one that is merely dependent on forbearance.

A very wide range of other people, who are not part of any of these groups, may also suddenly be criminalised. Under 19 TA relates to a duty to provide information about terrorist activity. Section19 goes well beyond requiring banks and other businesses to report any suspicion they might have that someone is laundering terrorist money or committing any of the other terrorist offences in ss 15–18. It applies to all employees or employers and means that if, during the course of their work, a person comes across information about, or become suspicious of, someone whom s/he suspects may be using money or property to contribute to the causes of terrorism, s/he will commit a criminal offence carrying a maximum penalty of five years' imprisonment if s/he does not report them. Section 38B Anti-Terrorism, Crime and Security Act 2001 broadens this provision immensely: it makes it an offence, subject to an unexplicated defence of reasonable excuse, for a person to fail to disclose to a police officer any information which s/he knows or believes *might* be of material assistance in preventing an act of terrorism or securing the apprehension or conviction of a person involved in such an act.

This disclosure offence is one of the most controversial in the Terrorism Act, but while it may be justifiable in relation to the knowledge of an imminent bomb attack, it clearly appears needlessly draconian when applied – via the s 1 definition of terrorism in the TA – to a much greater range of people. Anyone working with someone such as an anti-Ghadaffi activist who is active abroad in the manner now designated terrorist, or someone whose work happens to bring them into contact in some way with information related to activities linked to terrorism, has been placed in an invidious position. The offence also places journalists investigating the activities of certain groups, such as animal rights' campaigners, in a very difficult position, especially where they have contacts within the group. It would appear almost impossible for any investigative journalism to occur in such circumstances, without risk of incurring a five-year prison sentence. The provision requiring the surrender of information might mean that the identity of sources could not be protected. A defence is provided under s 19(3) which appears to be aimed *inter alia* at journalists: 'it is a defence for a person charged with an offence under subsection (2) to prove that he had a reasonable excuse for not making the disclosure'. This defence would allow a journalist to raise Convention points under the HRA. But it is clear that s 19 may be having a strong deterrent effect on investigative journalism in relation to extremist groups.

Section 1 TA acts not only as the 'trigger' applying the old offences to a wider range of groups; it also creates new offences of inciting terrorism abroad, which apply under ss 59, 60 and 61 to England and Wales, Northern Ireland and Scotland, respectively.

There are a number of possible methods of seeking to ensure that the HRA is complied within this context. They depend mainly on court action, but, it must also be remembered that the Home Secretary and other relevant members of the executive are bound by s 6 HRA to abide by the Convention. Articles 10 and 11 should therefore be taken into account in taking decisions to add groups to the list of those proscribed under the TA. In criminal proceedings on the broad application of the special terrorist offences under the TA the courts have the opportunity of interpreting them, under s 3 of the HRA, compatibly with the Convention rights. They must also discharge their duty under s 6 HRA. The approach of the courts towards the new legislation is clearly crucial. Traditionally, since terrorism has been viewed as threatening national security, the courts have adopted a deferential stance.

The notion of increasing the number of groups to be proscribed lay at the heart of the introduction of the TA. Clearly it was intended that a range of extremist Islamic groups would be proscribed, some, but not all, linked with Al Qu'aida, and that has already occurred. Other international groups have been proscribed, some that do not appear to create a security risk within the UK itself. A key issue therefore is the compatibility of the proscription of a range of groups with Art 10 and 11, especially taking the new glorification provisions into account, since the complete outlawing of a group constitutes *prima facie* a breach of those Articles. In findings as to proscription, therefore, the focus will be on the demands of para 2 of those articles. State interference with the Art 10 and 11 guarantees must be prescribed by law, have a legitimate aim, be necessary in a democratic society and be applied in a non-discriminatory fashion if it is to be justified. It can almost certainly be assumed that the exercise of the proscription power would be viewed domestically as prescribed by law since it is enshrined in primary legislation, although the 'quality' of proscription decisions should also be questioned.

In freedom of expression cases Strasbourg's main concern has unsurprisingly been with the 'necessary in a democratic society' requirement. In *Sidiropoulos v Greece* (1998) the Court considered the outlawing in Greece of an association called *the Home of Macedonian Civilisation* which had been formed in Macedonia. The authorities refused to register it, on the basis that it was viewed as intended to undermine Greece's national integrity, contrary to Greek law, since it intended to publicise the idea that there is a Macedonian minority in Greece. The Court indicated the stance it would take towards the aims of the state authorities – the preservation of national security and the prevention of disorder – in this context. They were found to be legitimate but the means used to further them – disallowing the registration of the group and therefore outlawing it – was found to be disproportionate to them and therefore unnecessary in a democratic society. Thus, proscription of a particular group, depending on the extent to which there was evidence that it threatens national security and public order, might be found domestically to violate these two Articles. Where, for example, a group presenting no risk to national security in the UK had been proscribed on the basis of its encouragement for another group operating abroad, it might be found that proscription was disproportionate to the aims in view.

'Certain of the proscription-linked offences strike directly at freedom of political expression, which, as indicated above, is viewed as one of the essential foundations of a democratic society', so that exceptions to it 'must be narrowly interpreted and the necessity for any restrictions . . . convincingly established' (*Observer and Guardian v. the United Kingdom* (1991)). Such offences include those of wearing any item which arouses a reasonable apprehension that a person is a member or supporter of a proscribed organisation, that of organising a meeting at which a member of a proscribed organisation is speaking, and that of soliciting support for such an organisation. The use of these offences is *prima facie* an interference with the guarantee under Art 10 since all, including the wearing of an item, involve exercises of expression. Obviously the view taken of the necessity of the interference would depend on the particular circumstances behind the charging of the offence in the instance before the court. But to take the example used above of a person meeting privately with two others and hearing a member of a proscribed group: it might be problematic to find that the necessity for the interference with freedom of expression in a democratic society had been convincingly established.[2]

As noted above, the offences of failing to report information to the police which might be of material assistance in preventing an act of terrorism, or of possessing information potentially useful in preventing someone carrying out such an act, curb journalistic investigation into the activities of a very wide range of groups, unless journalists are prepared to incur the risk of a lengthy prison sentence. These provisions afford very little recognition to the role of the media in investigating matters of public interest and informing the public. Strasbourg gives pre-eminence to the role of the press in a democracy (*Castells v Spain* (1992)). Restrictions placed on the press in performing this vital role have been subjected to the strictest scrutiny.

This essay will now turn to considering certain aspects of the pre-trial criminal justice regime for terrorist suspects, and its human rights implications. Controversially, under ss 44–47 of the TA blanket stop and search powers, not dependent on reasonable suspicion, can be operated by the police. They depend on authorizations covering a particular area, but the area can be very large: the whole of London has been covered by an authorisation for the last few years. Once the authorisation is in force anyone can be stopped and searched, even though nothing in their appearance or actions gives rise to reasonable suspicion that they are involved in terrorist activity. Under s 44(3) 'an authorisation under subsection (1) or (2) may be given only if the person giving it considers it expedient for the prevention of acts of terrorism.' The authorisation has to be given by a senior police officer. Authorisations apply to a specific area and are for a maximum of 28 days (although that period may be renewed). The provisions expressly confirm that reasonable suspicion remains irrelevant, under s 45. Vehicle stop and search authorisations, as well as pedestrian ones, have to be confirmed by the Secretary of State within 48 hours of their being made, or they cease to have effect. This appears to be a gesture in the direction of due process.

The Stop and Search Code – Code A (2006) – made under the Police and Criminal Evidence Act 1984 – has provisions governing these stops and searches; s 2.24 provides that when an authorisation under s 44 is given, a constable in uniform may exercise the powers only to stop and search for reasons connected with terrorism. It should be noted that breach of this Code does not render the search unlawful (unless Code provisions are also reproduced in the relevant statute and are viewed as mandatory – see *Osman v Director of Public Prosecutions* (1999)). Therefore a breach cannot give rise to any civil liability on the part of a police officer; it is conceivable, but extremely unlikely, that breach of the Code could lead to the inadmissibility in evidence of objects found during the search (*Khan (Sultan)* (1997)). So the only possible remedy is a disciplinary one that provides no redress for the victim of the search: the breach could only form part of a complaint about the conduct of the officers. Thus the Code has no firm legal underpinning.

So there are apparent safeguards surrounding the use of this stop and search power, but once they are scrutinised, it is doubtful whether they have the capacity to prevent an arbitrary use of the power. The uncertainty of the safeguards leaves open the possibility that the power could be used to harass other groups, such as protesters, or used in a racially or religiously discriminatory fashion. It might appear that the Human Rights Act could provide a check on the arbitrary and oppressive use of this power. This possibility was considered by the House of Lords in *R (on the application of Gillan) v Commissioner of Police for the Metropolis* ([2006] UKHL 12) in which two persons, a journalist on her way to report on a protest, and a protester, were stopped and searched near the site of the protest. The appellants argued that the stops and searches had constituted a breach of Art 5, Sched 1 HRA. Lord Bingham, who gave the leading judgment, sought to determine first whether the stops and searches were 'a deprivation of liberty' in Art 5(1) terms. He found that there was no deprivation of liberty in Art 5(1) terms.

However, Lord Bingham went on to consider the question whether, had there been a deprivation of liberty, it would have been justified as within Art 5(1)(b). He found that the statutory regime and the authorisation itself were 'prescribed by law' and that 'the respondents bring themselves within the exception, for the public are in my opinion subject to a clear obligation not to obstruct a constable exercising a lawful power to stop and search for articles which could be used for terrorism and any detention is in order to secure effective fulfilment of that obligation'. Thus Art 5 was deemed inapplicable, but even if it had been found to be applicable, the stops and searches would have been justified. Thus this judgment found not merely that the stops and searches were justified in Art 5 terms, it gave no encouragement at all to the raising of Art 5 arguments in relation to stop and search, in future.[3]

The maximum period of detention, applicable to a person arrested under s 41 of the TA, was seven days, but para 29, Sched 8 provides that it must be under a warrant issued by a 'judicial authority'. Under para 32, the warrant may be issued if there are reasonable grounds for believing that 'the detention of the person to whom the application relates is necessary to obtain relevant evidence whether by questioning him or otherwise or to preserve relevant evidence'. The detainee or his solicitor has the right to make written or oral representations under para 33(1). Thus, authorisation may not be merely 'on the papers'. The period was increased to 14 days by the Criminal Justice Act 2003, and then to 28 days by amendments under the Terrorism Act 2006. In requiring judicial authorisation for detention for up to seven days under s 41 and Sched 8 of the TA, the Government has sought to ensure that the new detention provisions comply with Art 5(3) as interpreted in *Brogan* (1989). One question which will probably be raised eventually in the domestic courts or at Strasbourg will be whether allowing a detention for 28 days, even with judicial authorisation, is in accordance with Art 5.

It is concluded that fundamental human rights have already been severely compromised by the current TA scheme. The anti-terrorist powers discussed have an impact on human rights that, it is argued, is out of proportion to their value in protecting against particular terrorist threats. The HRA has not had so far, as discussed above, a significant impact in curbing the tendency of the TA provisions, especially as amended in 2006, to lead to infringements of the Convention rights.

NOTES

1 It could be noted that there is a limited defence under s 11(2): 'it is a defence for a person charged with an offence under subsection (1) to prove that the organisation was not proscribed on the last (or only) occasion on which he became a member or began to profess to be a member, and that he has not taken part in the activities of the organisation at any time while it was proscribed'. But it is not a defence to prove that the defendant did not know that the organisation was proscribed or that it was engaged in activities covered by ss 1(1) and 3 of the Act.

2 It might be pointed that the offence under s 56 of the TA to direct 'at any level' a terrorist organisation is not confined to proscribed groups. If a minor figure in an organisation which fell within the wide definition of terrorism under s 1, but within its less serious aspects, was charged with this offence, a court which found that this interference with Art 11 was disproportionate to the aims pursued could interpret the terms used in s 56, especially 'directing' and 'at any level' under s 3 HRA so as to exclude such figures from the ambit of the section. For example, taking the terms together it could be argued that the term 'directing' qualifies 'at any level' so that only figures at some level within the *leadership* sector of the organisation are covered. The incitement offence under ss 59, 60 and 61 is similarly unconfined to members of proscribed groups. Taking the example used above of charging the offence in respect of persons at a public meeting denouncing a terrorist dictator, a court which viewed the interference with freedom of expression as, in the circumstances, disproportionate to the aims in view, could take the opportunity of construing the wording of the provisions

very strictly. In particular, where there was leeway to do so, on a very strict interpretation of the application of certain of the offences listed in s 59(2), it might be found that incitement merely of lesser, similar, but unlisted offences had occurred.

3 Other Convention points were raised, but Lord Bingham gave them short shrift. Assuming that the s 44 power was being used to harass protesters going to protest against the Arms Fair, a reasonable supposition, then it is hard to see that there is little in the argument that Arts 10 and 11 Sched 1 HRA might have been infringed. In relation to Arts 10 and 11 Lord Bingham merely found that the power to stop and search under s 44–45 may, if misused, infringe the Convention rights to free expression and free assembly protected by arts 10 and 11. But he found that if it did, and subject always to compliance with the 'prescribed by law' condition discussed below the restriction would fall within the heads of justification provided in Art 10(2) and 11(2)'. He found that the 'prescribed by law' condition was satisfied. But he failed entirely to deal with the key question under Arts10(2) and 11(2) – whether the use of the power in the instant cases was proportionate to the aim sought to be achieved – presumably the prevention of crime. Had he considered that question, it might have been argued that the use of the power against protesters at that particular time and place (where there was no particular reason – other than the protest itself – to expect acts of terrorism to occur or for protesters to be carrying articles to be used to perpetrate such acts), was disproportionate to the aim pursued.

Question 47

Critically evaluate the counter-terrorist initiatives of the government, introduced after 9/11, in Part 4 Anti-Terrorism, Crime and Security Act 2001 and under the Prevention of Terrorism Act 2005, taking account of the guarantees of the European Convention on Human Rights, received into UK law under the Human Rights Act 1998.

Answer plan

This is a fairly tricky essay question which asks you to deal with the controversial detention without trial scheme under Pt 4 of the Anti-Terrorism Crime and Security Act 2001, the findings of the House of Lords in relation to it in the *A and others* case (2004), and its replacement in the Prevention of Terrorism Act 2005. Questions as to the 2005 scheme have already been raised in relation to the Convention rights, so that aspect of the 2005 scheme must be dealt with. Essentially, the following points should be considered:

Check list

- Part 4, Anti-Terrorism Crime and Security Act 2001;
- special terrorism provisions in Prevention of Terrorism Act 2005;
- A and others (2004);
- Arts 5, 6, 8, 10, 11, 14 and 15 of the Convention;
- the HRA, especially ss 2, 3 and 6; relevant case law.

Answer

The problem faced by the government was presented after 9/11 to Parliament and a number of Parliamentary Committees in the following terms: a dilemma arises in respect of the presence of persons in the UK who are suspected of being international terrorists and as therefore posing a grave security problem, but who cannot be placed on trial due to the sensitivity of the evidence and the high standard of proof. At the same time they cannot be deported to their country of origin, because there are grounds to think that they would there be subject to torture or inhuman and degrading treatment, since to do so would violate Art 3 of the European Convention on Human Rights. The dilemma arose due to the decision of the European Court of Human Rights in *Chahal v UK* (1996) in which it found that a breach of Art 3 will arise where a country deports a person to another country, knowing that he or she will face a substantial risk of Art 3 treatment in that other country.

Article 5(1) of the Convention protects the right to liberty and security of the person, afforded further effect in domestic law under the Human Rights Act. There is an exception under Art 5(1)(f) allowing for detention of 'a person against whom action is being taken with a view to deportation or extradition', but it was considered that it would not cover lengthy detentions during which deportation proceedings would not be in being. Thus, the government presented itself as caught between the provisions of Art 3 and 5, in relation to a number of suspected international terrorists, including persons with links to Al Qaida, based in Britain, and therefore as having to find a compromise which would allow for their detention. The solution was to introduce a scheme allowing for indefinite detention without trial and at the same time to derogate from Art 5(1).

Under the detention without trial scheme under Pt IV Anti-Terrorism, Crime and Security Act 2001 (ACTSA) detention depended – in effect – on certification by the Home Secretary as a substitute for a trial in respect of non-British citizens (who were therefore subject to immigration controls). The government considered that the new Pt 4 ACTSA provisions would be incompatible with Art 5(1) of the Convention, afforded further effect in domestic law under the HRA, and therefore entered a derogation to Art 5(1), under s 14 HRA, within the terms of Art 15 of the Convention.

The House of Lords considered the detention scheme in *A and Others v Secretary of State for the Home Dept* (2004). They did conclude that it was open to the government to find that there was a state of emergency within the terms of Art 15 – that was viewed as a largely political judgment. On the question of proportionality – whether the measures went no further than required by the exigencies of the situation under Art 15 – the Lords made the point that s 21 and 23 ACTSA did not rationally address the threat to the security of the United Kingdom presented by Al-Qaeda terrorists and their supporters because the scheme did not address the threat presented by UK nationals, and it permitted foreign nationals suspected of being Al-Qaeda terrorists or their supporters to pursue their activities abroad if there was any country to which they were able to go, and also the sections permitted on their face the certification and detention of persons who were not suspected of presenting any threat to the security of the United Kingdom as Al-Qaeda terrorists or supporters.

Further, since the different treatment could not be justified, the scheme was found to violate Arts 14 and 5 read together on the basis of differentiating between groups of suspected international terrorists on the basis of nationality – this was found to be the key weakness of the scheme. The derogation order was quashed and a declaration of incompatibility between the Arts 14 and 5 and s 23 was made.

The Government accepted that it could no longer sustain the scheme – it could theoretically have continued the scheme in the face of an admitted violation of Art 5 (since the derogation order had been quashed) and of Art 5 and 14 read together – but it bowed to the pressure and introduced a new scheme under the Prevention of Terrorism Act 2005; in that Act Parliament repealed the key provisions of Pt 4 and introduced the new scheme.

The new scheme provides for lesser measures to be used – not detention without trial but control orders (although at their most stringent control orders can allow for detention without trial). Under s 1(3) a control order made against an individual can impose any obligations that the Secretary of State or the court considers necessary for purposes connected with preventing or restricting involvement by that individual in terrorism-related activity.

Literally any obligation up to and including house arrest can be imposed. A range of examples are given in s 1(4) but they are only illustrative examples – they include house arrest expressly or detention in any place; they include a prohibition or restriction on his use of specified services or specified facilities, or on his carrying on specified activities; this would include for example, not entering certain areas, not using the internet or phones; a restriction on his association or communications with specified persons or with other persons generally. So a range of control orders can be imposed but these fall into the categories of derogating control orders and non-derogating ones; the distinction between derogating ones and non-derogating is not made in the Act – a non-derogating order is merely defined as one made by the Secretary of state.

The nature of the obligations imposed by the orders means that other Articles apart from Art 5 are also clearly implicated, in particular Arts 8,10 and 11 – since communication and association are affected; obviously para 2 of these Articles could be invoked but only if the order satisfied the demands of proportionality in those paras. The derogating ones would require again a derogation from Art 5 since certain orders – in particular house arrest – are viewed as incompatible with the right to liberty; and possibly other Articles.

Under s 2 the Home Secretary can make a control order that imposes non-derogating obligations if he has reasonable grounds for suspecting that an individual is or has been involved in terrorist-related activity – this is similar to the standard of proof under Pt 4 of the ACTSA and so represents a standard well below the criminal standard of proof – the definition of terrorism is that from the 2000 Act; the order can be for up to 12 months. The courts have a greater role in the supervision of non-derogating control orders – it has to give permission – but the court cannot intervene if the Secretary of State certifies that order had to be made without permission due to urgency. Also appeal can be made to a court against the order. Section 4 also provides that in the case of an order imposing derogating obligations, the order must be made by the court on an application by the Secretary of State.

In *Secretary of State v MB* (2006) Judge Sullivan found, under s 3(10) of the Prevention of Terrorism Act 2005 in relation to a non-derogating control order made under s 2(1) of the Act, that the procedures in s 3 of the Act relating to the supervision by the court of non-derogating control orders made by the Secretary of State were incompatible with the respondents' right to a fair hearing under Art 6(1) of the European Convention on Human Rights ('the Convention') on the basis that the decision of the Home Secretary could only be quashed if it was obviously flawed. He therefore made a declaration of the incompatibility under s 4(2) of the Human Rights Act 1998, but decided under s 3(13) of the Act that the control order was to continue in force. In *Secretary of State for the Home Dept v MB* [2006] the Secretary of State appealed against this decision. It was found that the procedure could be found to be compatible with Article 6, relying on s 3 HRA: court had to consider whether there were reasonable grounds for suspicion, and that exercise differed from that of deciding whether a fact had been established according to a specified standard of proof. It was the procedure for determining whether reasonable grounds for suspicion existed that had to be fair if Sched. 1 Pt I and Art 6 of the 1998 Act was to be satisfied. Both Strasbourg and domestic authorities had accepted that there were circumstances where the use of closed material was compatible with Art 6 of the Convention. Article 6 of the Convention could not automatically require disclosure of the evidence of the grounds for suspicion. Reliance on closed material could only be on terms that appropriate safeguards were in place and the provisions of the 2005 Act for the use of a special advocate and rules of court constituted such appropriate safeguards. So the appeal was allowed.

In *Secretary of State for the Home Department v JJ, KK, GG, HH, NN, LL*, (2006) Judge Sullivan found, in respect of control orders imposing a range of obligations that the restrictions were 'the antithesis of liberty and equivalent to imprisonment'. 'Their liberty to live a normal life within their residences is so curtailed as to be non-existent for all practical purposes,' he said. Relying on *Guzzardi v Italy* (1980), he found that the control orders breached Art 5(1) ECHR. He found that they were in effect derogating control orders, not non-derogating ones. Therefore the government should have sought a derogation from Art 5(1). As it had not, the orders were incompatible with Art 5. Judge Sullivan found that the regime created by the orders was incompatible with Art 5 and quashed the orders. The Court of Appeal recently upheld this finding and the government has therefore had to accept that the current control order regime created an invasion of Art 5; it has therefore had to be modified. The non-derogating control orders regime can continue to be used, but, unless a derogation from Art 5 is sought, a less stringent regime has to be imposed on individuals, one that imposes restraints on freedom of movement, but does not go so far in doing so that it breaches the right to liberty under Art 5.

Further challenges to the control orders on human rights grounds are probable. If a derogation is sought from Art 5 in order to employ control orders allowing for house arrest, the impact of the orders on liberty would still have to be proportionate to the exigencies of the security situation under Art 15 ECHR. The decision of the House of Lords in *A and others*, mentioned above, indicates that the courts would be unlikely to accept that such control orders could be justified. It is clear therefore that the HRA has had a significant impact on the post- 9/11 counter-terrorist initiatives. A mounting tension can readily be discerned between the Labour government's increasingly authoritarian measures and the Convention rights, a tension which currently reaches its climax in the use of non-derogating control orders. Very broadly drawn definitions of terrorist activity may also be counter-productive; due to their human rights implications they may be playing a part in alienating the Muslim community, constructing it as a 'suspect community', and so making it more likely that some Muslims might be drawn into terrorist activity.

CHAPTER 12

FREEDOM OF ASSEMBLY AND PUBLIC ORDER

▌INTRODUCTION

This chapter is concerned with the conflict between the need on the one hand to maintain order and on the other to protect freedom of assembly. The topic lends itself readily to problem questions or essays, but in either case, its concern will be with those provisions of the criminal law most applicable in the context of demonstrations, marches or meetings. The common law power to prevent a breach of the peace is still extensively used. Students should be aware of recent decisions on this power. The Public Order Act 1986, as amended, is still the most significant statute, but it is also particularly important to bear in mind the public order provisions of the Criminal Justice and Public Order Act 1994. The Serious and Organized Crime Act 2005 ss 132–138 could be mentioned in a general question about freedom of assembly or in a specific question relating to demonstrations in the vicinity of Parliament. The Criminal Justice and Police Act 2001 could be mentioned in relation to harassing behaviour directed at persons in dwellings. The Racial and Religious Hatred Act 2006 adds Pt 3A to the Public Order Act, and would be relevant if issues of hate speech arise in a question. The relevance of any particular provision obviously depends on the wording of the question; there are a very large number of public order provisions and questions are unlikely to cover all of them. Police powers (covered in Chapter 11), may also be relevant.

Problem questions sometimes call on the student to discuss *any* issues which may arise, as opposed to considering criminal liability only, in which case, any tortious liability incurred by members of an assembly or by police officers may arise as well as questions of criminal liability. The possibility of judicial review of police decisions may also arise.

At the present time, the Human Rights Act 1998 is of course especially important and is relevant in all problem questions on public protest and assembly. Examiners will expect some discussion of its relevance and impact. Art 10 and 11 of the European Convention on Human Rights, which provide guarantees of freedom of expression and of peaceful assembly respectively, were received into UK law once the Human Rights Act 1998 came fully into force in 2000. (Note that Art 10 protects 'expression', not merely 'speech', thus covering many forms of expressive activity, including forms of public protest.) Therefore, Arts 10 and 11 and other Convention Articles relevant in this area are directly applicable in UK courts, and should be taken into account in interpreting and applying common law and statutory provisions affecting public protest. Section 3(1) of the HRA requires: 'So far as it is possible to do so, primary and subordinate legislation must be read and given effect in a way which is compatible with the Convention rights.' Section 3(2)(b) reads: 'this section does not affect the validity, continuing operation or enforcement of any incompatible primary legislation.' Section 3(1) goes well beyond the pre-HRA obligation to resolve ambiguity in statutes by reference to the Convention. All statutes affecting freedom of assembly and public protest therefore have to be interpreted so as to be in harmony with the Convention, if that is at all possible.

Under s 6, Convention guarantees are binding only against public authorities; these are defined as bodies which have a partly public function. In the context of public protest, this will normally mean that if the police, local authorities or other public bodies use powers deriving from any legal source in order to prevent or limit peaceful public protest, the protesters can bring an action against them under s 7(1)(a) of the HRA relying on Art 11, probably combined with Art 10. Section 7(1)(b) means that if the protesters are prosecuted or sued, they can rely on those Articles and can seek re-interpretation of the legal provision involved under s 3 HRA. Depending on the interpretation afforded to those Articles, including the exceptions to them, the protesters might be successful unless a statutory provision absolutely unambiguously supported the limitation or banning of the protest. Where a statute limiting/affecting public protest is applied, the court is likely to rely on ss 3 and 6 of the HRA; where a common law provision creating such a limitation is relevant, the court will rely on s 6 alone. (For further discussion, see Chapter 9.)

Checklist

Students should have general knowledge of the background to the Public Order Act 1986, as amended and the public order provisions of the Criminal Justice and Public Order Act 1994 and – in relation to question relating to demonstrations in the vicinity of Parliament or general questions about the current range of public order provisions – of the Serious and Organized Crime Act 2005; in particular, they should be familiar with the following areas:

- the freedom of assembly and public protest jurisprudence under Arts 10 and 11 of the European Convention on Human Rights;
- the Human Rights Act 1998, especially ss 3 and 6;
- the notice requirements under s 11 of the Public Order Act 1986;
- the conditions which can be imposed under ss 12 and 14 of the Act, as amended, on processions and assemblies;
- the banning power under ss 13 and 14A of the Act;
- liability under ss 3,4,4A and 5 of the Act;
- liability for assault on, or obstruction of, a police officer under s 89 of the Police Act 1996;
- the common law power to prevent a breach of the peace;
- public nuisance;
- the obstruction of the highway under s 137 of the Highways Act 1980;
- the public order provisions of Pt V and s 154 of the Criminal Justice and Public Order Act 1994.
- Section s 132–8 of the Serious and Organized Crime Act 2005 (only relevant if a question relates to demonstrations in the vicinity of Parliament);
- the Criminal Justice and Police Act 2001 (only relevant in relation to harassing behaviour directed at persons in dwellings);
- the Racial and Religious Hatred Act 2006 (only relevant if a question mentions hate speech).

Question 48

Section 3 of the Human Rights Act 1998 requires that statutes should be interpreted, if possible, so as to accord with the demands of the European Convention on Human Rights (the Convention). Is it fair to say that the restraints on assemblies of ss 11–14C of the Public Order Act 1986, as amended, create a balance between the public interest in freedom of assembly and in the need to maintain order which is in harmony with Arts 10 and 11 of the Convention, and that therefore no reinterpretation of those provisions under s 3 is necessary?

Answer plan

The Public Order Act (POA) 1986 remains the central statute in this area, but its amendment by the Criminal Justice and Public Order Act (CJPOA) 1994 created a significant new area of liability. The general public order scheme now created by the two statutes is very likely to appear on examination papers. This essay question requires a sound knowledge of certain key POA 1986 provisions which are particularly relevant to public assembly and protest. Section 16 POA was amended by the Anti-Social Behaviour Act 2003 so that an assembly is now a meeting of two or more persons in a public place. It also requires an awareness of the provisions of Arts 10 and 11 as interpreted at Strasbourg, and of their potential impact on this area of UK law under the HRA. It is suggested that a distinction should initially be drawn between prior and subsequent restraints contained in the POA 1986 as amended. The provisions in question operate to a significant extent as prior restraints.

Essentially, the following matters should be considered:

- the value of freedom of assembly;
- the provisions of Arts 10 and 11 as interpreted by Strasbourg;
- the provisions aimed specifically at processions and assemblies under ss 11, 12, 13, 14, 14A, 14B and 14C of the 1986 Act (as amended by the 1994 Act);
- the need for further protection of assembly by re-interpretation of the provisions under s 3 in accordance with the demands of Arts 10 and 11 as received into UK law under the HRA;
- conclusions.

Answer

The State and citizens have a legitimate interest in maintaining order, but citizens also have a legitimate interest in the protection of the freedoms of expression and assembly. The restraints available under ss 11–14C of the Public Order Act 1986 (POA) as amended by the Criminal Justice and Public Order Act 1994, affect demonstrations, marches and meetings. To an extent, the number of restraints available is unsurprising because the range of State interests involved is wider than any other expressive activity would warrant: they include the possibilities of disorder, of violence to citizens and of damage to property. Clearly, the State has a duty to protect citizens from the attentions of the mob. The need to give weight to these interests explains the general acceptance of freedom of assembly as a non-absolute right, even though it may be that violent protest is most likely to bring about change.

Public protest is tolerated in free societies due to its close links with freedom of speech; in particular, it fosters participation in the democracy. One aspect of this is the use of protest as a means of demonstrating to the government that it has strayed too far from the path of acceptability in policy-making. The question is where the balance is to be struck: what is the proper middle way between allowing free rein to the riotous mob on the one hand and on the other imposing an absolute prohibition on public meetings? The middle way clearly involves the use of controls; the need is to avoid introducing over-broad legislative provisions, and for the police and prosecuting authorities to apply restraints sensitively in order to avoid arbitrary suppression of freedom of assembly. Art 10 and 11 of the Convention, afforded further effect in domestic law under the Human Rights Act (HRA) 1998, seek to avoid such suppression in providing guarantees of freedom of expression and of peaceful assembly, subject to exceptions under Arts 10(2) and 11(2) which allow restraints on protests and demonstrations to be justified only if they are prescribed by law, have a legitimate aim, and are 'necessary in a democratic society'. The European Court of Human Rights has found that the right to organise public meetings is 'fundamental' (*Rassemblement Jurassien Unite Jurassienne v Switzerland (1979)*) and that the protection of free speech extends equally to ideas which 'offend, shock or disturb' (*Handyside v UK (1976)*). All forms of protest that can be viewed as the expression of an opinion fall within Art 10, according to the findings of the Court in *Steel v UK (1998)*. In *Ezelin v France (1991)*, the Court found that Art 11 had been violated; it found that the freedom to take part in a peaceful assembly is of such importance that it cannot be restricted in any way, so long as the person concerned (whose freedom of assembly has suffered interference through arrest, etc) does not himself commit any reprehensible act. Domestically, where protest is in question, there seems to be a preparedness, evident from the decision, in *DPP v Percy (2001)* to look to Art 10.

This essay will ask whether the UK controls under ss 11–14C of the POA 1986 as amended are in harmony with Arts 10 and 11, taking into account the above Strasbourg jurisprudence. In so doing, it will consider the varying effects of these prior restraints on freedom of assembly, taking into account their very significant extension under the CJPOA 1994. In particular, it will be borne in mind that prior restraints are especially restrictive since their use may mean that the whole purpose of the assembly – to express a point of view – is lost.

The POA 1986, as amended by ss 70 and 71 of the CJPOA 1994, contains various prior restraints on assemblies, which may mean that they cannot take place at all or can take place only under various limitations. These restraints are contained in ss 12, 13, 14, 14A, 14B and 14C of the Act. Sections 12 and 13 are underpinned by s 11, which provides that the organisers of a march (not a meeting) must give advance notice of it to the police. This statutory national notice requirement was imposed for the first time under the 1986 Act, although in some districts, a notice requirement was already imposed under local Acts. The notice must specify the date, time and proposed route of the procession and give the name and address of the person proposing to organise it. Under s 11(7), the organisers may be guilty of an offence if the notice requirement has not been satisfied or if the march deviates from the date, time or route specified. Clearly, s 11 may have some deterrence value to organisers; such persons obviously bear a heavy responsibility in ensuring that any deviation does not occur. It can be argued that the word 'any' should not be interpreted so strictly as to exclude spontaneous processions where a few minutes were available to give notice, because to do so would defeat the intention behind including the provision. If read in combination with the requirements as to giving notice by hand or in writing, it should be interpreted to mean 'any written notice' under s 3 of the HRA. If it were not so interpreted, it might be argued that s 11 breaches the guarantees of freedom of assembly under Art 11 and of expression under Art 10, since it could lead to the criminalisation of the organisers of a peaceful spontaneous march. Such an interpretation would seem to be in accordance with the findings in *Ezelin v France*.

Sections 12 and 13 grew out of the power under s 3 of the POA 1936 allowing the chief officer of police to impose conditions on a procession or apply for a banning order if he apprehended serious public disorder. The power to impose conditions on public assemblies under s 14 was an entirely new power. The power to impose conditions on processions under s 12 is much wider than the old power, as it may be exercised in a much wider range of situations. It is identical to the power under s 14 and can be exercised in one of four situations: the senior police officer in question must reasonably believe that serious public disorder, serious damage to property or serious disruption to the life of the community may be caused by the procession. The fourth 'trigger' condition, arising under ss 12 and 14(1)(b), consists of an evaluation of the purpose of the assembly rather than an apprehension that a particular state of affairs may arise. The senior police officer must reasonably believe that the purpose of the assembly is 'the intimidation of others with a view to compelling them not to do an act they have a right to do or to do an act they have a right not to do'. This fourth 'trigger' requires a police officer to make a political judgment as to the purpose of the group in question. It must be determined whether the purpose is coercive or merely persuasive. Asking police officers to make such a judgment clearly lays them open to claims of partiality in instances where they are perceived as being out of sympathy with the aims of the group in question.

'Serious disruption to the life of the community' is a very wide phrase and clearly offers the police wide scope for interpretation. It may be interpreted broadly where police officers wish to cut down the cost of the policing requirement for an assembly because of the conditions then imposed, such as requiring a limit on the numbers participating, might lead to a reduction in the number of officers who had to be present. In *R (Brehony) v Chief Constable of Greater Manchester (2005)* a regular demonstration had occurred outside a Marks and Spencers, protesting about the firm's support for the government of Israel; a counter-demonstration had also occurred, supporting the government. The Chief Constable had issued a notice under s 14 requiring the demonstration to move to a different location due to the disruption it would be likely to cause to shoppers over the Xmas period when the number of shoppers was likely to treble in number. The demonstrators sought judicial review of this decision; the judge refused the application on the basis that, in Arts 10 and 11 terms, the restraint was proportionate to the aim, of maintaining public order, pursued. This decision confirms that 'serious disruption to the life of the community' can mean mere anticipated inconvenience to shoppers. The decision indicates that ss 12 and 14 provide the police with extremely wide scope for interfering in demonstrations and marches.

The conditions that can be imposed if one of the above 'triggers' is thought to be present are very wide in the case of processions: *prima facie*, any condition may be imposed which appears necessary to the senior police officer in order to prevent the mischief envisaged occurring. Obviously, they are not completely unlimited; if the condition imposed bears no relationship to the mischief it was intended to avert, it may be open to challenge. The conditions which may be imposed under s 14 are much more limited in scope, presumably because it was thought that marches presented more of a threat to public order than meetings. In *DPP v Jones (2002)* conditions as to the movement of the assembly had been imposed; and were found to be *ultra vires* on the basis that they could only have been imposed under s 12; they could not be imposed under s 12 since the demonstration in question was clearly a static assembly, not a march.

The scope for challenging the conditions was very limited in the pre-HRA era: there was no method of appealing from them; it was only possible to have them reviewed for procedural errors or unreasonableness in the High Court. It was made clear in *Secretary of State for the Home Department ex p Northumbria Police Authority (1987)* that such a challenge would succeed only where a senior officer had evinced a belief in the existence of a 'trigger' which no reasonable officer could entertain: no presumption in favour of freedom of assembly would be imported. In the post-HRA era, a challenge could be mounted under s 7(1)(a) of the HRA, relying on Arts 10 and 11. The very fact that such an avenue of challenge is now available, and that the police as a public authority under s 6 of the HRA should take Arts 10 and 11 into account in imposing the conditions, provides an implied limitation on them, probably obviating the necessity of re-interpretation of the condition-imposing powers of ss 12(1) and 14(1) under s 3.

Under s 13, a ban must be imposed on a march if it is thought that it may result in serious public disorder. This reproduces the old power under s 3 of the

Public Order Act 1936. Assuming that a power was needed to ban marches expected to be violent, this power was nevertheless open to criticism, in that once a banning order had been imposed, it prevented all marches in the area it covered for its duration. Thus, a projected march likely to be of an entirely peaceful character would be caught by a ban aimed at a violent march. The Campaign for Nuclear Disarmament attempted to challenge such a ban after it had had to cancel a number of its marches (*Kent v Metropolitan Police Commissioner (1981)*), but failed due to the finding that an order quashing the ban could be made only if there were no reasons for imposing it at all. It is arguable that the 1986 Act should have limited the banning power to the particular marches giving rise to fear of serious public disorder, but this possibility was rejected by the government at the time on the ground that it could be subverted by organisers of marches who might attempt to march under another name. It would therefore, it was thought, have placed too great a burden on the police who would have had to determine whether or not this had occurred. However, in making this decision, it is arguable that too great a weight was given to the possible administrative burden placed on the police and too little to the need to uphold freedom of assembly.

Originally, the 1986 Act contained no power to ban assemblies, possibly because it was thought that such a power would be too draconian, but provision to allow for such bans was inserted into it by s 70 of the CJPOA 1994. The banning power, arising under s 14A, provides that a chief officer of police may apply for a banning order if he reasonably believes that an assembly is likely to be trespassory and may result in serious disruption to the life of the community or damage to certain types of buildings and structures. If an order is made, it will subsist for four days and operate within a radius of five miles around the area in question. Apart from these restrictions, this is a much wider power than that arising under s 13, since it is based on the very broad and uncertain concept of 'serious disruption to the life of the community'. Since it uses the same trigger as that operating under ss 12 and 14, it appears to leave a complete discretion to the police as to whether to ban or to impose conditions. Section 14A is backed up by s 14C (inserted into the 1986 Act by s 71 of the 1994 Act). Section 14C provides a very broad power to stop persons within a radius of five miles from the assembly if a police officer reasonably believes that they were on their way to it, and that is subject to a s 14A order. Thus, this power operates before any offence has been committed and hands the police a very wide discretion.

The meaning and ambit of s 14A were considered in *Jones and Lloyd v DPP (1997)*, which concerned an assembly on the road leading to Stonehenge, at a time when a s 14A order was in force. The key finding of the House of Lords was that since *the particular assembly in question* had been found by the tribunal in fact to be a reasonable user of the highway, it was therefore not trespassory and so not caught by the s 14A order. The Lords' conclusion was that the demands of this 'right' to assemble are satisfied, provided merely that an assembly on the highway is not invariably tortious. This interpretation did little, it is suggested, to ensure that s 14A is compatible with Arts 10 and 11, since it allows interferences with peaceful assemblies.

In general, it is argued that ss 12–14A appear to be out of accord with the demands of Arts 10 and 11 of the Convention. Sections 12 and 14 allow for the imposition of conditions on the basis of serious disruption of the life of the community – an aim not recognised in Arts 10 and 11. Sections 13 and 14A allow for the possibility of imposing blanket bans. Under all of those provisions, it is possible that those organising or taking part in protests and demonstrations can be subject to criminal penalties and hence to an interference with their Arts 10 and 11 rights, even though they themselves were behaving wholly peacefully. (For example, a march might be peaceful and yet arguably disruptive of the 'life' of the community under s 12; it might fall foul of a s 13 ban imposed due to the concerns generated by the projected march of a violent group.) Thus, the effects of ss 12–14A appear to be contrary to the statement of principle set out in *Ezelin*, above, since the arrest and conviction of demonstrators under them cannot be seen to be directly serving one of the legitimate aims of preventing public disorder or ensuring public safety under para 2 of Arts 10 and 11. It is therefore arguable that the use of bans or conditions always constitutes breaches of Arts 10 and 11 when they catch entirely peaceful protesters, since the 'legitimate aim' test is unsatisfied. Even if this is not accepted, on the basis that ss 12–14A have a more general aim in preventing disorder, it might be argued that the arrest of peaceful protesters is disproportionate to this legitimate aim.

On the other hand, there is a consistent line of case law from the European Commission on Human Rights which indicates that bans – and therefore *a fortiori* the imposition of conditions – on assemblies and marches are in principle compatible with Art 11, even where they criminalise wholly peaceful protests (*Pendragon v UK (1998); Chappell v UK (1988)*) or prevent what would have been peaceful demonstrations from taking place at all (*Christians Against Racism and Fascism v UK (1980)*).[1] A court which preferred the *Ezelin* stance and formed the view that blanket bans *per se* were essentially incompatible with the Convention could enforce this view through a radical re-interpretation of s 14A under s 3(1) of the HRA. It would entail reading into s 14A(5) the requirement that a given assembly, as well as being trespassory and within the geographical and temporal scope of a subsisting s 14A order, must also itself pose a threat of disorder, or otherwise satisfy one of the exceptions to Art 11. Since such an interpretation would mean that s 14A effectively ceased to bestow a power to impose blanket bans and is only doubtfully necessary under the Convention, it is, however, unlikely to be adopted.[2]

Under s 14A, attention will therefore probably focus upon scrutiny of the risk of serious disruption to the life of the community' in granting the original ban. This method could also be used to bring ss 12 and 14 into line with the Convention. Courts could be required to determine that the nature of the risk anticipated is one which would constitute one of the legitimate aims for limiting the primary rights under Arts 11 and 10. This vague and ambiguous phrase could be re-interpreted under s 3 of the HRA by reference to Arts 11(2) and 10(2) of the Convention. Given the terms of these criteria, the grounds for the ban/imposition of conditions would have to be justified either on the basis of protecting 'the rights of others' or because the 'serious disruption' feared amounted to 'disorder' for the purposes of Arts 11(2) and 10(2). If those aims were established, the ban/conditions would also have to be necessary and proportionate to them, on the basis that disruption that could be curbed without imposing a ban/conditions could not be viewed as 'serious'. Thus, s 3 could be used to limit and structure the tests allowing for the use of these curbs on protests. However, the decision in *Brehony* does not encourage the idea that the judiciary would be eager to take this course. *R(on the application of Gillan) v Commissioner of Metropolitan Police (2006)* also encourages a pessimistic view: the House of Lords found that, assuming that Art 10 was applicable in an instance in which a protester had been stopped and searched – arguably an interference that had occurred in order to impede him in joining the protest – the exception for the prevention of crime under para 2 was satisfied, without engaging in any proportionality analysis.

Section 13 could be re-interpreted under s 3 in order to achieve compatibility with Arts 10 and 11 in various ways. For example, it could be argued that a power to seek an order to ban all marches could be interpreted as a power to ban all espousing a particular message, using s 3 of the HRA creatively, as the House of Lords did in *R v A (2001)* and *Ghaidan v Mendoza (2004)*. Alternatively, the words 'or any class of public procession' used in s 13(1) could be utilised to afford leeway to include potentially disruptive marches (using 'disruptiveness' as the method of defining their membership of the class), and therefore to exclude marches expected to be entirely peaceful.

It is concluded that the far-reaching nature of the public order scheme under discussion argues strongly for establishing further protection for freedom of assembly under the HRA 1998, by re-interpretation of a number of the provisions under s 3. To say this is not to argue that the scheme is completely out of harmony with Arts 10 and 11. The scheme is to an extent pursuing legitimate aims – the prevention of disorder and crime – under those Articles, but insofar as certain of its provisions allow for interference with peaceful assemblies, it appears, as indicated, that in certain respects it goes further than is necessary in a democratic society. However, ironically, the very fact that the scheme employs imprecise phrases such as 'serious', possibly in an attempt to afford maximum discretion to the police, works against it in favour of freedom of protest, since it renders the task of re-interpretation under s 3 of the HRA relatively straightforward.

NOTES

1 The alternative argument could be pursued here: it would therefore be open to a court to follow the Commission case law on the basis that it is more directly applicable to ss 12–14A, since it deals directly with prior restraints, unlike *Steel* and *Ezelin*. On such an approach, the imposition of conditions under ss 12 or 14 or of bans under s 13 would be substantively unaffected by the HRA, since the police assessment of the need to impose the condition or seek the ban would be deferred to. In relation to s 14A, this approach would probably require the court to satisfy itself that there was some risk of disorder or property damage to justify the making of the original s 14A order.

2 There would be strong grounds to justify a departure from *DPP v Jones*, on the basis that it affords too precarious a level of protection to a fundamental right in allowing peaceful, non-obstructive protests to be interfered with merely because a magistrates' court has found the assembly to be 'unreasonable'. The question would then be how far a court wished to go in establishing a new approach to s 14A. The civil trespass finding could be modified: a court could find that if an assembly is peaceful and non-obstructive, it must always be termed reasonable and therefore non-trespassory, and so outside the terms of any s 14A order in force.

Question 49

Clare is a member of the City Youth Club. She and 40 other teenagers attend the youth club on Friday evening and are told that it has to close down that night due to sudden drastic cuts in funding imposed by the council. All the teenagers immediately walk out of the club in protest and assemble on the pavement outside. While they are angrily discussing the closure of the club, Edwin and Fred, two police officers in uniform, approach the group.

Clare begins to address the group, telling them that they must remain peaceful in order to air their grievances more effectively. Edwin tells her that she must disperse part of the group if she wants to hold a meeting. She ask some of the teenagers to leave, but takes no action when they make no attempt to do so. The meeting continues and becomes more heated. Clare then suggests that they should march through the town.

The group sets off, Clare leading. Traffic is held up for 10 minutes as the group enters the town. Edwin asks Clare to disperse half the group of marchers. Clare asks two of the teenagers to leave, but takes no further action when they fail to comply with her request. Edwin then says that she will have to give him the names and addresses of the members of the group. She refuses, and Edwin then informs Clare that he is arresting her for failing to comply with his orders.

Consider the criminal liability, if any, incurred by Clare.

Answer plan

This is a fairly typical problem question confined to a fairly narrow compass, dealing with issues which arise mainly but not entirely under the Public Order Act (POA) 1986 in respect of marches and assemblies. It also requires an awareness of the provisions of Arts 10 and 11 as interpreted at Strasbourg, and of their potential impact on UK law under the Human Rights Act (HRA) 1998. If any of the statutory provisions considered leave open any room at all for a different interpretation (not only on the grounds of ambiguity), they should be interpreted in harmony with Arts 10 and 11 of the European Convention on Human Rights (the Convention).

It is very important to note that the answer is confined to the question of possible criminal liability incurred by Clare. Possible tortious liability incurred by Clare or the police officers is therefore irrelevant, as is the possibility that Clare could seek to challenge the police decisions by way of judicial review. Breach of the peace is not technically a criminal offence, so it is also irrelevant. The demands of Arts 10 and 11 as received into UK law under the HRA 1998 will be relevant at a number of points.

The essential matters to be discussed are:

- introduction – mention the need to consider the HRA 1998 and the demands of Arts 10 and 11 of the Convention;
- notice requirements under s 11 of the POA 1986; take account of s 3 of the HRA;
- 'triggers' under ss 12 and 14 of the POA 1986; take account of s 3 of the HRA;
- conditions which can be imposed under ss 12 and 14 of the POA 1986 on processions and assemblies;
- liability which may arise under ss 12 and 14;
- public nuisance; take account of s 6 of the HRA;
- obstruction of the highway under s 137 of the Highways Act 1980; take account of s 3 of the HRA;
- conclusions – dependent on interpretation of statutory provisions based on the demands of Arts 10 and 11 as received into UK law under the HRA 1998.

Answer

Liability in this case arises mainly, but not exclusively, under the Public Order Act (POA) 1986. Since the question demands consideration of possible restrictions on protest and assembly, the requirements of Arts 10 and 11 as received into UK law under the HRA must be taken into account.

Under s 11 of the POA 1986, advance notice of a procession must be given if it falls within one of three categories. This march falls within s 11(1)(a), as it is intended to demonstrate opposition to the action of the local authority in closing the youth club. As no notice of the march was given, Clare may have committed an offence under s 11(7)(a) of the POA 1986 as she is the organiser of the march. However, the notice requirement does not apply under s 11(1) if it was not reasonably practicable to give any advance notice. This provision was intended to exempt spontaneous demonstrations such as this one from the notice requirements, but is defective due to the use of the word 'any'. This word would suggest that a phone call made five minutes before the march sets off would fulfil the requirements, thereby exempting very few marches. Although the march sets off suddenly, it is possible that Clare had time to make such a phone call; on a strict interpretation of s 11, she is therefore in breach of the notice requirements, as it was reasonably practicable for her to fulfil them. However, it can be argued that notice was informally and impliedly given to the police officers already on the scene, or alternatively that the term 'reasonably practicable' should be interpreted, under s 3 of the HRA, so as to exempt spontaneous processions from liability even where a few minutes were available to give notice, because to fail to do so would be out of harmony with Art 11, which protects freedom of peaceful assembly (*Ezelin v France (1991)*) since peaceful spontaneous marches could incur liability. The word "written" could be read into s11 relying on s 3 (*see Ghaidan v Mendoza (2004)*) and clearly there was insufficient time to give written notice. Thus, assuming that either argument was accepted by the court, liability would not arise under s 11.

Clare may be liable under s 14(4) of the POA 1986, as she was the organiser of a public assembly, but failed to comply with the condition imposed by the most senior police officer present at the scene (Edwin) to disperse part of the group (where the officers are of equal rank, this condition will be fulfilled when one of them issues an order). It should be noted that as the group was in a public place and comprised more than two persons, it constituted a public assembly under s 16 of the POA 1986, as amended. Edwin can impose conditions on the assembly only if one of four 'triggers' under s 14(1) is present. The third of these, and arguably the easiest to satisfy, provides that the police officer in question must reasonably believe that 'serious disruption to the life of the community' may be caused by the assembly. In the case of *Reid (1987)*, it was determined that the 'triggers' should be strictly interpreted: the words used should not be diluted. Clearly, it would be in accordance with Art 11, and indeed Art 10 (see *Steel v UK (1998)*) to adopt such an interpretation under s 3 of the HRA, since otherwise an interference with assemblies outside the legitimate aims of the second para of Arts 10 and 11 might be enabled to occur. In the instant case, a group of over 40 teenagers are gathered on the street in the evening; even if it could be argued that such a circumstance might cause some disruption in the community (in terms of noise or a blockage of the pavement), it is less clear that a reasonable person would expect the disruption to be serious.

In *R (Brehony) v Chief Constable of Greater Manchester (2005)* a regular demonstration had occurred outside a Marks and Spencers, protesting about the firm's support for the government of Israel; a counter-demonstration had also occurred, supporting the government. The Chief Constable had issued a notice under s 14 requiring the demonstration to move to a different location due to the disruption it would be likely to cause to shoppers over the Xmas period when the number of shoppers was likely to treble in number. The demonstrators sought judicial review of this decision; the judge refused the application on the basis that, in Art 10 and 11 terms, the restraint was proportionate to the aim, of maintaining public order, pursued. This decision confirms that 'serious disruption to the life of the community' can mean mere anticipated inconvenience to shoppers. On this argument, Edwin may have had a power to impose conditions on the assembly and the condition imposed is one allowed for under s 14 – to limit the number of persons in the assembly (see *DPP v Jones (2002)*). Liability may therefore arise under s 14(4) unless Clare could successfully argue that the failure to comply with the condition imposed arose due to circumstances beyond her control.

Will Clare incur liability under s 12(4) of the POA 1986, as she was the organiser of a public procession, but failed to comply with the conditions imposed by Edwin to provide the names and addresses of the group or to disperse part of it? Edwin can impose conditions on the procession only if one of the four 'triggers' under s 12(1) is present. The triggers are identical to those under s 14(1). The third of these may possibly arise, following *Brehony*. The group of teenagers was marching through the town; in such circumstances, it may be more readily argued that serious disruption to the life of the community may reasonably be apprehended. Such disruption could be argued for either on the basis that passers-by may be jostled by the group, especially if it has grown more excitable, or on the basis that traffic may be seriously disrupted. The fact that traffic has already been held up for 10 minutes may support a reasonable belief that such disruption may occur. Serious obstruction of the traffic might arguably amount to some disruption of the life of the community. Both possibilities taken together could found a reasonable apprehension that the life of the community will be seriously disrupted. However, courts are required under both ss 6 and 3 of the HRA to determine that the nature of the risk anticipated is one which would constitute one of the legitimate aims for limiting the primary rights under Arts 11 and 10. The vague and ambiguous phrase, 'serious disruption to the life of the community', could be re-interpreted under s 3 of the HRA by reference to Arts 11(2) and 10(2) of the Convention. The grounds for imposing the conditions would have to be justified, either on the basis of protecting 'the rights of others' or because the 'serious disruption' feared amounted to 'disorder' for the purposes of those second paragraphs. Following *Brehony* it seems probable that a court would be satisfied that serious disruption could reasonably be apprehended, and that in asserting a power to impose conditions the police did not breach Arts 10 or 11. However, the discretion as to the imposition of the conditions in s 12 could be viewed narrowly (either under Arts 10 or 11 or on ordinary principles of statutory construction). It could be argued that the restrictions are necessary in order to protect the rights of others. However, arguably, they are disproportionate to that aim, bearing in mind the importance of freedom of assembly (*Ezelin*). In particular, a requirement to provide names and addresses appears to be disproportionate to the aim in view, since it is unclear that it could serve that aim. In order to avoid breaching Arts 10 and 11, a court which took this view could adopt a strict interpretation of s 12, possibly finding either that the behaviour in question is not serious enough and/or that the condition could not be viewed as 'necessary'.

On the other hand, a court could rely on *Christians Against Racism and Fascism v UK (1980)*, in which a ban on a peaceful assembly was not found to breach Art 11. A *fortiori*, a mere imposition of conditions might be found to be proportionate within the terms of Art 11(2). Following this argument, and bearing *Brehony* in mind, Edwin would be entitled to impose conditions on the march. The conditions imposed would have to relate to the disruption apprehended; this may be said of the requirement to disperse half the group, but not of the order that Clare should disclose the names and addresses of the group. Thus, liability may arise only in respect of the failure to comply with the former condition. Clare made some attempt to comply with it but did not succeed; she would, therefore, following this argument, incur liability under s 12(4) unless she can show that the failure arose due to circumstances outside her control. Although the powers of an organiser to disperse members of a march are limited, it may be argued that in approaching only two members of the group, Clare made in any event a token effort only; it is therefore arguable that she has committed an offence under s 12(4).

Clare may further have incurred liability under s 137 of the Highways Act 1980, which provides that a person will be guilty of an offence if he 'without lawful authority or excuse in any way wilfully obstructs the free passage of the highway'. In *Nagy v Weston (1965)*, it was held that a reasonable use of the highway will constitute a lawful excuse, and that in order to determine its reasonableness or otherwise, the length of the obstruction must be considered, its purpose, the place where it occurred and whether an actual or potential obstruction took place. There is no evidence to suggest that the group assembled outside the youth club caused obstruction; however, the march did cause a brief obstruction of the highway. In

Arrowsmith v Jenkins (1963), it was held that minor obstruction of traffic can lead to liability under the Highways Act. However, the question of the purpose of the obstruction, mentioned in *Nagy*, was given greater prominence in *Hirst and Agu v Chief Constable of West Yorkshire (1986)*: it was said that courts should have regard to the freedom to demonstrate.

This approach was to an extent confirmed by *DPP v Jones* (1999), where the House of Lords recognised that a demonstration need not be treated as an improper use of the highway where it does not cause obstruction to other users. Such an approach is, of course, given added weight by the need for the courts to give appropriate weight, by virtue of s 3 of the HRA, to the rights of freedom of expression and assembly in Arts 10 and 11 of the Convention. One possibility would be to interpret the uncertain term 'excuse' in order to seek to ensure harmony between s 137 of the Highways Act and Arts 10 and 11 under s 3 of the HRA, since otherwise s 137 would allow interferences with peaceful, albeit obstructive, assemblies, arguably contrary to the findings of the European Court of Human Rights in *Steel* and in *Ezelin*. On this basis, the brevity of the obstruction and its purpose as part of a legitimate protest suggest that the march amounted to a reasonable use of the highway. The stronger argument seems to be that liability under the Highways Act for inciting the group to obstruct the highway will not be established.[1]

Clare may also have incited the group to commit a public nuisance by blocking the highway. However, according to *Clarke (1964)*, the disruption caused must amount to an unreasonable use of the highway in order to found liability for public nuisance. Thus, once obstruction has been shown, the question of reasonableness arises. In this instance, there has been some obstruction of the highway for 10 minutes. However, as has already been pointed out, it is arguable that to cause such a minor disruption for a legitimate purpose does not constitute an unreasonable use of the highway. It is unlikely that a use of the highway could be reasonable under the Highways Act but nevertheless able to amount to a public nuisance. This seemed to be accepted in *Gillingham Borough Council v Medway Dock Co (1992)*. This argument is strengthened by consideration of the duty of the court and the police officers, under s 6 of the HRA, to abide by the Convention rights which include the right to freedom of assembly. On this argument, liability for public nuisance will not arise.

Thus, in conclusion, Clare is most likely to attract liability under ss 14(4) and 12(4) of the POA 1986.

NOTE

1 It could be argued further that Clare's conduct could not be described as 'wilful', in the sense that at the point when the obstruction is caused, Edwin appears to be giving some sanction to the march and Clare may be relying on his official

connivance. Such a restrictive interpretation would offer a further means, under s 3 of the HRA, of limiting the application of s 137 to protesters.

Question 50

The Asian community in Northton become increasingly concerned about apparent racism in Northton City Council employment practices. A number of council workers have recently been made redundant; a disproportionate number of them are Asians. A group of 40 Asians decides to hold a demonstration outside the Civic Centre on the lawns and courtyard in front of it. On the day appointed, they assemble, appoint Ali and Rashid as their leaders, and shout at workers going into the Centre telling them not to go in but to join the demonstration. When the workers do not respond, some of the Asians, including Ali, become angrier; they shout and wave their fists threateningly at some of the workers, but make no attempt to impede them physically. Some of the workers appear to be intimidated.

One of the Asians, Sharma, tries to persuade workers not to enter the Civic Centre and to support the anti-racism protest, but eventually becomes involved in a heated argument with a group of white workers. He continues more angrily to attempt to persuade them not to enter; they threaten to beat him up if the Asian group continues with its efforts.

Three police officers arrive on the scene. One of them, John, arrests Sharma, stating that this is for breach of the peace since the group of white workers is about to become violent. Sharma tries to leave, pushing John aside in the process; John seizes Sharma's arm. Belinda, one of the police officers, orders Ali to disperse half of the group; when he makes no effort to comply, she says that she is arresting him for failing to comply with the order. She also orders Rashid to leave the area. He fails to do so.

Discuss.

Answer plan

This question is partly concerned with liability which may arise in respect of assemblies under the Public Order Act (POA) 1986, as amended, and under ss 68 and 69 of the Criminal Justice and Public Order Act (CJPOA) 1994. The common law power to prevent a breach of the peace is significant in the question. The statutory provisions considered should be interpreted in harmony with Arts 10 and 11 of the European Convention on Human Rights (the Convention) (and any other relevant Articles) under s 3 of the Human

Rights Act (HRA) 1998; the common law doctrine of breach of the peace must be interpreted and applied in accordance with the duty of the court under s 6 of the HRA. It should be borne in mind that the problem concerns an assembly only, and not a march. Further, the assembly is not taking place on the highway. Therefore, liability particularly associated with marches and with assemblies on the highway will not arise. Note that a broad, wide ranging discussion is called for due to the use of the word 'discuss'.

Essentially, the following matters should be discussed:

- introduction – a mention of the need to consider the HRA; demands of Arts 10 and 11 as received into UK law under the HRA;
- 'triggers' under s 14 of the Act;
- conditions which may be imposed under s 14; take account of s 3 of the HRA;
- liability under ss 3, 4, 4A and 5 of the POA 1986; take account of s 3 of the HRA (ss 3 and 4 are covered in the Notes);
- liability under ss 68 and 69 of the CJPOA 1994; take account of s 3 of the HRA;
- arrest for breach of the peace; s 6 of the HRA; liability under s 89(1) of the Police Act 1996;
- is there liability in tort?;
- conclusions.

Answer

Liability in this case may arise mainly, but not exclusively, under the Public Order Act 1986 (POA), as amended. Since the question demands consideration of possible restrictions on protest and assembly, the requirements of Arts 10 and 11 as received into UK law under the HRA must be taken into account. Art 14, which provides protection from discrimination in the context of another right, will also be considered briefly.

Ali may attract liability under s 14(4) of the POA 1986, as he was the organiser of a public assembly, but failed to comply with the condition imposed by the most senior police officer present at the scene (where the officers are of equal rank, this condition will be fulfilled when one of them issues an order) to disperse half of the group. It should be noted that as the group was in a public place and comprised more than two persons, it constituted a public assembly under s 16 of the POA

1986, as amended. Belinda can impose conditions on the assembly only if one of four 'triggers' under s 14(1) is present. Under s 14(1)(a), the police officer in question must reasonably believe that serious public disorder, serious damage to property or serious disruption to the life of the community may be caused by the assembly. The fourth 'trigger', arising under s 14(1)(b), consists of an evaluation of the purpose of the assembly rather than an apprehension that a particular state of affairs may arise. The senior police officer present must reasonably believe that the purpose of the assembly is 'the intimidation of others with a view to compelling them not to do an act they have a right to do or to do an act they have a right not to do'.

Possibly, the third 'trigger' could apply to this situation, but that point need not be considered because the fourth 'trigger' seems to be most clearly indicated: the Asians are trying to prevent persons entering the Civic Centre and are therefore trying to prevent persons doing something they have a right to do (in the sense that there is a right to pass along the highway to a place of work); the question is whether their actions have gone beyond what might be acceptable as part of a legitimate demonstration and could suggest an intention to intimidate. In the case of *Reid (1987)*, it was determined that the triggers should be strictly interpreted: the words used should not be diluted. In *Reid*, the defendants shouted, raised their arms and waved their fingers; it was determined that such behaviour might cause discomfort but not intimidation and that the two concepts could not be equated. In *News Group Newspapers Ltd v SOGAT 82 (1986)*, it was held that mere abuse and shouting did not amount to a threat of violence for the purposes of intimidation under s 7 of the Conspiracy and Protection of Property Act 1875. In the instant case, it could be argued that the Asians' behaviour in merely shouting at the Civic Centre workers could not amount to intimidation, but that in making threatening gestures with their fists, it crossed the boundary between discomfort and intimidation.

However, since the imposition of conditions, the arrest of Ali and (potentially) the imposition of criminal liability under s 14 create interferences with the rights under Arts 11 and 10 of assembly and expression (*Steel v UK (1998)*). Therefore, it must be asked whether the demands of s 14 as applied in this instance are in accordance with those rights. One possibility is that s 14(1)(b) could be re-interpreted under s 3 of the HRA by reference to Arts 10 and 11 of the Convention. The interference it represents (since it allows for the imposition of conditions) would have to be justified on the basis of protecting 'the rights of others'. It could be argued that the restriction is necessary in order to protect the rights of others, since that is precisely what s 14(1)(b) is aimed at, and that the requirements of s 14 in terms of applicability to this situation are proportionate to that aim. In *Ezelin v France (1991)*, the Court considered the issue of proportionality under Art 11 and found that the freedom to take part in a peaceful assembly is of such importance that it cannot be restricted in any way, so long as the person concerned does not himself commit any reprehensible act. It may be argued that the intimidation of others is reprehensible and that therefore the tests under Art 11(2) (and Art 10(2)) are satisfied by the application of s 14 in this instance, taking account of s 6 HRA. The lenient stance taken towards the application of the third trigger in *R (Brehony) v Chief Constable of Greater Manchester (2005)* indicates that this stance would probably also be taken here. In that instance the judge refused the application on the basis that, in Art 10 and 11 terms, the restraint was proportionate to the aim, of maintaining public order, pursued; the decision confirmed that 'serious disruption to the life of the community' can mean mere anticipated inconvenience to shoppers. Following this argument there appears to be no requirement to reinterpret s14 under s 3 HRA.

On that basis, it appears that Belinda had the power to impose a condition on the assembly, and the condition itself appears to relate quite closely to the mischief in question – the intimidation.[1] Ali made no effort to comply with the condition imposed. The question of whether the failure to comply with it arose due to circumstances beyond his control need not, therefore, be addressed. Thus, Ali's arrest appears to be justified under s 14(7) and he may be likely to incur liability under s 14(4). Other members of the Asian group who were aware of the condition may commit the offence under s 14(5).[2]

Ali, Rashid, and possibly other members of the Asian group may also incur liability under s 68 of the CJPOA 1994. The section requires, first, that the defendant has trespassed. This seems to be satisfied, since Ali, Rashid and the other protestors appear to have exceeded the terms of an implied licence to be in the courtyard, and the courtyard is not excluded from s 68 since it is arguably 'land in the open air' – it is clearly not part of the highway (s 68(5)(a)). Second, it must be shown that the defendant intended to disrupt or obstruct a lawful activity or to intimidate persons so as to deter them from that activity. This last requirement may also be satisfied by the Asians' behaviour in shouting at the workers entering the Civic Centre. It may perhaps be inferred that Ali and others did intend to intimidate the workers since they made threatening gestures towards them. The broad view of s 68 taken in *Winder (1996)* indicates that a court would not scrutinize the application of s 68 to the facts too closely. Rashid (and possibly other Asians aware of John's order that members of the assembly should disperse) may also commit the offence under s 69 of failing to leave land after a direction to do so is given, founded on a reasonable belief that the offence under s 68 is being committed. Belinda tells Rashid to leave the land and he refuses to do so.

However, these possibilities of liability under ss 68 and 69 must be considered in relation to the HRA. The European Court of Human Rights made a clear finding in *Steel* (1998), confirmed in *Hashman (2000)*, that protest which takes the form of physical obstruction nevertheless falls within the protection of Art 10 – and presumably Art 11. Thus, it is necessary to decide whether the interference with Ali's and the other protestors' Convention rights is justifiable under the second paragraphs of those Articles. If not, s 68 may require re-interpretation under s 3 so as to exclude behaviour such as that of Ali and Rashid, or possibly a declaration of incompatibility may eventually have to be made between s 68 and Arts 10 and 11 under s 4 of the HRA. In *Steel* the Court appeared to be readily convinced of the necessity and proportionality of the interferences with the two direct action protests complained of by the first two applicants. In contrast, the Court in *Ezelin (1991)* found that it was impossible to justify interferences with the freedom of peaceful assembly, unless the person exercising the freedom himself committed a 'reprehensible act'. Therefore, in order to reconcile the two decisions, it must be assumed either that *obstructive* protest, while it does fall within at least Art 10, does not constitute that class of purely 'peaceful' protest which, according to *Ezelin*, 'cannot be restricted in any way', or that any restriction is more readily justifiable. It seems clear from the findings in *Steel* as to the first and second applicants, and from the Commission decision in *G v federal Republic of Germany (1980)*, that where a protestor is engaged in obstructive, albeit nonviolent activity, arrest and imprisonment are in principle justifiable under the Convention. It is arguable therefore that s 68 is Convention compliant under s 3, and that the imposition of liability in this instance is compatible with the duty of the court under s 6 of the HRA. On this basis, liability under s 69 would also be established since it is dependent on establishing a reasonable belief that the offence under s 68 has been committed; this appears to be the case, bearing in mind that it has not been found necessary to re-interpret s 68 by reference to s 3 of the HRA.

It could also be argued that in shouting and waving their fists at the Civic Centre workers, Ali and the other demonstrators may incur liability under s 5 of the POA 1986. Their behaviour must amount to 'threatening, abusive or insulting words or behaviour or disorderly behaviour' which takes place 'in the hearing or sight of a person likely to be caused harassment, alarm or distress thereby'. These three terms must be given their ordinary meaning following *Brutus v Cozens (1973)*. The word 'likely' imports an objective test into the section: it is necessary to show that a person was present at the scene, but not that he actually experienced the feelings in question. The demonstrators shout and gesture aggressively; this behaviour may clearly be termed disorderly or even threatening, and it is arguable, given the width of the concept of harassment, that it would be likely to cause feelings of harassment, although probably not of alarm, to the workers. It appears then that the demonstrators may incur liability under s 5, subject to the argument below as to the *mens rea* requirement under s 6(4). On the same argument, liability under s 4A of the POA 1986 may be established, assuming that they *intended* to cause harassment and did cause it. It should be noted however that in *Dehal v DPP (2005)* it was found that s 4 should be interpreted restrictively when applied to public protest due to the impact of the HRA, Arts 10 and 11.

However, it is necessary to consider whether ss 4A and 5, interpreted as covering the behaviour in question, are compatible with Arts 10 and 11 under s 3 of the HRA (see *Percy v DPP (2001)*). Compatibility may be achieved by affording a broad interpretation to the defence of reasonableness in both sections (ss 5(3)(c) and 4A(3)(b)). It was determined in *DPP v Clarke (1992)* that the defence is to be judged objectively, and it will therefore depend on what a bench of magistrates considers reasonable. In that case, the behaviour of the protestors outside an abortion clinic was not found to be reasonable. The use of pictures and models of aborted foetuses appeared to contribute to this conclusion. This decision does not give much guidance to protestors seeking to determine beforehand the limits or meaning of 'reasonable' protest. As a deliberately ambiguous term, it obviously leaves enormous discretion to the judiciary to adopt approaches to its interpretation under s 3 of the HRA in accordance with Arts 10 and 11 as interpreted in *Steel*. Offensive words used by protestors could be found to fall within this defence, on the basis that in the context of a particular demonstration which had a legitimate political aim, such behaviour was acceptable and therefore reasonable (*Percy v DPP (2001)*). However, in the context under discussion, the demonstrators appear to have intended to intimidate others, rather than to make points which others could find offensive. It is arguable that the instant behaviour would fall outside the meaning of 'reasonable', even bearing the requirements of Arts 10 and 11 in mind.

Under s 6(4), it must be established in respect of s 5 that the defendant intended his words, etc, to be threatening, abusive or insulting or was aware that they might be. Under s 4A, intent to cause harassment alone is needed. In *DPP v Clarke (1992)*, it was found that to establish liability under s 5, it is insufficient to show only that the defendant intended to or was aware that he might cause harassment, alarm or distress; it must also be shown that he intended his conduct to be threatening, abusive or insulting or was aware that it might be. Both mental states have to be established independently. Thus, showing that the defendant was aware that he might cause distress was not found to be equivalent to showing that he was aware that his speech or behaviour might be insulting. Applying this subjective test, the magistrates acquitted the defendants and this decision was upheld on appeal. Using this test, it was found that anti-abortion protestors had not realised that their behaviour in shouting anti-abortion slogans, displaying plastic models of foetuses and pictures of dead foetuses would be threatening, abusive or insulting. This decision allows those who believe fervently in their cause, and therefore fail to appreciate that their protest may insult or offend others, to escape liability. It therefore places a significant curb on the ability of s 5 (and to an extent, impliedly of s 4A) to interfere with Art 10 and Art 11 rights. Persons participating in forceful demonstrations may sometimes be able to show that behaviour which could be termed disorderly and which might be capable of causing harassment to others was intended only to make a point, and that they had not realised that others might find it threatening, abusive or insulting. This does not appear to be the case here, since the threats appear to be used not in order to make a point forcefully, but to intimidate.

Sharma may have committed a breach of the peace or his behaviour might have given rise to a reasonable belief that a breach of the peace was threatened; breach of the peace is not in itself a criminal offence, but it would justify the arrest of Sharma by John. If the arrest was lawful, Sharma's action in pushing John away would be an assault on an officer in the execution of his duty, an offence under s 89(1) of the Police Act 1996. In *Howell (1981)*, the court said that a breach of the peace will arise if a positive act is done or is threatened to be done which: harms a person or, in his presence, his property, or is likely to cause such harm, or which puts a person in fear of such harm. In *Nicol v DPP (1996)*, it was found that a natural consequence of lawful conduct could be violence in another only where the defendant rather than the other person could be said to be acting unreasonably and, further, that unless rights had been infringed, it would not be reasonable for those others to react violently. However, in *Redmond-Bate v DPP (1999)*, it was found that, taking Art 10 into account, the court should ask where the threat was coming from; the person causing the threat should be arrested. In the instant case, following *Nicol*, a court might take the view that Sharma was acting unreasonably in attempting to dissuade the workers from entering their place of work, and that the workers' rights were infringed. On the other hand, the threat would appear to be coming from the white workers. Therefore, it may be argued that the police breached their duty under s 6 of the HRA in arresting Sharma, since they did not comply with Art 10 (and arguably Art 14 – the right to non-discrimination which arises in the context of another right). Further, the court's findings in *Steel v UK* (1998) may be taken to suggest that the power to prevent a breach of the peace may infringe Arts 5, 10 and 11 when used against an entirely peaceful protestor. The decision in *Laporte (2006)* would support this argument. In the instant case, Sharma may have remained peaceful, albeit 'heated' and angry. On this interpretation, therefore, which would accord with the court's duty to shape the common law in accordance with the Convention under s 6 of the HRA, Sharma should not have been arrested; therefore, he has not committed the offence under s 89(1) of the Police Act 1996. He could sue John in tort for assault if the arrest is found to be unlawful. Following this argument, it is therefore possible that if the protestors who used intimidatory tactics had been arrested for breach of the peace, their arrests would not have breached Art 10.

In conclusion, therefore, it appears that Ali may incur liability under ss 5, 4A and 14 of the POA 1986 and under s 68 of the CJPOA 1994. Sharma appears not to have committed a breach of the peace and not to have incurred liability under s 89(1) of the Police Act 1996; he may have a tort action for assault against John. Rashid will be likely to incur liability under ss 4A and 5 of the POA 1986 and under s 69 of the CJPOA 1994.[3] Other members of the Asian group, including Rashid and Sharma, may have committed an offence under s 14(5) of the POA 1986 and possibly under s 68 of the CJPOA 1994.

▌NOTES

1 In finding that the imposition of the condition in question did not itself breach Art 11, a court could rely on *Christians Against Racism and Fascism v UK (1980)*, in which a ban on a peaceful assembly was not found to breach Art 11. *A fortiori*, a mere imposition of conditions might be found to be proportionate within the terms of Art 11(2). As indicated, the conditions imposed must relate to the mischief apprehended or occurring, following both s 14(1)(b) (the condition must appear 'necessary' to prevent the intimidation) and the test of proportionality in Art 11(2); both are arguably satisfied by the requirement to disperse half the group.

2 Following the above argument in relation to s 14, Rashid and Sharma may be liable under s 14(5) of the 1986 Act for taking part in a public assembly and knowingly failing to comply with the condition imposed. However, this point cannot be settled as it is unclear from the facts whether or not they were aware of the condition imposed or, following *Vane v Yiannopoullos (1965)*, were wilfully blind as to its existence.

3 It might be worth considering the argument that a number of the Asians, including, of course, Ali and Rashid, also incur liability in respect of the offence of affray under s 3 of the POA 1986. In order to establish an affray, it must first be shown that the defendant used or threatened unlawful violence towards another, and second, that his conduct was such as would cause a person of reasonable firmness present at the scene to fear for his personal safety. As the Asians use threatening gestures, it may be argued that the first limb of s 3(1) is fulfilled, but a strong argument can be advanced that the second is not; due to the fact that the gestures are part of a demonstration, it is probable that a person of reasonable firmness would not fear unlawful violence, even though such a person might feel somewhat distressed. In *Taylor v DPP (1973)*, Lord Hailsham, speaking of the common law offence, said 'the degree of violence . . . must be such as to be calculated to terrify a person of reasonably firm character'. The Act of course refers to 'fear' as opposed to terror, but this ruling suggests that 'fear' should be interpreted restrictively. On this argument, no liability will arise in respect of s 3. Section 4 of the POA 1986 could also be considered, but for similar reasons liability is unlikely to be established, especially taking into account the need for a restrictive interpretation in this context (of a public protest) under s 3 of the HRA.

INDEX